Feminism/Postmodernism

Thinking Gender
Edited by Linda J. Nicholson

Also published in the series

Gender Trouble: Feminism and the Subversion of Identity
Judith Butler

Feminism/ Postmodernism

Edited and with an Introduction by Linda J. Nicholson

ROUTLEDGE
New York and London

First published in 1990 by

Routledge
an imprint of
Routledge, Chapman & Hall, Inc.
29 West 35 Street
New York, NY 10001

Published in Great Britain by

Routledge
11 New Fetter Lane
London EC4P 4EE

Library of Congress Cataloging-in-Publication Data

Feminism/postmodernism / edited by Linda J. Nicholson.
    p. cm.—(Thinking gender)
  Includes bibliographical references and index.
  ISBN 0-415-90058-1; ISBN 0-415-90059-X
  1. Feminism—Philosophy. 2. Postmodernism. I. Nicholson, Linda
J. II. Series
HQ1206.F453 1989
305.42'01—dc20   89-6432
                                           CIP

British Library Cataloguing in Publication Data

Feminism/postmodernism.—(Feminist theory series)
  1. Feminism related to postmodernism. 2. Culture
postmodernism related to feminism.
I. Nicholson, Linda, J. II. Series 305.4'2

ISBN 0-415-90058-1
ISBN 0-415-90059-x

To Philip, Linda, Andrew, Jennifer, and Peter Nicholson

Contents

Acknowledgments

I would like to thank Nancy Fraser, Steve Seidman, Marion Smiley, and Bernie Yack for their help with the introduction and with the organization of the book as a whole.

It is delightful when an editor also becomes a friend. Without the support of Maureen MacGrogan at Routledge, this book would not have been possible.

I would like to express appreciation for being able to reprint the following:

Jane Flax, "Postmodernism and Gender Relations in Feminist Theory," *Signs,* Vol. 12, No. 4. pp. 621–643.

Christine Di Stefano, "Dilemmas of Difference: Feminism, Modernity, and Postmodernism," *Women and Politics,* Vol. 8, No. 3/4, 1988, pp. 1–24.

Seyla Benhabib, "Epistemologies of Postmodernism: A Rejoinder to Jean-François Lyotard," *New German Critique,* No. 33, 1984, pp. 103–126.

Nancy Hartsock, "Foucault on Power: A Theory for Women?" *The Gender of Power: A Symposium,* ed. Monique Leijenaar (Leiden: Vakgroep Vrouwenstudies/Vena, 1987).

Donna Haraway, "A Manifesto for Cyborgs: Science, Technology, and Socialist Feminism in the 1980s," *Socialist Review,* Vol. 15, No. 80, 1985, pp. 65–107.

Andreas Huyssen, "Mapping the Postmodern," *New German Critique,* No. 33, 1984, pp. 5–52.

Iris Young, "The Ideal of Community and the Politics of Difference," *Social Theory and Practice,* Vol. 12, No. 1, Spring 1986, pp. 1–26.

Introduction

From the late 1960s to the mid-1980s, feminist theory exhibited a recurrent pattern: Its analyses tended to reflect the viewpoints of white, middle-class women of North America and Western Europe. The irony was that one of the powerful arguments feminist scholars were making was the limitation of scholarship which falsely universalized on the basis of limited perspectives. Moreover, feminists were becoming increasingly aware that a problem with existing scholarship was not only that it left out women's voices; rather, the voices of many social groups had been silenced. Yet, even in the context of this growing awareness of the oppressive politics of traditional scholarship and a sincere commitment to ensure wide-ranging inclusiveness in their own work, the tendency persisted.

In large part the problem was a consequence of the methodological legacies which feminist scholars inadvertently took over from their teachers. As Nancy Fraser and I note in "Social Criticism without Philosophy," not only did feminist scholars replicate the problematic universalizing tendencies of academic scholarship in general but, even more strikingly, they tended to repeat the specific types of questionable universalizing moves found in the particular schools of thought to which their work was most closely allied. Thus, Marxist-feminist scholarship suffered from the same kinds of faulty universalizations found in nonfeminist-Marxist scholarship, while feminist developmental psychologists replicated the specific types of universalizing mistakes present in developmental psychology.

But, while the specific manifestations of such universalizing tendencies in feminist theory might have been diverse, the underlying problem was the same. It was the failure, common to many forms of academic scholarship, to recognize the embeddedness of its own assumptions within a

1

specific historical context. Like many other modern Western scholars, feminists were not used to acknowledging that the premises from which they were working possessed a specific location.

To adequately diagnose this problem, both within feminist scholarship and within contemporary academic scholarship more generally, requires that we look back to trends which have dominated modern scholarship, trends which date back to the Enlightenment. The scholarship of modern Western culture has been marked by the attempt to reveal general, all-encompassing principles which can lay bare the basic features of natural and social reality. This attempt can be related to an earlier, more religiously based belief that the purpose of scholarship was to make evident the word of God as revealed in his creations. While the relation of God to the basic ordering principles of the universe grew increasingly distant, Western scholarship remained committed to the discovery of such principles.

One crucial consequence of this legacy was a vision of true scholarship as that which replicated "a God's eye view" as opposed to that which expressed the perspectives of particular persons or groups. To be sure, other ideals of scholarship have also surfaced within the modern West, such as those found in the traditions of romanticism, historicism, and hermeneutics. Nevertheless, an ideal of scholarship as transcending the perspective of any one human being or group has persisted as at least one highly powerful ideal.

A scholarly domain where this ideal has been pronounced is the discipline of philosophy, the most ancestral of contemporary disciplines. Moreover, modern philosophy has been marked not only by its universalizing mode but also by its strong belief in the independence of the adequacy of its pronouncements from the historical context of their genesis. Philosophy has undergone some important transformations over the past several centuries. With the emergence of the natural sciences, it lost its position as elaborator of the basic principles of nature. With the emergence of the social sciences in the late nineteenth and twentieth centuries, it also lost its position as elaborator of the basic principles of human nature and social reality. It retained, however, a position as elaborator of those basic principles by which all claims to knowledge were to be judged, and governance over those domains, such as ethics and aesthetics, which resisted description as "science." In short, it became the elaborator of standards governing the "true," the "good," and the "beautiful."

While the contemporary discipline of philosophy very clearly reflects this scholarly ideal of a "transcendent reason," other disciplines, such as those in the natural and social sciences, also contain important elements of this ideal. To be sure, the modern natural and social sciences have been marked more by the quest for a multitude of principles and laws than by a search for a basic few. Nevertheless, they have retained aspects of such an ideal in their allegiance to the norm of objectivity. While the meaning of this norm varies within the academy, one popular interpretation is that of inquiry immune to the nonacademic influences of politics or values.

Feminist scholarship emerged within an academic environment strongly governed by this norm. To gain legitimacy, feminists had to counter it, since many academics used the norm of objectivity to denounce the very idea of feminist scholarship. Feminist scholars responded by challenging the notion itself, arguing that what had most frequently been presented as objective because supposedly devoid of the influence of values, such as those related to gender, actually had reflected such values. Moreover, they claimed that such biases were inevitable; all scholarship reflected the perspectives and ideals of its creators. Avoiding narrowness in the academy could only be possible through ensuring the inclusion of a multitude of points of view.

Feminist scholars have not been alone in launching a criticism of the alleged neutrality of the academy. Scholars involved in other political movements, such as Marxism in the nineteenth and twentieth centuries and the movements of black and gay liberation in the twentieth century, have also questioned the supposed "God's eye view" of the academy. Such politically oriented criticisms of "objective scholarship" have been aided by more academically oriented discussions within philosophy of science about the "value-laden" aspect of theoretical inquiry.

Within the last decade, there have emerged even more radical arguments against claims of objectivity in the academy which have been tied to broad analyses of the limitations of modern Western scholarship. The proponents of such analyses, linked under the label of "postmodernists," have argued that the academy's ideal of "a God's eye view" must be situated within the context of modernity, a period whose organizing principles they claim are on the decline. The postmodernist critique of modernity is wideranging; it focuses on such diverse elements as the modern sense of the self and subjectivity, the idea of history as linear and evolutionary, and the modernist separation of art and mass culture. I will focus, for the moment, on the postmodernist critique of the idea of a transcendent reason.

Postmodernists have gone beyond earlier historicist claims about the inevitable "situatedness" of human thought within culture to focus on the very criteria by which claims to knowledge are legitimized. The traditional historicist claim that all inquiry is inevitably influenced by the values of the inquirer provides a very weak counter to the norm of objectivity. The response can be made that while values and culture might affect the choice of questions the scholar brings to her or his inquiry, they cannot affect the truth of falsity of the answers the scholar gives to such questions. This is because the criteria which determine the truth or falsity of such answers are themselves independent of the specific perspective of the inquirer. But the more radical move in the postmodern turn was to claim that the very criteria demarcating the true and the false, as well as such related distinctions as science and myth or fact and superstition, were internal to the traditions of modernity and could not be legitimized outside of those traditions. Moreover, it was argued that the very development and use of such criteria, as well as their extension to ever wider domains, had to be described as representing the growth and development of specific "regimes of power."

Postmodernists have focused on the growth of science and its widening influence over many spheres of life throughout modernity. They have claimed that in the name of "science," authority has become exercised in a variety of ways: in the disciplines, the media, popular advice manuals, and so on. By pointing to the element of power in such modern practices, postmodernists have extended the field where power has traditionally been viewed as operating, for example, from the state and the economy to such domains as sexuality and mental health.

Behind such practices, the postmodern argument continues, is the backdrop of science and those criteria separating science from superstition and myth. Such criteria, while often little thought about by practicing natural and social scientists or by those who view their work as inspired by science, serve as the "taken-for-granted" support of all such activity. It is mostly modern philosophers who have attempted to give meaning to such distinctions, to articulate general principles of knowledge, that is, an epistemology. This attempted construction of theories of knowledge within modern philosophy has paralleled the attempted construction of well-established theories of other important modern ideals, such as justice and beauty.

Therefore, the postmodern critique has come to focus on philosophy and the very idea of a possible theory of knowledge, justice, or beauty. The claim is that the pursuit itself of such theories rests upon the modernist conception of a transcendent reason, a reason able to separate itself from the body and from historical time and place. Postmodernists describe modern ideals of science, justice, and art, *as* merely modern ideals carrying with them specific political agendas and ultimately unable to legitimize themselves as universals. Thus, postmodernists urge us to recognize the highest ideals of modernity in the West as immanent to a specific historical time and geographical region and also associated with certain political baggage. Such baggage includes notions of the supremacy of the West, of the legitimacy of science to tell us how to use and view our bodies, and of the distinction between art and mass culture.

Feminism as Against Epistemology?

The above discussion represents a simplified summary of a range of positions which are more wide ranging, diverse, and less consistent than this brief overview might suggest. However, from this summary we can begin to see why "the postmodern turn" has become a pressing issue for feminist scholars. On the one hand, there are many points of overlap between a postmodern stance and positions long held by feminists. Feminists, too, have uncovered the political power of the academy and of knowledge claims. In general, they have argued against the supposed neutrality and objectivity of the academy, asserting that claims put forth as universally applicable have invariably been valid only for men of a particular culture, class, and race. They have further alleged that even the ideals which have given backing to these claims, such as "objectivity" and "reason," have reflected the values of masculinity at a particular point in history. Feminists have criticized other Enlightenment ideals, such as the autonomous and self-legislating self, as reflective of masculinity in the modern West. On such grounds, postmodernism would appear to be a natural ally of feminism.

Moreover, for some feminists, postmodernism is not only a natural ally but also provides a basis for avoiding the tendency to construct theory that generalizes from the experiences of Western, white, middle-class women. This position, qualified, is taken by Nancy Fraser and myself. As we note in "Social Criticism without Philosophy," postmodernism offers feminism some useful ideas about method, particularly a wariness toward generalizations which transcend the boundaries of culture and region. To be sure, transcendent generalizations within feminist theory have not been the same as those usually discussed by postmodernists. Feminist theorists have not attempted, by and large, the construction of cross-cultural theories of the true, the just, or the beautiful. On the contrary, feminist theorists have most frequently claimed to base their theories in observation and to acknowledge their construction as rooted in the concerns of the present.

Nevertheless, as we argue, because feminist theorists have frequently exhibited a too casual concern toward history and have used categories which have inclined the theories toward essentialism, many feminist theories of the late 1960s to the mid-1980s have been susceptible to the same kinds of criticisms as postmodernists make against philosophy. This point is evident in the attempts by many feminist theorists to locate "the cause" of women's oppression. Such attempts have ranged from Shulamith Firestone's very early appeal to biological differences between women and men, to the postulation by many influential feminist anthropologists in the 1970s of a cross-cultural domestic/public separation, to later appeals in the late 1970s and early 1980s to women's labor, to women's sexuality, and to women's primary responsibility for child bearing. In all of these cases, aspects of modern Western culture were postulated as present in all or most of human history. Such cultural projection can be found even in many instances of feminist theory which did not seek the ultimate cause of women's oppression, but which attempted to describe "a woman's distinctive perspective."

In "Postmodernism and Gender: Relations in Feminist Theory," Jane Flax argues a similar position. Flax does point to a lingering attraction among many feminists for an Enlightenment world view. As she notes, it is tempting for those who have been treated as incapable of autonomy and rationality to insist on the extension of these powers to themselves and to believe in reason as their ally in the struggle. Nevertheless, Flax argues that feminist theory more appropriately belongs in the terrain of postmodern philosophy. For one, feminist notions of the self, knowledge, and truth are too much at odds with those of the Enlightenment to fit comfortably within its boundaries. Moreover, she also points to the problems of feminist theory which does not adequately take to heart postmodern strictures against the search for ultimate causes or first principles. As she claims, underlying many feminist attempts to identify one aspect of human experience, such as production, sexuality, child rearing, or language, as the ultimate factor in women's oppression, is the hope of speaking from some Archimedean point. But such a hope places feminist theory at odds with its political ideals of inclusiveness. To try to identify unitary themes in the experiences or perspectives of women may require the suppression of voices different from our own. Flax claims that the assumption of such a standpoint may in part be a reflection of a way of thinking grounded in social domination. "Perhaps reality can have 'a' structure only from the falsely universalizing perspective of the dominant group. That is, only to the extent that one person or group can dominate the whole, will reality appear to be governed by one set of rules or be constituted by one privileged set of social relations."

Other feminist scholars are much more skeptical about the value of the postmodern turn for feminism. Christine Di Stefano's article is exemplary of this stance. One important set of concerns she raises can be grouped around the question: Is postmodernism a theory whose time has come for men but not women? Di Stefano raises the possibility that since men have had their Enlightenment, they can afford a sense of a decentered self and a humbleness regarding the coherence and truth of their claims. On the other hand, for women to take on such a position is to weaken what is not yet strong. One important arena which would suffer would be feminist politics. She raises the questions: Would not a politics of alliances, such as is suggested by postmodernism, be necessarily unreliable? Would it not be necessarily reactive rather than constructive and incapable of sustaining itself through time? Most fundamentally, does not the adoption of postmodernism really entail the destruction of feminism, since does not feminism itself depend on a relatively unified notion of the social subject "woman," a notion postmodernism would attack?

Sandra Harding also raises concerns about the critique of epistemology made by postmodernism. To this critique she counterposes two alternative feminist theories of scientific knowledge: feminist empiricism, the application of a traditional empiricist method to feminist concerns, and feminist standpoint theory, which views a feminist vantage point as more illuminating than any existing vantage point by cross-cultural standards. She points to some strong advantages each possesses, advantages which are lost by a postmodernist abandonment of epistemology. Briefly, she argues that feminism needs epistemology as a defense against both "objectivism" and "interpretivism." Feminism needs decision-making procedures which both valorize the importance of the social context of inquiry and yet also avoid relativism. An advantage of both feminist empiricism and feminist standpoint theory is that both leave intact traditional understandings of the cumulative nature of scientific research and thus the idea of some types of research as less false than others.

She also notes the many problems which both feminist empiricism and feminist standpoint theory possess. One is that feminist empiricism must remain inconsistent on the relation of politics to inquiry, as traditional empiricism has supported the norm of "value-free" research. Feminist standpoint theory has difficulties in elaborating linkages with the standpoints of oppressed groups other than women. Indeed, she claims that both theories have incorporated postmodernist elements to deal with such problems.

The view that postmodernism leads to relativism is also evident in the essay by Seyla Benhabib. Benhabib locates postmodernism as emerging out of a set of reactions to modern epistemology going back to the nineteenth century. She describes modern epistemology as operating with a threefold distinction: "the order of representations in our consciousness (ideas or sensations); the signs through which these 'private' orders were made public, namely, words, and that of which our representations were representations and to which they referred." The reactions against modern epistemology can therefore be identified as involving critiques of the modern subject, the modern object, and the modern concept of the sign. Conjointly these critiques have entailed a shift so "that the focus is no longer on the epistemic subject and the private contents of its consciousness but on the public signifying activities of a collection of subjects."

With such a shift, Benhabib has no objection. Her quarrel is with its elaboration in the writings of at least one prominent postmodernist, Jean-François Lyotard. Lyotard, according to Benhabib, identifies this rejection of modern epistemology, the epistemology of representation, with assertions about the incommensurability of language claims and the necessary locality and context-dependent nature of criteria of validity. For Benhabib, such an identification "either leads to a 'polytheism of values,' from which standpoint the principle of performativity or of emancipation cannot be criticized, or this philosophy does not remain wholly polytheistic but privileges one domain of discourse and knowledge over others as a hidden criterion." In short, for Benhabib, the kind of postmodernism found within the writings of Lyotard is either relativist or inconsistent.

The Politics of Location

While theorists such as Sandra Harding and Seyla Benhabib worry about postmodernism leading us down a relativist path, other feminists raise different kinds of concerns. Particularly disturbing to some is whether the category of gender can survive the postmodern critique. If postmodernism entails abandoning the use of cross-cultural categories, what then happens to the category of gender? Would any determinate generalizations be permitted in postmodern times? But if postmodernism entails the abandonment of all generalizations, would not the end result be a nominalist ontology and an individualist politics?

These kinds of questions appear in the essays by Nancy Hartsock and Susan Bordo. Both argue that theorizing needs some stopping points and that for feminists an important theoretical stopping point is gender. To invoke the ideal of endless difference is for feminism either to self-destruct or to finally accept an ontology of abstract individualism.

Susan Bordo also claims that postmodernism may effect the same kind of erasure of the body, and thus erasure of any positioning within space and time that was present in modernism. As she notes, in the Cartesian world view there is no room for the body, since the body, by situating any perspective, prevents the possibility of an all-encompassing perspective. However, she warns of the same endpoint resulting from a seemingly opposite stance. She points to the metaphors of continuous movement and dance present in postmodern writers and their description of the body as fragmented, changing and inviting a "confusion of boundaries." But since we real human beings possess bodies of limited mobility and flexibility, to portray them as otherwise is ultimately to negate them:

> What sort of body is it that is free to change its shape and location at will, that can become anyone and travel everywhere? If the body is a metaphor for our locatedness in space and time and thus for the finitude of human perception and knowledge, then the postmodern body is no body at all.

> The deconstructionist erasure of the body is not effected, as in the Cartesian version, through a trip to "nowhere," but in a resistance to the recognition that one is always *somewhere,* and limited.

The body can serve also as a metaphor for theory, since the location which bodies possess replicates the kind of cognitive location which theories provide. But as human bodies cannot be understood as endlessly mobile and flexible, so human understanding also possesses necessary boundaries and rigidities. As Bordo notes: "Reality itself may be relentlessly plural and heterogeneous, but human understanding and *interest* cannot be." Similarly, Nancy Hartsock also describes postmodernism as dangerously inviting the abandonment of theory:

> Somehow it seems highly suspicious that it is at the precise moment when so many groups have been engaged in "nationalisms" which involve redefinitions of the marginalized others that suspicions emerge about the nature of the 'subject,' about the possibilities for a general theory which can describe the work, about historical progress.

Thus, the dangers of postmodernism as seen by some feminists are those of both relativism and the abandonment of theory. While many reject the modernist "view from nowhere," they question whether postmodernism would not lead us to the equally problematic "view from everywhere." Are coherent theory and politics possible within a postmodern position?

The answer to this question might be positive if the kind of postmodernism feminists adopt is a carefully constructed one. As Nancy Fraser and I argue, postmodernism need not demand the elimination of all big theory, much less theory *per se,* to avoid totalization and essentialism. The key is to identify types of theorizing which are inimical to essentialism. Thus, theorizing which is explicitly historical, that is, which situates its categories within historical frameworks, less easily invites the dangers of false generalizations than does theorizing which does not. Thus, our criticisms of writers such as Chodorow are not based on the mere presence of generalizations within their theories as on the fact that the categories that they employ, such as mothering, are not situated within a specific cultural and historical context. Of course, the process of framing a phenomenon within a context is always one that can be further extended. Therefore, one could, theoretically, invoke this ideal to such an extent that all that is left viable are descriptions of particular events at particular points in time. However, that this ideal can be carried to such an extreme does not negate the wisdom of feminist scholars today moving in such a direction given the very extreme avoidance of history by many of the disciplines of the contemporary academy.

The conclusion, therefore, is that postmodernism must avoid any simple celebration of difference or of particularity for its own sake. This point also emerges in Elspeth Probyn's discussion of "location." By "location" Probyn refers to the process by which:

> knowledges are ordered into sequences which are congruent with pre-
> viously established categories of knowledge. Location then, delineates
> what we may hold as knowledge and, following, Foucault, renders
> certain experiences 'true' and 'scientific' while excluding others.

Lest, however, we are led to adopt a view of meaning construction as that which results only from imposition, Probyn reminds us that any "locale" is both a product of imposition (location) and is also the site of our desires. Thus:

> This is also to remember that we negotiate our locales; that we are
> continuously working to make sense of and articulate both place and
> event. Moreover, as we approach others' locales we must keep in mind
> that women are never simply fixed within locale. We may live within
> patriarchy but at different levels and in different ways the struggle to
> rearticulate locale continues.

One conclusion Probyn draws from these remarks is a warning against any simple celebration of locality. Any "locale" is rarely unproblematic but represents a process of contestation and negotiation. But this means that the extent to which we insist on difference and how we describe the "differences that make a difference" is itself a political act. Thus, Bordo is correct in noting that the mere abstract invocation of difference could theoretically be used in the service of conservative ends. The clear danger here is in viewing postmodernism as merely an invocation of certain abstract ideals, such as "difference" rather than viewing the postmodern invocation of difference as following from and being limited to the demands of specific political contexts.

But this demand that postmodernism situate its defense of specific values within an historical context obviously also follows from postmodernism's own methodological claims. It would not be difficult for postmodernists to carry out such an injunction with regard to the category of "difference." For example, the claim could be made that while the broad-category sweeps of modernity might have been liberatory at one point, by reacting against the particularistic way of thinking of earlier times, by the mid-part of the twentieth century such moves were also beginning to be used to justify reactive positions. Thus, the universalizing strategies of Enlightenment humanism began to be used in the United States and Western Europe against attempts to use race and gender as criteria in educational or employment policies. Twentieth-century Marxism has used the generalizing categories of production and class to delegitimize demands of women, black people, gays, lesbians, and others whose oppression cannot be reduced to economics. Thus, to raise questions now about the necessarily liberatory consequences of universalizing categories is to open spaces for movements otherwise shut out by them.

What, though about the argument that postmodernism reduces all discourse to rhetoric, that it allows no distinction between reason and power? Again, I believe that a carefully constructed postmodernism can deal with this problem. We can admit of the postmodern claim that conceptual distinctions, criteria of legitimation, cognitive procedural rules, and so forth are all political and therefore represent moves of power and also recognize that they represent a different type of power than is exhibited in, for example, physical violence or the threat of force. A postmodern feminism could thus both support certain procedural aspects of natural science or other reflexive criteria of validity claims, that is, "decision procedures to guide choices in theory, research, and politics," while also acknowledging such support as political and grounded in a particular cultural context.

The underlying thread of these remarks is that postmodernism must reject a description of itself as embodying a set of timeless ideals contrary to those of modernism; it must insist on being recognized as a set of viewpoints of a time, justifiable only within its own time. By doing so, of course, it opens itself up to objections by feminists and others of being potentially dangerous for our times. In short, as feminists, how do we assess the political implications of postmodernism?

The essay by Donna Haraway is helpful here. Haraway very clearly presents postmodernism as a viewpoint of our times, but as one neither wholly attractive nor abhorrent in so far as the period is one of both possibilities and foreclosures. To illuminate the mixed values of the present, she uses the metaphor of a Cyborg. A Cyborg is a phenomenon which violates certain previously dominant distinctions, particularly those between humans and animals, humans and machines, minds and bodies, and materialism and idealism. It rejects prior hopes of unity and wholeness as expressed in such ideals as unalienated labor, pre-Oedipal symbiosis, community as family , and female as goddess. Rather, it reveals a heightened consciousness of boundaries, whose dark side for her is an escalating individualism.

For Haraway, the postmodern is a period not only of changed ideals, metaphors, and hopes. It is also a period of changed structures of family, work relations, and class distinctions. Here, Haraway's position is similar to that of some theorists, such as Baudrillard, who describe the postmodern period as "post" modernization, where modernization refers to the process of industrialization and the growth of the nation state. For Haraway, some significant markers of such social-structural changes are the growing dominance of women-headed households, the erosion of gender as an organizing principle of some aspects of work life, and the emergence of a two-class system constituted on its underside by masses of women and people of color. It is a time where prior means of control and repression have given way to new forms. "Our dominations don't work by medicalization and normalization anymore; they work by networking, communications redesign, stress management."

But lest we become too gloomy about such a diagnosis of the present, Haraway also points to the political possibilities which the postmodern present makes available. "With no available original dream of a common language or original symbiosis promising protection from hostile "masculine" separation, . . . we are freed from the need to root politics in identification, vanguard parties, purity, or mothering." She argues that what has now become possible is a politics which embraces a recognition of the multiple, pregnant, and contradictory aspects of both our individual and collective identities. Such a politics no longer requires essential criteria of identification; rather, she claims, we are beginning to see instead the formation of political groupings which rest on the conscious negation of such criteria. For example, she points to the identifying phrase "women of color" as an example of such a postmodern identity, that is, an identity constructed out of a recognition of otherness and difference.

Andreas Huyssen, like Donna Haraway, describes the postmodern as a perspective within an historical condition. Like Haraway, he also sees certain critical and liberatory elements of postmodernism which are related to its rejection of that which had become oppressive in modernism.

For Huyssen there is no question that modernism was liberatory in its manifestations both as capitalist modernization and communist vanguardism. But tied to its emancipatory aspects were also its forms of oppression. Such forms became manifest in its architecture after 1945:

> After 1945, modernist architecture was largely deprived of its social vision and became increasingly an architecture of power and representation. Rather than standing as harbingers of promises of the new life, modernist housing projects became symbols of alienation and dehumanization, a fate they shared with the assembly line, that other agent of the new which had been greeted with exhuberant enthusiasm in the 1920s by Leninists and Fordists alike.

A most fundamental feature of modernist art has been its strong disdain of mass culture and its postulation of the aesthetic as a domain of life separate from both the political and the ordinary. Using this element of modernism as definitive, Huyssen examines various trends of aesthetic and theoretical rebellion from the 1960s to the present. His argument is that which most significantly defines the critical element in postmodernism is its challenge to modernism's hostility to mass culture. On such grounds, Huyssen distinguishes postmodernism from poststructuralism. Huyssen argues that the privileged position poststructuralist theorists give to aesthetics and the separation they make of art from life, reality, and history replicates crucial oppressive features of modernity:

> The insight that the subject is constituted in language and the notion that there is nothing outside the text have led to the privileging of the aesthetic and the linguistic which aestheticism has always promoted to justify its imperial claims. The list of 'no longer possibles' (realism, representation, subjectivity, history, etc. etc.) is as long in poststructuralism as it used to be in modernism, and it is very similar indeed.

Following these claims, Huyssen makes a distinction between writers such as Derrida and the late Barthes who have received warm receptions in American literature departments and the more political, and thus on Huyssen's criteria, more truly postmodern, writings of such theorists as Foucault, the early Baudrillard, Kristeva, and Lyotard.

Identity and Differentiation

The depiction of postmodernism as a set of perspectives with its own possibilities and dangers has implications going beyond what has traditionally been understood as "political." At stake also are issues of personal and social identity and how the "political" itself is to be defined. Anna Yeatman argues that such distinctions as between the "individual" and "society," between the "private" and the "public," between "emotion" and "reason," and between the "personal" and the "political" are distinctions both central to the modern world view and ones long recognized by feminists as antithetical to the needs of women. Yeatman also claims an affinity between the type of individualism created by modernity, that is, that which is rooted in private property and that which has been central to the modern subordination of women. It is this very individualism, she claims, which has necessitated the modern demand for normative universals:

> Instead of a divinely sanctioned, consensual moral order, there emerges the decentered world of a plurality of individual agents responsible for their own destinies. At the same time that this order of individualized agency undermines all religious presuppositions and secularizes our

reality, the primitive type of individuality involved necessitates that there be a single standard or norm of authority which subordinates the plurality of individualized agency, and renders it so many distinct versions of this sole authoritative voice. Accordingly, the implications of the modernist discovery of the existence of individualized and therefore plural values are contained in the face of the necessity to reduce this plurality to a single standard.

On the grounds, therefore, of sharing common enemies, Yeatman sees an affinity between feminism and postmodernism. However, she also sees dangers for feminism in certain versions of postmodernism, dangers which she aligns with relativism. One could extend her discussion to note that postmodernism might emerge as an extension of the individualism of modernity, only now deprived of its subordinating universals. The result would be the kind of absolute endorsement of particularity and difference that Bordo warns against. Following Haraway's description of the post-modern as an era of both dangers and possibilities, we could also say that such dangers, like the possibilities, emerge out of the specific features of the time. For Yeatman, such features include the increasing inability of privileged groups to use the universals of modernity to sustain their power. Or as suggested in the essay by Elspeth Probyn, they might even include the emergence of an attitude towards difference suggested by the experience of tourism: where diversity is experienced in its most superficial manifestations. In short, to move beyond modernist ideas of differentiation is to move in potentially many different directions.

Moreover, even knowing what it is to "move beyond modernist ideas" may not always be clear. For example, as Iris Young argues, one category to which leftists and feminists have frequently appealed to counter the alienation and individualism of modern Western society, has been that of "community." Insofar as feminists have often viewed the distinction between individual and community as also culturally associated with the distinctions of the masculine and the feminine, the calculative and the affective and the instrumental and the authentic, they have looked to "community" as expressing those ideals most positively and authentically female. Yet, Young warns us that the very ideal which community represents may be so tied within modernity to the individualism it seeks to reject, so as to negate its worth as a truly liberatory ideal:

> Like most such oppositions, moreover, individualism and community have a common logic underlying their polarity, which makes it possible for them to define each other negatively. Each entails a denial of difference and desire to bring multiplicity and heterogeneity into unity, though in opposing ways. Liberal individualism denies difference by positing the self as a solid, self-sufficient unity, not defined by or in

need of anything or anyone other than itself. Its formalistic ethic of rights denies difference by leveling all such separated individuals under a common measure of rights. Community, on the other hand, denies difference by positing fusion rather than separation as the social ideal.

Moreover, as Young notes, the ideal of community discourages the development of respect among people for those with whom they do not identify. By looking to small-town life as most exemplary of this ideal, it also negates the fact of the city as an historical given. Indeed, many of the same people who pay theoretical homage to the ideal of community also concretely enjoy the energy and diversity of the city as well as the very anonymity they might theoretically reject.

That any given category may not be obviously apparent as either "modern" or "postmodern" as well as either dangerous or liberatory is also made apparent in analyzing the category central to feminist discussions of social differentiation: gender. On the one hand, the recognition of this category as central in understanding human thought and behavior has been a major feminist accomplishment. Insofar as the use of this category represents a necessary refinement of the encompassing category of "humanity," this accomplishment might also be described as postmodern. However, in so far as the category is given substantive, cross-cultural content, there arises the possibility that it becomes totalizing and discriminating against the experiences and realities of some. Moreover, as Judith Butler demonstrates in "Gender Trouble, Feminist Theory, and Psychoanalytic Discourse," the dangers are not only that of shutting out the experiences of women not white, Western, middle-class and of the late twentieth century, but of constructing notions of self-identity which are implicitly heterosexist.

A central thesis of Judith Butler's essay is that gender identity is a regulative ideal which fundamentally assists the norm of heterosexuality. Psychoanalytic theory, in its diverse forms, including object relations theory and Lacanian and post-Lacanian theory, aids this regulative process. Such theory both "confers a false sense of legitimacy and universality to a culturally specific, and, in some contexts, culturally oppressive, version of gender identity" and contributes to the heterosexual ideal by intertwining gender identity and sexual orientation:

Within these appropriations of psychoanalytic theory, gender identity and sexual orientation are accomplished at once. Although the story of sexual development is complicated, and quite different for *the* girl than for *the* boy, it appeals in both contexts to an operative disjunction that remains stable throughout: One identifies with one sex and, in so doing, desires the other, that desire being the elaboration of that identity,

> the mode by which it creates its opposite and defines itself in that
> opposition. . . . Granted, it may well be a woman, male-identified,
> who desires another woman, or a man, female-identified, who desires
> another man, and it may also be a woman, male-identified, who desires
> a man, female-identified, or similarly, a man, female-identified, who
> desires a woman, male-identified. One either identifies with a sex or
> desires it, but only those two relations are possible.

Moreover, according to Butler, it is the very belief in gender identity
as a core unity which causes our sexual orientation, which keeps from
view the very political and disciplinary processes which produce the
ostensible coherence of gender identity. On these grounds, then, notions
of gender identity are not the point of our liberation but rather the grounding of our continuing oppression.

Following Butler's argument, we might speculate that a notion of gender
identity as the cause of sexual orientation became of use in the twentieth-
century West as a means to ensure widespread conformity with heterosexual norms in a context where the reproduction of children no longer
operated as sufficient motivation. However, more relevant here than explaining why a notion of gender identity could have come to be used in
controlling ways is the more methodological issue that the very categories
we use to liberate us may also have their controlling moment. The task
then is to be sensitive to the complexities of social demands and social
changes which can make the use of the very same category both dangerous
and liberating.

It is difficult to know whether to describe such a sensitivity as "modern"
or "postmodern." Certainly, the pragmatism, wariness toward absolutes,
and the recognition of complexities that such a sensitivity represents, are
all symptomatic of "the postmodern turn." On the other hand, as attitudes
of both theoretical and political practice, they also have clear roots within
modernity. In this sense, to describe such a sensitivity as modern or
postmodern may be less important than emphasizing its centrality to the
needs of feminism. At least with such a conclusion, I believe, all of the
contributors to this volume would surely agree.

Part I

Feminism As Against Epistemology?

1

Social Criticism without Philosophy: An Encounter between Feminism and Postmodernism

Nancy Fraser and *Linda J. Nicholson*

Feminism and postmodernism have emerged as two of the most important political-cultural currents of the last decade. So far, however, they have kept an uneasy distance from one another. Indeed, so great has been their mutual wariness that there have been remarkably few extended discussions of the relations between them.[1]

Initial reticences aside, there are good reasons for exploring the relations between feminism and postmodernism. Both have offered deep and far-reaching criticisms of the institution of philosophy. Both have elaborated critical perspectives on the relation of philosophy to the larger culture. And, most central to the concerns of this essay, both have sought to develop new paradigms of social criticism which do not rely on traditional philosophical underpinnings. Other differences notwithstanding, one could say that during the last decade feminists and postmodernists have worked independently on a common nexus of problems: They have tried to rethink the relation between philosophy and social criticism so as to develop paradigms of criticism without philosophy.

On the other hand, the two tendencies have proceeded from opposite directions. Postmodernists have focused primarily on the philosophy side of the prob-

This essay has previously appeared in *Communication*, Vol. 10, Nos. 3 and 4, 1988, pp. 345–366; *Theory, Culture and Society*, Vol. 5, Nos. 2 and 3, June 1988, pp. 373–394; *Universal Abandon? The Politics of Postmodernism*, ed. Andrew Ross (Minneapolis: University of Minnesota Press, 1988) pp. 83–104; *The Institution of Philosophy: A Discipline in Crisis?* ed. Avner Cohen and Marcelo Dascal (Peru, Illinois: Open Court Press, 1989). We are grateful for the helpful suggestions of many people, especially Jonathan Arac, Ann Ferguson, Marilyn Frye, Nancy Hartsock, Alison Jaggar, Berel Lang, Thomas McCarthy, Karsten Struhl, Iris Young, Thomas Wartenburg, and the members of SOFPHIA. We are also grateful for word-processing help from Marina Rosiene.

lem. They have begun by elaborating antifoundational metaphilosophical perspectives and from there have drawn conclusions about the shape and character of social criticism. For feminists, on the other hand, the question of philosophy has always been subordinate to an interest in social criticism. Consequently, they have begun by developing critical political perspectives and from there have drawn conclusions about the status of philosophy. As a result of this difference in emphasis and direction, the two tendencies have ended up with complementary strengths and weaknesses. Postmodernists offer sophisticated and persuasive criticisms of foundationalism and essentialism, but their conceptions of social criticism tend to be anemic. Feminists offer robust conceptions of social criticism, but they tend at times to lapse into foundationalism and essentialism.

Thus, each of the two perspectives suggests some important criticisms of the other. A postmodernist reflection on feminist theory reveals disabling vestiges of essentialism while a feminist reflection on postmodernism reveals androcentrism and political naivete.

It follows that an encounter between feminism and postmodernism will initially be a trading of criticisms. But there is no reason to suppose that this is where matters must end. In fact, each of these tendencies has much to learn from the other; each is in possession of valuable resources which can help remedy the deficiencies of the other. Thus, the ultimate stake of an encounter between feminism and postmodernism is the prospect of a perspective which integrates their respective strengths while eliminating their respective weaknesses. It is the prospect of a postmodernist feminism.

In what follows, we aim to contribute to the development of such a perspective by staging the initial, critical phase of the encounter. In the first section, we examine the ways in which one exemplary postmodernist, Jean-François Lyotard, has sought to derive new paradigms of social criticism from a critique of the institution of philosophy. We argue that the conception of social criticism so derived is too restricted to permit an adequate critical grasp of gender dominance and subordination. We identify some internal tensions in Lyotard's arguments, and we suggest some alternative formulations which could allow for more robust forms of criticism without sacrificing the commitment to antifoundationalism. In the second section, we examine some representative genres of feminist social criticism. We argue that in many cases feminist critics continue tacitly to rely on the sorts of philosophical underpinnings which their own commitments, like those of the postmodernists, ought in principle to rule out. We identify some points at which such underpinnings could be abandoned without any sacrifice of social-critical force. Finally, in a brief conclusion, we consider the prospects for a postmodernist feminism. We discuss some requirements which constrain the development of such a perspective, and we identify some pertinent conceptual resources and critical strategies.

Postmodernism

Postmodernists seek, *inter alia,* to develop conceptions of social criticism which do not rely on traditional philosophical underpinnings. The typical starting point for their efforts is a reflection on the condition of philosophy today. Writers like Richard Rorty and Jean-François Lyotard begin by arguing that Philosophy with a capital *P* is no longer a viable or credible enterprise. They go on to claim that philosophy and, by extension, theory in general, can no longer function to *ground* politics and social criticism. With the demise of foundationalism comes the demise of the view that casts philosophy in the role of *founding* discourse vis-à-vis social criticism. That "modern" conception must give way to a new "postmodern" one in which criticism floats free of any universalist theoretical ground. No longer anchored philosophically, the very shape or character of social criticism changes; it becomes more pragmatic, *ad hoc,* contextual, and local. With this change comes a corresponding change in the social role and political function of intellectuals.

Thus, in the postmodern reflection on the relationship between philosophy and social criticism, the term 'philosophy' undergoes an explicit devaluation; it is cut down to size, if not eliminated altogether. Yet, even as this devaluation is argued explicitly, the term 'philosophy' retains an implicit structural privilege. It is the changed condition of philosophy which determines the changed character of social criticism and of engaged intellectual practice. In the new postmodern equation, then, philosophy is the independent variable while social criticism and political practice are dependent variables. The view of theory which emerges is not determined by considering the needs of contemporary criticism and engagement. It is determined, rather, by considering the contemporary status of philosophy. This way of proceeding has important consequences, not all of which are positive. Among the results is a certain underestimation and premature foreclosing of possibilities for social criticism and engaged intellectual practice. This limitation of postmodern thought will be apparent when we consider its results in the light of the needs of contemporary feminist theory and practice.

Let us consider as an example the postmodernism of Jean-François Lyotard, since it is genuinely exemplary of the larger tendency. Lyotard is one of the few social thinkers widely considered postmodern who actually uses the term; indeed, it was he himself who introduced it into current discussions of philosophy, politics, society, and social theory. His book *The Postmodern Condition* has become the *locus classicus* for contemporary debates, and it reflects in an especially acute form the characteristic concerns and tensions of the movement.[2]

For Lyotard, postmodernism designates a general condition of contemporary Western civilization. The postmodern condition is one in which "grand narratives of legitimation" are no longer credible. By grand narratives he means overarching philosophies of history like the Enlightenment story of the gradual but steady progress of reason and freedom, Hegel's dialectic of Spirit coming to know itself, and, most importantly, Marx's drama of the forward march of human productive capacities via class conflict culminating in proletarian revolution. For Lyotard, these metanarratives instantiate a specifically modern approach to the problem of legitimation. Each situates first-order discursive practices of inquiry and politics within a broader totalizing metadiscourse which legitimates them. The metadiscourse narrates a story about the whole of human history which purports to guarantee that the pragmatics of the modern sciences and of modern political processes—the norms and rules which govern these practices, determining what counts as a warranted move within them— are themselves legitimate. The story guarantees that some sciences and some politics have the *right* pragmatics and, so, are the *right* practices.

We should not be misled by Lyotard's focus on narrative philosophies of history. In his conception of legitimating metanarrative, the stress properly belongs on the *meta* and not on the *narrative*. For what most interests him about the Enlightenment, Hegelian, and Marxist stories is what they share with other nonnarrative forms of philosophy. Like ahistorical epistemologies and moral theories, they aim to show that specific first-order discursive practices are well formed and capable of yielding true and just results. *True* and *just* here mean something more than results reached by adhering scrupulously to the constitutive rules of some given scientific and political games. They mean, rather, results which correspond to Truth and Justice as they really are in themselves independently of contingent, historical social practices. Thus, in Lyotard's view, a metanarrative is *meta* in a very strong sense. It purports to be a privileged discourse capable of situating, characterizing, and evaluating all other discourses but not itself to be infected by the historicity and contingency which render first-order discourses potentially distorted and in need of legitimation.

In *The Postmodern Condition,* Lyotard argues that metanarratives, whether philosophies of history or nonnarrative foundational philosophies, are merely modern and dépassé. We can no longer believe, he claims, in the availability of a privileged metadiscourse capable of capturing once and for all the truth of every first-order discourse. The claim to *meta* status does not stand up. A so-called metadiscourse is in fact simply one more discourse among others. It follows for Lyotard that legitimation, both epistemic and political, can no longer reside in philosophical metanarratives. Where, then, he asks, does legitimation reside in the postmodern era?

Much of *The Postmodern Condition* is devoted to sketching an answer to that question. The answer, in brief, is that in the postmodern era legitimation becomes plural, local, and immanent. In this era, there will necessarily be many discourses of legitimation dispersed among the plurality of first-order discursive practices. For example, scientists no longer look to prescriptive philosophies of science to warrant their procedures of inquiry. Rather, they themselves problematize, modify, and warrant the constitutive norms of their own practice even as they engage in it. Instead of hovering above, legitimation descends to the level of practice and becomes immanent in it. There are no special tribunals set apart from the sites where inquiry is practiced. Rather, practitioners assume responsibility for legitimizing their own practice.

Lyotard intimates that something similar is or should be happening with respect to political legitimation. We cannot have and do not need a single, overarching theory of justice. What is required, rather, is a "justice of multiplicities."[3] What Lyotard means by this is not wholly clear. On one level, he can be read as offering a normative vision in which the good society consists in a decentralized plurality of democratic, self-managing groups and institutions whose members problematize the norms of their practice and take responsibility for modifying them as situations require. But paradoxically, on another level, he can be read as ruling out the sort of larger-scale, normative political theorizing which, from a modern perspective at least, would be required to legitimate such a vision. In any case, his justice of multiplicities conception precludes one familiar, and arguably essential, genre of political theory: identification and critique of macrostructures of inequality and injustice which cut across the boundaries separating relatively discrete practices and institutions. There is no place in Lyotard's universe for critique of pervasive axes of stratification, for critique of broad-based relations of dominance and subordination along lines like gender, race, and class.

Lyotard's suspicion of the large extends to historical narrative and social theory as well. Here, his chief target is Marxism, the one metanarrative in France with enough lingering credibility to be worth arguing against. The problem with Marxism, in his view, is twofold. On the one hand, the Marxian story is too big, since it spans virtually the whole of human history. On the other hand, the Marxian story is too theoretical, since it relies on a *theory* of social practice and social relations which claims to *explain* historical change. At one level, Lyotard simply rejects the specifics of this theory. He claims that the Marxian conception of practice as production occludes the diversity and plurality of human practices; and that the Marxian conception of capitalist society as a totality traversed by one major division and contradiction occludes the diversity and plurality of contemporary societal differences and oppositions. But Lyotard does not conclude that such deficiencies can and should be remedied by a better social theory. Rather, he rejects the project of social theory *tout court*.

Once again, Lyotard's position is ambiguous, since his rejection of social theory depends on a theoretical perspective of sorts of its own. He offers a postmodern conception of sociality and social identity, a conception of what he calls "the social bond." What holds a society together, he claims, is not a common consciousness or institutional substructure. Rather, the social bond is a weave of crisscrossing threads of discursive practices, no single one of which runs continuously throughout the whole. Individuals are the nodes or posts where such practices intersect, and so, they participate in many practices simultaneously. It follows that social identities are complex and heterogeneous. They cannot be mapped onto one another nor onto the social totality. Indeed, strictly speaking, there is no social totality and *a fortiori* no possibility of a totalizing social theory.

Thus, Lyotard insists that the field of the social is heterogeneous and nontotalizable. As a result, he rules out the sort of critical social theory which employs general categories like gender, race, and class. From his perspective, such categories are too reductive of the complexity of social identities to be useful. There is apparently nothing to be gained, in his view, by situating an account of the fluidity and diversity of discursive practices in the context of a critical analysis of large-scale institutions and social structures.

Thus, Lyotard's postmodern conception of criticism without philosophy rules out several recognizable genres of social criticism. From the premise that criticism cannot be grounded by a foundationalist philosophical meta-narrative, he infers the illegitimacy of large historical stories, normative theories of justice, and social-theoretical accounts of macrostructures which institutionalize inequality. What, then, *does* postmodern social criticism look like?

Lyotard tries to fashion some new genres of social criticism from the discursive resources that remain. Chief among these is smallish, localized narrative. He seeks to vindicate such narrative against both modern totalizing metanarrative and the scientism that is hostile to all narrative. One genre of postmodern social criticism, then, consists in relatively discrete, local stories about the emergence, transformation, and disappearance of various discursive practices treated in isolation from one another. Such stories might resemble those told by Michel Foucault, although without the attempts to discern larger synchronic patterns and connections that Foucault sometimes made.[4] Like Michael Walzer, Lyotard evidently assumes that practitioners would narrate such stories when seeking to persuade one another to modify the pragmatics or constitutive norms of their practice.[5]

This genre of social criticism is not the whole postmodern story, however. For it casts critique as strictly local, *ad hoc,* and ameliorative, thus supposing a political diagnosis according to which there are no large-scale, systemic problems which resist local, *ad hoc,* ameliorative initiatives. Yet, Lyotard recognizes that postmodern society does contain at least one unfavorable structural tendency which requires a more coordinated response. This is the tendency to universalize instrumental reason, to subject *all* discursive practices indiscriminately to the single criterion of efficiency, or "performativity." In Lyotard's view, this threatens the autonomy and integrity of science and politics, since these practices are not properly subordinated to performative standards. It would pervert and distort them, thereby destroying the diversity of discursive forms.

Thus, even as he argues explicitly against it, Lyotard posits the need for a genre of social criticism which transcends local mininarrative. Despite his strictures against large, totalizing stories, he narrates a fairly tall tale about a large-scale social trend. Moreover, the logic of this story, and of the genre of criticism to which it belongs, calls for judgments which are not strictly practice-immanent. Lyotard's story presupposes the legitimacy and integrity of the scientific and political practices allegedly threatened by performativity. It supposes that one can distinguish changes or developments which are *internal* to these practices from externally induced distortions. But this drives Lyotard to make normative judgments about the value and character of the threatened practices. These judgments are not strictly immanent in the practices judged. Rather, they are metapractical.

Thus, Lyotard's view of postmodern social criticism is neither entirely self-consistent nor entirely persuasive. He goes too quickly from the premise that Philosophy cannot ground social criticism to the conclusion that criticism itself must be local, *ad hoc,* and nontheoretical. As a result, he throws out the baby of large historical narrative with the bathwater of philosophical metanarrative and the baby of social-theoretical analysis of large-scale inequalities with the bathwater of reductive Marxian class theory. Moreover, these allegedly illegitimate babies do not in fact remain excluded. They return like the repressed within the very genres of postmodern social criticism with which Lyotard intends to replace them.

We began this discussion by noting that postmodernists orient their reflections on the character of postmodern social criticism by the falling star of foundationalist philosophy. They posit that, with philosophy no longer able credibly to ground social criticism, criticism itself must be local, *ad hoc,* and untheoretical. Thus, from the critique of foundationalism, they infer the illegitimacy of several genres of social criticism. For Lyotard, the illegitimate genres include large-scale historical narrative and social-theoretical analyses of pervasive relations of dominance and subordination.[6]

Suppose, however, one were to choose another starting point for reflecting on postfoundational social criticism. Suppose one began, not with the condition of Philosophy, but with the nature of the social object one wished to criticize. Suppose, further, that one defined that object as the subordination of women to and by men. Then, we submit, it would be apparent that many of the genres rejected by postmodernists are necessary for social criticism. For a phenomenon as pervasive and multifaceted as male dominance simply cannot be adequately grasped with the meager critical resources to which they would limit us. On the contrary, effective criticism of this phenomenon requires an array of different methods and genres. It requires at minimum large narratives about changes in social organization and ideology, empirical and social-theoretical analyses of macrostructures and institutions, interactionist analyses of the micropolitics of everyday life, critical-hermeneutical and institutional analyses of cultural production, historically and culturally specific sociologies of gender, and so on. The list could go on.

Clearly, not all of these approaches are local and untheoretical. But all are nonetheless essential to feminist social criticism. Moreover, all can in principle be conceived in ways that do not take us back to foundationalism, even though, as we argue in the next section, many feminists have not wholly succeeded in avoiding that trap.

Feminism

Feminists, like postmodernists, have sought to develop new paradigms of social criticism which do not rely on traditional philosophical underpinnings. They have criticized modern foundationalist epistemologies and moral and political theories, exposing the contingent, partial, and historically situated character of what has passed in the mainstream for necessary, universal, and ahistorical truths. They have called into question the dominant philosophical project of seeking objectivity in the guise of a "God's eye view" which transcends any situation or perspective.[7]

However, if postmodernists have been drawn to such views by a concern with the status of philosophy, feminists have been led to them by the demands of political practice. This practical interest has saved feminist theory from many of the mistakes of postmodernism: Women whose theorizing was to serve the struggle against sexism were not about to abandon powerful political tools merely as a result of intramural debates in professional philosophy.

Yet, even as the imperatives of political practice have saved feminist theory from one set of difficulties, they have tended at times to incline it toward another. Practical imperatives have led some feminists to adopt modes of theorizing which resemble the sorts of philosophical metanarrative rightly criticized by postmodernists. To be sure, the feminist theories we have in mind here are not pure metanarratives; they are not ahistorical normative theories about the transcultural nature of rationality or justice. Rather, they are very large social theories—theories of history, society, culture, and psychology—which claim, for example, to identify causes and constitutive features of sexism that operate cross-culturally. Thus, these social theories purport to be empirical rather than philosophical. But, as we hope to show, they are actually quasi-metanarratives. They tacitly presuppose some commonly held but unwarranted and essentialist assumptions about the nature of human beings and the conditions for social life. In addition, they assume methods and concepts which are uninflected by temporality or historicity and which therefore function *de facto* as permanent, neutral matrices for inquiry. Such theories then, share some of the essentialist and ahistorical features of metanarratives: They are insufficiently attentive to historical and cultural diversity, and they falsely universalize features of the theorist's own era, society, culture, class, sexual orientation, and ethnic, or racial group.

On the other hand, the practical exigencies inclining feminists to produce quasi-metanarratives have by no means held undisputed sway. Rather, they have had to coexist, often uneasily, with counterexigencies which have worked to opposite effect, for example, political pressures to acknowledge differences among women. In general, then, the recent history of feminist social theory reflects a tug of war between forces which have encouraged and forces which have discouraged metanarrative-like modes of theorizing. We can illustrate this dynamic by looking at a few important turning points in this history.

When in the 1960s, women in the New Left began to extend prior talk about women's rights into the more encompassing discussion of women's liberation, they encountered the fear and hostility of their male comrades and the use of Marxist political theory as a support for these reactions. Many men of the New Left argued that gender issues were secondary because they were subsumable under more basic modes of oppression, namely, class and race.

In response to this practical-political problem, radical feminists such as Shulamith Firestone resorted to an ingenious tactical maneuver: Firestone invoked biological differences between women and men to explain sexism. This enabled her to turn the tables on her Marxist comrades by claiming that gender conflict was the most basic form of human conflict and the source of all other forms, including class conflict.[8] Firestone drew on the pervasive tendency within modern culture to locate the roots of gender differences in biology. Her coup was to use biologism to establish the primacy of the struggle against male domination rather than to justify acquiescence to it.

The trick, of course, is problematic from a postmodernist perspective in that appeals to biology to explain social phenomena are essentialist and monocausal. They are essentialist insofar as they project onto all women and men qualities which develop under historically specific social conditions. They are monocausal insofar as they look to one set of characteristics, such as women's physiology or men's hormones, to explain women's oppression in all cultures. These problems are only compounded when appeals to biology are used in conjunction with the dubious claim that women's oppression is the cause of all other forms of oppression.

Moreover, as Marxists and feminist anthropologists began insisting in the early 1970s, appeals to biology do not allow us to understand the enormous diversity of forms which both gender and sexism assume in different cultures. In fact, it was not long before most feminist social theorists came to appreciate that accounting for the diversity of the forms of sexism was as important as accounting for its depth and autonomy. Gayle Rubin aptly described this dual requirement as the need to formulate theory which could account for the oppression of women in its "endless variety and monotonous similarity."[9] How were feminists to develop a social theory adequate to both demands?

One approach which seemed promising was suggested by Michelle Zimbalist Rosaldo and other contributors in the influential 1974 anthropology collection, *Woman, Culture, and Society*. They argued that common to all known societies was some type of separation between a domestic sphere and a public sphere, the former associated with women and the latter with men. Because in most societies to date, women have spent a good part of their lives bearing and raising children, their lives have been more bound to the domestic sphere. Men, on the other hand, have had both the time and mobility to engage in those out of the home activities which generate political structures. Thus, as Rosaldo argued, while in many societies women possess some or even a great deal of power, women's power is always viewed as illegitimate, disruptive, and without authority.[10]

This approach seemed to allow for both diversity and ubiquity in the manifestations of sexism. A very general identification of women with the domestic and of men with the extra-domestic could accommodate a great deal of cultural variation both in social structures and in gender roles. At the same time, it could make comprehensible the apparent ubiquity of the assumption of women's inferiority above and beyond such variation. This hypothesis was also compatible with the idea that the extent of women's oppression differed in different societies. It could explain such differences by correlating the extent of gender inequality in a society with the extent and rigidity of the separation between its domestic and public spheres. In short, the domestic/public theorists seemed to have generated an explanation capable of satisfying a variety of conflicting demands.

However, this explanation turned out to be problematic in ways reminiscent of Firestone's account. Although the theory focused on differences between men's and women's spheres of activity rather than on differences between men's and women's biology, it was essentialist and monocausal nonetheless. It posited the existence of a domestic sphere in all societies and thereby assumed that women's activities were basically similar in content and significance across cultures. (An analogous assumption about men's activities lay behind the postulation of a universal public sphere.) In effect, the theory falsely generalized to all societies an historically specific conjunction of properties: women's responsibility for early child rearing, women's tendency to spend more time in the geographical space of the home, women's lesser participation in the affairs of the community, a cultural ascription of triviality to domestic work, and a cultural ascription of inferiority to women. The theory thus failed to appreciate that, while each individual property may be true of many societies, the conjunction is not true of most.[11]

One source of difficulty in these early feminist social theories was the presumption of an overly grandiose and totalizing conception of theory. Theory was understood as the search for the one key factor which would explain sexism cross-culturally and illuminate all of social life. In this sense, to theorize was by definition to produce a quasi-metanarrative.

Since the late 1970s, feminist social theorists have largely ceased speaking of biological determinants or a cross-cultural domestic/public separation. Many, moreover, have given up the assumption of monocausality. Nevertheless, some feminist social theorists have continued implicitly to suppose a quasi-metanarrative conception of theory. They have continued to theorize in terms of a putatively unitary, primary, culturally universal type of activity associated with women, generally an activity conceived as domestic and located in the family.

One influential example is the analysis of mothering developed by Nancy Chodorow. Setting herself to explain the internal, psychological dynamics which have led many women willingly to reproduce social divisions associated with female inferiority, Chodorow posited a cross-cultural activity, mothering, as the relevant object of investigation. Her question thus became: How is mothering as a female-associated activity reproduced over time? How does mothering produce a new generation of women with the psychological inclination to mother and a new generation of men not so inclined? The answer she offered was in terms of gender identity: Female mothering produces women whose deep sense of self is relational and men whose deep sense of self is not.[12]

Chodorow's theory has struck many feminists as a persuasive account of some apparently observable psychic differences between men and women. Yet, the theory has clear metanarrative overtones. It posits the existence of a single activity, mothering, which, while differing in specifics in different societies, nevertheless constitutes enough of a natural kind to warrant one label. It stipulates that this basically unitary activity gives rise to two distinct sorts of deep selves, one relatively common across cultures to women, the other relatively common across cultures to men. It claims that the difference thus generated between feminine and masculine gender identity causes a variety of supposedly cross-cultural social phenomena, including the continuation of female mothering, male contempt for women, and problems in heterosexual relationships.

From a postmodern perspective, all of these assumptions are problematic because they are essentialist. But the second one, concerning gender identity, warrants special scrutiny, given its political implications. Consider that Chodorow's use of the notion of gender identity presupposes three major premises. One is the psychoanalytic premise that everyone has a deep sense of self which is constituted in early childhood through one's interactions with one's primary parent and which remains relatively constant thereafter. Another is the premise that this deep self differs significantly for men and for women but is roughly similar among women, on the one hand, and among men, on the other hand, both across cultures and within cultures across lines of class, race, and ethnicity. The third premise is that this deep self colors everything one does; there are no actions, however trivial, which do not bear traces of one's masculine or feminine gender identity.

One can appreciate the political exigencies which made this conjunction of premises attractive. It gave scholarly substance to the idea of the pervasiveness of sexism. If masculinity and femininity constitute our basic and ever present sense of self, then it is not surprising that the manifestations of sexism are systemic. Moreover, many feminists had already sensed that the concept of sex-role socialization, an idea Chodorow explicitly criticized, ignored the depth and intractability of male dominance. By implying that measures such as changing images in school textbooks or allowing boys to play with dolls would be sufficient to bring about equality between the sexes, this concept seemed to trivialize and coopt the message of feminism. Finally, Chodorow's depth-psychological approach gave a scholarly sanction to the idea of sisterhood. It seemed to legitimate the claim that the ties which bind women are deep and substantively based.

Needless to say, we have no wish to quarrel with the claim of the depth and pervasiveness of sexism nor with the idea of sisterhood. But we do wish to challenge Chodorow's way of legitimating them. The idea of a cross-cultural, deep sense of self, specified differently for women and men, becomes problematic when given any specific content. Chodorow states that women everywhere differ from men in their greater concern with "relational interaction." But what does she mean by this term?

Certainly not any and every kind of human interaction, since men have often been more concerned than women with some kinds of interactions, for example, those which have to do with the aggrandizement of power and wealth. Of course, it is true that many women in modern Western societies have been expected to exhibit strong concern with those types of interactions associated with intimacy, friendship, and love, interactions which dominate one meaning of the late twentieth-century concept of relationship. But surely this meaning presupposes a notion of private life specific to modern Western societies of the last two centuries. Is it possible that Chodorow's theory rests on an equivocation on the term *relationship*?[13]

Equally troubling are the aporias this theory generates for political practice. While gender identity gives substance to the idea of sisterhood, it does so at the cost of repressing differences among sisters. Although the theory allows for some differences among women of different classes, races, sexual orientations, and ethnic groups, it construes these as subsidiary to more basic similarities. But it is precisely as a consequence of the request to understand such differences as secondary that many women have denied an allegiance to feminism.

We have dwelt at length on Chodorow because of the great influence her work has enjoyed. But she is not the only recent feminist social theorist who has constructed a quasi-metanarrative around a putatively cross-cultural female-associated activity. On the contrary, theorists like Ann Ferguson and Nancy Folbre, Nancy Hartsock, and Catharine MacKinnon have built similar theories around notions of sex-affective production, reproduction, and sexuality, respectively.[14] Each claims to have identified a basic kind of human practice found in all societies which has cross-cultural explanatory power. In each case, the practice in question is associated with a biological or quasi-biological need and is construed as functionally necessary to the reproduction of society. It is not the sort of thing, then, whose historical origins need be investigated.

The difficulty here is that categories like sexuality, mothering, reproduction, and sex-affective production group together phenomena which are not necessarily conjoined in all societies while separating off from one another phenomena which are not necessarily separated. As a matter of fact, it is doubtful whether these categories have any determinate cross-cultural content. Thus, for a theorist to use such categories to construct a universalistic social theory is to risk projecting the socially dominant conjunctions and dispersions of her own society onto others, thereby distorting important features of both. Social theorists would do better first to construct genealogies of the *categories* of sexuality, reproduction, and mothering before assuming their universal significance.

Since around 1980, many feminist scholars have come to abandon the project of grand social theory. They have stopped looking for *the* causes of sexism and have turned to more concrete inquiry with more limited aims. One reason for this shift is the growing legitimacy of feminist scholarship. The institutionalization of women's studies in the United States has meant a dramatic increase in the size of the community of feminist inquirers, a much greater division of scholarly labor, and a large and growing fund of concrete information. As a result, feminist scholars have come to regard their enterprise more collectively, more like a puzzle whose various pieces are being filled in by many different people than like a construction to be completed by a single grand theoretical stroke. In short, feminist scholarship has attained its maturity.

Even in this phase, however, traces of youthful quasi-metanarratives remain. Some theorists who have ceased looking for *the* causes of sexism still rely on essentialist categories such as gender identity. This is especially true of those scholars who have sought to develop gynocentric alternatives to mainstream androcentric perspectives but who have not fully abandoned the universalist pretensions of the latter.

Consider, as an example, the work of Carol Gilligan. Unlike most of the theorists we have considered so far, Gilligan has not sought to explain the origins or nature of cross-cultural sexism. Rather, she set herself the more limited task of exposing and redressing androcentric bias in the model of moral development of psychologist Lawrence Kohlberg. Thus, she argued that it is illegitimate to evaluate the moral development of women and girls by reference to a standard drawn exclusively from the experience of men and boys. She proposed to examine women's moral discourse on its own terms in order to uncover its immanent standards of adequacy.[15]

Gilligan's work has been rightly regarded as important and innovative. It challenged mainstream psychology's persistent occlusion of women's lives and experiences and its insistent but false claims to universality. Yet, insofar as Gilligan's challenge involved the construction of an alternative feminine model of moral development, her position was ambiguous. On the one hand, by providing a counterexample to Kohlberg's model, she cast doubt on the possibility of any single, universalist developmental schema. On the other hand, by constructing a female countermodel, she invited the same charge of false generalization she had herself raised against Kohlberg, although now from other perspectives such as class, sexual orientation, race, and ethnicity. Gilligan's disclaimers notwithstanding,[16] to the extent that she described women's moral development in terms of *a* different voice; to the extent that she did not specify which women, under which specific historical circumstances have spoken with the voice in question; and to the extent that she grounded her analysis in the explicitly cross-cultural framework of Nancy Chodorow, her model remained essentialist. It perpetuated in a newer, more localized fashion traces of previous more grandiose quasi-metanarratives.

Thus, vestiges of essentialism have continued to plague feminist scholarship, even despite the decline of grand theorizing. In many cases, including Gilligan's, this represents the continuing subterranean influence of those very mainstream modes of thought and inquiry with which feminists have wished to break.

On the other hand, the practice of feminist politics in the 1980s has generated a new set of pressures which have worked against metanarratives. In recent years, poor and working-class women, women of color, and lesbians have finally won a wider hearing for their objections to feminist theories which fail to illuminate their lives and address their problems. They have exposed the earlier quasi-metanarratives, with their assumptions of universal female dependence and confinement to the domestic sphere, as false extrapolations from the experience of the white, middle-class, heterosexual women who dominated the beginnings of the second wave. For example, writers like Bell Hooks, Gloria Joseph, Audre Lord, Maria Lugones, and Elizabeth Spelman have unmasked the implicit reference to white Anglo women in many classic feminist texts. Likewise, Adrienne Rich and Marilyn Frye have exposed the heterosexist bias of much mainstream feminist theory.[17] Thus, as the class, sexual, racial, and ethnic awareness of the movement has altered, so has the preferred conception of theory. It has become clear that quasi-metanarratives hamper rather than promote sisterhood, since they elide differences among women and among the forms of sexism to which different women are differentially subject. Likewise, it is increasingly apparent that such theories hinder alliances with other progressive movements, since they tend to occlude axes of domination other than gender. In sum, there is growing interest among feminists in modes of theorizing which are attentive to differences and to cultural and historical specificity.

In general, then, feminist scholarship of the 1980s evinces some conflicting tendencies. On the one hand, there is decreasing interest in grand social theories as scholarship has become more localized, issue-oriented, and explicitly fallibilistic. On the other hand, essentialist vestiges persist in the continued use of ahistorical categories like gender identity without reflection as to how, when, and why such categories originated and were modified over time. This tension is symptomatically expressed in the current fascination, on the part of U.S. feminists, with French psychoanalytic feminisms: The latter propositionally decry essentialism even as they performatively enact it.[18] More generally, feminist scholarship has remained insufficiently attentive to the *theoretical* prerequisites of dealing with diversity, despite widespread commitment to accepting it politically.

By criticizing lingering essentialism in contemporary feminist theory, we hope to encourage such theory to become more consistently postmodern. This is not, however, to recommend merely any form of postmodernism. On the contrary, as we have shown, the version developed by Jean-François Lyotard offers a weak and inadequate conception of social criticism without philosophy. It rules out genres of criticism, such as large historical narrative and historically situated social theory, which feminists rightly regard as indispensable. But it does not follow from Lyotard's shortcomings that criticism without philosophy is in principle incompatible with criticism with social force. Rather, as we argue next, a robust postmodern-feminist paradigm of social criticism without philosophy is possible.

Toward a Postmodern Feminism

How can we combine a postmodernist incredulity toward metanarratives with the social-critical power of feminism? How can we conceive a version of criticism without philosophy which is robust enough to handle the tough job of analyzing sexism in all its endless variety and monotonous similarity?

A first step is to recognize, *contra* Lyotard, that postmodern critique need forswear neither large historical narratives nor analyses of societal macrostructures. This point is important for feminists, since sexism has a long history and is deeply and pervasively embedded in contemporary societies. Thus, postmodern feminists need not abandon the large theoretical tools needed to address large political problems. There is nothing self-contradictory in the idea of a postmodern theory.

However, if postmodern-feminist critique must remain theoretical, not just any kind of theory will do. Rather, theory here would be explicitly historical, attuned to the cultural specificity of different societies and periods and to that of different groups within societies and periods. Thus, the categories of postmodern-feminist theory would be inflected by temporality, with historically specific institutional categories like the modern, restricted, male-headed, nuclear family taking precedence over ahistorical, functionalist categories like reproduction and mothering. Where categories of the latter sort were not eschewed altogether, they would be genealogized, that is, framed by a historical narrative and rendered temporally and culturally specific.

Moreover, postmodern-feminist theory would be nonuniversalist. When its focus became cross-cultural or transepochal, its mode of attention would be comparativist rather than universalizing, attuned to changes and contrasts instead of to covering laws. Finally, postmodern-feminist theory would dispense with the idea of a subject of history. It would replace unitary notions of woman and feminine gender identity with plural and complexly constructed conceptions of social identity, treating gender as one relevant strand among others, attending also to class, race, ethnicity, age, and sexual orientation.

In general, postmodern-feminist theory would be pragmatic and fallibilistic. It would tailor its methods and categories to the specific task at hand, using multiple categories when appropriate and forswearing the metaphysical comfort of a single feminist method or feminist epistemology. In short, this theory would look more like a tapestry composed of threads of many different hues than one woven in a single color.

The most important advantage of this sort of theory would be its usefulness for contemporary feminist political practice. Such practice is increasingly a matter of alliances rather than one of unity around a universally shared interest or identity. It recognizes that the diversity of women's needs and experiences means that no single solution, on issues like child care, social security, and housing, can be adequate for all. Thus, the underlying premise of this practice is that, while some women share some common interests and face some common enemies, such commonalities are by no means universal; rather, they are interlaced with differences, even with conflicts. This, then, is a practice made up of a patchwork of overlapping alliances, not one circumscribable by an essential definition. One might best speak of it in the plural as the practice of feminisms. In a sense, this practice is in advance of much contemporary feminist theory. It is already implicitly postmodern. It would find its most appropriate and useful theoretical expression in a postmodern-feminist form of critical inquiry. Such inquiry would be the theoretical counterpart of a broader, richer, more complex, and multilayered feminist solidarity, the sort of solidarity which is essential for overcoming the oppression of women in its "endless variety and monotonous similarity."

Notes

1. Exceptions are Jane Flax, "Gender as a Social Problem: In and For Feminist Theory," *American Studies/Amerika Studien,* June 1986, (an earlier version of the paper in this book); Sandra Harding, *The Science Question in Feminism* (Ithaca, NY: Cornell University Press, 1986) and "The Instability of the Analytical Categories of Feminist Theory," *Signs: Journal of Women in Culture and Society,* Vol. 11, No. 4, 1986, pp. 645–664; Donna Haraway, "A Manifesto for Cyborgs: Science, Technology, and Socialist Feminism in the 1980s," *Socialist Review,* No. 80, 1983, pp. 65–107; Alice A. Jardine, *Gynesis: Configurations of Women and Modernity* (Ithaca, NY: Cornell University Press, 1985); Jean-François Lyotard, "Some of the Things at Stake in Women's Struggles," trans. Deborah J. Clarke, Winifred Woodhull, and John Mowitt, *Sub-Stance,* No. 20, 1978; Craig Owens, "The

Discourse of Others: Feminists and Postmodernism," *The Anti-Aesthetic: Essays on Postmodern Culture,* ed. Hal Foster (Port Townsend, WA: Bay Press, 1983).

2. Jean-François Lyotard, *The Postmodern Condition: A Report on Knowledge,* trans. G. Bennington and B. Massumi (Minneapolis: University of Minnesota Press, 1984).

3. Ibid. Cf. Jean-François Lyotard and Jean-Loup Thebaud, *Just Gaming* (Minneapolis: University of Minnesota Press, 1987); also Jean-François Lyotard, "The Differend," *Diacritics,* Fall 1984, trans. Georges Van Den Abbeele, pp. 4–14.

4. See, for example, Michel Foucault, *Discipline and Punish: The Birth of the Prison,* trans. Alan Sheridan (New York: Vintage Books, 1979).

5. Michael Walzer, *Spheres of Justice: A Defense of Pluralism and Equality* (New York: Basic Books, 1983).

6. It should be noted that, for Lyotard, the choice of philosophy as a starting point is itself determined by a metapolitical commitment, namely, to antitotalitarianism. He assumes erroneously, in our view, that totalizing social and political theory necessarily eventuates in totalitarian societies. Thus, the "practical intent" that subtends Lyotard's privileging of philosophy (and which is in turn attenuated by the latter) is anti-Marxism. Whether it should also be characterized as neoliberalism is a question too complicated to be explored here.

7. See, for example, the essays in *Discovering Reality: Feminist Perspectives on Epistemology, Metaphysics, Methodology, and Philosophy of Science,* ed. Sandra Harding and Merrill B. Hintikka (Dordrecht, Holland: D. Reidel, 1983).

8. Shulamith Firestone, *The Dialectic of Sex* (New York: Bantam, 1970).

9. Gayle Rubin, "The Traffic in Women," *Toward an Anthropology of Women,* ed. Rayna R. Reiter, (New York: Monthly Review Press, 1975), p. 160.

10. Michelle Zimbalist Rosaldo, "Woman, Culture, and Society: A Theoretical Overview," *Woman, Culture, and Society,* ed. Michelle Zimbalist Rosaldo and Louise Lamphere (Stanford: Stanford University Press, 1974), pp. 17–42.

11. These and related problems were soon apparent to many of the domestic/public theorists themselves. See Rosaldo's self-criticism, "The Use and Abuse of Anthropology: Reflections on Feminism and Cross-cultural Understanding," *Signs: Journal of Women in Culture and Society,* Vol. 5, No. 3, 1980, pp. 389–417. A more recent discussion, which points out the circularity of the theory, appears in Sylvia J. Yanagisako and Jane F. Collier, "Toward a Unified Analysis of Gender and Kinship," *Gender and Kinship: Essays Toward a Unified Analysis,* ed. Jane Fishburne Collier and Sylvia Junko Yanagisako, (Stanford: Stanford University Press, 1987).

12. Nancy Chodorow, *The Reproduction of Mothering: Psychoanalysis and the Sociology of Gender* (Berkeley: University of California Press, 1978).

13. A similar ambiguity attends Chodorow's discussion of the family. In response to critics who object that her psychoanalytic emphasis ignores social structures, Chodorow has rightly insisted that the family is itself a social structure, one frequently slighted in social explanations. Yet, she generally does not discuss families as historically specific social institutions whose specific relations with other institutions can be analyzed. Rather, she tends to invoke the family in a very abstract and general sense defined only as the locus of female mothering.

14. Ann Ferguson and Nancy Folbre, "The Unhappy Marriage of Patriarchy and Capitalism," *Women and Revolution,* ed. Lydia Sargent (Boston: South End Press, 1981), pp. 313–338; Nancy Hartsock, *Money, Sex, and Power: Toward a Feminist Historical Materialism* (New York: Longman, 1983); Catharine A. MacKinnon, "Feminism, Marxism, Method, and the State: An Agenda for Theory," *Signs: Journal of Women in Culture and Society,* Vol. 7, No. 3, Spring 1982, pp. 515–544.

15. Carol Gilligan, *In a Different Voice: Psychological Theory and Women's Development* (Cambridge, MA: Harvard University Press, 1983).

16   Cf. Ibid., p. 2.

17. Marilyn Frye, *The Politics of Reality: Essays in Feminist Theory* (Trumansburg, NY: The Crossing Press, 1983); Bell Hooks, *Feminist Theory from Margin to Center* (Boston: South End Press, 1984); Gloria Joseph, "The Incompatible Menage à Trois: Marxism, Feminism and Racism," *Women and Revolution,* ed. Lydia Sargent (Boston: South End Press, 1981), pp. 91–107; Audre Lord, "An Open Letter to Mary Daly," *This Bridge Called My Back: Writings by Radical Women of Color,* ed. Cherríe Moraga and Gloria Anzaldúa (Watertown, MA: Persephone Press, 1981), pp. 94–97; Maria C. Lugones and Elizabeth V. Spelman, "Have We Got a Theory for You! Feminist Theory, Cultural Imperialism and the Demand for the Woman's Voice," *Hypatia, Women's Studies International Forum,* Vol. 6, No. 6, 1983, pp. 578–581; Adrienne Rich, "Compulsory Heterosexuality and Lesbian Existence," *Signs: Journal of Women in Culture and Society,* Vol. 5, No. 4, Summer 1980, pp. 631–660; Elizabeth Spelman, "Theories of Race and Gender: The Erasure of Black Women," *Quest,* Vol. 5, No. 4, 1980/81, pp. 36–62.

18. See, for example, Hélène Cixous, "The Laugh of the Medusa," trans. Keith Cohen and Paula Cohen, *New French Feminisms,* ed. Elaine Marks and Isabelle de Courtivron (New York: Schocken Books, 1981), pp. 245–261; Hélène Cixous and Catherine Clément, *The Newly Born Woman,* trans. Betsy Wing (Minneapolis: University of Minnesota Press, 1986); Luce Irigaray, *Speculum of the Other Woman* (Ithaca, NY: Cornell University Press, 1985) and *This Sex Which Is Not One* (Ithaca, NY: Cornell University Press, 1985); Julia Kristeva, *Desire in Language: A Semiotic Approach to Literature and Art,* ed. Leon S. Roudiez (New York: Columbia University Press, 1980) and "Women's Time," trans. Alice Jardine and Harry Blake, *Signs: Journal of Women in Culture and Society* Vol. 7, No. 1, Autumn

1981, pp. 13–35. See also the critical discussions by Ann Rosalind Jones, "Writing the Body: Toward an Understanding of l'Ecriture Féminine," *The New Feminist Criticism: Essays on Women, Literature and Theory*, ed. Elaine Showalter (New York: Pantheon Books, 1985), and Toril Moi, *Sexual/Textual Politics: Feminist Literary Theory* (London: Methuen, 1985).

2

Postmodernism and Gender Relations in Feminist Theory

Jane Flax

As the thought of the world, [philosophy] appears only when actuality is already there cut and dried after its process of formation has been completed. . . . When philosophy paints its grey in grey, then has a shape of life grown old. By philosophy's grey in grey it cannot be rejuvenated but only understood. The owl of Minerva spreads its wings only with the falling of the dusk.

[G. W. F. Hegel, preface to *Philosophy of Right*]

It seems increasingly probable that Western culture is in the middle of a fundamental transformation: A "shape of life" is growing old. In retrospect, this transformation may be as radical (but as gradual) as the shift from a medieval to a modern society. Accordingly, this moment in the history of the West is pervaded by profound yet little comprehended change, uncertainty, and ambivalence. This transitional state makes certain forms of thought possible and necessary, and it excludes others. It generates problems that some philosophies seem to acknowledge and confront better than others.

I think there are currently three kinds of thinking that best present (and represent) our own time apprehended in thought: psychoanalysis, feminist theory, and postmodern philosophy. These ways of thinking reflect and are partially constituted by Enlightenment beliefs still prevalent in Western (especially American) culture. At the same time, they offer ideas and insights that are only possible because of the breakdown of Enlightenment beliefs under the cumulative pressure of historical events such as the invention of the atomic bomb, the Holocaust, and the war in Vietnam.[1]

Each of these ways of thinking takes as its object of investigation at least one facet of what has become most problematic in our transitional state: how to understand and (re)constitute the self, gender, knowledge, social relations, and culture without resorting to linear, teleological, hierarchical, holistic, or binary ways of thinking and being. My focus here will be mainly on one of these modes of thinking: feminist theory. I will

39

consider what it could be, and I will reflect upon the goals, logics, and problematics of feminist theorizing as it has been practiced in the past fifteen years in the West. I will also place such theorizing within the social and philosophical contexts of which it is both a part and a critique.

I do not mean to claim that feminist theory is a unified or homogeneous discourse. Nonetheless, despite the lively and intense controversies among persons who identify themselves as practitioners concerning the subject matter, appropriate methodologies, and desirable outcome of feminist theorizing, it is possible to identify at least some of our underlying goals, purposes, and constituting objects.

A fundamental goal of feminist theory is (and ought to be) to analyze gender relations: how gender relations are constituted and experienced and how we think or, equally important, do not think about them.[2] The study of gender relations includes, but is not limited to, what are often considered the distinctively feminist issues: the situation of women and the analysis of male domination. Feminist theory includes an (at least implicit) prescriptive element as well. By studying gender we hope to gain a critical distance on existing gender arrangements. This critical distance can help clear a space in which reevaluating and altering our existing gender arrangements may become more possible.

Feminist theory by itself cannot clear such a space. Without feminist political actions, theories remain inadequate and ineffectual. However, I have come to believe that the further development of feminist theory (and hence a better understanding of gender) also depends upon locating our theorizing within and drawing more self-consciously upon the wider philosophical contents of which it is both a part and a critique. In other words, we need to think more about how we think about gender relations or any other social relations and about how other modes of thinking can help or hinder us in the development of our own discourses. In this paper, I will be moving back and forth between thinking about gender relations and thinking about how I am thinking—or could think—about them.

Metatheory

Feminist theory seems to me to belong within two, more inclusive, categories with which it has special affinity: the analysis of social relations and postmodern philosophy.[3] Gender relations enter into and are constituent elements in every aspect of human experience. In turn, the experience of gender relations for any person and the structure of gender as a social category are shaped by the interactions of gender relations and other social relations such as class and race. Gender relations thus have no fixed essence; they vary both within and over time.

As a type of postmodern philosophy, feminist theory reveals and contributes to the growing uncertainty within Western intellectual circles about the appropriate grounding and methods for explaining and interpreting human experience. Contemporary feminists join other postmodern philosophers in raising important metatheoretical questions about the possible nature and status of theorizing itself. Given the increasingly fluid and confused status of Western self-understanding, it is not even clear what would constitute the basis for satisfactory answers to commonly agreed upon questions within feminist (or other forms of social) theory.

Postmodern discourses are all deconstructive in that they seek to distance us from and make us skeptical about beliefs concerning truth, knowledge, power, the self, and language that are often taken for granted within and serve as legitimation for contemporary Western culture.

Postmodern philosophers seek to throw into radical doubt beliefs still prevalent in (especially American) culture but derived from the Enlightenment, such as the following:

1. The existence of a stable, coherent self. Distinctive properties of this Enlightenment self include a form of reason capable of privileged insight into its own processes and into the "laws of nature."

2. Reason and its "science"—philosophy—can provide an objective, reliable, and universal foundation for knowledge.

3. The knowledge acquired from the right use of reason will be "true"—for example, such knowledge will represent something real and unchanging (universal) about our minds and the structure of the natural world.

4. Reason itself has transcendental and universal qualities. It exists independently of the self's contingent existence (e.g., bodily, historical, and social experiences do not affect reason's structure or its capacity to produce atemporal knowledge).

5. There are complex connections between reason, autonomy, and freedom. All claims to truth and rightful authority are to be submitted to the tribunal of reason. Freedom consists of obedience to laws that conform to the necessary results of the right use of reason. (The rules that are right for me as a rational being will necessarily be right for all other such beings.) In obeying such laws, I am obeying my own best transhistorical part (reason) and hence am exercising my own autonomy and ratifying my existence as a free being. In such acts, I escape a determined or merely contigent existence.

6. By grounding claims to authority in reason, the conflicts between truth, knowledge, and power can be overcome. Truth can serve power without distortion; in turn, by utilizing knowledge in the service of power, both freedom and progress will be assured.

Knowledge can be both neutral (e.g., grounded in universal reason, not particular "interests") and also socially beneficial.

7. Science, as the exemplar of the right use of reason, is also the paradigm for all true knowledge. Science is neutral in its methods and contents but socially beneficial in its results. Through its process of discovery we can utilize the laws of nature for the benefit of society. However, in order for science to progress, scientists must be free to follow the rules of reason rather than pander to the interests arising from outside rational discourse.

8. Language is in some sense transparent. Just as the right use of reason can result in knowledge that represents the real, so, too, language is merely the medium in and through which such representation occurs. There is a correspondence between word and thing (as between a correct truth claim and the real). Objects are not linguistically (or socially) constructed; they are merely made present to consciousness by naming and the right use of language.

The relation of feminist theorizing to the postmodern project of deconstruction is necessarily ambivalent. Enlightenment philosophers such as Kant did not intend to include women within the population of those capable of attaining freedom from traditional forms of authority. Nonetheless, it is not unreasonable for persons who have been defined as incapable of self-emancipation to insist that concepts such as the autonomy of reason, objective truth, and beneficial progress through scientific discovery ought to include and be applicable to the capacities and experiences of women as well as men. It is also appealing, for those who have been excluded, to believe that reason will triumph—that those who proclaim such ideas as objectivity will respond to rational arguments. If there is no objective basis for distinguishing between true and false beliefs, then it seems that power alone will determine the outcome of competing truth claims. This is a frightening prospect to those who lack (or are oppressed by) the power of others.

Nevertheless, despite an understandable attraction to the (apparently) logical, orderly world of the Enlightenment, feminist theory more properly belongs in the terrain of postmodern philosophy. Feminist notions of the self, knowledge, and truth are too contradictory to those of the Enlightenment to be contained within its categories. The way(s) to feminist future(s) cannot lie in reviving or appropriating Enlightenment concepts of the person or knowledge.[4]

Feminist theorists enter into and echo postmodernist discourses as we have begun to deconstruct notions of reason, knowledge, or the self and to reveal the effects of the gender arrangements that lay beneath their neutral and universalizing facades.[5] Some feminist theorists, for example, have begun to sense that the motto of the Enlightenment, *"sapere aude—*'have courage to use your own reason,' "[6] rests in part upon a deeply gender-rooted sense of self and self-deception. The notion that reason is divorced from "merely contingent" existence still predominates in contemporary Western thought and now appears to mask the embeddedness and dependence of the self upon social relations, as well as the partiality and historical specificity of this self's existence. What Kant's self calls its "own" reason and the methods by which reason's contents become present or self-evident, are no freer from empirical contingency that is the so-called phenomenal self.[7]

In fact, feminists, like other postmodernists, have begun to suspect that all such transcendental claims reflect and reify the experience of a few persons — mostly white, Western males. These transhistoric claims seem plausible to us in part because they reflect important aspects of the experience of those who dominate our social world.

A Feminist Problematic

This excursus into metatheory has now returned us to the opening of my paper—that the fundamental purpose of feminist theory is to analyze how we think, or do not think, or avoid thinking about gender. Obviously, then, to understand the goals of feminist theory we must consider its central subject—gender.

Here, however, we immediately plunge into a complicated and controversial morass. For among feminist theorists there is by no means consensus on such (apparently) elementary questions as: What is gender? How is it related to anatomical sexual differences? How are gender relations constituted and sustained (in one person's lifetime and, more generally, as a social experience over time)? How do gender relations relate to other sorts of social relations such as class or race? Do gender relations have a history (or many)? What causes gender relations to change over time? What are the relationships between gender relations, sexuality, and a sense of individual identity? What are the relationships between heterosexuality, homosexuality, and gender relations? Are there only two genders? What are the relationships between forms of male dominance and gender relations? Could/would gender relations wither away in egalitarian societies? Is there anything distinctively male or female in modes of thought and social relations? If there is, are these distinctions innate or socially constituted? Are gendered distinctions socially useful or necessary? If so, what are the consequences for the feminist goal of attaining gender justice?[8]

Confronted with such a bewildering set of questions, it is easy to overlook the fact that a fundamental transformation in social theory has occurred. The single most important advance in feminist theory is that the existence of gender relations has been problematized. Gender can no longer be treated as a simple, natural fact. The assumption that gender relations are natural arose from two coinciding circumstances: the unexamined identification and confusion of (anatomical) sexual differences with gender relations, and the absence of active feminist movements. I will return to a consideration of the connections between gender relations and biology later in this chapter.

Contemporary feminist movements are in part rooted in transformations in social experience that challenge widely shared categories of social meaning and explanation. In the United States, such transformations include changes in the structure of the economy, the family, the place of the United States in the world system, the declining authority of previously powerful social institutions, and the emergence of political groups that have increasingly more divergent ideas and demands concerning justice, equality, social legislation, and the proper role of the state. In such a decentered and unstable universe it seems plausible to question one of the most natural facets of human existence—gender relations. On the other hand, such instability also makes old modes of social relations more attractive. The New Right and Ronald Reagan both call upon and reflect a desire to go back to a time when people and countries were in their "proper" place. The conflicts around gender arrangements become both the locus for and symbols of anxieties about all sorts of social-political ideas, only some of which are actually rooted primarily in gender relations.[9]

The coexistence of such social transformations and movements makes possible an increasingly radical and social, self-conscious questioning of previously unexamined facts and explanations. Thus, feminist theory, like all other forms of theory (including gender-biased ones), is dependent upon and reflects a certain set of social experiences. Whether, to what extent, and why feminist theory can be better than the gender-biased theories it critiques are questions that vex many writers.[10] In considering such questions, feminist theorists invariably enter the epistemological terrain shared in part with other postmodern philosophies. Hence, I wish to bracket these questions for now in order to consider more closely a fundamental category and object of investigation of feminist theory—gender relations.

Thinking in Relations

"Gender relations" is a category meant to capture a complex set of social processes. Gender, both as an analytic category and a social process, is relational. That is, gender relations are complex and unstable processes (or temporary totalities in the language of dialectics) constituted by and through interrelated parts. These parts are interdependent, that is, each part can have no meaning or existence without the others.

Gender relations are differentiated and (so far) asymmetric divisions and attributions of human traits and capacities. Through gender relations two types of persons are created: man and woman. Man and woman are posited as exclusionary categories. One can be only one gender, never the other or both. The actual content of being a man or woman and the rigidity of the categories themselves are highly variable across cultures and time. Nevertheless, gender relations so far as we have been able to understand them have been (more or less) relations of domination. That is, gender relations have been (more) defined and (imperfectly) controlled by one of their interrelated aspects—the man.

These relations of domination and the existence of gender relations themselves have been concealed in a variety of ways, including defining women as a "question" or the "sex" or the "other"[11] and men as the universal (or at least without gender). In a wide variety of cultures and discourses, men tend to be seen as free from or as not determined by gender relations. Thus, for example, academics do not explicitly study the psychology of men or men's history. Male academics do not worry about how being men may distort their intellectual work, while women who study gender relations are considered suspect (of triviality, if not bias). Only recently have scholars begun to consider the possibility that there may be at least three histories in every culture—his, hers, and ours. *His* and *ours* are generally assumed to be equivalents, although in contemporary work there might be some recognition of the existence of that deviant — woman (e.g., women's history).[12] However, it is still rare for scholars to search for the pervasive effects of gender relations on all aspects of a culture in the way that they feel obligated to investigate the impact of relations of power or the organization of production.

To the extent that feminist discourse defines its problematic as "woman," it, too, ironically privileges the man as unproblematic or exempted from determination by gender relations. From the perspective of social relations, men and women are both prisoners of gender, although in highly differentiated but interrelated ways. That men appear to be and (in many cases) are the wardens, or at least the trustees within a social whole, should not blind us to the extent to which they, too, are governed by the rules of gender. (This is not to deny that it matters a great deal—to individual men, to the women and children sometimes connected to them and to those concerned about justice—where men as well as women are distributed within social hierarchies.)[13]

Theorizing and Deconstruction

The study of gender relations entails at least two levels of analysis: of gender as a thought construct or category that helps us to make sense out of particular social worlds and histories, and of gender as a social relation that enters into and partially constitutes all other social relations and activities. As a practical social relation, gender can be understood only by close examination of the meanings of "male" and "female" and the consequences being assigned to one or the other gender within concrete social practices.

Obviously, such meanings and practices will vary by culture, age, class, race, and time. We cannot presume *a priori* that in any particular culture there will be a single determinant or cause of gender relations, much less that we can tell beforehand what this cause (or these causes) might be. Feminist theorists have offered a variety of interesting casual explanations including the sex/gender system, the organization of production or sexual division of labor, child-rearing practices, and processes of signification or language. These all provide useful hypotheses for the concrete study of gender relations in particular societies, but each explanatory scheme also seems to me to be deeply flawed, inadequate, and overly deterministic.

For example, Gayle Rubin locates the origin of gender systems in the "transformation of raw biological sex into gender."[14] However, Rubin's distinction between sex and gender rests in turn upon a series of oppositions that I find very problematic, including the opposition of "raw biological sexuality" and the social. This opposition reflects the idea predominant in the work of Freud, Lacan, and others that a person is driven by impulses and needs that are invariant and invariably asocial. This split between culture and natural sexuality may in fact be rooted in and reflect gender arrangements.

As I have argued elsewhere,[15] Freud's drive theory reflects in part an unconscious motive: to deny and repress aspects of infantile experience which are relational (e.g., the child's dependence upon and connectedness with its earliest caregiver, who is almost always a woman). Hence, in utilizing Freud's concepts, we must pay attention to what they conceal as well as reveal, especially the unacknowledged influences of anxieties about gender on his supposedly gender-neutral concepts (such as drive theory).

Socialist feminists locate the fundamental cause of gender arrangements in the organization of production or the sexual division of labor. However, this explanatory system also incorporates the historical and philosophical flaws of Marxist analysis. As Balbus convincingly argues,[16] Marxists (including socialist feminists) uncritically apply the categories Marx derived from his description of a particular form of the production of commodities to all areas of human life at all historical periods. Socialist feminists replicate this privileging of production and the division of labor with the concomitant assumptions concerning the centrality of labor itself. Labor is still seen as the essence of history and being human. Such conceptions distort life in capitalist society and surely are not appropriate to all other cultures.[17]

An example of the problems that follow from this uncritical appropriation of Marxist concepts can be found in the attempts by socialist feminists to widen the concept of production to include most forms of human activity. These arguments avoid an essential question: "Why widen the concept of production instead of dislodging it or any other singularly central concept from such authoritative power?"

This question becomes more urgent when it appears that, despite the best efforts of socialist feminists, the Marxist concepts of labor and production invariably exclude or distort many kinds of activity, including those traditionally performed by women. Pregnancy and child rearing or relations between family members more generally cannot be comprehended merely as "property relations in action."[18] Sexuality cannot be understood as an exchange of physical energy, with a surplus (potentially) flowing to an exploiter.[19] Such concepts also ignore or obscure the existence and activities of other persons as well—children—for whom at least a part of their formative experiences has nothing to do with production.

However, the structure of child-rearing practices also cannot serve as the root of gender relations. Among the many problems with this approach is that it cannot explain why women have the primary responsibility for child rearing; it can explain only some of the consequences of this fact. In other words, the child-rearing practices taken as causal already presuppose the very social relations we are trying to understand: a gender-based division of human activities and hence the existence of socially constructed sets of gender arrangements and the (peculiar and in need of explanation) salience of gender itself.

The emphasis that (especially) French feminists place on the centrality of language (e.g., chains of signification, signs, and symbols) to the construction of gender also seems problematic. [20] A problem with thinking about (or only in terms of) texts, signs, or signification is that they tend to take on a life of their own or become the world, as the claim that nothing exists outside of a text; everything is a comment upon or a displacement of another text, as if the model human activity is literary criticism (or writing).

Such an approach obscures the projection of its own activity onto the world and denies the existence of the variety of concrete social practices that enter into and are reflected in the constitution of language itself (e.g., ways of life constitute language and texts as much as language constitutes ways of life). This lack of attention to concrete social relations (including the distribution of power) results, as in Lacan's work, in the obscuring of relations of domination. Such relations (including gender arrangements) then tend to acquire an aura of inevitability and become equated with language or culture (the "law of the father") as such.

Much of French (including feminist) writing also seems to assume a radical (even ontological rather than socially constructed) disjunction between sign/mind/male/world and body/nature/female.[21] The prescription of some French feminists for the recovery (or reconstitution?) of female experience—"writing from the body"—seems incoherent given this sort of (Cartesian) disjunction. Since the body is presocial and prelinguistic, what could it say?

All of these social practices posited as explanations for gender arrangements may be more or less important, interrelated, or themselves partially constituted in and through gender relations depending upon context. As in any form of social analysis, the study of gender relations will necessarily reflect the social practices it attempts to understand. There cannot, nor should we expect there to be, a feminist equivalent to (a falsely universalizing) Marxism; indeed, the epistemologies of feminism undercut all such claims, including feminist ones.[22]

It is on the metatheoretical level that postmodern philosophies of knowledge can contribute to a more accurate self-understanding of the nature of our theorizing. We cannot simultaneously claim (1) that the mind, the self, and knowledge are socially constituted and that what we can know depends upon our social practices and contexts and (2) that feminist theory can uncover the truth of the whole once and for all. Such an absolute truth (e.g., the explanation for all gender arrangements at all times is X) would require the existence of an Archimedes point outside of the whole and beyond our embeddedness in it from which we could see (and represent) the whole. What we see and report would also have to be untransformed by the activities of perception and of reporting our vision in language. The object seen (social whole or gender arrangement) would have to be apprehended by an empty (ahistoric) mind and perfectly transcribed by/ into a transparent language. The possibility of each of these conditions existing has been rendered extremely doubtful by the deconstructions of postmodern philosophers.

Furthermore, the work of Foucault (among others) should sensitize us to the interconnections between knowledge claims (especially to the claim of absolute or neutral knowledge) and power. Our own search for an Archimedes point may conceal and obscure our entanglement in an episteme in which truth claims may take only certain forms and not others.[23] Any episteme requires the suppression of discourses that threaten to differ with or undermine the authority of the dominant one. Hence, within feminist theory a search for a defining theme of the whole or a feminist viewpoint may require the suppression of the important and discomforting voices of persons with experiences unlike our own. The suppression of these voices seems to be a necessary condition for the (apparent) authority, coherence, and universality of our own.

Thus, the very search for a root or cause of gender relations (or more narrowly, male domination) may partially reflect a mode of thinking that is itself grounded in particular forms of gender (and/or other) relations in which domination is present. Perhaps reality can have "a" structure only from the falsely universalizing perspective of the dominant group. That is, only to the extent that one person or group can dominate the whole will reality appear to be governed by one set of rules or be constituted by one privileged set of social relations. Criteria of theory construction such as parsimony or simplicity may be attained only by the suppression or denial of the experiences of the other(s).

The Natural Barrier

Thus, in order for gender relations to be useful as a category of social analysis we must be as socially and self-critical as possible about the meanings usually attributed to those relations and the ways we think about them. Otherwise, we run the risk of replicating the very social relations we are attempting to understand. We have to be able to investigate both the social and philosophical barriers to our comprehension of gender relations.

One important barrier to our comprehension of gender relations has been the difficulty of understanding the relationship between *gender* and *sex*. In this context, *sex* means the anatomical differences between male and female. Historically (at least since Aristotle), these anatomical differences have been assigned to the class of natural facts or biology. In turn, biology has been equated with the pre- or nonsocial. Gender relations then become conceptualized as if they are constituted by two opposite terms or distinct types of being — man and woman. Since man and woman seem to be opposites or fundamentally distinct types of being, gender cannot be relational. If gender is as natural and as intrinsically a part of us as the genitals we are born with, it follows that it would be foolish (or even harmful) to attempt either to change gender arrangements or not to take them into account as a delimitation on human activities.

Even though a major focus of feminist theory has been to denaturalize gender, feminists as well as nonfeminists seem to have trouble thinking through the meanings we assign to and the uses we make of the concept "natural."[24] What, after all, is the natural in the context of the human world?[25] There are many aspects of our embodiedness or biology that we might see as given limits to human action which Western medicine and science do not hesitate to challenge. For example, few Westerners would refuse to be vaccinated against diseases that our bodies are naturally susceptible to, although in some cultures such actions would be seen as violating the natural order. The tendency of Western science is to disenchant the natural world.[26] More and more the natural ceases to exist as the opposite of the cultural or social. Nature becomes the object and product of human action; it loses its independent existence. Ironically, the more such disenchantment proceeds, the more humans seem to need something that remains outside our powers of transformation. Until recently, one such exempt area seemed to be anatomical differences between males and females.[27] Thus, in order to save nature (from ourselves) many people in the contemporary West equate sex/biology/nature/gender and oppose these to the cultural/social/human. Concepts of gender then become complex metaphors for ambivalences about human action in, on, and as part of the natural world.

But the use of gender as a metaphor for such ambivalences blocks further investigation of them. For the social articulation of these equations is not really in the form I stated above but, rather, sex/biology/nature/ woman : cultural/social/man. In the contemporary West, women become the last refuge from not only the "heartless" world but also an increasingly mechanized and fabricated one as well.[28] What remains masked in these modes of thought is the possibility that our concepts of biology and nature are rooted in social relations; they do not merely reflect the given structure of reality itself.

Thus, in order to understand gender as a social relation, feminist theorists need to deconstruct further the meanings we attach to biology/sex/ gender/nature. This process of deconstruction is far from complete and certainly is not easy. Initially, some feminists thought we could merely separate the terms *sex* and *gender*. As we became more sensitive to the social histories of concepts, it became clear that such an (apparent) disjunction, while politically necessary, rested upon problematic and culture-specific oppositions, for example, the one between nature and culture or body and mind. As some feminists began to rethink these oppositions, new questions emerged: Does anatomy (body) have no relation to mind? What difference does it make in the constitution of my social experiences that I have a specifically female body?

Despite the increasing complexity of our questions, most feminists would still insist that gender relations are not (or are not only) equivalent to or a consequence of anatomy. Everyone will agree that there are anatomical differences between men and women. These anatomical differences seem to be primarily located in or are the consequence of the differentiated contributions men and woman make to a common biological necessity—the physical reproduction of our species.

However, the mere existence of such anatomical differentiation is a descriptive fact, one of many observations we might make about the physical characteristics of humans. Part of the problem in deconstruction of the meaning of biology/sex/gender/nature is that sex/gender has been one of the few areas in which (usually female) embodiment can be discussed at all in (nonscientific) Western discourses. There are many other aspects of our embodiedness that seem equally remarkable and interesting, for example, the incredible complexity of the structure and functioning of our brains, the extreme and relatively prolonged physical helplessness of the human neonate as compared to that of other (even related) species, or the fact that every one of us will die.

It is also the case that physically male and female humans resemble each other in many more ways than we differ. Our similarities are even more striking if we compare humans to, say, toads or trees. So why ought the anatomical differences between male and female humans assume such significance in our sense of our selves as persons? Why ought such complex human social meanings and structures be based on or justified by a relatively narrow range of anatomical differences?

One possible answer to these questions is that the anatomical differences between males and females are connected to and are partially a consequence of one of the most important functions of the species— its physical reproduction. Thus, we might argue, because reproduction is such an important aspect of our species life, characteristics associated with it will be much more salient to us than, say, hair color or height.

Another possible answer to these questions might be that in order for humans physically to reproduce the species, we have to have sexual intercourse. Our anatomical differences make possible (and necessary for physical reproduction) a certain fitting together of distinctively male and female organs. For some humans this "fitting together" is also highly desirable and pleasurable. Hence, our anatomical differences seem to be inextricably connected to (and in some sense even causative of) sexuality.

Thus, there seems to be a complex of relations that have associated, given meanings: penis or clitoris, vagina, and breasts (read distinctively male or female bodies), sexuality (read reproduction—birth and babies), sense of self as a distinct, differentiated gender—as either (and only) male or female person (read gender relations as a natural exclusionary category). That is, we believe there are only two types of humans, and each of us can be only one of them.

A problem with all these apparently obvious associations is that they may assume precisely what requires explanation—that is, gender relations. We live in a world in which gender is a constituting social relation and in which gender is also a relation of domination. Therefore, both men's and women's understanding of anatomy, biology, embodiedness, sexuality, and reproduction is partially rooted in, reflects, and must justify (or challenge) preexisting gender relations. In turn, the existence of gender relations helps us to order and understand the facts of human existence. In other words, gender can become a metaphor for biology just as biology can become a metaphor for gender.

Prisoners of Gender

The apparent connections between gender relations and such important aspects of human existence as birth, reproduction, and sexuality make possible both a conflating of the natural and the social and an overly radical distinction between the two. In modern Western culture and sometimes even in feminist theories, the words *natural* and *social* become conflated in our understanding of "woman." In nonfeminist and some feminist writings about women, a radical disjunction is frequently made between the natural and the social. Women often stand for/symbolize the body, "difference," the concrete. These qualities are also said by some feminist as well as nonfeminist writers to suffuse/define the activities most associated with women: nurturing, mothering, taking care of and being in relation with others, preserving. [29] Women's minds are also often seen as reflecting the qualities of our stereotypically female activities and bodies. Even feminists sometimes say women reason and write differently and have different interests and motives than men. [30] Men are said to have more interest in utilizing the power of abstract reason (mind), to want mastery over nature (including bodies), and to be aggressive and militaristic.

The reemergence of such claims even among some feminists needs further analysis. Is this the beginning of a genuine transvaluation of values or a retreat into traditional gendered ways of understanding the world? In our attempts to correct arbitrary (and gendered) distinctions, feminists often end up reproducing them. Feminist discourse is full of contradictory and irreconcilable conceptions of the nature of our social relations, of men and women and the worth and character of stereotypically masculine and feminine activities. The positing of these conceptions such that only one perspective can be correct (or properly feminist) reveals, among other things, the embeddedness of feminist theory in the very social processes we are trying to critique and our need for more systematic and self-conscious theoretical practice.

As feminist theorizing is presently practiced, we seem to lose sight of the possibility that each of our conceptions of a practice (e.g., mothering) may capture an aspect of a very complex and contradictory set of social relations. Confronted with complex and changing relations, we try to reduce these to simple, unified, and undifferentiated wholes. We search for closure, or the right answer, or the motor of the history of male domination. The complexity of our questions and the variety of the approaches to them are taken by some feminists as well as nonfeminists as signs of weakness or failure to meet the strictures of preexisting theories rather than as symptoms of the permeability and pervasiveness of gender relations and the need for new sorts of theorizing.

Some of the reductive moves I have in mind include the constricting of embodiedness to a glorification of the distinctively female aspects of our anatomy.[31] This reduction precludes considering the many other ways in which we experience our embodiedness (e.g., nonsexual pleasures, the processes of aging or pain). It also replicates the equating of women with the body—as if men did not have bodies also! Alternatively, there is a tendency simply to deny or neglect the meaningfulness or significance of any bodily experience within both women's and men's lives or to reduce it to a subset of relations of production (or reproduction).

Within feminist discourse, women sometimes seem to become the sole bearers of both embodiedness and difference. Thus, we see arguments for the necessity to preserve a gender-based division of labor as our last protection from a state power that is depersonalizing and atomizing.[32] In such arguments the family is posited as an intimate, affective realm of natural relations—of kinship ties, primarily between mothers, children, and female kin—and it is discussed in opposition to the impersonal realms of the state and work (the worlds of men). Alternatively, feminists sometimes simply deny that there are any significant differences between women and men and that insofar as such differences exist, women should become more like men (or engage in men's activities). Or, the family is understood only as the site of gender struggle and the reproduction of persons—a miniature political economy with its own division of labor, source of surplus (women's labor), and product (children and workers).[33] The complex fantasies and conflicting wishes and experiences women associate with family and home often remain unexpressed and unacknowledged. Lacking such self-analysis, feminists find it difficult to recognize some of the sources of our differences or to accept that we do not necessarily share the same past or share needs in the present.[34]

Female sexuality is sometimes reduced to an expression of male dominance, as when Catherine MacKinnon claims "gender socialization is the process through which women come to identify themselves as sexual beings, as beings that exist for men."[35] Among many other problems, such a definition leaves unexplained how women could ever feel lust for other women and the wide variety of other sensual experiences women claim to have—for example, in masturbation, breast feeding, or playing with children. Alternatively, the essence of female sexuality is said to be rooted in the quasi-biological primal bonds between mother and daughter.[36]

For some theorists, our fantasy and internal worlds have expression only in symbols, not in actual social relations. For example, Iris Young claims that gender differentiation as a category refers only to "ideas, symbols, and forms of consciousness."[37] In this view, fantasy, our inner worlds, and sexuality may structure intimate relations between women and men at home, but they are rarely seen as also entering into and shaping the structure of work and the state. Thus, feminist theory recreates its own version of the public/private split. Alternatively, as in some radical feminist accounts, innate male drives, especially aggression and the need to dominate others are posited as the motor that drives the substance and teleology of history.[38]

Feminist theorists have delineated many of the ways in which women's consciousness is shaped by mothering, but we often still see fathering as somehow extrinsic to men's and children's consciousness.[39] The importance of modes of child rearing to women's status and to women's and men's sense of self is emphasized in feminist theory; yet we still write social theory in which everyone is presumed to be an adult. For example, in two recent collections of feminist theory focusing on mothering and the family,[40] there is almost no discussion of children as human beings or mothering as a relation between persons. The modal "person" in feminist theory still appears to be a self-sufficient individual adult.

These difficulties in thinking have social as well as philosophical roots, including the existence of relations of domination and the psychological consequences of our current modes of child rearing. In order to sustain domination, the interrelation and interdependence of one group with another must be denied. Connections can be traced only so far before they begin to be politically dangerous. For example, few white feminists have explored how our understandings of gender relations and theory are partially constituted in and through the experiences of living in a culture in which asymmetric race relations are a central organizing principle of society.[41]

Furthermore, just as our current gender arrangements create men who have difficulties in acknowledging relations between people and experiences, they produce women who have difficulties in acknowledging differences within relations. In either gender, these social relations produce a disposition to treat experience as all of one sort or another and to be intolerant of differences, ambiguity, and conflict.

The enterprise of feminist theory is fraught with temptations and pitfalls. Insofar as women have been part of all societies, our thinking cannot be free from culture-bound modes of self-understanding. We as well as men internalize the dominant gender's conceptions of masculinity and femininity. Unless we see gender as a social relation rather than as an opposition of inherently different beings, we will not be able to identify the varieties and limitations of different women's (or men's) powers and oppressions within particular societies. Feminist theorists are faced with a fourfold task. We need to (1) articulate feminist viewpoints of/within the social worlds in which we live; (2) think about how we are affected by these worlds; (3) consider the ways in which how we think about them may be implicated in existing power/knowledge relationships; and (4) imagine ways in which these worlds ought to and can be transformed.

Since within contemporary Western societies gender relations have been ones of domination, feminist theories should have a compensatory as well as a critical aspect. That is, we need to recover and explore the aspects of social relations that have been suppressed, unarticulated, or denied within dominant (male) viewpoints. We need to recover and write the histories of women and our activities into the accounts and stories that cultures tell about themselves. Yet, we also need to think about how so-called women's activities are partially constituted by and through their location within the web of social relations that make up any society. That is, we need to know how these activities are affected but also how they effect, enable, or compensate for the consequences of men's activities, as well as their implication in class or race relations.

There should also be a transvaluation of values—a rethinking of our ideas about what is humanly excellent, worthy of praise, or moral. In such a transvaluation, we need to be careful not to assert merely the superiority of the opposite. For example, sometimes feminist theorists tend to oppose autonomy to being-in-relations. Such an opposition does not account for adult forms of being-in-relations that can be claustrophobic without autonomy—an autonomy that, without being-in-relations can easily degenerate into mastery. Our upbringing as women in this culture often encourages us to deny the many subtle forms of aggression that intimate relations with others can evoke and entail. For example, much of the discussion of mothering and the distinctively female tends to avoid discussing women's anger and aggression—how we internalize them and express them, for example, in relation to children or our own internal selves.[42] Perhaps women are not any less aggressive than men; we may just express our aggression in different, culturally sanctioned (and partially disguised or denied) ways.

Since we live in a society in which men have more power than women, it makes sense to assume that what is considered to be more worthy of praise may be those qualities associated with men. As feminists, we have the right to suspect that even praise of the female may be (at least in part) motivated by a wish to keep women in a restricted (and restrictive) place. Indeed, we need to search into all aspects of a society (the feminist critique included) for the expressions and consequences of relations of domination. We should insist that all such relations are social, that is, they are not the result of the differentiated possession of natural and unequal properties among types of persons.

However, in insisting upon the existence and power of such relations of domination, we should avoid seeing women/ourselves as totally innocent, passive beings. Such a view prevents us from seeing the areas of life in which women have had an effect, in which we are less determined by the will of the other(s), and in which some of us have and do exert power over others (e.g., the differential privileges of race, class, sexual preference, age, or location in the world system).

Any feminist standpoint will necessarily be partial. Thinking about women may illuminate some aspects of a society that have been previously suppressed within the dominant view. But none of us can speak for "woman" because no such person exists except within a specific set of (already gendered) relations—to "man" and to many concrete and different women.

Indeed, the notion of a feminist standpoint that is truer than previous (male) ones seems to rest upon many problematic and unexamined assumptions. These include an optimistic belief that people act rationally in their own interests and that reality has a structure that perfect reason (once perfected) can discover. Both of these assumptions in turn depend upon an uncritical appropriation of the Enlightenment ideas discussed earlier. Furthermore, the notion of such a standpoint also assumes that the oppressed are not in fundamental ways damaged by their social experience. On the contrary, this position assumes that the oppressed have a privileged (and not just different) relation and ability to comprehend a reality that is out there waiting for our representation. It also presupposes gendered social relations in which there is a category of beings who are fundamentally like each other by virtue of their sex—that is, it assumes the otherness men assign to women. Such a standpoint also assumes that women, unlike men, can be free of determination from their own participation in relations of domination such as those rooted in the social relations of race, class, or homophobia.[43]

I believe, on the contrary, that there is no force or reality outside our social relations and activity (e.g., history, reason, progress, science, some transcendental essence) that will rescue us from partiality and differences. Our lives and alliances belong with those who seek to further decenter the world—although we should reserve the right to be suspicious of their motives and visions as well.[44] Feminist theories, like other forms of postmodernism, should encourage us to tolerate and interpret ambivalence, ambiguity, and multiplicity as well as to expose the roots of our needs for imposing order and structure no matter how arbitrary and oppressive these needs may be.

If we do our work well, reality will appear even more unstable, complex, and disorderly than it does now. In this sense, perhaps Freud was right when he declared that women are the enemies of civilization.[45]

Notes

1. For a more extended discussion of these claims, see my forthcoming book, *Thinking Fragments: Psychoanalysis, Feminism, and Postmodernism in the Contemporary West* (Berkeley, CA: University of California Press, forthcoming 1990).

2. Representative examples of feminist theories include *Home Girls: A Black Feminist Anthology,* ed. Barbara Smith (New York: Kitchen Table: Women of Color Press, 1983); *This Bridge Called My Back,* ed. Cherrie Moraga and Gloria Anzaldua (Watertown, MA: Persephone Press, 1981); Elizabeth Abel, Marianne Hirsch, and Elizabeth Langland, *The Voyage In: Fictions of Female Development* (Hanover, NH, and London: University Press of New England, 1983); *Capitalist Patriarchy and the Case for Socialist Feminism,* ed. Zillah R. Eisenstein (New York: Monthly Review Press, 1979); *Feminism and Materialism,* ed. Annette Kuhn and Ann Marie Wolpe, (Boston: Routledge & Kegan Paul, 1978); Hunter College Women's Studies Collective, *Women's Realities, Women's Choices* (New York: Oxford University Press, 1983); *New French Feminisms,* ed. Elaine Marks and Isabelle de Courtivron, (New York: Schocken Books, 1981); *Mothering: Essays in Feminist Theory,* ed. Joyce Trebilcot, (Totowa, NJ: Rowman & Allanheld, 1984); *Sexual Meanings: The Cultural Construction of Gender and Sexuality,* ed. Sherry B. Ortner and Harriet Whitehead, (New York: Cambridge University Press, 1981); Nancy C. M. Hartsock, *Money, Sex, and Power* (New York: Longman, Inc., 1983); *The Powers of Desire: The Politics of Sexuality,* ed. Ann Snitow, Christine Stansell, and Sharon Thompson, (New York: Monthly Review Press, 1983); *Discovering Reality: Feminist Perspectives on Epistemology, Metaphysics, Methodology, and Philosophy of Science,* ed. Sandra Harding and Merill B. Hintikka, (Boston: D. Reidel Publishing Co., 1983); Carol C. Gould, *Beyond Domination: New Perspectives on Women and Philosophy* (Totowa, NJ: Rowman & Allanheld, 1984); Isaac D. Balbus, *Marxism and Domination* (Princeton, NJ: Princeton University Press, 1982); Alison Jaggar, *Feminist Politics and Human Nature* (Totowa, NJ: Rowman and Allanheld, 1983).

3. Sources for and practitioners of postmodernism include Friedrich Nietzsche, *On the Genealogy of Morals* (New York: Vintage, 1969) and *Beyond Good and Evil* (New York: Vintage, 1966); Jacques Derrida, *L'écriture et la différence* (Paris: Editions du Seuil, 1967); Michel Foucault, *Language, Counter-Memory, Practice* (Ithaca, NY: Cornell University Press, 1977); Jacques Lacan, *Speech and Language in Psychoanalysis* (Baltimore: Johns Hopkins University Press, 1968) and *The Four Fundamental Concepts of Psychoanalysis* (New York: W.W. Norton & Co., 1973); Richard Rorty, *Philosophy and the Mirror of Nature* (Princeton, NJ: Princeton University Press, 1979); Paul Feyerabend, *Against Method* (New York: Schocken,

1975); Ludwig Wittgenstein, *On Certainty* (New York: Harper & Row, 1972) and *Philosophical Investigations* (New York: Macmillan Publishing Co., 1970); Julia Kristeva, "Women's Time," *Signs: Journal of Women in Culture and Society,* Vol. 7, No. 11, Autumn 1981, pp. 13–35; and Jean-François Lyotard, *The Postmodern Condition* (Minneapolis: University of Minnesota Press, 1984).

4. In "The Instability of the Analytical Categories of Feminist Theory," *Signs,* Vol. 11, No. 4, Summer 1986, pp. 645–664, Sandra Harding discusses the ambivalent attraction of feminist theorizing to both sorts of discourse. She insists that feminist theorists should live with the ambivalence and retain both discourses for political and philosophical reasons. However, I think her argument rests in part on a too uncritical appropriation of a key Enlightenment equation of knowing, naming, and emancipation.

5. Examples of such work include Alice A. Jardine, *Gynesis: Configurations of Woman and Modernity* (Ithaca, NY: Cornell University Press, 1985); Donna Haraway, "A Manifesto for Cyborgs: Science, Technology, and Socialist Feminism in the 1980s," *Socialist Review,* No. 80, 1983, pp. 65–107; Kathy E. Ferguson, *The Feminist Case Against Bureaucracy* (Philadelphia: Temple University Press, 1984); and Luce Irigaray, *Speculum of the Other Woman* (Ithaca, NY: Cornell University Press, 1985).

6. Immanuel Kant, "What is Enlightenment?" in *Foundations of the Metaphysics of Morals* (Indianapolis: Bobbs-Merrill Co., 1959), p. 85.

7. For critiques of the mind (reason)/body split, see Naomi Scheman, "Individualism and the Objects of Psychology," in Harding and Hintikka, eds. (see Note no. 2); Susan Bordo, "The Cartesian Masculinization of Thought," *Signs* Vol. 11, No. 3, Spring 1986, pp. 439–456; Nancy C. M. Hartsock, "The Feminist Standpoint: Developing the Ground for a Specifically Feminist Historical Materialism," in Harding and Hintikka, eds.; Caroline Whitbeck, "Afterword to the 'Maternal Instinct,' " in Joyce Trebilcot, ed. (see Note no. 2); and Dorothy Smith, "A Sociology for Women," *The Prison of Sex: Essays in the Sociology of Knowledge,* ed. J. Sherman and E.T. Beck (Madison: University of Wisconsin Press, 1979).

8. These questions are suggested by Judith Stacey, "The New Conservative Feminism," *Feminist Studies,* Vol. 9, No. 3, Fall 1983, pp. 559–583, and Nancy Chodorow, "Gender, Relation, and Difference in Psychoanalytic Perspective," *The Future of Difference,* ed. Hester Eisenstein and Alice Jardine (1980, reprint, New Brunswick, NJ: Rutgers University Press, 1985).

9. On the appeal of New Right ideology to women, see Judith Stacey (Note no. 8).

10. Harding discusses these problems in detail. See Note no. 4. See also Sandra Harding, "Is Gender a Variable in Conceptions of Rationality? A Survey of Issues," in Carol C. Gould, (Note no. 2), and "Why Has the Sex/Gender Become Visible Only Now?" in Harding and Hintikka, eds., and Alison Jaggar (Note no. 2), pp. 353–394. Since within modern Western cultures

science is the model for knowledge that is simultaneously neutral/objective yet socially useful/powerful (or destructive), much epistemological inquiry has focused on the nature and structure of science. Compare Hilary Rose, "Hand, Brain, and Heart: A Feminist Epistemology for the Natural Sciences," *Signs* Vol. 9, No. 1, Autumn 1983, pp. 73–90; and Helen Longino and Ruth Doell, "Body, Bias, and Behavior: A Comparative Analysis of Reasoning in Two Areas of Biological Science, *Signs* Vol. 9, No. 2, Winter 1983, pp. 206–227.

11. For example, the Marxist treatments of the "woman question" from Engels onward, or existentialist, or Lacanian treatment of woman as the "other" to man.

12. On this point, see Joan Kelly, "The Doubled Vision of Feminist Theory," *Feminist Studies* Vol. 6, No. 2, Summer 1979, pp. 216–227; and also Judith Stacey and Barrie Thorne, "The Missing Feminist Revolution in Sociology," *Social Problems* Vol. 32, No. 4, April 1985, pp. 301–316.

13. Compare Phyllis Marynick Palmer, "White Women/Black Women: The Dualism of Female Identity and Experience in the United States," *Feminist Studies* Vol. 9, No. 11, Spring 1983, pp. 151–170.

14. This is Gayle Rubin's claim in "The Traffic in Women: Notes on the 'Political Economy' of Sex," in *Toward an Anthropology of Women*, ed. Rayna Rapp Reiter (New York: Monthly Review Press, 1975).

15. I develop this argument in "Psychoanalysis as Deconstruction and Myth: On Gender, Narcissism and Modernity's Discontents," in *The Crisis of Modernity: Recent Theories of Culture in the United States and West Germany*, ed. Kurt Shell (Boulder, CO: Westview Press, 1986).

16. See Balbus (Note no. 2), Chapter 1, for a further development of these arguments. Despite Balbus's critique of Marx, he still seems to be under Marx's spell on a metatheoretical level when he tries to locate a root of all domination—child-rearing practices. I have also discussed the inadequacy of Marxist theories in "Do Feminists Need Marxism?" *Building Feminist Theory*, ed. Quest Staff (New York: Longman, Inc., 1981), and "The Family in Contemporary Feminist Thought: A Critical Review," ed. Jean Bethke Elshtain, *The Family in Political Thought* (Amherst, MA: University of Massachusetts Press, 1982), pp. 232–239.

17. Marx may replicate rather than deconstruct the capitalist mentality in his emphasis on the centrality of production. Compare Albert O. Hirschman, *The Passions and the Interests* (Princeton, NJ: Princeton University Press, 1977) for a very interesting discussion of the historical emergence and construction of a specifically *capitalist* mentality.

18. Annette Kuhn, "Structure of Patriarchy and Capital in the Family," in Kuhn and Wolpe, eds. (Note no. 2), p. 53.

19. Ann Ferguson, "Conceiving Motherhood and Sexuality: A Feminist Materialist Approach," in Joyce Trebilcot, ed. (Note no. 2), pp. 156–158.

20. The theories of French feminists vary, of course. I am focusing on a

predominant and influential approach within the variations. For further discussion of French feminisms, see the essays in *Signs,* Vol. 7, No. 1, Autumn 1981, and *Feminist Studies,* Vol. 7, No. 2, Summer 1981.

21. Domna Stanton, in "Difference on Trial: A Critique of the Maternal Metaphor in Cixous, Irigaray, and Kristeva," *The Poetics of Gender,* ed. Nancy Miller (New York: Columbia University Press, 1986), discusses the ontological and essentialist aspects of these writers' work.

22. Catherine MacKinnon, in "Feminism, Marxism, Method, and the State: An Agenda for Theory," *Signs,* Vol. 7, No. 3, Spring 1982, pp. 515–544, seems to miss this basic point when she makes claims such as: "The defining theme of the whole is the male pursuit of control over women's sexuality — men not as individuals nor as biological beings, but as a gender group characterized by maleness as socially constructed, of which this pursuit is definitive" (p. 532). On the problem of the Archimedes point, see Myra Jehlen, "Archimedes and the Paradox of Feminist Criticism," *Signs,* Vol. 6, No. 4, Summer 1981, pp. 575–601.

23. Compare Michel Foucault, *Power/Knowledge,* ed. Colin Gordon (New York: Random House, 1981).

24. But see the work of Evelyn Fox Keller on the gendered character of our views of the natural world, especially her essays "Gender and Science," in Harding and Hintikka, eds. (Note no. 2), and "Cognitive Repression in Physics," *American Journal of Physics,* Vol. 47, 1979, pp. 718–721.

25. In *Public Man, Private Woman,* Jean Bethke Elshtain provides an instructive instance of how allegedly natural properties (of infants) can be used to limit what a "reflective feminist" ought to think. In Elshtain's recent writings it becomes (once again) the responsibility of women to rescue children from an otherwise instrumental and uncaring world. Elshtain evidently believes that psychoanalytical theory is exempt from the context-dependent hermeneutics she believes characterize all other kinds of knowledge about social relations. She utilizes psychoanalytic theory as a warrant for absolute or foundational claims about the nature of "real human needs" or "the most basic human relationships" and then bases political conclusions on these "natural" facts. See Jean Bethke Elshtain, *Public Man, Private Woman* (Princeton, NJ: Princeton University Press, 1981), pp. 314, 331.

26. See Max Weber, "Science as a Vocation," *From Max Weber,* ed. H.H. Gerth and C. Wright Mills (New York: Oxford University Press, 1958), and Max Horkheimer and Theodor W. Adorno, *Dialectic of Enlightenment* (New York: Herder & Herder, 1972).

27. I say "until recently" because of developments in medicine such as sex change operations and new methods of conception and fertilization of embryos.

28. As in the work of Christopher Lasch, *Haven in a Heartless World* (New York: Basic Books, 1977). Lasch's work is basically a repetition of the ideas stated earlier by members of the Frankfurt School, especially Hork-

heimer and Adorno. See, for example, the essay "The Family" in *Aspects of Sociology,* Frankfurt Institute for Social Research (Boston: Beacon Press, 1972).

29. Compare Sara Ruddick's essays, "Maternal Thinking" and "Preservative Love and Military Destruction: Some Reflections on Mothering and Peace," both in Joyce Trebilcot, ed. (Note no. 2).

30. On women's "difference," see the essays in Eisenstein and Jardine, eds. (Note no. 8), and Marks and de Courtivron (Note no. 2); also Carol Gilligan, *In a Different Voice* (Cambridge, MA: Harvard University Press, 1982), and Donna Stanton (Note no. 21).

31. As in, for example, Hélène Cixous, "Sorties," *The Newly Born Woman,* ed. Hélène Cixous and Catherine Clément (Ithaca, NY: Cornell University Press, 1986).

32. See, for instance, Jean Bethke Elshtain (Note no. 25), and Jean Bethke Elshtain, ed. (Note no. 16), pp. 7–30.

33. This seems to be the basic approach characteristic of socialist-feminist discussions of the family. See, for example, the essays by Ann Ferguson (Note no. 19) and Annette Kuhn (Note no. 18).

34. See, for example, Barbara Smith's discussion of the meanings of *home* to her in the introduction to *Home Girls* (Note no. 2). Smith's definition contrasts strongly with the confinement and exploitation some middle-class white women associate with *home*. See, for example, Michele Barrett and Mary McIntosh, *The Anti-Social Family* (London: Verso, 1983), and Heidi I. Hartmann, "The Family as the Locus of Gender, Class, and Political Struggle: The Example of Housework," *Signs* Vol. 6, No. 3, Spring 1981, pp. 366–394.

35. Catherine MacKinnon (Note no. 22), p. 531.

36. This seems to be Adrienne Rich's argument in "Compulsory Heterosexuality and Lesbian Existence," *Signs* Vol. 5, No. 4, Summer 1980, pp. 631–660. See also Donna Stanton (Note no. 21) on this point.

37. Iris Young, "Is Male Gender Identity the Cause of Male Domination?" in Joyce Trebilcot, ed. (Note no. 2), p. 140. In this essay, Young replicates the split Juliet Mitchell posits in *Psychoanalysis and Feminism* (New York: Pantheon Books, 1974) between kinship/gender/superstructure and class/production/base.

38. As in Shulamith Firestone, *The Dialectic of Sex* (New York: Bantam Books, 1970), and Catherine MacKinnon (Note no. 22).

39. On this point, see Nancy Chodorow and Susan Contratto, "The Fantasy of the Perfect Mother," *Rethinking the Family,* ed. Barrie Thorne and Marilyn Yalom (New York: Longman, Inc., 1983)

40. Joyce Trebilcot, ed. (Note no. 2), and Thorne and Yalom, eds. (Note no. 39).

41. But see the dialogues between Gloria I. Joseph and Jill Lewis, *Common*

Differences: Conflicts in Black and White Feminist Perspectives (New York: Doubleday & Co., 1981), and Marie L. Lugones and Elizabeth V. Spelman, "Have We Got a Theory For You," *Women and Values,* ed. Marilyn Pearsall (Belmont, CA: Wadsworth Publishing Co., 1986), and Phyllis Marynick Palmer (Note no. 13). Women of color have been insisting on this point for a long time. Compare the essays in Barbara Smith, ed. (Note no. 2), and Cherríe Moraga and Gloria Anzaldúa, eds. (Note no. 2). See also Audre Lorde, *Sister Outsider* (Trumansburg, NY: Crossing Press, 1984).

42. Compare the descriptions of mothering in Joyce Trebilcot, ed. (Note no. 2), especially the essays by Whitbeck and Ruddick.

43. For contrary arguments, see Jaggar (Note no. 10), and also Nancy C.M. Hartsock, "The Feminist Standpoint" (Note no. 7).

44. I discuss the gender biases and inadequacies of postmodern philosophy in *Thinking Fragments* (Note no. 1). See also Naomi Schor, "Dreaming Dissymmetry: Barthes, Foucault, and Sexual Difference," *Men in Feminism,* ed. Alice Jardine and Paul Smith (New York: Methuen, 1987).

45. Sigmund Freud, *Civilization and Its Discontents* (New York: W. W. Norton & Co., 1961), pp. 50–51.

3

Dilemmas of Difference: Feminism, Modernity, and Postmodernism

Christine Di Stefano

Whether we choose to characterize the contemporary age as modern or postmodern, most of us are prepared to admit or to defend the notion that few aspects of the human condition are *basic* in the ontological or transhistorical sense. While a few social theorists have been more willing than others to take seriously some of the enduring aspects of human experience which issue from the existentially imposed limits, requirements, and possibilities of the body and psyche, most subscribe to modernist notions which stress history, cultural specificity and variability, and the essentially *conventional* nature of social and political life. Whether for better or for worse, humanity inhabits a sociopolitical environment of its own (yet often unwitting) making. This has been the theoretical starting point for theorists such as Rousseau, Marx, and de Beauvoir; each begins with the assumption that it is a humanly authored history which holds the key to understanding the fate of modern peoples. Postmodernism has taken things one step further by subjecting the tenets and truisms of secular humanism to even further scrutiny. In applying and extending the modernist insistence on the essentially conventional nature of sociopolitical arrangements and their (increasingly important) representations, postmodernism renders the conventional into the arbitrary and promotes a politics and theory of disbelief toward the language of rights, rationality, interests, and autonomy as

Earlier versions and portions of this paper were delivered to the Northwest Women's Studies Association Conference, Eastern Washington University, Cheney, WA, October 17 and 18, 1986, and to the Annual Meeting of the American Political Science Association, the Palmer House, Chicago, September 3–6, 1987. I am grateful to the various panel organizers, participants, and audiences for helpful criticism and encouragement. Special thanks to Tom Dalglish, Susan Hekman, and Lisa Orlando for notably generous and detailed critical responses.

presumed characteristics of a humanistic self that was thought to provide the legitimizing foundation for modern social life.

Contemporary Western feminism is firmly, if ambivalently, located in the modernist ethos, which made possible the feminist identification and critique of gender. Although it was a long time in the making, Western feminism was finally able to deconstruct the presumably fixed and universal association between femininity and the biology of reproduction. Nancy Chodorow's (1978) re-definition of mothering as an institutionalized social practice with its own mode of historical reproduction is, along with Simone de Beauvoir's *The Second Sex,* a quintessential exemplar of modernist feminist inquiry and critique. The concept of gender has made it possible for feminists to simultaneously explain and delegitimize the presumed homology between biological and social sex differences. At the same time, however, gender (rather than sex) differences have emerged as highly significant, salient features which do more to divide and distinguish men and women from each other than to make them parts of some larger, complementary, humanistic whole. In other words, the feminist analysis of gender has undone one version of a presumably basic difference, thought to be rooted in nature, and come up with another, albeit more debatably basic than the previous one.

Gender Differences: How Basic Are They?

Research on gender suggests, among other things, that men and women in contemporary Western societies are differently constituted as modern human subjects; that they inhabit, experience, and construct the sociopolitical world in different, often incommensurable ways; that we are just beginning to perceive and to understand the heretofore suppressed feminine dimensions of public and private life; and that what has passed as a gender neutral vocabulary of reason, morality, cognitive development, autonomy, justice, history, theory, progress, and enlightenment is imbued with masculine meaning (Balbus, 1982; Belenky et al., 1986; Bernard, 1981; Bordo, 1986; Chodorow, 1978; Dinnerstein, 1976; Di Stefano, 1984; Flax, 1983; Fraser, 1985b; Gilligan, 1982; Hartsock, 1983; Hirschman, 1987; Irigaray, 1985; Keller, 1985; Lloyd, 1986; Miller, 1976; O'Brien, 1981). Cross-cultural research on gender reveals several important findings that may be summed up in the following way: On the one hand, gender seems to be a nearly universal feature of all human societies. On the other hand, the actual contents of gender definitions have an astonishingly wide-ranging cross-cultural variability, and it is not always the case that "difference" translates into "unequal."[1] The good news, for feminists at any rate, is that these findings have helped to destabilize domestic notions of difference that construct and impinge on women's and men's life chances. The bad news is gender seems to be a stubbornly ubiquitous feature of culture. In short, it is both more and less of an obstacle to achieving parity between the sexes than many of us had previously imagined.

Questions such as "How basic are gender differences?" emerge out of engagement with this literature and serve as significant grounds of contestation within contemporary Western feminism. At issue are a linked set of theoretical and strategic questions concerning the enterprise of feminist theory and the kinds of political demands and activities that feminists should pursue on behalf of women. Those who believe that gender differences are significantly basic (in the modernist sense that they are strong conventions which help to constitute men and women as incommensurably different subjects) are more likely to pursue a politics of difference which can speak to women's alienated (with respect to dominant, male-stream culture) but also potentially critical identity and be employed on behalf of a reconstituted, nonmasculinist social order. Those who do not see gender as basic in this deep and constitutive sense are more likely to argue for a politics of equality based on some presumption of eventual, attainable, and desirable androgyny; that is, on the basis of an identity which transcends gender difference.

How basic, then, are gender differences? If, by the word *basic,* we mean inescapable or overdetermined, they are basic indeed, inhabiting and structuring the arenas of culture, social structure, and subjectivity to produce a world that is simultaneously gender divided (masculine versus feminine) and gender dominated (masculine). Construed in this way, gender differences pose a radical challenge to the humanist Enlightenment legacy which has come under increasing feminist scrutiny as a masculinist legacy. But recently, gender itself has come under critical scrutiny from new intellectual and political quarters, which charge that gender and its cohort of core assumptions and terms are guilty of the same totalization with which humanism was previously charged. On this view, gender is implicated in a disastrous and oppressive fiction, the fiction of "woman," which runs roughshod over multiple differences among and within women who are ill-served by a conception of gender as basic. For some writers, gender is no more and perhaps not even as basic as poverty, class, ethnicity, race, sexual identity, and age, in the lives of women who feel less divided from men as a group than, for example, from white or bourgeois or Anglo or heterosexual men *and* women (Hooks, 1984; Jordan, 1981; Lorde, 1984). The argument here is that a notion of gender as basic merely serves to reify, rather than to critically contest, transform, and escape the imposed myth of difference, while it ignores other crucial and as yet subjugated arenas of difference.

Is a conception of gender as basic just another, slightly more qualified, version of humanism, a totalizing fiction which should be deconstructed and opposed in the name of a difference that serves no theoretically unifying master? Or can and should it be deployed as part of the ongoing challenge to masculinist hegemony? Which theoretical tack best serves the contemporary needs of women in Western society?

In posing these questions, I have deliberately departed from the empirical territory that often houses the issue of how basic gender differences are. While it is certainly the case that there are some well-established empirical parameters for the answer, I want to argue that this question carries an irreducible theoretical and normative core, one which is not susceptible to strictly empirical resolution. In asking how basic gender differences *are,* we are also asking how basic *we want them to be* for particular purposes and ends. This is really what the feminist debate about gender these days is all about. It could not be otherwise, since gender itself is a product of and a contribution to modernist discourse; it is about conventional forms of meaning, practice, and representation and not at all about foundations, whether natural or metaphysical.

One way of posing the "how basic" question is to explore how various conceptions of gender difference that range across a continuum of less to more basic commit us to particular theoretical and political agendas. This chapter will pursue this tack with reference to the current modernist/ postmodernist controversy, which carries important implications for feminist gender theory. At issue in each theoretical debate is the question of our relationship to and assessment of the enlightened modernist legacy.[2]

Debates about gender differences are, I believe, embedded in three strategic forms for posing the relationship between contemporary Western feminism and the Enlightenment legacy of humanistic rationalism: (1) feminist rationalism, (2) feminine anti-rationalism, and (3) feminist postrationalism. *(Humanism* or *modernism* could be substituted for *rationalism* in this particular scheme.) Each position, as I will try to show, utilizes a particular notion of gender difference and generates specific insights and problems as viewed from the vantage points of the other two. Feminist rationalism, which uses a minimalist notion of gender difference, enables a critique of sexism as an irrational and hence illegitimate set of beliefs and practices. Feminine anti-rationalism, committed to a stronger version of gender difference, levels its protest against the rational/masculine : irrational/feminine construct and attempts to revalorize, rather than to overcome, traditional feminine experience, and to reconceive the meaning of *rational* in a manner that will take account of women's traditional activities. Feminist postrationalism rejects the terms and strategies of the previous two and argues that feminism must initiate a thoroughgoing break with the rationalist paradigm by simultaneously disengaging from the assumptions of generic humanism on the one hand and feminism construed as a theory and politics for the subject "woman" on the other. In this third approach, gender is treated with greater care than it is in the first, but with more suspicion than in the second. Three texts will be especially helpful here and central to the following discussion: Carol McMillan's *Women, Reason and Nature*, Genevieve Lloyd's *The Man of Reason*, and Sandra Harding's *The Science Question in Feminism*. As with any attempt to schematize a complex debate, these three positions are necessarily artificial and overly simplistic. Nevertheless, I believe that the scheme works well enough to help us identify prevailing tendencies and currents. Hopefully, whatever clarity is produced within this schematic frame will not have been purchased at the expense of important nuances and hybrid or alternative positions.

Dilemmas of Gender and Rationality

The *rationalist* position takes the Enlightenment view of rationality and humanism at its word and as its starting point. On this view, common respect is due to all people because they are rational. The human capacity for rationality is precisely what distinguishes us from the realm of nature which, not incidentally, is not accorded respectful treatment. Women have been unfairly excluded from the respect which they are due as human beings on the basis of an insidious assumption that they are less rational and more natural than men. "Difference" has been used to legitimize the unequal treatment of women and therefore must be repudiated theoretically and practically in order for women to assume their rightful place in society as the nondifferentiated equals of men.[3]

Anti-rationalism comes face to face with the denigration of feminized nature within rationalism and attempts to revalorize the feminine in the light of this denigration. Significantly, the terms of this valorization are the terms of the excluded and denigrated "other": Anti-rationalism celebrates the designated and feminized irrational, invoking a strong notion of difference against the gender-neutral pretensions of a rationalist culture that opposes itself to nature, the body, natural contingency, and intuition. This project sees itself as a disloyal opposition and envisions a social order that would better accomodate women in their feminized difference rather than as imperfect copies of the Everyman.[4]

Finally, *postrationalism* refuses the linguistic and conceptual currency of rationalism altogether. Eschewing a position either within or outside of the rationalist framework, for or against difference, postrationalism attempts to transcend the discourse of rationalism and to offer new, decentered, and admittedly partial or fractured narratives of opposition. Here, difference is simultaneously upheld and deconstructed: A proliferation of differences is counterposed to the singular difference of gender, and suspicion is cast on difference as an artifact of the very system of domination to which it is ostensibly opposed. While this strategy is theoretically appealing, it is also complex and unnerving, inhabiting a constantly shifting ground of emerging and dissolving differences.[5]

A very interesting example of feminine anti-rationalism is Carol McMillan's *Women, Reason and Nature: Some Philosophical Problems With Feminism,* which has been justly criticized as an anti-feminist text. A crucial flaw in the analysis is her thin version of feminist theory, which she believes is adequately captured by (her version of) the work of Simone de Beauvoir and Shulamith Firestone. Her consequent indictment of feminism as a co-conspirator in the rationalist project which devalues women and the feminine in the name of a masculinist rationalism is, therefore, weak. Nevertheless, her critical reading of rationalism is instructive in several respects.

McMillan takes aim at the classical Cartesian version of reason and morality, which has been housed within a dichotomous structure that is all too familiar to us: It begins with the subject-object dyad and culminates in the opposition between reason and emotion-intuition. Within this framework, women and the feminine have carried the brunt of guilt by association with the irrational. McMillan's quarrel with feminism is that it uncritically accepts the rationalist division between (feminine) intuitive and (masculine) rational knowledge. This is manifested in the various attempts of feminists to break the link between women, nature, and irrationality rather than to contest the dichotomous construct within which these links are housed. According to McMillan, "what feminists need to acknowledge is that the whole rationalist enterprise was able to get off the ground only because a spurious contrast was made between rationality and intuition, between reason and emotion" (pp. 55–56). This contrast nourished the idea that "reasoning is the peculiar prerogative of masculine pursuits, and therefore of the male sex" (p. 56). Hence, "the idea of sexists that women cannot reason and the idea of feminists that they do not reason because they have never been given the necessary educational opportunities rest on the same misconceptions" (p. 56). McMillan's argument is a cry for greater sensitivity to the interpretive nuances of complex feminine lives. On this view, the everyday life practices of women, particularly in their reproductive and child-rearing roles, merit reevaluation as complex, rational, thoughtful, and important activities. "If the critical fact of womanhood . . . is that women bear children and men do not, then surely a new sense of the worth of women should involve, above all, a revaluation of the maternal role" (p. 102). To criticize such lives and the sexual division of labor according to which they are organized is to apply a foreign (i.e., masculine, rationalist) standard of evaluation. Feminism, then, is judged guilty in the following terms: "Far from being either radical or revolutionary [feminism] reveals itself to be perhaps the most articulate expression of the philosophy of a society in which human life is continually trivialized and cheapened for the sake of extraneous, abstract aims" (p. 78).

For McMillan, the feminist demand for control over reproduction, for reproductive rights, plays into and out of the rationalist conception of a human agency pitted over and against the natural realm of necessity. Rather than reading biology as a problem to be mastered and therefore overcome, she proposes that we treat it as a condition to be embraced "more fully, and with more justice." As for the sexual division of labor within the household, "we have to look for ways in which value can be placed upon femininity without resorting to money or 'masculine' activities as our frame of reference" (pp. 204–105). In other words, neither wages for housework nor paid labor outside the home qualify as solutions to the problem of the underevaluation of women's work. For this problem, according to McMillan, is ultimately related to rationalist conceptions of what counts in the human scheme of things. Capitulating to the ethos of this conception will not serve the interests of women.

We need to stop assuming, argues McMillan, in line with the voluntarist account of human agency and rationality, that social restrictions such as sex roles are necessarily bad, that is, unjustified infringements on free choice and self-determination. Even though they are conventions, these cultural artifacts are not merely arbitrary impositions. Rather, they seek to make sense out of the givens of life; in this case, they seek to make sense out of the ontological givens of reproductive sex differences. According to McMillan, the restriction of women to the domestic sphere is a violation of their rights *only if* domestic activities are devalued. This is a strange way of putting it, since we might want to ask whether the restriction of women to the domestic sphere would have existed in the *first place,* if such activities had not already been devalued. That is, does devaluing give way to the restriction or does the restriction give way to the devaluing? Obviously, there is no way to answer this question concerning the origins of a denigrated and separate female sphere with any satisfactory sense of closure. McMillan's answer to this unarticulated question of origins locates the devaluation of the feminine in a philosophical framework (rationalism) rather than in a visceral world of power/knowledge relations. Hence, an appreciation of the political fact that conventions preclude, even as they construct, certain choices never enters into her discussion of women's estate. The very notion of choice is, for McMillan, implicated in the rationalist understanding of agency as a manipulative power exercised over events and brute necessity. McMillan's repudiation of choice is refracted in her criticism of the feminist call for reproductive freedom. Abortion is viewed as a denial and destruction of life. The technology of birth control is criticized (in many ways, rightly so) for its damaging effects on female bodies and sexuality.

McMillan's analysis is similarly marred by a heterosexist conception of sexuality. Presumably, it is only members of the two opposite sexes who interact sexually. A good part of the reason for this oversight is related to her argument that all conventions seek to make sense out of real or basic facts of life. In her insistence that social conventions such as motherhood are not merely arbitrary inventions, she goes to the other extreme and claims that they all aim to make sense out of a nature that is sexually dimorphous and devalued by rationalism. There is no sense here that conventions often take on complex lives and histories of their own, which often bear little resemblance to their functional roots. Equally problematic, we find no appreciation of the fact that conventions often help to produce and constitute the very facts and problems which they ostensibly help us to make sense of or which they stand as solutions to. Among feminists, a favorite example of this phenomenon is the genealogy of the "woman question." We can add others: The convention of heterosexuality is implicated in the "problem" of homosexuality; the nineteenth-century "problem" of the spinster was effectively the progeny of the nuclear family from which she was excluded.

In her eagerness to problematize the inherited patterns of rationalist thought which undermine and devalue the feminine, McMillan manages to deproblematize femininity altogether. By insisting that femininity has its own appropriate criteria of rationality, agency, motivation, morality, and worth, McMillan would have us invoke these so as to valorize feminine experience. Unfortunately, her anti-rationalist critique, potentially useful to feminists, particularly those attempting to develop a theory and politics of eco-feminism (King, 1981), ends up confirming the very fears that have kept so many of us within rationalism for lack of a *viable* alternative. The view from here suggests that rationalism, along with its thin version of gender differences, provides a safer foothold than the paradoxically conformist anti-rationalist alternative. Thankfully, our choices do not reduce to these two.

Genevieve Lloyd's *The Man of Reason* offers a more sophisticated and feminist treatment of gender differences and masculine rationality. In this critical review of the Western philosophical tradition, Lloyd explores the ideal of Reason as it has been formulated by the "great" philosophers. Her conclusion is that the ideal of a sexually neutral Reason is radically misconceived. Like McMillan, Lloyd sees that "rationality has been conceived as transcendence of the feminine" and that "women cannot easily be accomodated into a cultural ideal which has defined itself in opposition to the feminine" (p. 104). In contrast to McMillan, however, Lloyd makes the additional and critically crucial observation that "the 'feminine' itself has been partly constituted by its occurence within this structure" (p. 105). Within Lloyd's scheme, the "different but equal" approach advocated by McMillan seriously overestimates its own radicalness vis à vis the discourse it would challenge. For, "the idea that women have their own distinctive kind of intellectual or moral character [and worth] has itself been partly formed within the philosophical tradition to which it may now appear to be a reaction" (p. 105). The effort to valorize the feminine as an essentially different kind of rationality and agency unrecognized by rationalism "will occur in a space already prepared for it by the intellectual tradition it seeks to reject" (p. 105).

Lloyd's analysis, then, urges us to approach the various exclusions of the feminine from Reason as a less than straightforward discrimination, for Western philosophy has permitted or required feminine traits (as it defines them) to be simultaneously preserved and downgraded. "Making good the lacks in male consciousness, providing it with a necessary complementation by the 'feminine,' is a large part of what the suppression, and the correlative constitution, of 'womankind' has been all about" (p. 105). The important difference here between McMillan and Lloyd is that whereas McMillan thinks that ideals of Reason have merely *reflected* sexual difference, Lloyd asserts that they have also helped to *constitute* the terms and content of that difference. The feminine, then, has also been constituted through its exclusion. If many of the critical strengths of female/feminine difference derive from that exclusion, these strengths will survive only so long as they are not used to assert a positive rival norm.

The temptation to do so, however, is enormous. This is not simply a matter of fighting fire with fire, a strategic counterweight to the devaluation and oppression of things female and feminine. Rather, the critical acuity and insight produced by the voice of the other provides a visceral, tangible sense of alternatives to the one-dimensional rationalist horror show. The poet Carolyn Kizer has put it this way: "Witnessing: woman's role and art. What would we—all of us—lose if women succeeded in entering the arena as the equals of men, at the expense of that witnessing? . . . the view from the sidelines has produced a precious hoard" (Kizer, 1986, p. 11). In her "Declaration of an Independence I Would Just as Soon Not Have," June Jordan raises similar concerns about an assimilative feminism whose image of liberation is cast in the dominant white masculine mode:

> Will we liberate ourselves so that the caring for children, the teaching, the loving, healing, person-oriented values that have always distinguished us will be revered and honored at least commensurate to the honors accorded bank managers, lieutenant colonels, and the executive corporate elite? Or will we liberate ourselves so that we can militantly

> abandon those attributes and functions, so that we can despise our own
> warmth and generosity even as men have done, for ages? (p.120)

What, then, are we to do with gendered difference? A strict rationalist
response dictates its denial and elimination in the service of a universal
humanism. The anti-rationalist response seems to call for its reification.
Lloyd reminds us of two important things here: While difference cannot
be denied, because rationalist sameness already presupposes a *particular*
gendered version of itself, the outsider witness (the feminized Other) is
not innocent. She is also a product of rationalist, masculinist discourse.

Where does all of this leave us with respect to the modern, rationalist
legacy? McMillan's solution—a feminized model of agency and rationality on the model of the mother in labor—is no solution here. But neither,
argues Lloyd, is a thoroughgoing repudiation of the categories of reason,
truth, and logic: "The claim that Reason is male need not at all involve
sexual relativism about truth, or any suggestion that principles of logical
thought valid for men do not hold also for female reasoners" (p. 109).
Lloyd believes that "philosophers can take seriously feminist dissatisfaction with the maleness of Reason without repudiating either Reason or
Philosophy" (p. 109). But does Lloyd protest a bit too loudly? Has she
perhaps underestimated the implications of her analysis? What is "Reason"
or "Philosophy," stripped of its androcentric content and associations,
which, as Lloyd has demonstrated, is ubiquitous throughout the history
of Western philosophical discourse? Can these terms even be *thought*
without the residues of that content? Unfortunately, Lloyd does not pursue
these questions. However, a parallel set of questions concerning the theory
and practice of science has been raised by Sandra Harding in *The Science
Question in Feminism*.

But first, a brief review of the issues thus far covered is in order. The
political counterpart to rationalism commits us to equality and to the
elimination of gender differences, but this equality, as McMillan has
suggested, is constituted within a set of terms that disparage things female
or feminine. Lloyd would add that these terms have also created, and not
merely reflected, the female and the feminine. Anti-rationalism attempts
to revalorize the feminine, with the nasty effect of failing to criticize it.
Hence, anti-rationalism tends to slide into anti-feminism. The dilemma
seems to be this: Give up rationalism and its cohort assumption of human
sameness and we surrender an existing vocabulary of and claim to Enlightenment humanism and rationalism; embrace it and we endorse the modernist misogynous sensibility as we lose a critical vantage point on that
sensibility. The choice seems to be one between a politics and epistemology of identity (sameness) or difference. Yet, as Lloyd reminds us, such
a choice is only a pseudo-choice, since it comes to us already framed as

such, prepackaged by a gendered narrative of *us* and *them*. On this view, difference appeals to mistakenly essentialized identities as much as identity does. We seem, then, to be stuck in a vicious discursive cycle. The only way out (if such exists) is provided by a strategy that may be termed postrationalist or postmodernist. While this strategy solves many of the problems entailed and engendered by the rationalist and anti-rationalist agendas, it generates a formidable one of its own. I call this problem the "postfeminist tendency," an inclination which is fostered by a refusal to systematically document or privilege any particular form of difference or identity against the hegemonic mainstream.

Postmodernism/Postfeminism?

According to Sandra Harding, the feminist challenge to Western culture's intellectual and social frameworks inevitably reaches to the very foundations of our cultural-epistemological systems. Like McMillan and Lloyd, she argues that "what we took to be humanly inclusive problematics, concepts, theories, objective methodologies, and transcendental truths are in fact far less than that. Indeed, these products of thought bear the mark of their collective and individual creators, and the creators in turn have been distinctively marked as to gender, class, race, and culture" (p. 15). In Harding's account, the feminist challenge is even more threatening to the social and epistemological order than McMillan and Lloyd seem to think, for the conspiratorial ubiquity of gender and (scientific) rationality dovetail to promote the suspicion that an appropriate model of rationality—of methodical knowledge-seeking—has yet to be specified, much less realized in practice. On this view, the inherited vocabularies of the feminine and of Reason, of difference and identity, are equally suspicious. There is insufficient space for critical recuperation in either enterprise.

Harding argues that feminist critiques of modern science have taken three forms: feminist empiricism, feminist standpoint theories, and, more recently, feminist postmodernism. Feminist empiricism corresponds quite neatly with rationalism. (It is also the epistemological counterpart to liberalism and liberal-feminism). It identifies sexism and androcentrism as *social biases* which are correctable by stricter adherence to the existing norms of scientific inquiry. Hence, sexist science is portrayed as bad science rather than science as usual. But feminist empiricism unwittingly deconstructs its terms of endearment to rationalism by revealing that sexist bias is an internal rather than accidental or secondary feature of scientific research procedures. The epistemological paradoxes of feminist empiricism are addressed by the feminist standpoint approach, which is willing to acknowledge the intimate gendered dimensions of rational inquiry. Here, the gender specific and differentiated perspective of women is advanced as a *preferable* grounding for inquiry—preferable because the experience and perspective of women as the excluded and exploited other is judged to be more inclusive and critically coherent than that of the masculine group (Hartsock, 1983, pp. 231–251). While the feminist standpoint approach is willing to embrace an open relationship between knowledge and gendered interests, it still shares—with feminist empiricism—an urge for generalizable, universal knowledge. Minimally, such knowledge should be universal for the group "women." Maximally, it should be able to subsume the partial and perverse understandings of masculine inquiry within its horizon of explanation and interpretation. As Harding points out, feminist standpoint theories are vulnerable to the suspicion that "women" do not exist as a sufficiently coherent social subject. If differences between women—differences secured on the basis of race, class, sexuality, culture, and ethnicity—are sufficient to override feminine commonalities of experience and interest, then *a* feminist standpoint, like *the* feminist movement (Hooks, 1984), is a potentially oppressive and totalizing fiction, just as humanism has been. More disturbing still is this question: "Is the feminist standpoint project still too firmly grounded in the historically disastrous alliance between knowledge and power characteristic of the modern epoch? Is it too firmly rooted in a problematic politics of essentialized identities?" (p. 27). Harding's question suggests that femin*ist* standpoint theories, like femin*ine* standpoint theories, are stuck in an overly literal loyalty to the reified account of gender and rationality bequeathed by modern rationalist philosophy and culture.

For Harding, feminist postmodernism goes even further to challenge the assumptions of feminist empiricism and feminist standpoint theories. While postmodernism opposes "the dangerous fiction of the naturalized, essentialized, uniquely 'human' (read 'manly') and . . . the distortion and exploitation perpetrated on behalf of this fiction" (p. 26), it embraces a skepticism regarding generalizable and universal claims of *any* sort, including those of feminism. Furthermore, it cultivates a suspicion toward any overly coherent theory. Feminist postmodernism, then, is "an epistemology that justifies knowledge claims only insofar as they arise from enthusiastic violation of the founding taboos of Western humanism" (p. 193). The political counterpart to this epistemology of "permanent partiality" is a "politics of solidarity" of "fragmented selves and oppositional consciousness" (pp. 195–196), enacting "a refusal of the delusion of return to an 'original unity' " (p. 193). This original unity designates the fiction of wholeness applied to the self, to the group, to the ideal of a comprehensive politics or theory, to the epistemological problem of the subject-object relationship, and to the political vision of communal (totalitarian) utopia. "Why not," asks Harding:

> seek a political and epistemological solidarity in our oppositions to the
> fiction of the naturalized, essentialized, uniquely "human" and to the
> distortions, perversions, exploitations, and subjugations perpetrated on
> behalf of this fiction? Why not explore the new possibilities opened up
> by recognition of the permanent partiality of the feminist point of view?
> (p. 193)

For many reasons, this is an attractive reformulation of a feminist politics and theory of difference. The affinities between contemporary feminism and postmodern theory have been noticed by others as well (Ferguson, 1984; Flax, 1986; Fraser, 1985a; Fraser and Nicholson, 1988; Hekman, 1987; Meese, 1986; Owens, 1983). What they share, according to Jane Flax, is "a profound skepticism regarding universal (or universalizing) claims about the existence, nature and powers of reason, progress, science, language and the 'subject / self' " (Flax, 1986, p. 3). If gender has been the original impetus for this skepticism, then it may also be the case that it is time to give up the comforts and closures of the concept for a more radical and decentered attention to multiple differences, none of which merit theoretical privileging over others.

But from other feminist quarters, the postmodern call to give up the privileging of gender, along with subject-centered forays into women's ways of thinking, acting, and reconceiving theory and politics, is met with suspicion and hostility. As Nancy Hartsock has asked, Why is it, just at the moment in Western history when previously silenced populations have begun to speak for themselves and on behalf of their subjectivities, that the concept of the subject and the possibility of discovering/creating a liberating "truth" become suspect? (Hartsock, 1987). In other words, is postmodernism merely a sophisticated version of the sour grapes phenomenon? Jane Flax (1987) suggests that postmodern theory is perhaps no less immune from the repressive and prohibitory functions practiced by other theories. In this case, she argues, the postmodernist suspicion of the subject effectively prohibits the exploration of (a repressed) subjectivity by and on behalf of women. Like Wendy Brown (1987), she believes that the subject under fire from postmodernism may be a more specifically masculine self than postmodern theorists have been willing to admit. With Nancy Hartsock, she is "deeply suspicious of the motives of those who counsel such a move at the moment when women have just begun to remember their selves and claim an agentic subjectivity" (p. 106).

The feminist case against postmodernism would seem to consist of several related claims. First, that postmodernism expresses the claims and needs of a constituency (white, privileged men of the industrialized West) that has already had an Enlightenment for itself and that is now ready and willing to subject that legacy to critical scrutiny. Secondly, that the objects of postmodernism's various critical and deconstructive efforts have been the creations of a similarly specific and partial constituency (beginning with Socrates, Plato, and Aristotle). Third, that mainstream postmodernist theory (Derrida, Lyotard, Rorty, Foucault) has been remarkably blind and insensitive to questions of gender in its own purportedly politicized rereadings of history, politics, and culture. Finally, that the postmodernist project, if seriously adopted by feminists, would make any semblance of a feminist politics impossible. To the extent that feminist politics is bound up with a specific constituency or subject, namely, women, the postmodernist prohibition against subject-centered inquiry and theory undermines the legitimacy of a broad-based organized movement dedicated to articulating and implementing the goals of such a constituency.[6]

Harding herself is ambivalent and cautious about the feasibility of a feminist postmodern politics. In recognizing "the permanent partiality of the feminist point of view," she admits that we may become dangerously vulnerable to the hegemonic power of science and its epistemological strategies. Politically, we might add, this weakness translates into a vulnerability to modern state and disciplinary power. Another problem is that "robust" solidarities of opposition (rather than of shared identity) may be psychologically and politically unreliable, unable to generate sufficient attachment and motivation on the part of potential activists. Can this solidarity be anything other than a local and negative solidarity, a solidarity of *resistance* rather than of substantive *alternatives?* If we are encouraged to embrace fractured identities, we are inevitably drawn to the forbidden question: Fractured with respect to *what?* Can fractured identities be embraced without the parallel construction of new fictions of counter-identity? The epistemological attractiveness of decentered knowledge-seeking lies precisely in the fact that it bears little resemblance to current conceptions of knowledge and rationality which, as we now appreciate, have been intimately bound up with modes of domination and illicit power. But this attractiveness carries a political liability and question of significant proportions: Is a postmodern politics—a political opposition capable of sustaining itself through time—seriously conceivable?[7]

Harding's attempt to delineate the contours of a feminist postmodern politics is an instructive example of the difficulties attached to the effort. In the following passage, for example, she retains key features of the discourse she seeks to deconstruct, precisely to preserve some familiar sense of political plausibility: "I argue for the primacy of fragmented identities but only for those *healthy* ones constructed on a *solid* and *non-defensive core identity,* and only within a *unified* opposition, a *solidarity* against the culturally dominant forces for unitarianism" (p. 247, my emphasis). Harding has smuggled a forbidden vocabulary into her analysis, a vocabulary whose connotative context lies in the very modernist, humanist, rationalist discourse she is presumably repudiating. Criteria such as these, of "health," "solidity," "non-defensiveness," "identity," and "unity" partake of the very ontology disallowed by postmodernism; they all require standards of normalcy, of judgement, of hierarchical distinctions which must be rooted within some organizing and legitimating ground or framework. Harding invokes them, I believe, to dodge the potentially anti-political and anti-feminist implications of postmodernism. As a result, the specter of a completely deconstructed rationality and its cohort, a deracinated politics, is held at bay. Harding argues as if we can have our cake and eat it too—that is, as if the critical deconstructive insights of postmodernism can be explicitly, defensibly, and plausibly harnessed to a progressive and substantive feminist politics.

Such a harnessing would be a remarkable achievement indeed. The nagging question is whether the uncertain promise of a political linkage between feminism and postmodernism is worth the attendant potential risks. These risks exist not merely at the currently speculative level of wondering whether feminism without a subject and standpoint of some sort can survive. They are also palpably present in the existing language of postmodernism which has reappropriated the political vocabulary of "pluralism" to describe its version of theory as a huge "conversation" among a variety of fractured participants (Rorty, 1979). Yet, as Craig Owens (1983) has astutely remarked: "Pluralism . . . reduces us to being an other among others; it is not a recognition, but a reduction to [sic] difference to absolute indifference, equivalence, interchangeability . . ." (p. 58). It is as if postmodernism has returned us to the falsely innocent indifference of the very humanism to which it stands opposed; a rerun, in updated garb, of the modernist case of the incredible shrinking woman.

For the time being, then, postmodernism is as entrenched in the dilemmas of difference as are the modernist and anti-modernist alternatives. Within each framework, the fate of the female subject is instructive: In the rationalist framework, *she* dissolves into *he* as gender differences are collapsed into the (masculine) figure of the Everyman. The political counterparts to this collapsing of difference are liberalism and orthodox Marxism. Anti-rationalism preserves the figure of the differentiated female subject, but *she* is preserved at the expense of her transformation and liberation from the conventions of femininity. We can detect the echoes of radical feminism and of New Right anti-feminism here. With postrationalism, *she* dissolves into a perplexing plurality of differences, none of which can be theoretically or politically privileged over others. But as Martin Jay (1985) has pointed out, in our haste to deconstruct hierarchical distinctions such as gender as harmful illusions, we may fail to grasp "their tenacious rootedness in an objective world created over time and deeply resistant to change" (p. 140), and we will avoid the difficult and important question: Are some differences more basic than others?

By reference to postmodernism's own championing of an alternative to unified theoretical coherence, we should insist that the theoretical and political dilemmas of difference are well worth pondering. As yet, they remain stubbornly persistent and elusive, suggesting that gender is basic in ways that we have yet to fully understand, that it functions as "a difference that makes a difference," even as it can no longer claim the legitimating mantle of *the* difference. The figure of the shrinking woman may perhaps be best appreciated and utilized as an aporia within contemporary theory: as a recurring paradox, question, dead end, or blind spot to which we must repeatedly return, because to ignore her altogether is to risk forgetting and thereby losing what is left of her. The alternatives, such as they exist without her, consist of generic (hu)manism, reified femininity, or postmodern pluralism.

Notes

1. See the following sources for excellent discussions of gender-related research in anthropology: A classic exposition of the cross-cultural variability of gender conceptions and practices is still *(pace* Derek Freeman) Mead (1963). Two of the most highly influential anthologies in feminist anthropology are R. Reiter (1975) and M. Rosaldo and L. Lamphere (1974). A more recent anthology is S. Ortner and H. Whitehead (1981). For an extensive comparison of cross-cultural data and an effort to identify the factors most likely to issue in the cultural subordination of women, see P. Sanday (1981). For important critiques of the mistaken universalization of the female/nature: male/culture opposition originally advanced by S. Ortner (1974), see the collection of essays edited by C. MacCormack and M. Strathern (1980). An interesting discussion of the ways in which *difference* may serve women better than *equality* may be found in Y. Murphy and R. Murphy (1974).

2. As Iris Young has pointed out to me, this chapter is vulnerable to the criticism that *modernity* and *postmodernism* are treated in overly generalized terms and suffer from insufficient specification. For example, a wide variety of theorists and philosophers, including Descartes, Hobbes, Kant, Marx, and J.S. Mill qualify as modern thinkers, even though the differences among them are substantial and significant. Furthermore, an overly monolithic account of modernity fails to recognize the counter-discourses which it has spawned: Hegel and Rousseau come to mind here. Postmodernism is a similarly diversified phenomenon. Theorists such as Gadamer, Foucault, Derrida, and Rorty are not interchangeable figures who inhabit a neatly singular discursive domain. Since the primary focus of this chapter is feminist theory—more specifically, feminist debates concerning the status of gender differences—I have depicted the modern and postmodern in broad

brush strokes. While particular strands of modern and postmodern theory would benefit from careful and sustained feminist interrogations, that is not the purpose of this chapter. Rather, I have chosen to situate the modern-postmodern controversy as a backdrop to contemporary feminist theory and discussion. Within the limited space of an article, I see no way to pursue both strategies simultaneously. In short, I have decided to privilege feminist theory here.

3. Classic (but also internally contradictory) expositions of this strategy include the following: John Stuart Mill, *The Subjection of Women,* in A. Rossi (1970), and M. Wollestonecraft (1975). See also A. Jaggar (1983), Chapter 7, for a discussion of liberalism that links up in close ways with this description of rationalism.

4. For contemporary examples of feminist anti-egalitarianism, see H. Eisenstein and A. Jardine (1980). For a good review of the theme of difference in the literature of second-wave feminism, see H. Eisenstein (1983). For a philosophical (but not feminist) exploration of problems with egalitarian thinking, see E. Wolgast (1980). For an earlier exposition of similar themes by a nineteenth-century feminist, see M. Fuller (1971).

5. For a compelling, sophisticated, and politically sensitive exploration of deconstructive feminist approaches to difference, see E. Meese (1986).

6. Many of these themes are implicated in the modernist-postmodernist controversy. See the following sources for helpful discussions of the issues: J. Arac (1986), S. Benhabib (1984), R. Bernstein (1985), W. Connolly (1985), N. Fraser (1985a), J. Habermas (1983), A. Huyssen (1984), M. Jay (1984–85), C. Taylor (1984), J. Whitebook (1981–82), R. Wolin (1984–85).

7. See A. J. Polan (1984) for an interesting discussion of politics and time.

References

Arac, J., ed. 1986. *Postmodernism and Politics.* Minneapolis: University of Minnesota.

Balbus, I. 1982. *Marxism and Domination,* Princeton: Princeton University Press.

Belenky, M. et al. 1986. *Women's Ways of Knowing: The Development of Self, Voice, and Mind.* New York: Basic Books.

Benhabib, S. 1984. "Epistemologies of Postmodernism: A Rejoinder to Jean-Francois Lyotard." *New German Critique* 33: 103–126.

Bernard, J. 1981. *The Female World.* New York and London: The Free Press.

Bernstein, R., ed. 1985. *Habermas and Modernity.* Cambridge, MA: The MIT Press.

Bordo, S. 1986. "The Cartesian Masculinization of Thought." *Signs* 11 (3): 439–456.

Brown, W. 1987. "Where is the Sex in Political Theory?" *Women & Politics* 7 (1): 3–23.

Chodorow, N. 1978. *The Reproduction of Mothering*. Berkeley, CA: University of California Press.

Connolly, W. 1985. "Taylor, Foucault, and Otherness." *Political Theory* 13 (3): 365–376.

Dinnerstein, D. 1976. *The Mermaid and the Minotaur*. New York: Harper & Row.

Di Stefano, C. 1984. "Gender and Political Theory: Masculinity as Ideology in Modern Political Thought." Unpublished doctoral dissertation, University of Massachusetts, Amherst, MA.

————— 1989. "Rereading J.S. Mill: Interpolations from the (M)otherworld." *Discontented Discourses: Feminism/Textual Intervention/Psychoanalysis*. Edited by M. Barr & R. Feldstein. (pp 160–172). Urbana, IL: University of Illinois Press.

Eisenstein, H. 1983. *Contemporary Feminist Thought*. Boston: G.K. Hall.

Eisenstein, H. and Jardine, A., eds. 1980. *The Future of Difference*. Boston: G.K. Hall.

Ferguson, K. 1984. *The Feminist Case against Bureaucracy*. Philadelphia: Temple University Press.

Flax, J. 1983. "Political Philosophy and the Patriarchal Unconscious: A Psychoanalytic Perspective on Epistemology and Metaphysics." In *Discovering Reality: Feminist Perspectives on Epistemology, Metaphysics, Methodology, and Philosophy of Science*. Edited by S. Harding and M. B. Hintikka, pp. 245–281. Dordrecht and Boston: D. Reidel.

————— 1986. "Gender as a Social Problem: In and for Feminist Theory." *Amerikastudien/American Studies* 31: 193–213.

————— 1987. "Re-membering the Selves: Is the Repressed Gendered? *Michigan Quarterly Review* 26 (1): 92–110.

Foucault, M. 1980. *Power/Knowledge: Selected Interviews and Other Writings*. Trans, C. Gordon. New York: Pantheon.

Fraser, N. 1984. "The French Derrideans: Politicizing Deconstruction or Deconstructing the Political?" *New German Critique* 33: 127–154.

————— 1985a. "Michel Foucault: A Young Conservative?" *Ethics* 96: 165–184.

————— 1985b. "What's Critical about Critical Theory? The Case of Habermas and Gender." *New German Critique* 35: 97–131.

Fraser, N. and L. Nicholson, 1989. Social Criticism Without Philosophy: An Encounter between Feminism and Postmodernism.

Fuller, M. 1971 (1855). *Woman in the Nineteenth Century*. New York: W.W. Norton.

Gilligan, C. 1982. *In a Different Voice: Psychological Theory and Women's Development*. Cambridge, MA and London: Harvard University Press.

Habermas, J. 1983. Modernity—An Incomplete Project. In *The Anti-Aesthetic*. Edited by H. Foster, pp. 3–15. Port Townsend, WA: Bay Press.

Harding, S. 1986. *The Science Question in Feminism*. Ithaca and London: Cornell University Press.

Hartsock, N. 1983. *Money, Sex, and Power: Toward a Feminist Historical Materialism*. New York and London: Longman.

———— 1987. "Rethinking Modernism: Minority vs. Majority Theories." *Cultural Critique* 7: 187–206.

Hekman, S. 1987. "Feminism and Liberalism." Unpublished manuscript.

Hirschman, N. *Rethinking Obligation: A Feminist Method For Political Theory*. Ithaca: Cornell University Press (forthcoming).

Hooks, B. 1984. *Feminist Theory: From Margin to Center*. Boston: South End Press.

Huyssen, A. 1984. "Mapping the Postmodern." *New German Critique* 33: 5–52.

Irigaray, L. 1985. *Speculum of the Other Woman*. Ithaca: Cornell University Press.

Jaggar, A. 1983. *Feminist Politics and Human Nature*. Totawa, NJ: Rowman and Allanheld.

Jay, M. 1984–1985. "Hierarchy and the Humanities: The Radical Implications of a Conservative Idea." In *Telos* 62: 131–144.

Jordan, J. 1981. "Declaration of an Independence I Would Just As Soon Not Have." *Civil Wars*, 115–121. Boston: Beacon Press.

Keller, E. 1985. *Reflections on Gender and Science*. New Haven and London: Yale University Press.

King, Y. 1981. "Feminism and the Revolt of Nature." In *Heresies* 13: 12–16.

Kizer, C. 1986. "Two women, Terrified." (Review of E. Clark, *Camping Out*). *New York Times Book Review*, May 14, p. 11.

Lloyd, G. 1984. *The Man of Reason: "Male" and "Female" in Western Philosophy*. Minneapolis: University of Minnesota Press.

Lorde, A. 1984. *Sister Outsider*. Trumansburg, NY: The Crossing Press.

Lyotard, J. 1984. *The Postmodern Condition: A Report on Knowledge*. Minneapolis: University of Minnesota Press.

MacCormack, C., and Strathern, M., eds. 1980. *Nature, Culture and Gender*. Cambridge: Cambridge University Press.

McMillan, C. 1982. *Women, Reason and Nature: Some Philosophical Problems with Feminism*. Princeton: Princeton University Press.

Mead, M. 1963. *Sex and Temperament*. New York: Morrow Quill Paperbacks.

Meese, E. 1986. *Crossing the Double-Cross: The Practice of Feminist Criticism*. Chapel Hill and London: University of North Carolina Press.

Miller, J. 1976. *Toward a New Psychology of Women*. Boston: Beacon Press.

Murphy, Y., and Murphy, R. 1974. *Women of the Forest*. New York: Columbia University Press.

O'Brien, M. 1981. *The Politics of Reproduction*. Boston: Routledge and Kegan Paul, 1974.

Ortner, S. "Is Female to Male as Nature is to Culture?" In *Woman, Culture, and Society*. Edited by M. Rosaldo and L. Lamphere, pp. 67–87. Stanford, CA: Stanford University Press, 1981.

Ortner, S., and Whitehead, H., eds. *Sexual Meanings: The Cultural Construction of Gender and Sexuality*. Cambridge: Cambridge University Press.

Owens, C. 1983. "The Discourse of Others: Feminists and Postmodernism." In *The Anti-Aesthetic*, edited by H. Foster, pp. 57–82. Port Townsend, WA: Bay Press.

Polan, A.J. 1984. *Lenin and the End of Politics*. Berkeley, CA: University of California Press.

Reiter, R., ed. 1975. *Toward an Anthropology of Women*. New York and London: Monthly Review Press.

Rorty, R. 1979. *Philosophy and the Mirror of Nature*. Princeton: Princeton University Press.

Rosaldo, M.Z. 1980. "The Use and Abuse of Anthropology: Reflections on Feminism and Cross-Cultural Understanding." *Signs*, 5 (3): 389–417.

Rosaldo, M., and Lamphere, L., eds. 1974. *Woman, Culture and Society*. Stanford, CA: Stanford University Press.

Rossi, A., ed. 1970. *Essays on Sex Equality*. Chicago and London: The University of Chicago Press.

Sanday, P. 1981. *Female Power and Male Dominance: On the Origins of Sexual Inequality*. Cambridge: Cambridge University Press.

Taylor, C. 1984. "Foucault on Freedom and Truth." *Political Theory* 12: 152–83.

Whitebook, J. 1981–1982. "Saving the Subject: Modernity and the Problem of the Autonomous Individual." *Telos* 50: 79–102.

Wolgast, E. 1980. *Equality and the Rights of Women*. Ithaca: Cornell University Press.

Wolin, R. 1984–1985. "Modernism vs. Postmodernism." *Telos* 62: 9–29.

Wollestonecraft, M. 1975 (1792). *A Vindication of the Rights of Women*. New York: W.W. Norton.

4

Feminism, Science, and the Anti-Enlightenment Critiques

Sandra Harding

At the center of an emerging controversy in U.S. feminism lies the question of whether there should be feminist sciences and epistemologies. Feminists in the scientific traditions have attempted to reform and transform the theories and practices of these traditions in order to create less partial and less distorted representations of the world than the mainstream, androcentric ones. They want less false stories about nature and social life; they want scientific explanations that can provide useful guides to improving the conditions of women. In addition to producing new theories and empirical studies, they have developed feminist empiricism and the feminist standpoint epistemologies as justificatory strategies for the new scientific projects. In important ways, these tendencies continue what have come to be labeled modernist and Enlightenment projects. These labels would appear to be appropriate for the feminist science and epistemology projects since they envision emancipatory possibilities for the harnessing of power to knowledge.

Other feminists indebted to darker, less optimistic, European traditions of skepticism about the beneficial effects of the agendas of the Enlightenment and modernity are beginning to add the feminist science and epistemology projects to their mainstream targets of criticism. They ask whether it is realistic to imagine that the scientific traditions can be harnessed in ways that will advance women's situations.

Here I want to show why it would be accurate and useful to conceptualize as lying *within* each of our feminisms some of the oppositions that have surfaced in this controversy but that are usually thought to occur only between the science and postmodernist projects. But my concern in doing so is also to defend the viability and progressiveness of the feminist science and epistemology projects against their postmodernist critics. My way of doing this will be to show that valuable postmodernist agendas are also to be found in these science projects, and to argue that—both for better and worse—feminist criticisms of Enlightenment tendencies are certainly not free of Enlightenment projects.[1]

Should There Be Feminist Sciences?

I take as my starting point the importance of fundamental insights and agendas of both feminist groups. In nonfeminist worlds, of course, science agendas and the Enlightenment critiques are opposed to each other. According to the Enlightenment critics, science embodies the intellectual and political sins of the Enlightenment (e.g., Lyotard, 1984; Rorty, 1979; Foucault, 1981). According to Enlightenment defenders, these postmodernist critics are attempting to undermine the harnessing of science for democratic, anti-racist, ecologically sound, anti-militarist, and other progressive ends; or, even if this is not what the postmodernists consciously intend, their positions have that consequence (e.g., Habermas 1983).[2]

Within feminist theory this opposition is replicated. For instance, Jane Flax (1989) argues that in spite of understandable ambivalence toward Enlightenment projects, feminism is, and should recognize that it is, solidly on the terrain of the postmodern. The feminist standpoint epistemology is one of the theories she criticizes in this respect; it is still too firmly and uncritically grounded in faulty Enlightenment assumptions. She writes:

> the notion of *a* feminist standpoint that is truer than previous (male) ones seems to rest upon many problematic and unexamined assumptions. These include an optimistic belief that people act rationally in their own interests and that reality has a structure that perfect reason (once perfected) can discover. Both of these assumptions in turn depend upon an uncritical appropriation of . . . Enlightenment ideas. . . . Furthermore, the notion of such a standpoint also assumes that the oppressed are not in fundamental ways damaged by their social experience. On the contrary, this position assumes that the oppressed have a privileged (and not just different) relation and ability to comprehend a reality that is "out there" waiting for our representation. It also presupposes gendered social relations in which there is a category of beings who are fundamentally like each other by virtue of their sex—that is, it assumes the otherness men assign to women. Such a standpoint also assumes that women, unlike men, can be free of determination from their own participation in relations of domination such as those rooted in the social relations of race, class, or homophobia. (p. 56)

The charge of "essentializing women," and thereby eradicating or silencing the voices of women of color, is frequently made against the feminist science and epistemology projects. Donna Haraway (1989) argues that the standpoint epistemology, like other kinds of socialist feminist theory, is guilty of this theoretical and political error:

> women's labor in the household and women's activity as mothers generally, i.e., reproduction in the socialist feminist sense, entered theory on the authority of analogy to the Marxian concept of labor. The unity of women here rests on an epistemology based on the ontological structure of "labor." Marxist/socialist feminism does not "naturalize" unity; it is a possible achievement based on a possible standpoint rooted in social relations. The essentializing move is in the ontological structure of labor or of its analogue, women's activity. (p. 200)

However, other feminist theorists (including some attempting to redirect the science traditions) argue that feminists must be wary of the anti-Enlightenment criticisms. They state, or clearly imply, that feminists are making a big mistake in adopting postmodernist postures. Luce Irigaray (1985) asks if postmodernism is the "last ruse" of patriarchy. Nancy Hartsock (1987) writes:

> In our efforts to find ways to include the voices of marginal groups, we might expect helpful guidance from those who have argued against totalizing and universalistic theories such as those of the Enlightenment. . . . Despite their apparent congruence with the project I am proposing, these theories, I contend, would hinder rather than help its accomplishment. . . . For those of us who want to understand the world systematically in order to change it, postmodernist theories at their best give little guidance. . . . At their worst, postmodernist theories merely recapitulate the effects of Enlightenment theories—theories that deny marginalized people the right to participate in defining the terms of interaction with people in the mainstream. (pp. 190–191)

Christine Di Stefano argues against the location of feminism fully in the terrain of the postmodern, claiming that an important strength of feminist theory and politics is to be found in its modernist insistence on the importance of gender. She writes:

> Contemporary Western feminism is firmly, if ambivalently, located in the modernist ethos, which made possible the feminist identification and critique of gender. . . . The concept of gender has made it possible for feminists to simultaneously explain and delegitimize the presumed homology between biological and social sex differences. At the same time, however, gender (rather than sex) differences have emerged as highly significant, salient features which do more to divide and distin-

guish men and women from each other than to make them parts of some larger, complementary, "humanistic" whole.[3] (p. 64)

She provides a succinct summary of key aspects of the feminist case against postmodernism:

> First, postmodernism expresses the claims and needs of a constituency (white, privileged men of the industrialized West) that has already had an Enlightenment for itself and that is now ready and willing to subject that legacy to critical scrutiny. Secondly, . . . the objects of postmodernism's various critical and deconstructive efforts have been the creations of a similarly specific and partial constituency (beginning with Plato). Third, . . . mainstream postmodernist theory (Derrida, Lyotard, Rorty, Foucault) has been remarkably blind and insensitive to questions of gender in its own purportedly politicized rereading of history, politics, and culture. And finally, . . . the postmodernist project, if seriously adopted by feminists, would make any semblance of a feminist politics impossible. To the extent that feminist politics is bound up with a specific constituency or "subject," namely, women, the postmodernist prohibition against subject-centered inquiry and theory undermines the legitimacy of a broad-based organized movement dedicated to articulating and implementing the goals of such a constituency. (pp. 30–31)

Flax and Di Stefano noted the ambivalence of feminist theorists toward the choice between modernism and postmodernism. In light of the problems feminists on each side point out in the other side's position, one can understand such ambivalence. My argument is that such an ambivalence should be much more robust and principled than that identified by the theorists cited above.[4] They attribute a tentative, hesitant, reluctant ambivalence on the part of feminists—one frequently not even articulated—with respect to which side of this dispute feminism should be on. Their own analyses often explore and nourish ambivalence in this dispute. However, the principled ambivalence for which I argue is self-conscious and theoretically articulated. It is a positive program. There is a tendency among the critics of feminist ambivalence to attribute this attitude to a failure to understand what is really at issue. In contrast, I think that the rationale for feminist ambivalence here should refer not primarily to feminist error, or even exclusively to intellectual and political inadequacies in the mainstream debate. More important in generating this ambivalence are tensions and contradictions in the worlds in which feminists move. From this perspective, at least some of the tensions between the scientific and postmodernist agendas are desirable; they reflect different, sometimes conflicting, legitimate political and theoretical needs of women today.

In the mainstream postmodernist discourses, Western epistemology and its "policing of thought" have been primary targets of criticism. I begin here by asking an apparently naive question: Why do feminists need epistemology at all? Why not just accept the position of Rorty, Lyotard, Foucault, and other critics that there has already been far too much policing of thought, that epistemology invariably legitimates exploitative and ig-norance-producing links between knowledge and power? Why not just agree to avoid such risks by refusing to develop any feminist theories of knowledge?

Justificatory Needs

Considered from sociological and historical perspectives, epistemolo-gies are justificatory strategies. Like moral codes, they present themselves as challenging "might make right"—this time in the domain of knowledge claims. Foucault, Rorty, and other critics have pointed out epistemologies that end up rationalizing the legitimacy of the beliefs of the powerful. But not all theories of knowledge have that end, or epistemology would be only an honorific used to designate the winners in such struggles. For example, feminists could continue to develop theories of knowledge al-though male domination continued to take new forms and, in significant ways, increase in power (horrible as that is to contemplate). In such a case, feminist epistemology would not be rationalizing the beliefs of the powerful.

At any rate, once we note that epistemologies are justificatory strategies, then we are led to ask questions about the hostile environment that creates the perception that one needs a theory of knowledge at all. Perhaps epistemologies are created only under pressure from a hostile environment. After all, why would anyone bother to articulate a *theory* of knowledge if her beliefs and the grounds for those beliefs were not challenged?

First, feminists need a defense against, and an alternative, positive program to, the traditional discourses of both objectivism and "interpreta-tionism."[5] Objectivism insists that scientific claims can be produced only through dispassionate, disinterested, value-free, point-of-viewless, objec-tive inquiry procedures, and that research generated or guided by feminist concerns obviously cannot meet such standards. Objectivism places women and feminists firmly outside a tightly defended barricade within which is claimed to lie all there is of reason, rationality, scientific method, truth, and guides to social policy that avoid privileging special interests. These objectivist discourses are to be found not only in the sciences, but also in every scholarly discipline. They are used to devalue and justify calculated ignorance about any thought, research, or scholarship that begins and proceeds by asking questions from the perspective of women's activities. They are also to be found in the state and its judicial systems (MacKinnon, 1982–83), in the social welfare and health care systems, in every location where male dominance defends itself in modern Western cultures. Feminists are not alone in finding their projects wrongly devalued by these discourses; critics of capitalism and racism also point to objectivism's support of the status quo (e.g., Staples, 1973; Rose and Rose, 1979). Moreover, the objectivist discourses are not just the territory of intellectuals and academics; they are official dogma of the age. They stand to the feminist science and epistemology projects in much the same way as medieval theology stood to Copernican astronomy, Newtonian physics, and the new philosophies these would require.

Feminists also need epistemological resources to deal with the loyal opposition to objectivism—here to be called interpretationism. This discourse also discounts feminist knowledge claims in scientific and everyday contexts. It does so by taking the position that while feminists certainly have a right to their interpretation of who contributed what to the dawn of human history, or why rape occurs, or the causal role of family forms in historical change, that is just their opinion. The conflicting interpretations made by nonfeminists are equally defensible. For the sake of the argument, interpretationists can even graciously give feminism the point that these conflicting understandings originate in different social experiences. However, they then go on to insist that since there is no way to decide "objectively" between the two, there is no reason why people who are not already convinced of feminist claims should support them.[6] This position functions to justify the silencing of women/feminists no less than its objectivist twin by refusing to recognize existing power relations of male dominance and the dynamics that insure intimate relations between partial and perverse beliefs and social power. The authors of interpretationist texts pretend that they are just plain folks like women, feminist critics, and everyone else. They pretend that no one can detect that as researchers and as reporters with access to publication, public policy, and university classrooms they are in positions of relatively great political power.

Neither of these two dominant justificatory strategies work for feminists. When women appeal to "the facts" to justify their claims in ways parallel to those routinely used by men, impressions of impartiality, disinterest, value-neutrality do not arise (especially not for men). When women appeal to their interpretations of evidence, instead of this appeal having the meaning "this is a good (or plausible, justifiable, reasonable) interpretation," it asserts only that "this is just my interpretation." Instead of certifying the evidence, the strategy has the effect of discounting it.[7] Objectivism and interpretationism do not allow feminists to generate scientific problems, to define what should count as empirical evidence, and to determine what constitutes an adequate explanation or understanding.

Woman the knower can find no place in either of these two, intimately linked, mainstream epistemologies.

Thus, the development of feminist justificatory strategies serves a second need also: the need for a decision procedure articulable to feminists—to ourselves, to each other—to guide choices in theory, research, and politics. That is, when traditional grounds for knowledge claims are not available, there is not only the problem of justifying one's claims to others, but also the problem of justifying them to oneself and to those who might prove sympathetic to feminist goals. This need is easily discernible in research reports and political statements, where feminists struggle to articulate the grounds on which a claim that is controversial within feminist circles should be found reasonable, rational, empirically supported, desirable, and so on. Jane Flax formulates well an analogous point in discussing the problem of the therapist who finds flawed all of the theories she could draw upon as resources to decide what to tell her distressed patient. There is no guide that is unquestionably believable to the therapist for her to use in choosing her words. The decision she makes has real consequences: The patient will make crucial choices depending on what the therapist says. Moreover, the therapist can't just walk away from the situation and decide to take up some occupation where decision procedures are clearer: She cares about the patient; she wants the patient to get better (Flax, forthcoming book). I think that this is an excellent analogue to "the feminist's epistemological problem": What theory of knowledge can provide a justifiable guide to practical decisions that have effects on women's lives? Neither objectivism nor interpretationism serves women well. What could serve better?

This question leads to another. Who are "ourselves"? Who are the women to whom feminist theory and politics should be accountable? As everyone knows, women are not homogenous—we differ most importantly by class, race, culture, and sexual orientation. Here I draw attention only to the fact that two distinct difference agendas appear to wind in and out of much of these discussions (that is, in addition to attention to difference between the genders). On the one hand, there is difference as diversity and variety: the valuable feminist vision of understanding differences between women as richness and opportunity for cultural enhancement and understanding rather than as a threat to the self of the speaker. This vision is expressed in contemporary life in, for instance, the appreciation of Puerto Rican feminists for the culture and experience of Mexican women. These two culturally differing groups of women have not stood in dominance relations to each other: "Difference" is simply cultural variation. On the other hand, there is the existence of differences due to structures of domination that appears in criticism of white Western women's participation in and benefit from race, class, and cultural exploitation.[8] "We women" are both diverse and, often, in domination rela-tions—consciously or not—with each other. We need theories of knowl-edge that recognize these differences and, along with substantive feminist theories, motivate and enable us to work against exploitative relations between women.

This brings us to the final but not least justificatory need. Feminists have developed justificatory strategies that value feminist perspectives as resources for organizing to end male domination. Feminist sciences and epistemologies should help to bring to consciousness less mystified under-standings of women's and men's situations so that these understandings can energize and direct women and men to struggle on behalf of eliminat-ing the subordination of women in all of its race, class, and cultural forms.

Each of the feminist epistemologies does not respond equally to all of these needs. Nevertheless, I think that these needs have provided important constraints within which justificatory strategies have been constructed. Feminist epistemologies are embattled. They struggle to create space for feminist voices within worlds—academic, intellectual, social, economic, state policy, judicial practice, health care—that continually try to squeeze them out, isolate them, and co-opt them.

Postmodern Tendencies in Feminist Theories of Scientific Knowledge

In response to these needs, two main justificatory strategies in the natural and social sciences have been developed—feminist empiricism and the feminist standpoint theories. As I have discussed these epistemologies elsewhere, I will delineate each with just enough detail to enable me to point out how they do respond to some of the perceived justificatory needs mentioned earlier and how each begins to move out of the terrain of the Enlightenment.[9]

Feminist Empiricism

Feminist empiricism is the justificatory strategy that has been used primarily by researchers in biology and the social sciences. Feminist empiricists argue that sexism and androcentrism in scientific inquiry are entirely the consequence of badly done science. Sexist and androcentric distortions in the results of research in biology and the social sciences are caused by social biases. These prejudices are the result of hostile attitudes and false beliefs due to superstitions, ignorance, or mis-education. Andro-centric biases enter the research process particularly at the stage when scientific problems are identified and defined, and when concepts and hypotheses are formulated. But they also appear in the design of research and in the collection and interpretation of data. Sexist and androcentric biases can be eliminated by stricter adherence to the existing methodological norms of scientific inquiry.

Feminist empiricists try to use to feminist advantage the strategies of those who respond to feminist criticisms with such (patently false) remarks as: "Everyone knows that permitting only men to interview only men about both men's and women's beliefs and behaviors is just plain bad science." (Of course, this is the science upon which 99% of the claims of the social sciences rest and to which no one objected before the women's movement.) "Everyone knows that both sexes contributed to the evolution of our species." (Try to find that recognition in standard biology texts.) They argue that the women's movement alerts everyone to the social blinders, the distorted and clouded lenses, through which we have been experiencing the world around (and within) us. The women's movement creates the conditions that make better science possible—that makes the sciences of today better able to achieve the goals of the founders of modern science. Sociologists Marcia Millman and Rosabeth Moss Kanter (1975) make this argument in the following way:

> Movements of social liberation . . . make it possible for people to see the world in an enlarged perspective because they remove the covers and blinders that obscure knowledge and observation. In the last decade no social movement has had a more startling or consequential impact on the way people see and act in the world than the women's movement. . . . We can see and plainly speak about things that have always been there, but that formerly were unacknowledged. Indeed, today it is impossible to escape noticing features of social life that were invisible only ten years ago. (p. vii)

Other feminist empiricists point out that the women's movement creates the opportunity for there to be more women researchers and feminist (male and female) ones, who are more likely than men or sexists to notice androcentric biases.[10]

This theory of knowledge meets an important range of justificatory needs. For one thing, its appeal is obvious as a defense against objectivism and interpretationism. Many of the claims emerging from feminist research in biology and the social sciences are capable of—and have already begun—accumulating better empirical support than the androcentric ones they would replace. This research better meets the overt standards of "good science" than do the purportedly gender-blind studies. I think that the weight of this empirical support should be valued more highly than the ideal of value-neutrality that was advanced only in order to increase empirical support for hypotheses. It is not that all feminist claims are automatically to be preferred because they are feminist; rather, when the results of such research show good empirical support, the fact that they were produced through politically guided research should not count against them. Moreover, it is difficult for interpretationism to gain a hold against feminist empiricism. The feminist results of research are not simply as good as the sexist claims they replace; they conflict with the sexist claims, and the feminist argument is that anyone should be able to see that the evidence supports the feminist claims over the sexist ones.

Moreover, feminist empiricism appears to leave intact a great deal of scientists' and philosophers' traditional understandings of the principles of adequate scientific research. It appears to challenge mainly the incomplete way scientific method has been practiced, not the norms of science themselves. Many scientists will admit that the social values and political agendas of feminists raise new issues, enlarge the scope of inquiry, and reveal cause for greater care in the conduct of research. But the logic of the research process and of scientific explanation appear to rest fundamentally untouched by these challenges. This conservatism enables feminist criticisms to be heard by people who are just now developing interest in feminist research and scholarship and who might well be leery of more radical claims. Feminist empiricism stays close to the kinds of justificatory appeals that are already respected in the natural and social sciences.

This epistemology is not particularly welcoming to issues of race, class, or cultural differences in women as subjects of knowledge—that is, between women as agents of knowledge. It does not invite analysis of these differences, tending to express feminist concerns in terms that imply homogeneity among feminist agents of knowledge. However, it must be noted that the kind of argument Millman and Kanter made should be equally convincing with respect to the positive effects of anti-racist and working-class movements on the growth of knowledge. Thus, feminist empiricism can be used to argue for the importance of other emancipatory political movements, in addition to feminism, to the growth of knowledge. Moreover, for empirical social scientists, the conservatism of feminist empiricism may well appear to offer the most effective grounds for defending controversial claims about race, class, and cultural differences in women as objects of research.

In these ways, feminist empiricism satisfies a range of the perceived justificatory needs mentioned earlier. Many feminist critics certainly think that it is far too conservative. It is these dissatisfactions that have motivated development of the standpoint epistemologies by some and the turn by others to criticisms of the Enlightenment vision that shines so clearly through this feminist theory of knowledge.

However, I think a case can be made that even this conservative justificatory strategy begins to undermine Enlightenment assumptions in significant ways. I do not want to overstate the case here. Feminist empiricists certainly would be far more comfortable within an Enlightenment world, extinct though that possibility be, than they are in the more treacherous contemporary epistemological terrain. By no means do I wish to suggest that feminist empiricists are self-consciously or paradigmatically postmodern. In fact, they unanimously ignore or inveigh against postmodernist projects in feminism. My argument, instead, is that significant dimensions of the break between modernity and postmodernism can be found within this stance. There are tendencies in these thinkers that lead them firmly out of the terrain of the Enlightenment on which they have intended to ground their arguments.

These steps toward postmodernism are forced, I think, by the subject, the ideal knower, of feminist empiricism. She is a woman scientist working in the environment of the present women's movement. Or, at least, this knower begins his/her analyses from the objective situation of such a woman scientist. (That is, there is nothing in the structure of this epistemology that forbids men from producing feminist research. However, what is ideal about knowers for feminist empiricists arises from the actual situation of women researchers, e.g., their situations as women working now make them more likely than men to detect and speak about the topics of concern to feminist researchers.) I am suggesting that the knowing subject of feminist empiricism inadvertently but inevitably is in tension with Enlightenment assumptions. A woman scientist cannot be the Enlightenment's transhistorical, unitary individual, and the present feminist environment makes it difficult for women scientists to avoid stumbling upon this fact. This "failure" is the source of hidden riches in feminist empiricism.

The consciousness of the ideal knower is not unitary because the feminism of this epistemology undermines its empiricism, although its defenders clearly intend to hang on to whatever they can of the empiricism. Feminist empiricism holds on to the idea that a goal of science is to produce less biased, more objective claims, but it also insists on what is overtly forbidden in empiricism—the importance of analyzing and assigning different epistemological values to the social identities of inquirers. (In its institutional memory, paternal empiricism recollects that this is what it objected to in medieval knowledge-seeking; this is what it objected to in Lysenkoism and Nazi science.) The ideal agent of knowledge, the ideal scientist, is not a disembodied mind, but one located in history. The historical location of researchers—during and after feminism—is what permits them to create less biased, more objective accounts in biology and the social sciences, although individual initiative clearly is necessary to the production of such accounts since not everyone these days produces them. Consequently, this epistemology challenges the idea that knowledge-seeking is usefully conceptualized as an activity of individuals in isolation from their social milieux. I think my thoughts, but it is my culture that observes through my eyes and arranges and rearranges thoughts in my mind. Moreover, scientific method both is and isn't problematic for feminist empiricists. On the one hand, they claim simply to be following the principles of inquiry even more rigorously than their androcentric predecessors who failed to control for gender bias in the research process in numerous ways. On the other hand, they point out that without the challenge of feminism, scientific method couldn't detect or eliminate sexist and androcentric biases. They seem to be saying that scientific method is intrinsically incapable of doing what it was supposedly constructed to do.

Inquirers beneficially shaped by history (and not just, or even, the history of science), but producing less-false belief; shaped by culture in ways advantageous to the growth of knowledge, but nevertheless individual thinkers; using scientific method more rigorously, and also undermining faith in it—the feminism and the empiricism of this position are in tension with each other. The ideal knower expresses this tension; although in the writings of the researchers in biology and the social sciences who adopt this justificatory strategy, the tension must be suppressed all the more because it is not analyzed. (Indeed, it cannot be analyzed with only the impoverished and mystifying theoretical resources of empiricism.)

For these reasons, I think it is reasonable to see feminist empiricism as inadvertently taking steps toward reconstructing both the ideal knower and the ideal of objectivity in ways uncongenial to Enlightenment assumptions. It is a mistake to see this position as simply a repetition of an androcentric epistemology.

Feminist Standpoint Theory

Even though the feminist empiricists do insist, I believe, on the importance of the historical identity of the ideal knower, it would certainly be hard to defend their understanding of history and of the material dimensions of social identity as rich enough to do justice to the distinctiveness of feminism's potential and actual contributions to the growth of knowledge. A second major line of justification of feminist research is provided by the standpoint theorists.[11] They explicitly develop some of the notions that appear only dimly in feminist empiricist assumptions, and they also take these in directions that empiricists—even feminist empiricists—would never accept. Indeed, one way to think of the standpoint theories is as analyses and explanations of the research generated by feminist empiricists. The standpoint theorists have tended to stress their differences from empiricist theories of knowledge, and this stress is necessary in order to highlight what is really valuable about these theories. However, there are some tendencies they share.

Knowledge, they observe, is supposed to be grounded in experience. But what has counted as knowledge in modern, Western cultures originates in and is tested against only a certain limited and distorted kind of social experience. The experiences arising from the activities assigned to women, understood through feminist theory, provide a starting point for developing potentially more complete and less distorted knowledge claims than do men's experiences (Hartsock, 1983; Smith, 1974, 1987; Rose, 1983).[12]

Consider Dorothy Smith's form of this argument. In our society, women have been assigned the kinds of work that men do not want to do. Several aspects of this division of activity by gender have consequences for what can be known from the perspective of men's and women's activities. "Women's work" relieves men of the need to take care of their bodies or of the local places where they exist, freeing men to immerse themselves in the world of abstract concepts. The labor of women thereby articulates and shapes men's concepts of the world into those appropriate for administrative work. Moreover, the more successfully women perform their work, the more invisible does it become to men. Men who are relieved of the need to maintain their own bodies and the local places where these bodies exist can now see as real only what corresponds to their abstracted mental world. Men see "women's work" as not real human activity—self-chosen and consciously willed—but only as natural activity, an instinctual labor of love. Women are thus excluded from men's conceptions of culture. Furthermore, women's actual experiences of their own activities are incomprehensible and inexpressible within the distorted abstractions of men's conceptual schemes. Women are alienated from their own experience by the use of the dominant conceptual schemes.

However, for women sociologists (we can generalize here—for women inquirers, scientists, researchers, theorists), a "line of fault" opens up between their experiences and the dominant conceptual schemes. This disjuncture is the break along which much major work in the women's movement has focused. The politics of the women's movement has drawn attention to the lack of fit between women's experiences and the dominant conceptual schemes. It is to the "bifurcated consciousness" of women researchers that we should attribute the origins of the greater adequacy of the results of feminist inquiry. Looking at nature and social relations from the perspective of "men's work" can provide only partial and distorted understandings. (Of course, only white, Western, professional/managerial-class men are permitted this work, although it is the goal of more widespread ideals of masculinity.) Research that is capable of explaining social life in ways that are useful to anyone besides administrators must recover the understanding of women, men, and social relations available from the perspective of women's activities.

To give an example that Smith discusses, the concept "housework," which appears in historical, sociological, and economic studies, at least permits the recognition that what women do at home is neither instinctual activity nor a labor of love. However, it conceptualizes this activity on an analogy with the division of men's activities into paid work and leisure. Is housework work? Yes! However, it has no fixed hours or responsibilities, no qualifications, wages, days off for sickness, retirement, or retirement benefits. Is it leisure? No, although even under the worst of conditions it has rewarding and rejuvenating aspects. As social scientists and liberal political philosophers use the term, housework includes raising one's children, entertaining friends, caring for loved ones, and other activities not appropriately understood through the wage-labor/leisure construct. Smith argues that this activity should be analyzed through concepts that arise from women's experience of it, not with concepts selected to account for men's experience of their work. Moreover, our understanding of men's activities also is distorted by reliance on conceptual schemes arising only from the activities of men in the administrative classes. How would our understanding of men's activities in domestic life, warfare, or the economy be expanded and transformed if it were structured by questions and concepts arising from those activities assigned predominantly to women that make possible men's participation in domestic life, warfare, and the economy?

This justificatory strategy has the virtue of providing a general theory of the greater adequacy of research that begins in questions arising from the perspective of women's activities, and that regards this perspective as an important part of the data on which the evidence for all knowledge claims should be based. The standpoint theorists reassert the possibility of science providing less distorted representations of the world around us, but not a science that myopically beatifies a mythical method and thus is unable to counter the sexist, racist, and class biases built into the very social structure and agendas of science.

This theory of knowledge resolves more satisfactorily certain problems with feminist empiricism. It sets within a larger social theory its explanation of the importance of the origin of scientific problems (of the context of discovery) for the eventual picture of science. It eschews blind allegiance to scientific method, concluding that no method, at least in the sciences' sense of this term, is powerful enough to eliminate social biases that are as widely held as the scientific community itself. In claiming that inquiry from the standpoint of women (or the feminist standpoint) can overcome the partiality and distortion of the dominant androcentric/bourgeois/Western sciences, it directly undermines the point-of-viewlessness of objectivism while refusing the relativism of interpretationism. The advocates of this justificatory strategy explicitly call for women of color, working-class women, and lesbians to be present among the women whose experiences generate inquiry. They all discuss the limitations of sciences emerging only from white, Western, homophobic, academic feminisms. In this respect, they take a more actively critical stance toward the homogeneity of women assumed by much feminist inquiry. Moreover, the importance of political activism to the advance of understanding is conceptualized far more richly by the standpoint theorists. For instance, Nancy Hartsock (1983) says:

> Women's lives, like men's, are structured by social relations which manifest the experience of the dominant gender and class. The ability to go beneath the surface of appearances to reveal the real but concealed social relations requires both theoretical and political activity. Feminist theorists must demand that feminist theorizing be grounded in women's material activity and must as well be part of the political struggle necessary to develop areas of social life modeled on this activity. (p. 304)

There are many interesting and difficult issues this epistemology raises.[13] I will not identify or attempt to resolve these here since my focus is instead on how this epistemology incorporates anti-Enlightenment tendencies. How are important dimensions of the transition from modernity to postmodernism reasonably seen as lying within this theoretical tendency, not just as between it and the more readily identified feminist postmodernist critics? I think that standpoint theory explicitly articulates, develops, and pushes to more radical conclusions the anti-Enlightenment tendencies that were only implicit in feminist empiricism.

Where feminist empiricists are ambivalent about the Enlightenment faith in scientific method—it both is and isn't part of the problem for feminist researchers—the feminist standpoint theorists are unambivalently opposed to the idea that a-historical principles of inquiry can insure ever more perfect representations of the world. They challenge the possibility of such a "science machine" or algorithm for producing true representations.

Moreover, these writers theorize not just the importance of feminist politics being located in the historical environment in which science occurs, as the feminist empiricists attempt to do, but the permeation of science as an institution and a system of thought by political life. Like the empiricists, they hold that movements for social liberation advance the growth of knowledge. The bourgeois revolution of the fifteenth to seventeenth centuries—the movement from feudalism to modernity—made it possible for modern science itself to emerge. The proletarian movement of the nineteenth and early twentieth centuries permitted an understanding of the effects of class struggles on conceptions of nature and social relations. The post-1960 decline (or, at least, transformation) of North Atlantic colonialism creates the possibilities for widespread understandings of how racism shapes thought. The international women's movement is just the most recent of these emancipatory movements. But the reason why science advances at these moments is not primarily because "ideas are in the air." They get in the air because of changes in concrete social relations. It is actual administrative/managerial activities which tend to produce abstract masculinity; it is caring labor that tends to produce stereotypically feminine concerns and thought patterns; and it is participation in both that makes possible feminist concerns and patterns of thought. So the point about my culture observing through my eyes is, here, that my actual daily activities, structured by social divisions of activity by gender, set limits on what I (and, therefore, my culture) can see. Movements of social liberation make possible new kinds of human activity, and it is on the basis of this activity that new sciences can emerge.[14] This historical account conflicts with the Enlightenment's own explanations of the history of science, but it does so without asserting the perfection of thought at any moment in that history.

Furthermore, the standpoint epistemologies specifically articulate the intuition of feminist empiricism that a unitary consciousness is an obstacle to understanding. All refer to the importance of the gap between women's consciousness and the social order. They speak of women's alienation from our behavior, of the line of fault of women's consciousness, of women's bifurcated consciousness. This focus of the epistemologists is supported by the recurring report in the social sciences that women's behavior is a much less reliable guide to their belief than is men's behavior to their belief. It is supported by sociological, psychological, and economic analyses of the dysfunctionality of the social order for women.

For these reasons, it is reasonable to see feminist standpoint theory as in tension with central Enlightenment assumptions. Reality does not have a structure, for the social order is made up of many structures that both overlap and conflict—androcentrism, racism, and class oppression, to mention just three. But from the perspective of a feminist standpoint, some of these structures become visible for the first time. The oppressed are indeed damaged by their social experience, but what is a disadvantage in terms of their oppression *can* become an advantage in terms of science: Starting off from administrative/managerial activity in order to explain the world insures more partial and distorted understandings than starting off from the contradictory activities of women scientists. Women are, indeed, like each other by virtue of their sex and also by virtue of the otherness that men assign to women. Of course, they differ by race, class, culture, and other important social features; in important respects, they are more like men in their own race, class, culture than like women in other races, and so on. But standpoint theory does not require any kind of feminine essentialism, as this frequently mentioned critique supposes. It *analyzes* the essentialism that androcentrism assigns to women, locates its historical conditions, and proposes ways to counter it. Standpoint theory does not assume that women are different from men in that they are free of participation in race, class, and homophobic social relations.[15] These theorists constantly call for more vigorous feminist analysis of and politics against these forms of oppression.

The Modernity of Feminist Postmodernism

However a specifically feminist alternative to Enlightenment projects may develop, it is not clear how it could completely take leave of Enlightenment assumptions and still remain feminist. The critics are right that feminism (also) stands on Enlightenment ground. Most obviously, critics of the feminist epistemologies join those they criticize in believing in the desirability and the possibility of social progress, and that improved theories about ourselves and the world around us will contribute to that progress. Thus, within feminism, the disagreement is over other matters, such as what those theories should say and who should get to define what counts as social progress. In this respect it is misleading to assume that the line between feminist supporters and critics of Enlightenment assumptions is as broadly drawn as many take it to be in the nonfeminist discourses.

I quoted earlier a number of criticisms that contribute to the "feminist case against postmodernism." The point of these critics is that feminists should not adopt the postmodernist agenda because it undermines important feminist projects in significant ways. I think *feminist postmodernism* has important contributions to make to feminist theory and politics. But here I want to note two ways in which it appears to subscribe to too many Enlightenment assumptions. Paradoxically, feminist postmodernists adhere to some powerful Enlightenment assumptions that even the feminist empiricists do not.

For one thing, in criticizing the very goal of an improved, specifically feminist science and epistemology, they appear to agree with Enlightenment tendencies that all possible science and epistemology—anything deserving these names—must be containable within modern, androcentric, Western, bourgeois forms. However, we are certainly entitled to skepticism about this assumption. It is virtually impossible to specify significant commonalities between the industrialized production of knowledge that characterizes research in the natural sciences and much of the social sciences today and the craft tinkering that produced Galileo's astronomy and Newton's physics. Obviously, science has changed immensely even during modernity (See Harding 1986, p. 68ff). Why can't it continue to change in the future? Why aren't scientific projects formulated for specifically feminist ends an important part of such change? Moreover, the high cultures of Asia and Africa—those that existed prior to the rise of the North Atlantic cultures—had sophisticated sciences and technologies by the standards of their day (See Goonatilake, 1984; Rodney, 1982; Van Sertima, 1986). The extent of human rationality is neither restricted to—nor perhaps paradigmatically exhibited by—the modern West. If other institutions and practices of gaining knowledge have existed outside the modern, bourgeois, androcentric West, why must desirable forms of science and knowledge be restricted to the dominant ones in the modern West?

Additionally, the postmodernist critics of feminist science, like the most positivist of Enlightenment thinkers, appear to assume that if one gives up the goal of telling one true story about reality, one must also give up trying to tell less false stories. They assume a symmetry between truth and falsity. Yet, even Thomas Kuhn argued that it would be better to understand the history of science in terms of increasing distance from falsity rather than closeness to truth. Kuhn's work has certainly been responsible for radical shifts in understandings of the history of science— I do not mean to undervalue its importance. But it did not propose the kinds of shifts in our theories of scientific knowledge that the feminist epistemologies require. If even such relatively traditional thinking about science can propose that truth and falsity need not always be regarded as symmetrical, as opposite poles of the same continuum, this certainly should be a real option within feminist thought. Feminist inquiry can aim to produce less partial and perverse representations without having to assert the absolute, complete, universal, or eternal adequacy of these representations. Isn't that how we should take the feminist Enlightenment critics' own analyses?

I have been arguing that both the feminist science thinkers and their feminist postmodernist critics stand with one foot in modernity and the other in the lands beyond. Moreover, that link to the past has problematic and fruitful aspects for both projects. The tensions between Enlightenment and postmodernist tendencies occur between them, but they also occur in different ways within each project.

An epistemology—this kind of social theory—is a justificatory strategy. Important differences between the feminist science and epistemology projects and the feminist Enlightenment critiques are generated in large part by the different intellectual and social contexts in which they each explore, expand, and defend consequences of the emergence of feminist explanations of nature and social life. These tendencies have different histories, different audiences, and, therefore, different projects. Memories of other disputes muddy the psychic grounds on which they meet. Each should be understood as an attempt to escape damaging limitations of the dominant social relations and their conceptual schemes. These projects are incomplete—we haven't yet figured out how to escape such limitations. Most likely, we are not yet in an historical era when such vision should be possible. At this moment in history, our feminisms need both Enlightenment and postmodernist agendas—but we don't need the same ones for the same purposes or in the same forms as do white, bourgeois, androcentric Westerners.

Notes

1. Jane Flax, Donna Haraway, and Linda Nicholson have provided helpful criticisms and comments on my arguments. Their own positions are significantly different from the ones I take here.

    This chapter develops further and in different directions projects begun in earlier writings. In *The Science Question in Feminism* (1986) I argued that all of the feminist standpoint writings challenge dichotomies fundamental to the history of modern Western thought and practice. They challenge emotional versus intellectual and manual activity; sensuous, concrete, and relational versus abstract activity; unconscious (and repressed) versus conscious projects; ideas arising from everyday life versus those arising from administrative work; socially caused false beliefs versus true beliefs with no social origins. I argued that consequently in these respects they are in opposition to projects of modernity and the Enlightenment. There and in my article in *Science, Morality and Feminist Theory* (1987) I suggested reasons to think that feminism does not need the feminine, truth, or the transcendental subject of history and science—all dear to the heart of the Enlightenment. This chapter adds items to the list of postmodernist characteristics to be found in the feminist standpoint epistemologies, points to at least hints of such characteristics even in the far more conservative feminist empiricist framework, and begins an analysis of the modernity of feminist postmodernism. Because the feminist scientific epistemologies are still too recently articulated as such for it to be reasonable to assume familiarity with them, I must briefly review some of their central features in order to defend them. I have analyzed them in *The Science Question in Feminism;* key features of that analysis are repeated in my article in *APA Feminism and Philosophy Newsletter* (1987) and in the concluding essay in *Feminism and Methodology: Social Science Issues* (1987).

2. The borders and character of postmodernism, its two forms, its relation to modernism (and modernization) are themselves the topic of continual de-

bate. For one useful guide to the debates, see Huyssen, 1989. But among the issues central to the feminist postmodernist critiques of the feminist science and epistemology projects are skepticism about beliefs in:

> The existence of a stable, coherent self. . . . Reason and its "science"—philosophy—can provide an objective, reliable, and universal foundation for knowledge. . . . The knowledge acquired from the right use of reason will be "True". . . . Reason itself has transcendental and universal qualities. . . . Freedom consists in obedience to laws that conform to the necessary results of the right use of reason. . . . By grounding claims to authority in reason, the conflicts between truth, knowledge, and power can be overcome. Truth can serve power without distortion; in turn, by utilizing knowledge in the service of power both freedom and progress will be assured. Knowledge can be both neutral (e.g., grounded in universal reason, not particular "interests") and also socially beneficial. . . . Science, as the exemplar of the right use of reason, is also the paradigm for all true knowledge. Science is neutral in its methods and contents but socially beneficial in its results. . . . Language is in some sense transparent. . . . Objects are not linguistically (or socially) constructed, they are merely *made present* to consciousness by naming and the right use of language. (Flax, 1989, pp. 41–42)

3. I do not mean to oversimplify the analyses either of Di Stefano or of Flax (Note No. 2). Both share my project of trying to weave together some of the fundamental contributions of feminist social theory and of the postmodernist Enlightenment critiques while also developing a critical analysis of *other* strains in feminism and postmodernism. They and I each arrive at this project from different starting points, and our analyses head off in other directions, and sometimes conflict as well. (Flax's discussion of these issues is book-length: see her article in this book and her forthcoming book.)

4. See my book *The Science Question in Feminism* (1986) and Alison Wylie's article (1987).

5. I use the awkward neologism *interpretationism* rather than *relativism* here since relativism is a consequence, but not always the intent, of interpretationism. In philosophic circles, its advocates refer to it as *intentionalism,* though that term is not widely understood outside philosophy. The assumptions of interpretationism can be found in much ethnomethodology, participant-observer research, and phenomenological studies in the social sciences.

6. This position is relativist, so the *defense* of it is always made in bad faith (or ignorance). A consistent relativist would not try to argue for, to assert against alternative opinions, objectivity-assuming claims about his views. The fact of assertion conflicts with the position asserted, as a long stream of philosophic critics of relativism have pointed out.

7. M.F. Belenky et al. (1986) point out that a woman's claim that "It's my

opinion . . ." means that it is just her opinion; a man's identical sentence means he's got a right to his opinion.

8. I think that one tension between the feminist science and epistemology projects and their anti-Enlightenment critics arises over how to conceptualize differences between women in ways that are not themselves ideological. Are both kinds of differences between women theorized, conceptualized, given metaphysical space—not just called for and said to be welcome— within both theoretical tendencies?

9. The following descriptions of these two epistemologies are taken with but slight modification from my article in the *APA Feminism and Philosophy Newsletter*. My original discussion of them was in *The Science Question in Feminism* (1986). The issue of the postmodernist tendencies in the epistemologies was raised in Chapter 6 and begins where I left off there.

10. Because those whom I have called feminist empiricists frequently take themselves to be doing nothing epistemologically unusual—they are simply adhering very strictly to the norms of science—they tend not to articulate this theory of knowledge as such. Examples can be found in reports of substantive feminist research, especially in their obligatory sections on methods. Fausto-Sterling (1985, p. 208) intentionally frames her critical evaluation of sex-difference research as addressing a problem of "poorly done science." She also provides an excellent discussion of the value of the women's movement to the creation of good science.

11. There have also been several kinds of feminist critiques of androcentric epistemology that are at least partially independent of these two developed positive theories of knowledge. More radical than the feminist criticisms of "bad science" are those that take as their target Western generalizations from masculine to human in the case of ideal reason. For the standpoint theorists, this criticism provides one motivation for the development of a feminist epistemology. But several important critics appear to intentionally stop short of such a theoretical program. Philosophers such as Genevieve Lloyd (1984) and Sara Ruddick (1980) and scientists such as Evelyn Fox Keller (1984) criticize what has come to be called "abstract masculinity." They point out how ideals of Western rationality, including scientific thought, distort, and leave partial our understandings of nature and social relations. These ideals devalue contextual modes of thought and emotional components of reason. Empirical support for this criticism is provided by psychological studies. Best known is Carol Gilligan's (1982) study of women's moral reasoning. Since scientific reason includes normative judgments (e.g., about which is the most interesting or potentially fruitful hypothesis or research program to pursue), Gilligan's work is highly suggestive for feminist thought about scientific knowledge. More recently, the analysis by Mary Belenky et al. (1986) of developmental patterns in women's thinking about reason and knowledge points to gender bias in philosophic and scientific ideals and suggests its origins in gendered experience. I mention these here because it is important to recognize that not all feminist thought about science and knowledge, even within what I am calling the

science traditions, has ended up inside the two feminist theories of knowledge discussed above.

12. Jane Flax made arguments very close to this in her article in my book *Discovering Reality* (1983). I took her to be developing a kind of feminist standpoint theory in my book *The Science Question in Feminism* (see p. 151–155). As the passages I cited in the opening section indicate, recently she has clearly distinguished her own assumptions from what she takes to be central standpoint ones.

13. I have discussed some of them in *The Science Question in Feminism* (1986). The feminist postmodernists quoted earlier raise others. See also the positive discussion of this epistemology's potential as "the feminist appropriation of Lukacs" in Jameson's article in *Rethinking Marxism* (1988).

14. Thus, the standpoint theorists construct exactly the kind of sociology of *knowledge*—not just of error—called for by the "strong programme" in the sociology of knowledge (and some of Dorothy Smith's work predates these calls). (See *Knowledge and Social Imagery* by David Bloor, 1977). But they avoid the scientific and a-political (or, rather, conservatively political) claims of the strong programme that belief is entirely a consequence of social relations: They construct an epistemology, not just a sociology.

15. However, it does not actually place these relations at the center of its theorizing. That is a problem.

References

Belenky, M. F. et al. 1986. *Women's Ways of Knowing: The Development of Self, Voice, and Mind*. New York: Basic Books.

Bloor, David. 1977. *Knowledge and Social Imagery*. London: Routledge & Kegan Paul.

Bordo, Susan R. 1987. *The Flight to Objectivity: Essays on Cartesianism and Culture*. Albany, NY: State University of New York Press.

Di Stefano, Christine. 1987. "Postmodernism/Postfeminism?: The Case of the Incredible Shrinking Woman." Paper read at 1987 meetings of American Political Science Association, Chicago, September 3–6, 1987. This is an earlier version of "Dilemmas of Difference: Feminism, Maternity, and Postmodernism" in this book.

Fausto-Sterling, Anne. 1985. *Myths of Gender: Biological Theories About Women and Men*. New York: Basic Books.

Flax, Jane. 1983. "Political Philosophy and the Patriarchal Unconscious: A Psychoanalytic Perspective on Epistemology and Metaphysics," in *Discovering Reality: Feminist Perspectives on Epistemology, Metaphysics, Methodology and Philosophy of Science*. Edited by Sandra Harding and Merrill Hintikka. Dordrecht: Reidel Publishing Co., 1983.

———. 1989. "Postmodernism and Gender Relations in Feminist Theory," in this book.

————. Forthcoming, 1990. *Thinking Fragments: Psychoanalysis, Feminism, and Postmodernism in the Contemporary West*. Berkeley, CA: University of California Press.

Foucault, Michel. 1981. *Power/Knowledge*. Edited by Colin Gordon. New York: Random House.

Fraser, Nancy, and Linda Nicholson. 1989. "Social Criticism Without Philosophy: An Encounter Between Feminism and Postmodernism," in this book.

Gilligan, Carol. 1982. *In a Different Voice: Psychological Theory and Women's Development*. Cambridge, MA: Harvard University Press.

Goonatilake, Susantha. 1984. *Aborted Discovery: Science and Creativity in the Third World*. London. Zed Books Ltd.

Habermas, Jurgen. 1983. "Modernity—An Incomplete Project," in *The Anti-Aesthetic: Essays on Postmodern Culture*. Edited by Hal Foster. Port Townsend, WA: Bay Press. See also the collection of essays in *Habermas and Modernity*. Edited by Richard Bernstein. Cambridge, MA: MIT Press, 1985.

Haraway, Donna. 1989. "A Manifesto for Cyborgs: Science, Technology, and Socialist Feminism in the 1980s," in this book.

Harding, Sandra. 1986a. *The Science Question in Feminism*. Ithaca: Cornell University Press; Milton Keynes, England: Open University Press.

————. 1986b. "The Instability of the Analytical Categories of Feminist Theory." *Signs: Journal of Women in Culture and Society*. 11 (4): 645–664.

————. 1987a. "Ascetic Intellectual Opportunities: Reply to Alison Wylie." In *Science, Morality and Feminist Theory*. Edited by M. Hanen and K. Nielsen. Calgary: University of Calgary Press.

————. 1987b. "Feminism and Theories of Scientific Knowledge." *APA Feminism and Philosophy Newsletter* 1:9–14.

————., ed. 1987c. *Feminism and Methodology: Social Science Issues*, Bloomington: Indiana University Press.

———— and Merrill Hintikka, eds. 1983. *Discovering Reality: Feminist Perspectives on Epistemology, Metaphysics, Methodology and Philosophy of Science*. Dordrecht: Reidel Publishing Co.

Hartsock, Nancy. 1987. "Rethinking Modernism: Minority vs. Majority Theories." *Cultural Critique* 7:187–206.

————. 1983. "The Feminist Standpoint: Developing the Grounds for a Specifically Feminist Historical Materialism." In *Discovering Reality*. Edited by S. Harding and M. Hintikka. See also Chapter 10 of N. Hartsock's *Money, Sex, and Power*. Boston: Northeastern University Press, 1985.

Huyssen, Andreas. 1989 in this book.

Irigaray, Luce. 1985. *The Sex Which Is Not One*. Translated by Catherine Porter. Ithaca: Cornell University Press.

Jameson, Fredric. 1988. *"History and Class Consciousness* as an 'Unfinished Project'." *Rethinking Marxism* (1):49–72.

Keller, Evelyn Fox. 1984. *Reflections on Gender and Science*. New Haven: Yale University Press.

Kuhn, Thomas S. 1970. *The Structure of Scientific Revolutions,* 2nd ed. Chicago: University of Chicago Press.

Lloyd, Genevieve. 1984. *The Man of Reason: "Male" and "Female" in Western Philosophy*. Minneapolis: University of Minnesota Press.

Lyotard, Jean-François. 1984. *The Post-Modern Condition*. Minneapolis: University of Minnesota Press.

MacKinnon, Catharine. 1982–1983. "Feminism, Marxism, Method and The State," Parts 1 & 2. *Signs: Journal of Women in Culture and Society* 7 (3):515–544 8 (4):635–658.

Millman, Marcia and Rosabeth Moss Kanter. 1975. Editor's Introduction in *Another Voice: Feminist Perspectives on Social Life and Social Science*. New York: Anchor Books.

Rodney, Walter. 1982. *How Europe Underdeveloped Africa*. Washington, DC: Howard University Press.

Rorty, Richard. 1979. *Philosophy and the Mirror of Nature*. Princeton: Princeton University Press.

Rose, Hilary. 1983. "Hand, Brain and Heart: A Feminist Epistemology for the Natural Sciences." *Signs: Journal of Women in Culture and Society* 9 (1):73–90.

———— and Steven Rose, ed. 1979. *Ideology of/in the Natural Sciences*. Cambridge, MA: Schenkman.

Ruddick, Sara. 1980. "Maternal Thinking." *Feminist Studies* 6, (2):342–369.

Smith, Dorothy. 1974. "Women's Perspective as a Radical Critique of Sociology." *Sociological Inquiry* 44:7–13.

————. 1987. *The Everyday World as Problematic: A Feminist Sociology*. Boston: Northeastern.

Staples, Robert. 1973. "What is Black Sociology? Toward a Sociology of Black Liberation." In *The Death of White Sociology*. Edited by J. A. Ladner. New York: Random House.

Van den Daele, W. 1977. "The Social Construction of Science." In *The Social Production of Scientific Knowledge*. Edited by E. Mendelsohn, P. Weingart, R. Whitley. Dordrecht: Reidel Publishing Co.

Van Sertima, Ivan. 1986. *Blacks in Science: Ancient and Modern*. New Brunswick, NJ: Transaction Books.

Wylie, Alison. 1987. "The Philosophy of Ambivalence." In *Science, Morality and Feminist Theory*. Edited by M. Hanen and K. Nielsen. Calgary: University of Calgary Press.

5

Epistemologies of Postmodernism:
A Rejoinder to Jean-François Lyotard

Seyla Benhabib

In the recent, flourishing debate on the nature and significance of postmodernism, architecture seems to occupy a special place.[1] It is tempting to describe this situation through a Hegelianism: It is as if the *Zeitgeist* of an epoch approaching its end has reached self-consciousness in those monuments of modern architecture of steel, concrete, and glass. Contemplating itself in its objectifications, Spirit has not "recognized" and thus "returned to itself" but has recoiled in horror from its own products. The visible decay of our urban environment, the uncanniness of the modern megalopolis, and the general dehumanization of space appear to prove the Faustian dream to be a nightmare. The dream of an infinitely striving self, unfolding its powers in the process of conquering externality, is one from which we have awakened. Postmodernist architecture, whatever other sources it borrows its inspiration from, is undoubtedly the message of the end of this Faustian dream, which had accompanied the self-understanding of the moderns from the beginning.[2]

The end of the Faustian dream has brought with it a conceptual and semiotic shift in many domains of culture. This shift is not characterized by a moral or political critique of the Faustian aspects of modernity, but by the questioning of the very conceptual framework that made the Faustian dream possible in the first place. The following statement by Peter Eisenman, one of the key figures in the modernist/postmodernist constellation in architecture, captures the elements of this new critique quite precisely:

> Architecture since the fifteenth century has been influenced by the assumption of a set of symbolic and referential functions. These can be

I would like to thank Andreas Huyssen and Wolf Schäfer for comments and criticisms.

collectively identified as the classical . . . 'Reason,' 'Representation'
and 'History,' 'Reason' insists that objects be understood as rational
transformations from a self-evident origin. 'Representation' demands
that objects refer to values or images external to themselves. . . .
'History' assumes that time is made up of isolatable historical moments
whose essential characteristics can and should be abstracted and represented. If these classical assumptions are taken together as imperatives
they force architecture to represent the spirit of its age through a
rationally motivated and comprehensible sign system. . . . But if these
'imperatives' are simply 'fictions' then the classical can be suspended
and options emerge which have been obscured by classical
imperatives. . . .[3]

Eisenman's statement describes rather accurately the conceptual self-
understanding of postmodernism, not only in architecture, but in contemporary philosophy as well. In fact, if one were to substitute the word
philosophy for *architecture* in the first paragraph of Eisenman's statement,
it could serve as a pithy summary of Jean-François Lyotard's *The Postmodern Condition: A Report on Knowledge*.[4] For Lyotard as well the demise
of the Faustian ideal signifies the end of the "grand narrative" of the
moderns and of the epistemology of representation on which it has been
based. "I will use the term *modern* to designate any science that legitimates
itself with reference to a metadiscourse of this kind making an explicit
appeal to some grand narrative," writes Lyotard, "such as the dialectics
of Spirit, the hermeneutics of meaning, the emancipation of the rational
or working subject, or the creation of wealth" (p. xxiii). Like Eisenman,
in the suspension of the classical, Lyotard sees the emergence of cognitive
and social options which had been obscured by the "classical imperatives."
He defines the new cognitive option variously as "paralogy" (p. 60 ff.),
"agonistics" (p. 16), and "recognition of the heteromorphous nature of
language games" (p. 66). The new social option is described as a "temporary contract," supplanting permanent institutions in the professional,
emotional, sexual, cultural, family, and international domains, as well as
in political affairs (p. 66).

Lyotard offers these cognitive and social options as alternatives that are
authentic to the experience of postindustrial societies and to the role of
knowledge within them. The hold of the classical episteme upon contemporary consciousness, however, tends to channel our cognitive as well as
our practical imagination in two directions. In the first place, society is
conceived of as a functional whole (p. 11), and the condition of knowledge
appropriate to it is judged as "performativity." Performativity is the view
that knowledge is power, that modern science is to be legitimated through
the increase in technological capacity, efficiency, control, and output it
enables (p. 47). The ideal of the theorists of performativity, from Hobbes

to Luhmann, is to reduce the fragility intrinsic to the legitimation of power by minimizing risk, unpredictability, and complexity. Not only is knowledge power, but power generates access to knowledge, thus preparing for itself a self-perpetuating basis of legitimacy. "Power . . . legitimates science and the law on the basis of their efficiency, and legitimates this efficiency on the basis of science and law. . . . Thus the growth of power, and its self-legitimation, are now taking the route of data storage and accessibility, and the operativity of information" (p. 47).

The second alternative is to view society as divided into two, as an alienated, bifurcated totality, in need of reunification. The corresponding epistemic vision is critical as opposed to functional knowledge. Critical knowledge is in the service of the subject; its goal is not the legitimation of power but the enabling of empowerment (pp. 12 ff.). It seeks not to enhance the efficiency of the apparatus but to further the self-formation of humanity, not to reduce complexity but to create a world in which a reconciled humanity recognizes itself. For Lyotard, the contemporary representative of this nineteenth-century ideal, born out of the imagination of a German thinker, Wilhelm von Humboldt, is Jürgen Habermas (p. 32). Had it been von Humboldt's ideal to have philosophy restore unity to learning via the development of a language game linking all the sciences together as moments in the becoming of Spirit (p. 33), it is Habermas's purpose to formulate a metadiscourse which is "universally valid for language games" (p. 65). The goal of such discourse is not so much the *Bildung* of the German nation, as it had been for von Humboldt, but the attainment of consensus, transparency, and reconciliation. Lyotard comments: "The cause is good, but the argument is not. Consensus has become an outmoded and suspect value. We must . . . arrive at an idea and practice of justice that is not linked to that of consensus" (p. 66).

Can Lyotard convince? Is his project to formulate the outlines of a postmodern episteme, beyond the dualism of functional and critical knowledge, beyond instrumental reason and critical theory, viable? What are the epistemological options opened by the demise of the classical episteme of representation?

The Crisis of the Representational Episteme

Modern philosophy began with the loss of the world.[5] The decision of the autonomous bourgeois subject to take nothing and no authority for granted, whose content and strictures had not been subjected to rigorous examination, and that had not withstood the test of "clarity and distinctness," began with the withdrawal from the world. It was still possible for Descartes in the seventeenth century to describe this withdrawal in the language of Stoicism and Spanish Jesuit philosophy as an ethical and religious gesture, either as a "suspension" of the involvement of the self with the world (Stoicism) or as the withdrawal of the soul to a communion with itself (Jesuit teaching of meditation). These were stages on the road to an equilibrium with the cosmos or necessary for the purging of the soul in preparation for the truth of God. The future development of modern epistemology succeeded in repressing this ethical and cultural moment to the point where the typical reductions on which the classical episteme of representation rested could emerge. The corporeal, ethico-moral self was reduced to a pure subject of knowledge, to consciousness, or to mind. The object of knowledge was reduced to "matters of fact" and "relations of ideas," or to "sensations" and "concepts." The question of classical epistemology from Descartes to Hume, from Locke to Kant was how to make congruous the order of representations in consciousness with the order of representations outside the self. Caught in the prison-house of its own consciousness, the modern epistemological subject tried to recover the world it had well lost.[6] The options were not many: Either one reassured oneself that the world would be gained by the direct and immediate evidence of the senses (empiricism) or one insisted that the rationality of the creator or the harmony of mind and nature would guarantee the correspondence between the two orders of representations (rationalism).

Whether empiricist or rationalist, modern epistemologists agreed that the task of knowledge, whatever its origins, was to build an adequate representation of things. In knowledge, mind had to "mirror" nature.[7] Charles Taylor points out, "When we hold that having X is having a (correct) representation of X, one of the things we establish is the neat separation of ideas, thoughts, descriptions and the like, on the one hand, and what these ideas, etc. are about on the other."[8] Actually, modern epistemology operated with a threefold distinction: the order of representations in our consciousness (ideas and sensations); the signs through which these "private" orders were made public, namely, words; and that of which our representations were representations, and to which they referred.[9] In this tradition, meaning was defined as "designation"; the meaning of a word was what it designates, while the primary function of language was denotative, namely, to inform us about objectively existing states of affairs. The classical episteme of representation presupposed a spectator conception of the knowing self, a designative theory of meaning, and a denotative theory of language.

Already in the last century three directions of critique of the classical episteme, leading to its eventual rejection, formed themselves. Stylizing somewhat, the first can be described as the critique of the modern epistemic subject, the second as the critique of the modern epistemic object, and the third as the critique of the modern concept of the sign.

The critique of the Cartesian, spectator conception of the subject begins with German Idealism and continues with Marx and Freud to Horkheimer in 1937 and to Habermas in *Knowledge and Human Interests*.[10] This tradition substitutes for the spectator model of the self the view of the active, producing, fabricating humanity, creating the conditions of objectivity confronting it through its own historical activity. The Hegelian and Marxist tradition also shows that the Cartesian ego is not a self-transparent entity and that the epistemic self cannot reach full autonomy as long as the historical origin and social constitution of the clear and distinct ideas it contemplates remain a mystery. This critique joins hands with the Freudian one which likewise shows that the self is not transparent to itself, for it is not "master in its own house" (*Herr im eigenen Haus*). It is controlled by desires, needs, and forces whose effects upon it shape both the contents of its clear and distinct ideas, as well as its capacity to organize them. The historical and psychoanalytic critique of the Cartesian ego sees the task of reflection neither as the withdrawal from the world nor as access to clarity and distinctness, but as the rendering conscious of those unconscious forces of history, society, and the psyche. Although generated by the subject, these necessarily escape its memory, control, and conduct. The goal of reflection is emancipation from self-incurred bondage.

The second line of criticism can be most closely associated with the names of Neitzsche, Heidegger, and Adorno and Horkheimer in *Dialectic of Enlightenment*. The modern episteme is viewed as an episteme of domination. For Nietzsche modern science universalizes Cartesian doubt. Modern knowledge divides the world into the realm of appearance on the one hand and that of essence, or things-in-themselves, on the other.[11] This dualistic vision is internalized by the subject of knowledge who in turn is split into body and mind, the senses and the conceptual faculty. Nietzsche has no difficulty in showing that in this sense modern science signifies the triumph of Platonism. Heidegger drives the error underlying the modern episteme of representation further back than its Platonic origins, to a conception of being as presence, as what is available and present to the consciousness of the subject.[12] This conception of being as presence-to reduces the manyness of the appearances by making them available to a sovereign consciousness. By reducing appearances to what is present to it, this consciousness attains the option of controlling them. In a spirit that is quite akin to Heidegger's in the *Dialectic of Enlightenment,* Adorno and Horkheimer argue that it is the "concept," the very unit of thought in the Western tradition that imposes homogeneity and identity upon the heterogeneity of material. This drive for identity of conceptual thought culminates in the technical triumph of Western ratio, which can only know things in that it comes to dominate them. "The Enlightenment relates to things as the dictator to humans."[13]

The third tradition of criticism is initiated by Ferdinand de Saussure

112 / Seyla Benhabib

and Charles Sanders Peirce and given sharper contours by Frege and Wittgenstein in our century. They argue that it is impossible to make sense of meaning, reference, and language in general when the view of linguistic signs as "private marks"[14] prevails. Instead, the public and shared character of language is a beginning point. Both de Saussure and Peirce point out that there is no *natural* relation between a sound, the word it represents in a language, and the content it refers to. For Peirce, the relation of the sign, of which words are but one species, to the signified is mediated by the interpretant.[15] For de Saussure, it is within a system of differential relations that certain sounds get arbitrarily frozen to stand for words.[16] Language is that sedimented set of relations which stands ideally behind the set of enunciations called *parole*. This move in the analysis of language from the private to the public, from consciousness to sign, from the individual word to a system of relations among linguistic signs, is followed by Frege and Wittgenstein, insofar as they too argue that the unit of reference is not the word but the sentence (Frege) and that meaning can only be understood by analyzing the multiple contexts of use (Wittgenstein).

The epistemological juncture at which Lyotard operates is characterized by the triumph of this third tradition. Whether in analytic philosophy, contemporary hermeneutics, or French poststructuralism, the paradigm of language has replaced the paradigm of consciousness. This shift has meant that the focus is no longer on the epistemic subject nor on the private contents of its consciousness but on the public, signifying activities of a collection of subjects. Not only has there been a shift in the size of the interrogated epistemic unit from idea, sensation, and concept to the threefold character of the sign as signifier, signified, and interpretant (Peirce), but also to language and parole (Saussure) or to language games as "forms of life" (Wittgenstein). The identity of the epistemic subject has changed as well: The bearer of the sign cannot be an isolated self— there is no private language, as Wittgenstein has observed; either it is a community of selves whose identity extends as far as their horizon of interpretations (Gadamer) or it is a social community of actual language users (Wittgenstein). This enlargement of the relevant epistemic subject is one option. A second option, followed by French structuralism, is to deny that, in order to make sense of the epistemic object, one need appeal to an epistemic subject at all. The subject is replaced by a system of structures, oppositions, and *différances* which, to be intelligible, need not be viewed as products of a living subjectivity at all.[17]

Lyotard wants to convince that the destruction of the episteme of representation allows only one option, namely, a recognition of the irreconcilability and incommensurability of language games and the acceptance that only local and context-specific criteria of validity can be formulated.

One must accept, in other words, an "agonistics" of language: " . . . to speak is to fight, in the sense of playing, and speech-acts fall within the domain of a general agonistics" (p. 10). This cognitive option yields a "polytheism of values," and a politics of justice beyond consensus, characterized by Lyotard vaguely as the "temporary contract."

The shift in contemporary philosophy from consciousness to language, from the order of representations to that of speech-acts, from denotation to performance need not lead to a polytheism of values and ultimately to Wittgenstein's dictum that "philosophy leaves everything as it is.[18] In order to see that the decline of the episteme of representation allows another alternative besides Lyotard's polytheism and agonistics of language, it is necessary to examine the self-contradictoriness of Lyotard's program more carefully. Lyotard wants to deny the choice between instrumental and critical reason, between performativity and emancipation. But his agonistic philosophy either leads to a polytheism of values, from which standpoint the principle of performativity or emancipation cannot be criticized, or this philosophy does not remain wholly polytheistic but privileges one domain of discourse and knowledge over others as a hidden criterion. The choice is still between an uncritical polytheism and a self-conscious recognition of the need for criteria of validity, and the attempt to reflexively ground them. Lyotard cannot escape the Scylla of uncritical polytheism nor the Charybdis of criteriological dogmatism.

Truth: The Future of an Illusion?

The differences between Lyotard's agonistics of language and the program of universal or "transcendental pragmatics," formulated by Apel and Habermas serve as a good beginning point in developing this dilemma.[19] Insofar as both Lyotard's agonistics and the program of pragmatics reject the denotative function of language, they signal a turn to its performative aspects. This turn is accompanied by a redefinition of knowledge as argumentative, discursive practice. Whereas Habermas distinguishes between the "know-how" embedded in the pre-theoretical life-world and the implicit rules of communicative competence which guide each competent speaker of a language, Lyotard emphasizes the "narrativity" of a mode of knowledge repressed and marginalized by science. He defines this as a "know-how, knowing how to live, how to listen" (*savoir-faire, savoir-vivre, savoir-écouter*, p. 19). For Habermas, discursive knowledge is *continuous* with everyday communicative practices; already everyday communication functions as its own reflexive medium through acts of interrogation, disagreement, questioning, and puzzling. In discourses we do not enter a Platonic heaven of ideas, but we "bracket" certain constraints of space and time, suspend belief in the truth of propositions, in the rightness of norms, and the truthfulness of our partners, and examine everyday convictions in which we have lost belief. For Lyotard, by contrast, "discourse" and "narrative knowledge" are radically discontinuous. Narrative knowledge appears to be in need of no legitimation. Lyotard describes the pragmatics of narrative knowledge such that it *eo ipso* seems to preclude the kind of questioning, puzzling, and disagreement which everyday communicative practices in fact always already allow (p. 27).

Although Lyotard describes his philosophy of language as "pragmatics" as well—albeit an agonistic one—"rhetorics" would be a more adequate characterization of the view he develops. Both pragmatics and rhetorics emphasize the performative as opposed to denotative uses of language, and both take as unit of analysis not the proposition but the speech-act. The pragmatic theory of speech-acts maintains that every act of communication is directed toward certain "validity claims" (*Geltungsansprüche*). Validity claims can be formulated with respect to the truth of statements, the rightness of norms, and the truthfulness of speaking subjects.[20] By contrast, the rhetorics of language Lyotard espouses does not distinguish between *raising a validity claim* and *forcing* someone to believe in something, between the coordination of action among participants on the basis of conviction generated through agreement and the manipulative influencing of the behavior of others. Lyotard misses the boat when he accuses Habermas of reducing all language games to the metagame of truth. In the theory of universal pragmatics, truth claims are one among two other validity claims, namely, rightness and truthfulness, and are not privileged in any way.[21] The issue then is not whether Habermas privileges the metagame of truth, but which view of language is more adequate: one that sees language as a *cognitive* medium through which norms of action coordination, patterns of interpretation of cultures, and frameworks for the exploration of our needs and desires are generated,[22] or a view that regards language as an *evocative* medium, in which validity and force, reasoned belief and manipulated opinion, can no longer be distinguished?

Is this a fair charge against Lyotard? Let us look more closely. A long passage in which Lyotard explains his pragmatics of language is revealing in this regard:

> A denotative utterance such as "The university is sick," made in the context of a conversation or an interview, positions its sender (the person who utters the statement), its addressee (the person who receives it), and its referent (what statement it deals with) in a specific way; the utterance places (and exposes) the sender in the position of "knower" . . . (If) we consider a declaration such as "The university is open," pronounced by a dean or rector at convocation, it is clear that the

previous specifications no longer apply. . . . The distinctive feature of this second, "performative" utterance is that *its effect upon the recipient coincided with its enunciation. . . .* That this is so is not subject to discussion or verification on the part of the addressee, who is immediately placed within the new context created by the utterance. As for the sender, he must be invested with the authority to make such a statement. Actually, we could say it the other way around: the sender is dean or rector—that is, *he is invested with the authority to make this kind of statement—only insofar as he can directly affect both the referent (the university) and the addressee (the university staff) in the manner I have indicated.* (p. 9, my emphasis)

This lengthy passage in which Lyotard explicates the pragmatic dimension of language games betrays that he no longer distinguishes between power and validity. The "sender" is defined as the one invested with the authority to make a certain kind of statement, but then this authority is said to be invested in him "only insofar as he can affect both the referent . . . and the addressee." But surely the *investment* of authority in someone or in an institution and the *effective exercise* of this authority are two different things. The first is a matter of *validity,* the second a matter of *power.* Just as the one invested with authority may not be effective in exercising it, there may be others effective in exercising authority but not invested with the right to exercise it. Lyotard seems to imply that only the one who effectively exercises authority is also invested with the title to it. If this is so, however, all authority would be charismatic and dependent, that is, upon the individual qualities and characteristics of a special individual, and not liable to justification through procedure, rules, and grounds. Power and validity, might and right would then be indistinguishable.

Lyotard writes, "the utterance places (and exposes) the sender in the position of the 'knower' . . . the addressee is put in the position of having to give or refuse his assent." (p. 9). The difference between universal and transcendental pragmatics and Lyotard's agonistics turns around the question as to how this "giving" or "refusing" of assent is to be understood. Lyotard regards this to be a consequence of a language game with many moves and does not specify the process whereby assent is generated or refusal obtained. But surely there is a distinction between agreeing and giving in; consenting and being persuaded to do so; presenting reasons to convince and blackmailing; refusing and being obstinate. Lyotard actually does not eliminate these distinctions altogether, for he writes, "to speak is to fight, in the sense of playing, and speech-acts fall within the domain of a general agonistics. *This does not necessarily mean that one plays in order to win"* (p. 10, my emphasis). The question is, why not? Why isn't language simply a sphere through which the universal power game is carried out? Why isn't all conversation seduction? All consensus conquest?

All agreement the result of delusion, of a *narcissisme à deux,* as Lacan would have it?[23] Despite a certain ambivalence, Lyotard cannot escape these conclusions.

The line between truth and deception, consensus and coercion disappears in Lyotard's agonistics, for, to speak with J. L. Austin, Lyotard cannot differentiate between illocutionary and perlocutionary speech-acts. According to Austin, "the illocutionary act . . . has a certain *force* in saying something; the perlocutionary act . . . is the *achieving* of certain *effects* by saying something"[24] (my emphasis). For example, *in* saying I would shoot someone, I threaten them (illocutionary act); *by* saying I would shoot someone, I alarm them (perlocutionary). The consequences attained by an illocutionary act can be stated at the beginning of a statement in the form of an *explicit* intention, "I threatened to shoot him"; in the case of a perlocutionary statement, however, the speaker can only attain the desired effect as long as his or her intentions are not explicitly made part of the speech-act.[25] If it is my goal to alarm someone, I do not begin a statement by saying, "I want to alarm you that." In this case my act would be illocutionary and intended with the purpose of apprehending you about a certain state of affairs. This in turn leaves open the possibility that you may assent or refuse to respond in the way I desire you to. In perlocutionary acts, however, the speaker wants to generate a certain effect upon the hearer *regardless* of the assent or dissent of the latter. In fact, it is necessary to achieve certain effects that the intentions of the speaker not be revealed. For Lyotard, the primary use of speech is perlocutionary. The use of speech to affect and influence the hearer, for whatever purposes, is the paradigm. But then the agonistics of language can no longer distinguish between manipulative and nonmanipulative uses of speech. The consequence of this position is that not truth alone, but all claims to validity are at best pious wishes, at worst illusions fabricated to deceive.

It is not difficult to show that any theory which denies the claims to truth and the possibility of distinguishing between it and sheer manipulative rhetoric would be involved in a "performative self-contradiction."[26] This may not be terribly difficult, but it does not settle the issue either. For, from Nietzsche's aphorisms, to Heidegger's poetics, to Adorno's stylistic configurations, and to Derrida's deconstructions, we have examples of thinkers who accept this performative self-contradiction and who self-consciously draw the consequences from it by seeking a new way of writing and communicating. That, following this tradition, Lyotard has not experimented with style in *The Postmodern Condition* may be more the result of accident than of conceptual consistency. We must seek to approach Lyotard's presuppositions through yet another route.

Science: The Same Old Dream

In a recent article on "Habermas and Lyotard on Postmodernity," Richard Rorty has described the impasse between Habermas and Lyotard as follows: "To put the opposition in another way, the French writers whom Habermas criticizes are willing to drop the opposition between 'true consensus' and 'false consensus,' or between 'validity' and 'power,' in order not to have to tell a metanarrative in order to explicate 'true' or 'valid.' But Habermas thinks that if we do drop the idea of the 'better argument' . . . we shall have only a 'context-dependent' sort of social criticism."[27] Rorty observes that Lyotard would respond to Habermas's claim that even the sciences are propelled beyond themselves toward self-reflection, by responding that "Habermas misunderstands the character of modern science."[28] Indeed, Lyotard's discussion of postmodern science is intended to accomplish a most peculiar function. This is also the point at which we see that Lyotard avoids the performative self-contradiction of stylistic self-deconstruction à la Derrida, by falling into dogmatism, that is, by privileging a knowledge-practice above others to serve as their criterion while failing to justify this explicitly.

Drawing from such diverse sources as Gödel's metamathematical research, quantum mechanics, microphysics, and catastrophe theories, in an obscure discussion, Lyotard attempts to show that the pragmatics of postmodern scientific knowledge has little to do with performativity or instrumental criteria (p. 54).[29] Lyotard writes, "Postmodern science . . . is theorizing its own evolution as discontinuous, catastrophic, nonrectifiable, and paradoxical. *It is changing the meaning of the word knowledge, while expressing how such a change can take place.* It is provoking not the known, but the unknown" (p. 60, my emphasis). This epistemic privileging of mathematical and natural science is problematical. It avoids a series of questions which any serious epistemological theory would have to face. The distinction between the natural, social, and human sciences (*Geisteswissenschaften*) is completely ignored. It remains to be shown that problems of concept formation, formulation of lawlike generalities, procedures of verification, the interaction between pre-theoretical and theoretical cognition in the social and human sciences can be illuminated by the model of postmodern knowledge Lyotard proposes.[30] The privileging of developments in mathematical and natural science does not break with the tradition of modern science which simply ignores the knowledge claims and problems of the human and social sciences. More significant is the question, "What is the relationship between the antimodel of pragmatics of science, and society? Is it applicable to the vast clouds of language material constituting a society? . . . Is it an impossible ideal of an open community?" (p. 64). Lyotard's answer to this question is incoherent. On the one hand, he admits that social and scientific pragmatics are different, for social pragmatics is not as simple as scientific pragmatics, "but is a monster formed by the interweaving of heteromorphous classes of utterances" (p. 65). On the other hand, the postmodern epistemology of science is said to approach the practice of narrativity (*le petit récit*). In other words, either Lyotard privileges natural and mathematical science, thus falling into traditional scientific dogmatism, or there is a criterion of knowledge, transcending modern natural science, and with reference to which science itself is legitimized, and which in turn needs to be defended. It would appear that narrative knowledge is such a criterion.

Indeed, Rorty as well interprets Lyotard as wanting to diminish the distance between scientific and narrative knowledge.[31] In Lyotard's construction of narrativity, Rorty discovers affinities with his own contextual-pragmatism. Closing fronts with Lyotard, he writes that "the trouble with Habermas is not so much that he provides a meta-narrative of emancipation as that he feels the need to legitimize, that he is not content to let the narratives which hold our culture together do their stuff. He is scratching where it does not itch."[32] Rorty's argument is revealing for two reasons. First, it indicates that epistemological questions flow into assessments of culture and society. Whether "the narratives which hold our culture together do their stuff" is an empirical question. Likewise, whether critical theory "scratches where it does not itch" depends upon our understanding of the problems, struggles, crises, conflicts, and miseries of the present. Epistemological issues are indeed closely linked with moral and political ones.

In the second place, we must note that Lyotard himself is not as sanguine as Rorty about the validity and continuing role of narrative in modern society and culture. Narrative knowledge, far from being an alternative to the modern scientific one, is sometimes described as if it were "premodern" knowledge, a historically lost mode of thought.[33] Yet, narrative knowledge is also viewed as the "other" of discursive knowledge—not its historical past but its contemporaneous other. Narrative knowledge, to use a phrase of Bloch's, is the "non-contemporaneous contemporary" of discursive knowledge. The scientist "classifies them as belonging to a different mentality: savage, primitive, underdeveloped, backward, alienated, composed of opinions, customs, authority, prejudice, ignorance, ideology. Narratives are fables, myths, legends, fit only for women and children" (p. 27). Is the meaning of Lyotard's postmodernist epistemology then a gesture of solidarity with the oppressed? A gesture toward the recognition of the otherness of the other? This may seem so, but Lyotard constructs the epistemology of narrative knowledge in such a way that it can no longer challenge scientific knowledge, let alone provide a criterion transcending it. Narrative knowledge belongs to the ethnological museum of the past.

"Narrative knowledge," writes Lyotard, "does not give a priority to the question of its own legitimation in that it certifies itself in the pragmatics of its own transmission without having recourse to argumentation and proof" (p. 27). This global characterization of narrative knowledge as prereflexive, as a self-sustaining whole, flattens the internal contradictions and tensions which affect narrative no less than discursive practices.[34] It also implies that all change in this episteme must come from without, through violence. Such an episteme has no self-propelling or self-correcting mechanism. But, in fact, this is to condemn the subjects of this episteme to ahistoricity, to deny that they inhabit the same place with us. We do not interact with them as equals, we inhabit a space in which we observe them as ethnologists and anthropologists, and we treat them with distance and indifference. But if this is not so, if indeed narrative knowledge is the other of *our* mode of knowledge, then Lyotard must admit that narrative and scientific knowledge are not merely incommensurable, but that they can and do clash, and that sometimes the outcome is less than certain.[35] To admit this possibility would mean that "narrative" and "discursive" practices occupy the same epistemic space, that both raise claims to validity, and that an argumentative exchange between them is not only possible but desirable. You cannot respect the otherness of the other if you deny the other the right to enter into a conversation with you, if you do not discard the objective indifference of an ethnologist and engage with the other as an equal. Instead of reckoning with this dilemma of recognition and distance, acceptance and tolerance, Lyotard agrees with Wittgenstein that philosophy must leave everything as is:

> It is therefore impossible to judge the existence or validity of narrative knowledge on the basis of scientific knowledge and vice versa: the relevant criteria are different. All we can do is gaze in wonderment at the diversity of discursive species, just as we do at the diversity of plant and animal species. Lamenting the "loss of meaning" in postmodernity boils down to mourning the fact that knowledge is no longer principally narrative. Such a reaction does not necessarily follow. Neither does an attempt to derive or engender (using operators like development) scientific knowledge from narrative knowledge, as if the former contained the latter in an embryonic state (pp. 26–27).

If we cannot lament the passing away of narrative knowledge nor indicate a possible line of transition from one knowledge type to another, then in fact narrative knowledge possesses no epistemic priority to scientific knowledge. Equipped with "undecidables, 'fracta' catastrophes and pragmatic paradoxes," we can face the brave, new world of postmodernity.

Thus, in the final analysis, Lyotard avoids performative self-contradiction, or simply incoherence, by privileging one practice of knowledge to serve as a criterion over others. This criterion is provided by the model of a discontinuous, fractured, and self-destabilizing epistemology, said to characterize modern mathematical and natural science. We may have woken from the Faustian dream but not from the scientific one!

Let us return once more to the question, what are the options opened in the present by the demise of the episteme of representation?

The Politics of Postmodernism

As Fredric Jameson has remarked, "The problem of postmodernism . . . is at one and the same time an aesthetic and a political one. The various positions which can logically be taken on it, whatever terms they are couched in, can always be shown to articulate visions of history, in which the evaluation of the social moment in which we live today is the object of an essentially political affirmation or repudiation."[36] Jean-François Lyotard's political trajectory led him from the *Socialisme ou Barbarie* group to a farewell to Marx and Freud and to the embracing of Nietzsche in *Economié Libidinale* (1974). Casting aside the mask of the social critic as simply a disguise for clerical and Christian values, Lyotard put on "the mask of paganism, polytheism."[37] "So you would challenge Spinozist or Nietzschean ethics, which separates the movements of being-more and those of being-less, of action and reaction?—Yes, but let us be aware of an entire morality and an entire politics, with their sages, militants, courts and jails, taking advantage of these dichotomies to appear again. . . . We do not speak as liberators of desire."[38]

Lyotard writes as a disillusioned Marxist, as one who has discovered that the grand metanarrative of history leads to an "entire morality and an entire politics." Lyotard prefers the Spinozist or Nietzschean conatus of being, the drive of the will to preserve itself, to the republic of virtue and terror. In fact, for Lyotard this choice between a polytheism of desire and a republic of terror appears so compelling that no one who has ever spoken in the name of humanity, history, emancipation, and unity can escape its curse. Terror did not begin with the citizen's committees of the French Revolution nor with the banning of the Mensheviks and Social Revolutionaries from the revolutionary Dumas. No, it is not Pol Pot or Stalin, but Kant and Hegel who lie at its origin. This total loss of historical perspective in the rhetoric of disillusionment leads Lyotard to finish his essay "What is Postmodernism?" on the following note:

"Finally, it must be clear that it is our business not to supply reality but to invent allusions to the conceivable which cannot be presented. And it is not to be expected that this task will effect the last reconciliation between language games . . . and that only the transcendental illusion (that of Hegel) can hope to totalize then into a real unity. But Kant also knew that the price to pay for such an illusion is terror. The nineteenth and twentieth centuries have given us as much terror as we can take. We have paid a high enough price for the nostalgia of the whole and the one, for the reconciliation of the concept and the sensible, of the transparent and communicable experience. Under the general demand for slackening and for appeasement, we can hear the mutterings of the desire for a return of terror, for the realization of the fantasy to seize reality. The answer is: Let us wage a war on totality; let us witness to the unpresentable, let us activate the differences and save the honor of the name" (p. 82).

Surely, Lyotard knows that under the heading of "Absolute Freedom and Terror," Hegel in Chapter 6 of the *Phenomenology of Spirit* provided one of the most brilliant discussions of terror in the history of modern political thought.[39] Surely, he also knows (or should know) that Habermas and Wellmer, whom he accuses of propagating a "nostalgia for the whole and the one," are not German neo-Romantics, but thinkers who have insisted upon the need to revitalize whatever fragile tradition of participatory, civil-libertarian, democratic resources the Federal German Republic possesses. Why then this misunderstanding? What is at stake?

As with the crisis of the representational episteme, the demise of the metanarrative of traditional Marxism suggests diverse possibilities, among which the return to Nietzsche and Spinoza is one among many, and not the most compelling one. Whereas the demise of the episteme of representation initiated a shift from the philosophy of consciousness to the philosophy of language, from denotation to performance, from the proposition to the speech-act, the demise of the metanarrative of traditional Marxism opens the possibility of post-Marxist radical, democratic politics. The issue is whether the conceptual polytheism and agonistics proposed by Lyotard aids in this project or whether indeed under the guise of postmodernism, a "young conservatism"[40] is not establishing itself among the avant-garde of the 1980s.

Lyotard's project is ambivalent. His defense of the morally uncompromising gesture of the aesthetic avant-garde, his insistence upon the spirit of innovation, experimentation, play, and his call "to activate differences and save the honor of the name" (p. 82) could be constituents of a post-Marxist radical, democratic politics. Indeed, *The Postmodern Condition* intends to sketch "the outline of a politics that would respect both the desire for justice and the desire for the unknown" (p. 67). Yet, insisting upon the incommensurability of language games, in the name of polytheism, may generate moral and political indifference; the call for innovation, experimentation, and play may be completely dissociated from social reform and institutional practice, and the activation of differences may not amount to a democratic respect of the right of the other to be, but to a conservative plea to place the other, because of her otherness, outside the pale of our common humanity and mutual responsibility.

The moral debate between Lyotard and the tradition of critical theory concerns the nature of the *minimum cognitive and moral commitments* necessary to keep the fronts clear between a post-Marxist radical, democratic politics and a postmodernist, young conservatism. Critical social theory at the present defines these cognitive and moral criteria as the defense of a communicative, discursive concept of reason, the acceptance that knowledge should serve moral autonomy, and the recognition that intentions of the good life cannot be dissociated from the discursive practice of seeking understanding (*Verständigung*) among equals in a process of communication free from domination. Admittedly, whether a nonfoundationalist justification of these commitments, which also avoids the metanarratives which Lyotard so effectively dismantles, is possible needs to be investigated. This is surely Lyotard's challenge to the program of a critical social theory at the present. Only Lyotard's agonistic theory of language and paralogistic theory of legitimation cannot serve as a basis for a post-Marxian radical, democratic politics. The political alternatives that follow from Lyotard's epistemology are twofold: The first is a vaguely defined neoliberal pluralism; the second, a contextual pragmatism.

Lyotard ends his essay on the postmodern condition with a plea to "give the public free access to memory and data banks" (p. 67). This is justified on the grounds that it would prevent the total computerization of society and supply groups "discussing metaprescriptives" with the information they need to make knowledgeable decisions. "Language games would then be games of perfect information at any moment. But they would also be non-zero sum games" (p. 67). Despite Lyotard's caveat that his task is not to supply reality with models but "to invent allusions to the conceivable which cannot be presented" (p. 81), the reader might well want to know who these groups discussing metaprescriptives are. Are they social movements, citizens' groups, institutions, interest groups, or lobbies? How far would the demand "to give the public free access to memory and data banks" go? Can IBM or any other multinational corporation democratize its trade secrets and technical information? Is the military likely to democratize its procedures of acquiring, processing, and storing information? It is not incumbent upon Lyotard to provide a blueprint of the society of the future, but this image of a society with free access to data banks on the part of competing groups whose identity remains unclear is hardly "the outline of a politics that would respect both the desire for justice and the desire for the unknown." Lyotard ends up with a neoliberal interest group pluralism plus the democratization of computers.[41]

Surely, there is much in the traditional liberal conceptions of pluralism, tolerance, and the public competition of ideals that would need to be incorporated into a post-Marxist radical, democratic politics. Yet, the difficulty with political liberalism, old and new, is the neglect of the *structural* sources of inequality, influence, resource, and power among competing groups. In the absence of radical, democratic measures redressing economic, social, and cultural inequalities and forms of subordination, the pluralistic vision of groups Lyotard proposes remains naive. It would fail to redress the plight of those for whom the question of the democratization of information is a luxury, simply because, as marginalized groups in our societies, they fail even to have access to organizational let alone informational resources. At the present, these groups include increasing numbers of women, minorities, foreigners, unemployed youth, and the elderly.

Lyotard's neoliberal interest group pluralism is naive in yet another way. The assumption that language games would be games of perfect information suggests that language games do not compete, struggle with, or contradict one another, not in the sense of jousting in a tournament, but in the actual sense of struggling to delegitimize, overpower, and silence the language game of the other. To take a concrete example: Lyotard cannot maintain that the current attempt of conservative, pro-life groups to establish a "new reverence for life and creation," to deny the moral legitimacy of abortion, to even ask science to provide exact criteria as to when the fetus becomes a person, are "narratives" in our culture that point to a happy polytheism of language games. The polytheism of language games either assumes that culture and society are harmonious wholes or that the struggles within them are plays only. But there are times when philosophy cannot afford to be a "gay science," for reality itself becomes deadly serious. To deny that the play of language games may not turn into a matter of life and death and that the intellectual cannot remain the priest of many gods but must take a stance is cynical.

The second political gesture which follows from Lyotard's agonistics of language games was described as "contextual-pragmatist." Actually, it is Richard Rorty who articulates this position most clearly. His view, however, is a perfectly logical consequence of Lyotard's claim that "narratives . . . thus define what has the right to be said and done in the culture in question, and since they are themselves a part of that culture, they are legitimated by the simple fact that they do what they do" (p. 23). Rorty agrees with Lyotard that Habermas's difficulty is that "he scratches where it does not itch."[42] This means that neither our culture nor our societies need justification or criticism, adoration or reprimand. We have to satisfy ourselves with context-immanent criteria that the political practices of Western democracies provide us with.[43] Rorty further advocates the development of a "de-theoreticized sense of community," the growth of an "analogue of civic virtue—tolerance, irony, and a willingness to let spheres of culture flourish without worrying too much about their 'common ground,' their unification. . . ."[44] This admirable demand, to use an expression of another decade, "to let a hundred flowers bloom," is motivated by a desire to depoliticize philosophy. "Then one might see," writes Rorty, "the canonical sequence of philosophers from Descartes to Nietzsche as a distraction from the history of concrete social engineering which made the North Atlantic culture what it is now, with all its glories and all its dangers."[45]

Perhaps one should admire the honesty of one of the leading philosophers of the Anglo-American culture in this sad avowal of the marginality to which the "glorious North Atlantic culture" reduces philosophical thought. Yet, Rorty's statement is sad in another way. It reveals the internalization by an intellectual of the distrust and disparagement of intellectuals, accompanying the modern temperament from Edmund Burke to Norman Podhoretz. In fact, it reveals the internalization of the charge that were it not for the *Weltschmerz* of a few "pessimistic and too exclusively German individuals"[46] and those influenced by them, we would not have an adversary culture in this country. Isn't there indeed a curious convergence between postmodernism and "young conservatism"?

Thus, the agonistics of language games leads to its own paralogisms. On the one hand, there is Lyotard's faith in the aesthetic avant-garde intellectuals as messengers of the "sublime" and harbingers of the way to the "unknown"; on the other hand, there is Rorty's advice to abandon the "illusion of the intellectuals as a revolutionary vanguard"[47] and to return to a strange synthesis of Deweyian pragmatism and British conservatism.

Hence, there follows the frustrating eclecticism of postmodernism in philosophy and elsewhere. Just as the postmodern architects of the "Chicago Seven" can cite classical, oriental, and Renaissance themes and details all in one breath in their plans for Chicago townhouses,[48] contemporary philosophy, dazzled by the dissolution of the episteme of representation, is anxious to cite American pragmatism, French Nietscheanism, British conservatism, and Heideggerian wisdom all in one breath. It is likely that we will have to live with this polytheism and dazzling "play of surfaces," as Jameson had named them, for some time to come. Nor is it unwelcome that the frozen fronts of philosophy are becoming fluid again. Only it is necessary that we think the epistemic alternatives created by the present also to their moral and political ends. For questions of truth, as Lyotard admits and Rorty denies, are still matters of justice as well.

The paradigm shift in contemporary philosophy from consciousness to language, from the denotative to the performative, from the proposition to the speech-act, need not lead to a self-contradictory polytheism and to a vision of politics incapable of justifying its own commitment to justice. This paradigm shift can also lead to an epistemology and politics which recognizes the lack of metanarratives and foundational guarantees but which nonetheless insists on formulating minimal criteria of validity for our discursive and political practices. The struggle over what lies beyond the classical imperative remains unresolved. In this sense, the definition of postmodernity may be that of a future which we would like to think of as our past.

Notes

1. Paolo Portoghesi, *After Modern Architecture* (New York: Rizzoli, 1982), p. 7ff.

2. Cf. M. Berman, *All That Is Solid Melts Into Air* (New York: Simon and Schuster, 1982), pp. 37ff., 60–71.

3. Peter Eisenman, accompanying text to exhibit piece, "Cite Unseen," in "Revision der Moderne," Deutsches Architekturmuseum, Summer 1984, Frankfurt am Main. For some of the difficulties in characterizing Eisenman's work, cf. Charles A. Jencks, *Late-Modern Architecture and Other Essays* (New York: Rizzoli, 1980), pp. 13, 137ff.

4. Jean-Francois Lyotard, *The Postmodern Condition: A Report on Knowledge,* trans. Geoff Bennington and Brian Massouri, forward by F. Jameson (Minneapolis: University of Minnesota Press, 1984). All future references in the text are to this edition. Appended to the English translation is also the essay "Answering the Question: What is Postmodernism," trans. R. Durand, originally in *Critique,* No. 419, April 1982.

5. Cf. H. Arendt's statement: "Descartes' philosophy is haunted by two nightmares which in a sense became the nightmares of the whole modern age, not because this age was so deeply influenced by Cartesian philosophy, but because their emergence was almost inescapable once the true implications of the modern world view were understood. These nightmares are very simple and very well known. In the one, reality, the reality of the world as well as of human life, is doubted. . . . The other concerned . . . the impossibility for man to trust his senses and his reason." *The Human Condition* (Chicago: University of Chicago Press, 1973), eighth printing, p. 277.

6. I borrow the phrase from R. Rorty's well-known article, "The World Well Lost," which argues that the conclusion to be drawn from contemporary epistemological disputes about conceptual frameworks is that "The notion of the 'world' that is correlative with the notion of a 'conceptual framework' is simply the Kantian notion of a thing-in-itself. . . ." Originally published

in *Journal of Philosophy* (1972), reprinted in *Consequences of Pragmatism* (Minneapolis: University of Minnesota Press, 1982), p. 16.

7. Richard Rorty, *Philosophy and the Mirror of Nature* (Princeton: Princeton University Press, 1979), p. 131ff.

8. Charles Taylor, "Theories of Meaning," Daves Hickes Lecture, Proceedings of the British Academy (Oxford: Oxford University Press, 1982), p. 284.

9. Thomas Hobbes, *Leviathan,* ed. C. B. McPherson (Baltimore: Penguin Books, 1971), p. 101ff. Cf. M. Foucault, *The Order of Things: An Archeology of the Human Sciences* (New York: Random House, 1973), First Vintage Books edition: "In its simple state as an idea, or an image, or a perception, associated with or substituted for another, the simplifying element is not a sign. It can become a sign only on condition that it manifests, in addition, the relation that links it to what it signifies. It must represent, but that representation, in turn, must also be represented within it" (p. 64).

10. The transition from *consciousness* to *self-consciousness,* from *representation* to *desire* in Chapter 3 of Hegel's *Phenomenology of Spirit* contains also a critique of the spectator conception of the knowing subject. Hegel's point is that an epistemological standpoint confined to the spectator conception of the self cannot solve the questions it raises; most notably, it cannot explain the genesis and becoming of an object of knowledge. It is only insofar as the knowing self is also an acting one that it can destroy the myth of the given in knowledge (Hegel, *Phenomenology of Spirit,* trans. with an analysis and foreword by J. N. Findlay [Oxford: Clarendon Press, 1977], pp. 104–110). Cf. "He does not see how the sensuous world around him is not given direct from all eternity, ever the same, but is the product of industry and of the state of society, and indeed in the sense that it is an historical product, the result of the activity of a whole succession of generations," K. Marx and F. Engels, *The German Ideology,* ed. and intro. by R. Pascal (New York: International Publishers, 1969), p. 35. M. Horkheimer, "Traditional and Critical Theory," *Critical Theory,* trans. M. J. O'Connell et al. (New York: Herder and Herder, 1972), pp. 188–244. J. Habermas, *Knowledge and Human Interests,* trans. J. Shapiro (Boston: Beacon Press, 1972), pp. 1–65. S. Freud, "A Difficulty in the Path of Psychoanalysis," *Standard Edition* (London: Hogarth, 1953), Vol. 17, pp. 137–144. For this reading of Freud, I am much indebted to Paul Ricoeur, *Freud and Philosophy: An Essay on Interpretation,* trans. Denis Savage (New Haven: Yale University Press, 1977), pp. 419–459.

11. Friedrich Nietzsche, "The Genealogy of Morals," *The Birth of Tragedy and the Genealogy of Morals,* trans. F. Golffing (New York: Doubleday, 1958), p. 289ff.

12. Martin Heidegger, *Being and Time,* trans. John Macquarrie and Edward Robinson (New York: Harper and Row, 1962), pp. 47ff.; "Die Frage nach der Technik?" *Vorträge und Aufsätze* (Stuttgart: Gunther Neske, 1974), fourth ed., p. 27ff.

13. M. Horkheimer and Th. Adorno, *Dialektik der Aufklärung* (Frankfurt am Main: Fischer Verlag, 1980), p. 12, originally published in Amsterdam 1947.

14. Cf. Wittgenstein's critique of the "naming" theory of meaning and of the impossibility of viewing language as a private game in *Philosophical Investigations*, trans. G. E. M. Anscombe (New York: MacMillan Company, 1965), tenth printing, pp. 27–32, 38, 39, 180, 199ff.

15. Charles Sanders Peirce, "Some Consequences of Four Incapabilities," *Selected Writings*, ed. and with an intro. and notes by Philip Wiener (New York: Dover Publications, 1966), pp. 53–54; K.-O. Apel, "From Kant to Peirce: The Semiotical Transformation of Transcendental Logic," *Toward a Transformation of Philosophy*, trans. G. Adey and D. Frisby (London: RKP, 1980), pp. 77–93.

16. Ferdinand de Saussure, *Course in General Linguistics*, ed. by C. Bally and A. Sechehaye, trans. and intro. by Wade Baskin (New York: McGraw Hill, 1959), p. 67ff.

17. Cf. Manfred Frank, *Was ist Neostrukturalismus?* (Frankfurt am Main: Suhrkamp, 1984), pp. 71ff., 83ff., 259. Pierre Bourdieu and J. C. Passeron, "Sociology and Philosophy in France since 1945: Death and Resurrection of a Philosophy without the Subject," *Social Research*, Vol. 34, No. 1, Spring 1983, pp. 162–212.

18. Wittgenstein, *Philosophical Investigations*, pp. 124, 49e.

19. K.-O. Apel, "Sprechakttheorie und transzendentale Sprachpragmatik zur Frage ethischer Normen," in *Sprachpragmatik und Philosophie*, ed. K.-O. Apel (Frankfurt am Main: Suhrkamp, 1976), pp. 10–81; J. Habermas, "Was heisst Universalpragmatik?" ibid., pp. 184–273, English translation by T. McCarthy, "What is Universal Pragmatics?" in *Communication and the Evolution of Society* (Boston: Beacon Press, 1979), pp. 1–69.

20. J. Habermas, "An Excursus on Theory of Argumentation," *The Theory of Communicative Action*, Vol. 1, trans. T. McCarthy (Boston: Beacon Press, 1984), p. 23ff.

21. One of Habermas's main purposes in developing a theory of discourse and argumentation was to formulate a concept of the validity of ethical norms, which avoided the dogmatism of natural law theories (that confuse moral validity and factual assertions) and the arbitrariness of emotivism (that reduced moral claims to statements of taste). Cf. "Zwei Bemerkungen zum praktischen Diskurs," *Konstruktionen versus Positionen*, ed. Kuno Lorenz (Berlin: Walter de Gruyter, 1979); "Wahrheitstheorien," *Wirklichkeit und Reflexion*, ed. H. Fahrenbach (Pfullingen: Neske, 1973), pp. 211–265.

22. Against Lyotard's reading, I want to emphasize that linguistically mediated communicative action serves *three* functions: first, the coordination of social action among individuals; second, the socialization and individuation of members of a human group; and third, the appropriation of cultural tradition and the generation of meaning and symbolic patterns which define the

hermeneutic horizon of a culture. Cf. Habermas, *The Theory of Communicative Action,* pp. 100–101, 136ff.

23. Quoted in Frank, *Was ist Neostrukturalismus?,* p. 111.

24. J. L. Austin, *How to do Things with Words* (Cambridge, MA: Harvard University Press, 1962), p. 120.

25. Admittedly, the interpretation of the distinction between *illocutionary* and *perlocutionary* acts is controversial (cf. Austin, *How to do Things with Words,* pp. 120ff.). The difficulty with Lyotard's interpretation of Austin's thesis appears to be that he conflates the illocutionary force of an utterance with the producing of certain effects, intended or otherwise, by means of an utterance. Thus, he describes a "performative utterance" as one whose "effect upon the recipient coincided with its enunciation" (*The Postmodern Condition,* p. 9). Austin, however, identifies an illocutionary act as an act we perform in saying something (*How to do Things with Words,* p. 99), and the description of which can figure in the first person indicative as "I pronounce that," "I warn you that," "I inform you that," etc. In his valuable article, "Intention and Convention in Speech Acts," P. F. Strawson clarifies in fact how irrelevant the achieving of certain effects upon the hearer is to the identifying of illocutionary acts; he shifts the focus instead to the overt intention of the speaker and the recognition by his hearers of this intention, regardless of how they choose to respond to it, *Philosophical Review,* No. 73, 1964, pp. 439–460.

26. Habermas, "The Entwinement of Myth and Enlightenment: Rereading the *Dialectic of Enlightenment*," *New German Critique,* Vol. 26, Spring-Summer 1982.

27. Rorty, "Habermas and Lyotard on Postmodernity," *Praxis International,* Vol. 4, No. 1, April 1984, p. 33.

28. Ibid.

29. This argument is somewhat unconvincing because Lyotard does not distinguish between the internal *cognitive dynamics of science* and its *social* uses. Performativity, or what is known as "scientism" in the tradition of critical theory, is a view that legitimizes science by an appeal to—although not exclusively—its social-technological uses. That scientism is not an adequate theory of the natural sciences has been argued forcefully by others like Mary Hesse, *Revolutions and Reconstructions in the Philosophy of Science* (Bloomington: Indiana University Press, 1980). However, in attacking this ideology, Lyotard ignores the social reality it expresses. The fact that postmodern natural science operates with a discontinuous epistemology of instabilities does not decide the question of its social role. Lyotard emphasizes the internal, cognitive dynamics of modern science while ignoring its social-technological aspects. For the distinction between the cognitive and social dynamics of science, cf. G. Böhme et al., *Finalization of Science,* ed. W. Schafer (Boston: D. Reidel Publishing, 1983), pp. 3–11.

30. For a recent statement of problems and issues, cf. R. J. Bernstein, *The*

Restructuring of Social and Political Theory (Philadelphia: University of Pennsylvania Press, 1976).

31. Rorty, "Habermas and Lyotard on Postmodernity," p. 34.

32. Ibid.

33. Frank, *Was ist Neostrukturalismus?*, p. 106.

34. Cf. E. Gellner, "Concepts and Society," *Rationality*, ed. B. R. Wilson (New York: Harper and Row, Publishers, 1970), pp. 18–50; P. Bourdieu, *Outline of a Theory of Practice*, trans. Richard Nice (Cambridge: Cambridge University Press, 1979), pp. 22–30.

35. In portraying this relationship, Lyotard adopts the *observer's* point, the standpoint of the curator of an ethnological museum of the past. Had he adopted the *participant's* perspective, he would have had to concede that "gazing in wonderment at the variety of discursive species" is hardly the attitude to take when confronted with the moral and epistemic problems that the coexistence of incompatible discursive modes pose for us qua children of the modern West. In this essay, I am only arguing that these modes of thought cannot harmoniously coexist in one epistemic space, that their very presence next to each other poses moral as well as cognitive problems, or that the question of validity inevitably confronts us, and that we cannot extricate ourselves from an answer by gazing in wonderment at the plurality of language games and life-forms. For a recent statement of these thorny questions, cf. *Rationality and Relativism*, ed. by Steven Lukes and Martin Hollis (Cambridge: MIT Press, 1984).

36. Fredric Jameson, "The Politics of Theory: Ideological Positions in the Postmodernism Debate," *New German Critique*, No. 33 (Fall 1984), pp. 53–66.

37. I adopt this phrase from Vincent Descombes, *Modern French Philosophy* (New York: Cambridge University Press, 1980), p. 184.

38. Lyotard, *Economié Libidinale*, pp. 54–55, as cited by Descombes, p. 185.

39. *Hegel's Phenomenology of Spirit*, pp. 355–364. Indeed, it is this condemnation of the Terror that leads Hegel "to conceptually legitimize the revolutionizing reality without the Revolution itself." Habermas, "Hegel's Critique of the French Revolution," *Theory and Practice*, trans. John Viertel, (Boston: Beacon Press, 1971), p. 123ff.

40. J. Habermas, "Modernity versus Postmodernity," *New German Critique*, Vol. 22, Winter 1981, p. 13. In his "Questions and Counter-questions," *Praxis International*, Vol. 4, No. 3 (1984), pp. 229–249. Habermas has modified this charge somewhat, but it strikes me as being quite accurate for at least one possible implication of the postmodernist epistemological positions.

41. Albrecht Wellmer makes a similar point in his "On the Dialectic of Modernism and Postmodernism," *Praxis International*, Vol. 4, No. 4 (1985), pp. 337–362.

42. Rorty, "Habermas and Lyotard on Postmodernity," p. 34.

43. Ibid., p. 35.

44. Ibid., p. 38.

45. Ibid., p. 41.

46. Ibid., p. 38.

47. Ibid., p. 35. This is a curious demand, since the whole revival of critical theory in Europe as well as in this country, and certainly a main political impetus behind Habermas's and Wellmer's works, was the abandonment and critique by the Student Movement and of the New Left of the illusion of a revolutionary vanguard. It is as if some French and American intellectuals are suffering a lapse of memory in the 1980s, accusing the Student Movement and the New Left of attitudes that they did most to combat.

48. Cf. the works of the Chicago School (Stanley Tigerman, Frederick Read, Peter Pran, Stuart Cohen, Thomas Beeby, Anders Nerheim) exhibited at "Die Revision der Moderne," Deutsches Architekturmuseum, Frankfurt, Summer 1984.

Part II
The Politics of Location

6

Feminism, Postmodernism, and Gender-Scepticism

Susan Bordo

Contemporary Feminism and Gender-Scepticism

Recently, I heard a feminist historian claim that there were absolutely no common areas of experience between the wife of a plantation owner in the pre-Civil War South and the female slaves her husband owned. Gender, she argued, is so thoroughly fragmented by race, class, historical particularity, and individual difference, as to self-destruct as an analytical category. The "bonds of womanhood," she insisted, is a feminist fantasy, born out of the ethnocentrism of white, middle-class academics.

A central point of a recently published book by a feminist philosopher is the refutation of all feminist attempts to articulate a sense in which the history of philosophy reveals distinctively "male" perspectives on reality.

The writing of this chapter was made possible by the generous support of the Rockefeller Foundation and the American Council of Learned Societies/Ford Foundation. Written while I was in residence at the Duke University/University of North Carolina Center for Research on Women, it has benefitted greatly from my participation in the Duke/UNC communities, especially from almost daily conversation with LeeAnn Whites, and from the insights and suggestions of friends and colleagues there who read and commented on earlier drafts: Ted Koditschek, Jean O'Barr, Lynne Tirrell, Jane Tompkins, and Mary Wyer. I am grateful to Mario Moussa and Linda Robertson for their help in enabling me to shape and clarify later drafts, at a point when I was beginning to lose my own distance and focus on the piece. I would also like to thank Pat Keane, Edward Lee, Bruce Shefrin, and Linda Nicholson for their comments and suggestions. Finally, it is impossible to adequately acknowledge the contribution of Lynne Arnault, for whose friendship, insight, ability to help me untie my intellectual knots, and deep philosophical and practical engagement with the issues of importance to both of us, I am constantly grateful.

All such attempts, the author argues, "do violence" to the history of philosophy and "injustice" to the "extremely variegated nature" of male experience. Indeed, any attempt to "cut" reality and perspective along gender lines is methodologically flawed and essentializing.

For some feminist literary theorists, gender has become a "discursive formation," inherently unstable and continually self-deconstructing. The meaning of gender is constantly "deferred," endlessly multiple. We must "get beyond the number two," as one writer has described it, and move toward a "dizzying accumulation of narratives." (A new journal is entitled *Genders.*) Not to do so is to perpetuate a hierarchical, binary construction of reality.

In the November 1987 issue of *Ms.* magazine, an article appeared on the art of Georgia O'Keeffe. It included the text of a letter from O'Keeffe to Mabel Luhan:

> "I thought you could write something about me that the men can't—
> What I want written—I do not know—I have no definite idea of what
> it should be—but a woman who has lived many things and who sees
> lines and colors as an expression of living—might say something that
> a man can't—I feel there is something unexplored about woman that
> only a woman can explore—Men have done all they can do about it.
> Does that mean anything to you — or doesn't it?"

The article itself, written by a staff reporter, begins: "Georgia O'Keeffe. The woman of our century who made it clear once and for all that painting had no gender."

In the 1970s, the feminist imagination was fueled by the insight that the template of gender could disclose aspects of culture and history previously concealed. The male-normative view of the world, feminists argued, had obscured its own biases through its fictions of unity (History, Reason, Culture, Tradition, and so forth). Each of those unities was shown to have a repressed shadow—an *Other* whose material history, values, and perspective had yet to be written.

Today, many feminists are critical of what they now see as the oversimplifications and generalizations of this period in feminism. Challenges have arisen—sometimes emotionally charged—targeted against earlier classics of feminist theory and their gendered readings of culture and history. Where once the prime objects of academic feminist critique were the phallocentric narratives of our male-dominated disciplines, now feminist criticism has turned to its own narratives, finding them reductionist, totalizing, inadequately nuanced, valorizing of gender difference, unconsciously racist, and elitist. It seems possible to discern what may be a new drift within feminism, a new scepticism about the use of gender as an analytical category.

Such scepticism is by no means universal; contemporary feminism remains a diverse and pluralist enterprise. Nor does gender-scepticism take one characteristic form. Rather, it has emerged (as my opening montage suggests) across disciplines and theoretical affiliations, speaking in different voices and crystallized around different concerns. Naming and criticizing such a phenomenon is a slippery, perilous business. Yet, it is my contention that there is an important cultural formation here, the analysis of which must become a pressing concern for feminists.

Like all cultural formations, feminist gender-scepticism is complexly constructed out of diverse elements—intellectual, psychological, institutional, and sociological. Arising not from monolithic design but from an interplay of factors and forces, it is best understood not as a discrete, definable position which can be adopted or rejected, but as an emerging coherency which is being fed by a variety of currents, sometimes overlapping, sometimes quite distinct. In this chapter, I will critically examine four such currents and the (sometimes unintentional) routes by which they empty into the waters of gender-scepticism.

The first current is the result of a recent academic marriage which has brought indigenous feminist concerns over the ethnocentrisms and unconscious racial biases of gender theory into a theoretical alliance with (a highly programmatic appropriation of) the more historicist, politically oriented wing of poststructuralist thought (e.g., Foucault, Lyotard). This union, I will argue, has contributed to the development of a new feminist "methodologism" which lays claims to an authoritative critical framework, legislating "correct" and "incorrect" approaches to theorizing identity, history, and culture. This methodologism, which eschews generalizations about gender *a priori* on theoretical grounds, is in danger of discrediting and disabling certain kinds of feminist cultural critique; it also often implicitly (and mistakenly) supposes that the adoption of a "correct" theoretical approach makes it possible to *avoid* ethnocentrism.

The second current which I discuss in this chapter is the result of certain feminist appropriations of deconstructionism. Here, a postmodern recognition of *interpretive* multiplicity, of the indeterminacy and heterogeneity of cultural meaning and meaning-production, is viewed as calling for new narrative approaches, aimed at the adequate representation of textual "difference." From this perspective, the template of gender is criticized for its fixed, binary structuring of reality and is replaced with a narrative ideal of ceaseless textual play. But this ideal, I will argue, while arising out of a critique of modernist epistemological pretensions to adequately represent reality, remains animated by its *own* fantasies of attaining an epistemological perspective free of the locatedness and limitations of embodied existence—a fantasy that I call a "dream of everywhere."

Through the critical concerns raised in these sections of my chapter, I hope to encourage caution among those who are ready to wholeheartedly celebrate the emergence of "postmodern feminism." The programmatic appropriation of poststructuralist insight, I will argue, in shifting the focus of crucial feminist concerns about the representation of cultural diversity from practical contexts to questions of adequate theory, is highly problematic for feminism. Not only are we thus diverted from attending to the professional and institutional mechanisms through which the politics of exclusion operate most powerfully in intellectual communities, but we also deprive ourselves of still vital analytical tools for critique of those communities and the hierarchical, dualistic power structures that sustain them.[1]

If this is so, what are the mechanisms which have drawn feminists into participation with such a development? The last two currents I examine provide foci for examining such issues, through an exploration of the *institutions* of knowledge/power that still dominate in our masculinist public arena and that now threaten, I will argue, to harness and tame the visionary and critical energy of feminism as a movement of cultural resistance and transformation.

From The "View from Nowhere" to Feminist Methodologism

Let me begin with a story, told from my perspective as a feminist philosopher, about the emergence of gender analytics and the difficulties into which it later fell.[2]

In 1979, Richard Rorty's *Philosophy and the Mirror of Nature* burst on the philosophical scene in the United States. Its author, established and respected within the very traditions he now set out to deconstruct, was uniquely situated to legitimate a simple yet subversive argument. That argument, earlier elaborated in different ways by Marx, Nietzsche, and Dewey, and being developed on the continent in the work of Derrida and Foucault, held that ideas are the creation of social beings rather than the (more or less adequate) representations or "mirrorings" of nature.

Rorty's presentation of this argument was philosophically elegant, powerful, and influential. But it was not Rorty, rebellious member of the club (or indeed, *any* professional intellectual voice), who was ultimately responsible for uncovering the pretensions and illusions of the ideals of epistemological objectivity, foundations, and neutral judgment. That uncovering first occurred, not in the course of philosophical conversation, but in political practice. Its agents were the liberation movements of the sixties and seventies, emerging not only to make a claim to the legitimacy of marginalized cultures, unheard voices, suppressed narratives, but also to expose the perspectivity and partiality of the official accounts. Now those accounts could no longer claim to descend from the heavens of pure rationality or to reflect the inevitable and progressive logic of intellectual or scientific discovery. They had to be seen, rather, as the products of historically situated individuals with very particular class, race, and gender interests. The imperial categories which had provided justification for those accounts—Reason, Truth, Human Nature, History, Tradition—now were displaced by the (historical, social) questions: *Whose* truth? *Whose* nature? *Whose* version of reason? *Whose* history? *Whose* tradition?

Feminism, appropriately enough, initiated the cultural work of exposing and articulating the *gendered* nature of history, culture, and society. It was a cultural moment of revelation and relief. The category of the "human"—a standard against which all difference translates to lack, insufficiency—was brought down to earth, given a pair of pants, and reminded that it was not the only player in town. Our students still experience this moment of critical and empowering insight when, for example, they learn from Gilligan (1982) and others that the language of "rights" is not the ethical discourse of God or Nature, but the ideological superstructure of a particular construction of masculinity.[3]

Gender theorists Dinnerstein (1977), Chodorow (1978), Gilligan (1982), and many others uncovered patterns that resonate experientially and illuminate culturally. They cleared a space, described a new territory, which radically altered the male-normative terms of discussion about reality and experience; they forced recognition of the difference gender makes. Academic disciplines were challenged, sometimes in their most basic self-conceptions and categories—as in philosophy, which has made an icon of the ideal of an abstract, universal reason, a reason without race, class, gender, or history (the "view from nowhere," to borrow Thomas Nagel's [1986] apt phrase). There *is* no view from nowhere, feminists insisted; indeed, the "view from nowhere" may *itself* be a male construction of the possibilities for knowledge.[4]

The unity of the "gendered human," however, often proved to be as much a fiction as the unity of abstract, universal "man." In responding to the cultural imperative to describe the difference gender makes, gender theorists (along with those who attempted to speak for a "black experience" uninflected by gender or class) often glossed over other dimensions of social identity and location, dimensions which, when considered, cast doubt on the proposed gender (or racial) generalizations. Chodorow (1978), for example, has frequently been criticized for implicitly elevating one pattern of difference between men and women, characteristic at most of a particular historical period and form of family organization, to the status of an essential "gender reality." Since the patterns described in gender analysis have often been based on the experiences of white, middle-class men and women, such accounts are guilty, feminists have frequently pointed out, of perpetuating the same sort of unconscious privilegings and exclusions characteristic of the male-normative theories they criticize.

As was the case when the first challenges were presented to the imperial unities of the phallocentric world view, the agents of critical insight into the biases of gender theory were those excluded and marginalized: women of color, lesbians, and others who found their history and culture ignored in the prevailing discussions of gender. What I wish to emphasize here is that these challenges, arising out of concrete experiences of exclusion, were neither grounded in a conception of adequate "theory" nor did they demand a theoretical response. Rather, as new narratives began to be produced, telling the story of the diversity of women's experiences, the chief imperative was to *listen,* to become aware of one's biases, prejudices, and ignorance, to begin to stretch the borders of what Minnie Bruce Pratt (1984) calls "the narrow circle of the self." For academics, this required, too, that we stretch the established borders of required curriculum, course reading lists, lecture series, research designs, student and faculty recruitment, and so forth.

We also *should* have learned that while it is imperative to struggle continually against racism and ethnocentrism in all its forms, it is impossible to be "politically correct." For the dynamics of inclusion and exclusion (as history had just taught us) are played out on multiple and shifting fronts, and all ideas (no matter how "liberatory" in some contexts or for some purposes) are condemned to be haunted by a voice from the margins, already speaking (or perhaps presently muted but awaiting the conditions for speech), awakening us to what has been excluded, effaced, damaged.[5] However, nothing in the indigenous feminist critique of early gender theory, it should be noted, declared the theoretical impossibility of discovering common ground among diverse groups of people or insisted that the abstraction of gender coherencies across cultural difference is *bound* to lapse into a pernicious universalization. It is only recently, as feminism has become drawn into what Barbara Christian (1988) has called the "race for theory," that problems of racism, ethnocentrism, and ahistoricism have become wedded to general methodological concerns about the legitimacy of gender generalization and abstraction.

Frequently (although not exclusively[6]), the categories of postmodern thinkers have been incorporated in statements of these concerns. Nancy Fraser and Linda Nicholson, for example, urge feminists to adopt a "postmodern-feminist theory" of identity, in which general claims about "male" and "female" reality are eschewed in favor of "complexly constructed conceptions . . . treating gender as one relevant strand among others, attending also to class, race, ethnicity, age, and sexual orientation" (p. 35). Conceptions of gender (and, presumably, of race, class, sexual orientation, and so forth) that are not constructed in this way are totalizing, that is, they crease a false unity out of heterogeneous elements, relegating the submerged elements to marginality. Much past feminist theory, Fraser and Nicholson argue, is guilty of this. Like the "grand narratives of legitimation" (of the white, male, Western intellectual tradition) which Lyotard and others have criticized, the narratives of gender analysis harbor, either fully (e.g., Chodorow) or in "trace" form (e.g., Gilligan), "an overly grandiose and totalizing conception of theory" (p. 29). Donna Haraway, too, describes gender theory in the same terms used by postmodernists to criticize phallocentric culture: appropriation, totalization, incorporation, suppression.

These proposals for more adequate approaches to identity begin from the invaluable insight that gender forms only one axis of a complex, heterogeneous construction, constantly interpenetrating, in historically specific ways, with multiple other axes of identity. I want to question, however, the conversion of this insight into *the* authoritative insight, and from there into a privileged critical framework, a "neutral matrix" (to borrow Rorty's term), legislating the appropriate terms of all intellectual efforts, capable of determining who is going astray and who is on the right track. This is a result that Fraser and Nicholson would also deplore, given their obvious commitment to feminist pluralism; their ideal is that of a "tapestry composed of threads of many different hues" (p. 35). Sharing this ideal, I question whether it is best served through a new postmodern-feminist theoretical agenda.

Certainly, feminist scholarship will benefit from more local, historically specific study and from theoretical projects analyzing the relations of diverse axes of identity. Too often, however (e.g., in grant, program, and conference guidelines and descriptions), this has translated to the coercive, mechanical requirement that *all* enlightened feminist projects attend to "the intersection of race, class, and gender." What happened to ethnicity? Age? Sexual orientation? On the other hand, just how many axes *can* one include and still preserve analytical focus or argument? Even more troubling is the (often implicit, sometimes explicit) dogma that the only "correct" perspective on race, class, and gender is the affirmation of difference; this dogma reveals itself in criticisms which attack gender generalizations as *in principle* essentialist or totalizing. Surely, such charges should require concrete examples of *actual* differences that are being submerged by any particular "totality" in question.

We also need to guard against the "view from nowhere" supposition that if we employ the right method we can avoid ethnocentrism, totalizing constructions, and false universalizations. No matter how local and circumscribed the object or how attentive the scholar is to the axes that constitute social identity, some of those axes will be ignored and others selected. This is an inescapable fact of human embodiment, as Nietzsche was the first to point out: "The eye . . . in which the active and interpreting forces, through which alone seeing becomes seeing *something,* are supposed to be lacking [is] an absurdity and a nonsense. There is *only* a perspectival seeing, *only* a perspectival knowing" *(On The Genealogy of Morals,* p. 119). This selectivity, moreover, is never innocent. We always "see" from points of view that are invested with our social, political, and personal interests, inescapably "centric" in one way or another, even in the desire to do justice to heterogeneity.

Nor does attentiveness to difference assure the adequate representation of difference. Certainly, we often err on the side of exclusion and thus submerge large areas of human history and experience. But attending *too* vigilantly to difference can just as problematically construct an Other who is an exotic alien, a breed apart. As Foucault has reminded us, "everything is dangerous"—and every new context demands that we reassess the "main danger" (1983, p. 232). This requires a "hyper- and pessimistic activism," not an alliance with one, true theory. For no theory—not even one which measures its adequacy in terms of justice to heterogeneity, locality, complexity—can place itself beyond danger.

Indeed, it is possible, as we all know, to advance the most vociferously anti-totalizing theories, and yet to do so in the context of an intellectual discourse and professional practice (governing hiring, tenure, promotion, publications, etc.) whose very language requires membership to understand, and that remains fundamentally closed to difference (regarding it as "politically incorrect," "theoretically unsophisticated," "unrigorous" and so forth). We deceive ourselves if we believe that postmodern theory is attending to the "problem of difference" so long as so many concrete others are excluded from the conversation. On the other hand, in the context of a practice which is attentive to issues of exclusion and committed to developing the conditions under which many voices can speak and be heard, clear, accessible, stimulating general hypotheses can be dialogically invaluable. Such ideas reconfigure the realities we take for granted; they allow us to examine our lives freshly; they bring history and culture to new life and invite our critical scrutiny. Showing a bold hand, they can encourage difference to reveal itself as well.

In terms of such practical criteria, feminist gender theory deserves a somewhat different historical evaluation than is currently being written.[7] Certainly, it is undeniable that such theory, as Fraser and Nicholson persuasively argue, has overly universalized. (Chodorow's work, for example, requires careful historical circumscription and contextualization; it then becomes enormously edifying for certain purposes). The reasons for this, as I suggested earlier, reflect the historical "logic" conditioning the emergence of contemporary feminist thought and are not *merely* symptomatic of the ethnocentrism of white, middle-class feminists. We all— postmodernists especially—stand on the shoulders of this work (and on the shoulders of those who spoke, often equally univocally, for black experience and culture). Could we now speak of the differences that inflect *gender* if gender had not first been shown to make a difference?

While in theory, all "totalizing" narratives may be equal, in the context of Western history and the actual relations of power characteristic of that history, key differences distinguish the universalizations of gender theory from the metanarratives arising out of the propertied, white, male, Western intellectual tradition. That tradition, we should remember, reigned for thousands of years and was able to produce powerful works of philosophy, literature, art, and religion before *its* hegemony began to be dismantled, under great protest. Located at the very center of power, at the intersection of three separate axes of privilege—race, class, and gender—that tradition had little stake in the recognition of difference (other than to construct it as inferior or threatening Other). This is not to say that this tradition is univocal. Rather, my point is that it produced no self-generated practice of self-interrogation and critique of its racial, class, and gender biases— because they were largely invisible to it.

Feminist theory—even the work of white, upper-class women—is not located at the *center* of cultural power. The axes whose intersections form the cultural locations of feminist authors give some of us positions of privilege, certainly; but *all* of us, as women, also occupy subordinate positions, positions in which we feel ignored or denigrated. Contemporary feminism, emerging out of that recognition, has from the beginning exhibited an interest in restoring to legitimacy that which has been marginalized and disdained, an interest, I would suggest, that has affected our intellectual practice significantly. As an "outsider" discourse, that is, a movement born out of the experience of marginality, contemporary feminism has been unusually attuned to issues of exclusion and invisibility. This does not mean, of course, that the work of feminists has not suffered deeply from class, racial, and other biases. But I find Donna Haraway's charge (p. 199) that "white feminists . . . were forced kicking and screaming to notice" those biases to be remarkable. It is a strange (perhaps postmodern) conception of intellectual and political responsiveness that views white feminism, now critically scrutinizing (and often utterly discrediting) its conceptions of "female" reality and morality and its "gendered" readings of culture *barely more than a decade after they began to be produced,* as "resistant" to recognizing its own fictions of unity.

In the context of our specific history, assessing where we are now, I believe that feminism stands less in danger of the "totalizing" tendencies of feminists than of an increasingly paralyzing anxiety over falling (from what grace?) into ethnocentrism or "essentialism". (The often-present implication that such a fall indicates deeply conservative and racist tendencies, of course, intensifies such anxiety). Do we want to delegitimate *a priori* the exploration of experiential continuity and structural common ground among women? Journals and conferences are now becoming dominated by endless debates about method, reflections on how feminist scholarship should proceed, where it has gone astray, and so forth. We need to consider the degree to which this serves, not the empowerment of diverse cultural voices and styles, but the academic hegemony (particularly in philosophy and literary studies) of detached, metatheoretical discourse.[8] If we wish to empower diverse voices, we would do better, I believe, to shift strategy from the methodological dictum that we foreswear talk of "male" and "female" realities (which, as I will argue later, can still be edifying and useful), to the messier, more slippery, practical struggle to create institutions and communities that will not permit *some* groups of people to make determinations about reality for *all*.

The View from Nowhere and the Dream of Everywhere

In theory, deconstructionist postmodernism stands against the ideal of disembodied knowledge and declares that ideal to be a mystification and an impossibility. There is no Archimedean viewpoint; rather, history and culture are texts, admitting an endless proliferation of readings, each of which is itself unstable. I have no dispute with this epistemological critique or with the metaphor of the world-as-text as a means of undermining various claims to authoritative, transcendant insight into the nature of reality. The question remains, however, how the human knower is to negotiate this infinitely perspectival, destabilized world. Deconstructionism answers with constant vigilant suspicion of all determinate readings of culture and a partner aesthetic of ceaseless textual play as an alternative ideal. Here is where deconstruction may slip into its own fantasy of escape from human locatedness—by supposing that the critic can become wholly protean by adopting endlessly shifting, seemingly inexhaustible vantage points, none of which are "owned" by either the critic or the author of a text under examination.

Deconstructionism has profoundly affected certain feminist approaches to gender as a grid for the reading of culture. Such readings, they argue, only reproduce the dualistic logic which has held the Western imagination in its grip. Instead, contemporary feminism should attempt, as Susan Suleiman (1986) describes it, "to get beyond, not only the number one—the number that determines unity of body or of self—but also to get beyond the number two, which determines difference, antagonism and exchange . . ." (p. 24). "One is too few," as Donna Haraway writes, "but two are too many." (p. 219). The "number one" clearly represents for Suleiman the fictions of unity, stability, and identity characteristic of the phallocentric world view. The "number two" represents the grid of gender, which feminists have used to expose the hierarchical, oppositional structure of that world view. "Beyond the number two" is no other number, but "endless complication" and a "dizzying accumulation of narratives." Suleiman here refers to Derrida's often-quoted interview with Christy Mac-Donald (1982), in which he speaks of "a 'dream' of the innumerable, . . . a desire to escape the combinatory . . . to invent incalculable choreographies" (p. 76).

Such images from Derrida have been used in a variety of ways by feminists. Drucilla Cornell and Adam Thurschwell (1987) present it as a utopian vision of human life no longer organized by gender duality and hierarchy. But Suleiman presents it as offering an *epistemological* or narrative ideal. As such, key contrasts with traditional (most particularly, Cartesian) images of knowing immediately are evident. Metaphors of dance and movement have replaced the ontologically fixing stare of the motionless spectator. The lust for finality is banished. The dream is of "incalculable choreographies," not the clear and distinct "mirrorings" of nature, seen from the heights of "nowhere." But, I would argue, the philosopher's fantasy of transcendence has not yet been abandoned. The historical specifics of the modernist, Cartesian version have simply been replaced with a new postmodern configuration of detachment, a new imagination of disembodiment: a dream of being *everywhere*.

My point can best be seen through examination of the role of the body—that is, the metaphor of the body—in these (seemingly contrasting) epistemologies of "nowhere" and "everywhere." For Cartesian epistemology, the body—conceptualized as the site of epistemological limitation, as that which fixes the knower in time and space and therefore situates and relativizes perception and thought—requires transcendence if one is to achieve the view from nowhere, God's eye-view. Once one has achieved that view (has become *object*-ive), one can see nature as *it* really is, undistorted by human perspective. For postmodern Suleiman, on the other hand, there is no escape from human perspective, from the process of human making and remaking of the world. The body, accordingly, is reconceived. No longer an obstacle to knowledge (for "knowledge" in the Cartesian sense is an impossibility, and the body is incapable of being

144 / Susan Bordo

"transcended" in pursuit of it), the body is seen instead as the vehicle of the human making and remaking of the world, constantly shifting location, capable of revealing endlessly new "points of view" on things.

Beneath the imagery of a *moving* (but still unified) body is the deeper postmodern imagery of a body whose *own* unity has been shattered by the choreography of multiplicity. For the "creative movement" (as Suleiman describes it) of human interpretation, of course, "invents" (and reinvents) the body itself. Donna Haraway imaginatively and evocatively describes this fragmented postmodern body through the image of the Cyborg, which becomes a metaphor for the "disassembled and reassembled, postmodern collective and personal self [which] feminists must code" (p. 205). The Cyborg is not only culturally "polyvocal"; she (?) "speaks in tongues" (p. 223). Looking at it via the imagery of archetypal typology rather than science fiction, the postmodern body is the body of the mythological "Trickster," the shape-shifter: "of indeterminate sex and changeable gender . . . who continually alters her/his body, creates and recreates a personality . . . [and] floats across time" from period to period, place to place. (Smith-Rosenberg, 1985, p. 291).

The appeal of such archetypes is undeniable. Set against the masculinist hubris of the Cartesian ideal of the magisterial, universal knower whose privileged epistemological position reveals reality as it is, the postmodern ideal of narrative "heteroglossia" (as Haraway calls it) appears to celebrate a "feminine" ability to identify with and enter into the perspectives of others, to accept change and fluidity as features of reality. At a time when the rigid demarcations of the clear and distinct Cartesian universe are crumbling, and the notion of the unified "subject" is no longer tenable, the Trickster and the Cyborg invite us to "take pleasure" (as Haraway puts it) in the "confusion of boundaries" (p. 191), in the fragmentation and fraying of the edges of the self that have already taken place.

However, the spirit of epistemological *jouissance* which is suggested by the images of Cyborg, Trickster, the metaphors of dance, and so forth, also obscures the located, limited, inescapably partial, and *always* personally invested nature of human "story making." This is not merely a theoretical point. Deconstructionist readings that enact this protean fantasy are continually "slip-slidin' away"; through paradox, inversion, self-subversion, facile and intricate textual dance, they often present themselves (maddeningly, to one who wants to enter into critical dialogue with them) as having it any way they want. They refuse to assume a shape for which they must take responsibility.

Recognition of this responsibility, on the other hand, forces one to take a more humble approach to the project of embracing heterogeneity. That project, taken as anything other than an ideal of social *process,* is self-deconstructing. The imagination of "justice" to heterogeneity, entertained as an epistemological (or narrative) goal, devours its own tail. For the appreciation of difference requires the acknowledgment of some *limit* to the dance, beyond which the dancer cannot go. If she were able to go there, there would *be* no difference, nothing which eludes. To deny the unity and stability of identity is one thing. The epistemological fantasy of *becoming* multiplicity—the dream of limitless multiple embodiments, allowing one to dance from place to place and self to self—is another. What sort of body is it that is free to change its shape and location at will, that can become anyone and travel everywhere? If the body is a metaphor for our locatedness in space and time and thus for the finitude of human perception and knowledge, then the postmodern body is no body at all.

The deconstructionist erasure of the body is not affected, as in the Cartesian version, through a trip to "nowhere," but in a resistance to the recognition that one is always *somewhere,* and limited. Here, it becomes clear that to overcome Cartesian hubris, it is not sufficient to replace metaphors of spectatorship with metaphors of dance; it is necessary to relinquish all fantasies of epistemological conquest, not only those that are soberly fixed on necessity and unity but also those that are intoxicated with possibility and plurality. Despite the explicit rejection of conceptions of knowledge that view the mind as a "mirror of nature," deconstruction-ism reveals a longing for adequate representations—unlike Cartesian con-ceptions, but no less ambitiously, of a relentlessly heterogeneous reality.[9]

The Retreat from Female Otherness

The preceding discussion of the body as epistemological metaphor for locatedness has focused on deconstructionism's *theoretical* deconstruction of locatedness. In the next two sections of this chapter, I want to shift gears and pursue the issue of locatedness—or rather, the denial of locat-edness—in more concrete directions.

It is striking to me that there often is a curious selectivity at work in contemporary feminist criticisms of gender-based theories of identity. The analytics of race and class—the two other giants of modernist social critique—do not seem to be undergoing the same deconstruction. Rather, it is my impression that feminists infrequently demand the same attentive-ness to difference, or the same sensitivity to issues of interpretation and textuality from the analytics of race and class that we do from the analytics of gender. When women of color construct "white feminists" as a unity, without attention to the class, ethnic, and religious differences that situate and divide us, white feminists tend to accept this (as I believe they should) as enabling crucial sorts of criticisms to be made. It is usually acknowledged, too, that the experience of being a person of color in a racist culture creates some similarities of position across class and gender.

At the very least, the various notions of identity that have come out of race consciousness are regarded as what Nietzsche would call "life-enhancing [i.e. edifying] fictions." Donna Haraway, for example, applauds the homogenizing unity "women of color" as "a cyborg identity, a potent subjectivity synthesized from fusions of outsider identities" (p. 216).

I have heard feminists insist, too, that race and class each have a "material base" that gender lacks. When the suggestion is made that perhaps such a material base exists for gender, in women's reproductive role, the wedges of cultural diversity and multiple interpretation suddenly are produced. Women have perceived childbearing, as Jean Grimshaw points out, "as both the source of their greatest joy and as the root of their worst suffering" (p. 73); she concludes that the differences in various social constructions of reproduction, the vast disparities in women's experiences of childbirth, and so forth preclude that the practices of reproduction can meaningfully be interrogated as a source of insight into the difference gender makes. Why, it must be asked, are we so ready to deconstruct what have historically been the most ubiquitous elements of the gender axis, while so willing to defer to the authority and integrity of race and class axes as fundamentally *grounding* ?[10]

In attempting to answer this question, I will no longer focus on postmodern theory, for the current of gender-scepticism which I am exploring here is not particularly characteristic of postmodern feminism. Rather, it flows through all theoretical schools of feminist thought, revealing itself in different ways. In place of my previous focus on postmodernism, I will organize my discussion instead around a heuristic distinction between two historical moments of feminist thought, representing two different perspectives on "female otherness."

A previous generation of feminist thought (whose projects, of course, many feminists continue today) set out to connect the work that women have historically done (typically regarded as belonging to the "material," practical arena, and thus of no epistemological or intellectual significance) with distinctive ways of experiencing and knowing the world. As such, the imagination of female alterity was a "life-enhancing" fusion, providing access to coherent visions of utopian change and cultural transformation. Within this moment, too, a developing feminist focus on the role of mothering in the construction of infant gender identity (and thus of culture) was central to the ongoing feminist deconstruction of the phallocentric world view. (Within that world view it is the father/theologian/philosopher who is the sole source of morality, logic, language).

The feminist recovery of female otherness from the margins of culture had both a "materialist" wing (Ruddick, Hartsock, Rich, and others) and a psychoanalytic wing (Dinnerstein, Chodorow, Kristeva, Cixous,

Irigaray), the latter attempting to reconstruct developmental theory with the pre-Oedipal mother rather than the phallic father at its center. I think it is instructive to note the difference in the way that feminists once described this work from the way it is often described now. In a 1982 *Diacritics* review of Dinnerstein, Rich, and Chodorow, Coppelia Kahn describes what these authors have in common:

> To begin with, they all regard gender less as a biological fact than as a social product, an institution learned through and perpetuated by culture. And they see this gender system not as a mutually beneficial and equitable division of roles, but as a perniciously symbiotic polarity which denies full humanity to both sexes while meshing—and helping to create—their neuroses. Second, they describe the father-absent, mother-involved nuclear family as creating the gender identities which perpetuate patriarchy and the denigration of women. . . . They question the assumption that the sexual division of labor, gender personality, and heterosexuality rest on a biological and instinctual base. . . . They present, in effect, a collective vision of how maternal power in the nursery defines gender so as to foster patriarchal power in the public world. (p. 33).

In a 1987 talk, Jean Grimshaw describes these same texts as depicting motherhood "as a state of regression" in which the relation between mother and child is "idealized" in its symbiotic nondifferentiation.[11] Chodorow's lack of historical specificity was not the issue here, but her portrayal, as Grimshaw saw it, of a suffocating reality as a cozy, blissful state and an implicit criticism of women who do not experience maternity in this way. Similarly, Toril Moi, in a talk devoted to reviving Freud's view of reason *against* the revisions of feminist object relations theory, describes that theory as involving "an idealization of pre-Oedipal mother-child relations," a "biologistic" view of development, and a "romanticization of the maternal."[12] Are Grimshaw and Moi discussing the same works as Kahn?

Of course, the answer is *no*. For the context has changed, and these texts are now being read by these critics from the perspective of a different concrete situation than that which existed when Kahn produced her reading of Chodorow, Dinnerstein, and Rich. My point is not that Kahn's reading was the "correct" one (for there is no timeless text against which to measure historical interpretations). Rather, I wish to encourage confrontation with the present context. It is the present context that has supplied the specters of "biologism," "romanticization," and "idealization." The dangers that we are responding to are not in the texts, but in our social reality and in ourselves.

In speaking of social reality, I am not *only* referring to the danger of feminist notions of male and female realities or perspectives entering into a conservative *Zeitgeist* where they will function as an ideological mooring for the reassertion of traditional gender roles. In a time of great backlash against changes in gender-power relations, that danger is certainly real enough. What I am primarily interested in here, however, are the changing meanings of female Otherness for women, as we attempt to survive, in historically unprecedented numbers, within our still largely masculinist public institutions.

Changes in the professional situation of academic feminists over the last ten years may be exemplary here. A decade ago, the exploration and revaluation of that which has been culturally constructed as "female" set the agenda for academic feminists of many disciplines, at a time when feminism was just entering the (white, male) academy and had not yet been integrated into it or professionalized by it. We were outsiders, of suspect politics (most of us had been "political" feminists before or during our professional training), and inappropriate sex (a *woman* philosopher?). Then, to be a feminist academic was to be constantly aware of one's Otherness; one could not forget that one was a woman even if one tried. The feminist imagination was fueled precisely by what it was never allowed to forget: The analysis of the historical construction of male power and female Otherness became our theoretical task.

Today, on the other hand, we have been "accepted." That is, it has been acknowledged (seemingly) that women can indeed "think like men," and those women who are able to adopt the prevailing standards of professional "balance," critical detachment, rigor, and the appropriate insider mentality have been rewarded for their efforts. Those who are unable or unwilling to do so (along with those men who are similarly unable or unwilling) continue to be denied acceptance, publications, tenure, promotions. At this juncture, women may discover that they have a new investment in combating notions that gender locates and limits.

In such a world any celebration of "female" ways of knowing or thinking may be felt by some to be a dangerous alliance professionally and perhaps a personal regression as well. For, within the masculinist institutions we have entered, relational, holistic, and nurturant attitudes continue to be marked as flabby, feminine, and soft. In this institutional context, as we are permitted "integration" into the public sphere, the category of female Otherness, which has spoken to many feminists of the possibility of institutional and cultural change, of radical transformation of the values, metaphysical assumptions, and social practices of our culture, may become something from which we wish to dissociate ourselves. We need instead to establish our leanness, our critical incisiveness, our proficiency at clear and distinct dissection.

I was startled, at a conference last year, by the raw hostility of a number of responses to a talk on "female virtue"; I have often been dismayed at the anger which (white, middle-class) feminists have exhibited toward the work of Gilligan and Chodorow. This sort of visceral reaction to theorists of gender difference (unlike the critiques discussed in the first section in this chapter) is not elicited by their ethnocentrism or ahistoricism; it is specifically directed against what is perceived as their romanticization of female values — empathy, mothering, and so forth. Such a harsh critical stance is protection, perhaps, against being tarred by the brush of female Otherness, of being contaminated by things "female." Of course, to romanticize *anything* is the last thing that any rigorous scholar would do. Here, disdain for female "sentimentality" intersects, with both the modern fashion for the cool and the cult of professionalism in our culture.

Gender-Scepticism and the Reproduction of Male Knowledge/Power

Generalizations about gender can obscure and exclude. Of course, this is true. I would suggest, however, that such determinations cannot be made by methodological fiat but must be decided from context to context. The same is true of the representation of heterogeneity and complexity. There are dangers in too wholesale a commitment to either dual *or* multiple grids.

Too relentless a focus on historical heterogeneity, for example, can obscure the transhistorical hierarchical patterns of white, male privilege that have informed the creation of the Western intellectual tradition.[13] More generally, the deconstruction of dual girds can obscure the dualistic, hierarchical nature of the actualities of power in Western culture. Contemporary feminism, like many social movements arising in the 1960s, developed out of the recognition that to live in our culture is not (despite powerful social mythology to the contrary) to participate equally in some free play of individual diversity. Rather, one always finds oneself located within structures of dominance and subordination—not least important of which have been those organized around gender. Certainly, the duality of male/female is a discursive formation, a social construction. So, too, is the racial duality of black/white. But as such, each of these dualities has had profound consequences for the construction of experience of those who live them.

The danger that I have spoken of above can be detected—between the lines, as it were — in the following excerpt from Jean Grimshaw's *Philosophy and Feminist Thought* (1986):

> The experience of gender, of being a man or a woman, inflects much
> if not all of people's lives. . . . But even if one is always a man or a
> woman, one is never *just* a man or a woman. One is young or old, sick

or healthy, married or unmarried, a parent or not a parent, employed or unemployed, middle class or working class, rich or poor, black or white, and so forth. Gender of course inflects one's experience of these things, so the experience of any one of them may well be radically different according to whether one is a man or a woman. But it may also be radically different according to whether one is, say, black or white or working class or middle class. The relationship between male and female experience is a very complex one. Thus there may in some respects be more similarities between the experience of a working-class woman and a working-class man—the experience of factory labor for example, or of poverty and unemployment—than between a working-class woman and a middle-class woman. But in other respects there may be greater similarities between the middle-class woman and the working-class woman—experiences of domestic labor and childcare, of the constraints and requirements that one be "attractive," or "feminine," for example.

Experience does not come neatly in segments, such that it is always possible to abstract what in one's experience is due to "being a woman" from that which is due to "being married," "being middle class" and so forth. (pp. 84–85)

Grimshaw emphasizes, absolutely on target, that gender never exhibits itself in pure form but in the context of lives that are shaped by a multiplicity of influences, which cannot be neatly sorted out. This doesn't mean, however, (as Grimshaw goes on to suggest) that abstractions or generalizations about gender are methodologically illicit or perniciously homogenizing of difference. Certainly, we will never find the kind of theoretical neatness which Grimshaw, nostalgic for a Cartesian universe of clear and distinct segments, requires of such abstraction. But, as anyone who has taught courses in gender knows, there are many junctures at which, for example, women of color and white women discover profound *commonalities* in their experience, as well as differences.[14] One can, of course, adjust one's methodological tools so that these commonalities become indiscernable under the finely meshed grid of various interpretations and inflections (or the numerous counterexamples which can always be produced). But what then becomes of social critique? Theoretical criteria such as Grimshaw's, which measure the adequacy of representations in terms of their "justice" to the "extremely variegated nature" of human experience (p. 102), must find nearly *all* social criticism guilty of methodologically illicit and distorting abstraction. Her inflection argument, although designed to display the fragmented nature of gender, in fact deconstructs race, class, and historical coherencies as well. For (although race, class, and gender are privileged by current intellectual convention), the inflections that modify experience are endless, and *some* item of difference can always be produced which will shatter any proposed generalizations. If generalization is only permitted in the *absence* of multiple inflections or interpretive possibilities, then cultural generalizations of *any* sort—about race, about class, about historical eras—are ruled out. What remains is a universe composed entirely of counterexamples, in which the way men and women see the world is purely as *particular* individuals, shaped by the unique configurations that form that particularity.[15]

It is no accident, I believe, that feminists are questioning the integrity of the notion of "female reality" just as we begin to get a foothold in those professions which could be most radically transformed by our (historically developed) Otherness and which have been historically most shielded from it. Foucault constantly reminds us that the routes of individual interest and desire do not always lead where imagined and may often sustain unintended and unwanted configurations of power. Could feminist gender-scepticism, in all its multifaceted "deployment" (to continue the Foucauldian motif), now be operating in the service of the reproduction of white, male knowledge/power?

If so, it will not be the result of conspiracy, but a "strategy," as Foucault would say, "without strategists," operating through numerous, noncentralized processes: through the pleasure of joining an intellectual community and the social and material rewards of membership; through the excitement of engagement in culturally powerful and dominant theoretical enterprises; through our own exhaustion with maintaining an agonistic stance at the institutions where we work; through intellectual boredom with stale, old talk about male dominance and female subordination; through our postmodern inclination to embrace the new and the novel; through the genuine insights that new theoretical perspectives offer; through our feminist commitments to the representation of difference; even (most ironically) through out "female" desire to heal wounds of exclusion and alienation.

More coercively, we may be required to abandon our "female" ways of knowing and doing through the demands of "professionalism" and its exacting, "neutral" standards of rigor and scholarship. The call to professionalism is especially powerful, almost irresistible for an academic. In the classical traditions of our culture, "the man of reason" provided the model of such "neutrality" (a neutrality that feminists have exposed as an illusion and a mystification of its masculinist biases.) Today, however, the category of the "professional" functions in much the same way; it may be the distinctively twentieth-century refurbishing of the view from nowhere.

It is striking—and chilling—to learn how many of the issues confronting professional women today were constructed in virtually the same terms in debates during the 1920s and 1930s, when the social results of the first feminist wave were being realized. Then as now, there was a strong backlash, particularly among professional women, against feminist talk about gender difference. "We're interested in people now—not men and women," declared a Greenwich Village female literary group, proclaiming itself (in 1919) as "post-feminist" (Cott, p. 282). The "New Woman" of the twenties, like her counterpart today, was glamorized for her diversity, equal to that of men: "The essential fact about the New Women is that they differ among themselves, as men do, in work and play, in virtue, in aspiration and in rewards achieved. They are women, not woman," wrote Leta Hollingworth (Cott, p. 277). "The broad unsexual world of activity lies before every human being," declared Miriam Ford (Cott, p. 281).

Professional women in particular shunned and scorned the earlier generation of activist women, who had made themselves a "foreign, irritating body" to prevailing institutions and who attempted to speak for an alternative set of empathic, relational "female" values (Cott, p. 231). Instead, women were urged to adopt the rationalist, objectivist standards they found in place in the universities and professions they entered, to aspire to "excellence" and "forgetfulness of self" rather than gender consciousness (Cott, p. 232), to develop a "community of interest between themselves and professional men [rather than] between themselves and non-professional women" (Cott, p. 237). Professional women saw in the "neutral" standards of objectivity and excellence the means of being accepted as "humans," not women. In any case, as Cott points out, to have mounted a strategy *against* those standards (to expose them as myths, to offer other visions) would have surely "marked them as outsiders" (p. 235).

In a culture that is *in fact* constructed by gender duality, however, one *cannot* simply be "human." This is no more possible than it is possible that we can "just be people" in a racist culture. (It is striking, too, that one hears this complaint from whites—"why can't we just be people; why does it always have to be 'black' this and 'white' that . . ."—only when *black* consciousness asserts itself.) Our language, intellectual history, and social forms are "gendered"; there is no escape from this fact and from its consequences on our lives. Some of those consequences may be unintended, may even be fiercely resisted; our deepest desire may be to "transcend gender dualities"; to not have our behavior categorized as "male" *or* "female." But, like it or not, in our present culture, our activities *are* coded as "male" or "female" and will function as such within the prevailing system of gender-power relations. The adoption of the "professional" standards of academia is no more an activity devoid of gender politics than the current fashion in women's tailored suits and large-shouldered jackets is devoid of gender meaning. One cannot be "gender neutral" in this culture.

One might think that postmodernism, which has historicized and criticized the liberal notion of the abstract "human," would be an ally here.

This is partially so. But the postmodern critique of liberal humanism is mitigated by its tendencies, discussed earlier, to insist on the "correct" destabilization of general categories of social identity: race, class, gender, and so forth. Practically—that is, in the context of the institutions which we are trying to transform—the most powerful strategies against liberal humanism have been those that demystify the "human" (and its claims to "neutral" perspective) *through* general categories of social identity, which give content and force to the notions of social interest, historical location, and cultural perspective. Now, we are being advised that the strongest analyses along such lines—for example, classic feminist explorations of the consequences of female-dominated infant care or of the "male" biases of our disciplines and professions—are to be rejected as resources for understanding history and culture. Most of our institutions have barely begun to absorb the message of modernist social criticism; surely, it is too soon to let them off the hook via postmodern heterogeneity and instability. This is not to say that the struggle for institutional transformation will be served by univocal, fixed conceptions of social identity and location. Rather, we need to reserve *practical* spaces for both generalist critique (suitable when gross points need to be made) and attention to complexity and nuance. We need to be pragmatic, not theoretically pure, if we are to struggle effectively with the inclination of institutions to preserve and defend themselves against deep change.

Of course, it is impossible to predict the cultural meanings that one's gestures will take on and the larger formations in which one will find one's activities participating. Nonetheless, history does offer some cautions. The 1920s and 1930s saw a fragmentation and dissipation of feminist consciousness and feminist activism, as women struggled with what Nancy Cott calls "the dilemma of twentieth-century feminism": the tension between the preservation of gender consciousness and identity (as a source of political unity and alternative vision) and the destruction of "gender prescriptions" (p. 239) which limit human choice and possibility. The "postfeminist" consciousness of the twenties and thirties, in *pursuit* of an ideal world undermined by gender dualities, cut itself adrift from the moorings of gender identity. This was culturally, historically understandable. But we thus, I believe, cut ourselves off from the source of feminism's transformative possibilities—possibilities that then had to be revived and reimagined again four decades later. The deconstruction of gender analytics, I fear, may be participating in a similar cultural moment of feminist fragmentation, coming around again.

Notes

1. This is not to say that I disdain the insights of poststructuralist thought (which I often apply in my own work). My argument here is addressed to

certain programmatic uses of those insights. Much poststructuralist thought (the work of Foucault in particular) is better understood, I would argue, as offering interpretive *tools* and *historical* critique rather than theoretical frameworks for wholesale adoption.

2. My discussion here is focused on the emergence of gender analytics in North America. The story, told in the context of France and England, would be different in many ways.

3. It must be noted, however, that Gilligan does *not* view the different "voices" she describes as essentially or only related to gender. She "discovers" them in her clinical work exploring gender difference, but the chief aim of her book, as she describes it, is to "highlight a distinction between two modes of thought" which have been culturally reproduced along (but not only along) genderlines (p. 2).

4. The literature here is large and growing all the time. For a representative bibliography, see *APA Newsletter on Feminism and Philosophy,* March 1989. For one of the earliest and best collections of articles dealing with the feminist critique of metaphysics and epistemology, see S. Harding and M. Hintikka.

5. Recently, I presented a paper discussing some consequences of the fact that the classical philosophical canon has been dominated by white, privileged males. But they have also, as was pointed out to me afterward by Bat-Ami Bar On, overwhelmingly been Christian. As a Jew myself, I had to think long and hard about what *that* exclusion of mine meant, and I was grateful to be enabled, by Ami's insight, to do so. This is, of course, the way we learn; it is not a process that should be freighted (as it often is nowadays) with the constant anxiety of "exposure" and political discreditation.

6. Jean Grimshaw (1986) is an example of a feminist who expresses these theoretical concerns via the categories and traditional formulations of problems of the Anglo-American analytic style of philosophizing, rather than those of continental poststructuralist thought.

7. The Fraser and Nicholson article, which exhibits a strong, historically informed appreciation of past feminist theory, is fairly balanced in its critique. In contrast, other recent travels through the same literature have sometimes taken the form of a sort of demolition derby of previous feminist thought—portrayed in reductive, ahistorical, caricatured, and downright distorted terms, and presented, from the enlightened perspective of advanced feminist method, as hopelessly inadequate.

8. See Barbara Christian, "The Race For Theory," (1988) for an extended discussion of such dynamics and the way in which they sustain the exclusion of the literatures and critical styles of peoples of color.

9. Haraway elides these implications by a constant and deliberate ambiguity about the nature of the body she is describing: It is both "personal" and "collective." Her call for "polyvocality" seems at times to be directed toward feminist culture as a collectivity, at other times, toward individual

feminists. The image she ends her piece with, of a "powerful infidel hetero-glossia" to replace the old feminist dream of a "common language," sounds like a cultural image — until we come to the next line, which equates this image with that of "a feminist speaking in tongues." I suggest that this ambiguity, although playful and deliberate, nonetheless reveals a tension between her imagination of the Cyborg as liberatory "political myth" and a lingering "epistemologism" which presents the Cyborg as a model of "correct" perspective on reality. I applaud the former and have problems with the latter.

10. In speaking of "the practice of reproduction," I have in mind not only pregnancy and birth, but menstruation, menopause, nursing, weaning, and spontaneous and induced abortion. I do not deny, of course, that all of these have been constructed and culturally valued in diverse ways. But does that diversity utterly invalidate any abstraction of significant points of general contrast between female and male bodily realities? The question, it seems to me, is to be approached through concrete exploration, not decided by theoretical fiat.

11. "On Separation from and Connection to Others: Women's Mothering and the Idea of a Female Ethic," Keynote Address, 10th Annual Conference of the Canadian Society for Women in Philosophy, University of Guelph, September 1987.

12. "Philosophy, Psychoanalysis and Feminism," University of North Carolina Women's Studies lecture series, Chapel Hill, October 1987.

13. In another paper ("Feminist Scepticism and the 'Maleness' of Philosophy"), I discuss these points in more detail.

14. In my experience as a teacher, these commonalities have come to light not only in discussion of the works of writers such as Ntozake Shange and Toni Morrison but also through exploration of the work of those feminist theorists most often accused of white, middle-class bias and gender essentialism, e.g., Nancy Chodorow and Carol Gilligan.

15. Lynne Arnault makes a similar point in "The Uncertain Future of Feminist Standpoint Epistemology" (unpublished paper).

References

Susan Bordo. "Feminist Scepticism and the 'Maleness' of Philosophy." *The Journal of Philosophy* 85(11)(1988): 619–626. (Please note: This printed version is an abstract of a longer talk, delivered at the Eastern Meetings of the American Philosophical Association, December 1988, the text of which is available upon request from the author.)

Barbara Christian. 1988. "The Race for Theory." *Feminist Studies* 14 (1): 67–69.

Nancy Cott. 1987. *The Grounding of Modern Feminism.* New Haven, CT: Yale University Press. 1987.

Nancy Chodorow. 1978. *The Reproduction of Mothering*. Berkeley, CA: University of California Press.

Drucilla Cornell and Adam Thurschwell. 1987. "Feminism, Negativity, Intersubjectivity." In *Feminism as Critique*, ed. Seyla Benhabib and Drucilla Cornell. Minneapolis: University of Minnesota Press, pp. 143–162.

Jacques Derrida and Christie V. McDonald. 1982. "Choreographies." *Diacritics* 12(2): 66–76.

Dorothy Dinnerstein. 1977. *The Mermaid and the Minotaur*. New York: Harper & Row.

Michel Foucault, "On the Geneology of Ethics," Interview with Foucault in Hubert Dreyfus and Paul Rabinow. 1983. *Michel Foucault: Beyond Structuralism and Hermeneutics*. Chicago: University of Chicago Press.

Nancy Fraser and Linda Nicholson. 1989. "Social Criticism without Philosophy: An Encounter between Feminism and Postmodernism." in this book.

Carol Gilligan. 1982. *In A Different Voice*. Cambridge, MA: Harvard University Press.

Jean Grimshaw. 1986. *Philosophy and Feminist Thinking*. Minneapolis: University of Minnesota Press.

Donna Haraway. 1989. "A Manifesto for Cyborgs: Science, Technology, and Socialist Feminism in the 1980s," in this book.

Sandra Harding and Merril Hintikka. 1983. *Discovering Reality: Feminist Perspectives on Epistemology, Metaphysics, Methodology, and Philosophy of Science*. Dordrecht: Reidel.

Coppelia Kahn. 1982. "Excavating 'Those Dim Minoan Regions': Maternal Subtexts in Patriarchal Culture," *Diacritics* 12(3): 32–41.

Thomas Nagel. 1986. *The View From Nowhere*. Oxford: Oxford University Press.

Friedrich Nietzsche. 1969. *On the Genealogy of Morals*. New York: Vintage.

Elly Bulkin, Minnie Bruce Pratt and Barbara Smith. 1984. *Yours in Struggle: Three Feminist Perspectives on Anti-Semitism and Racism*. Brooklyn, NY: Long Haul Press.

Richard Rorty. 1979. *Philosophy and the Mirror of Nature*. Princeton: Princeton University Press.

Carroll Smith-Rosenberg. 1985. *Disorderly Conduct*. Oxford: Oxford University Press.

Susan Suleiman. 1986. "(Re)Writing the Body: The Politics and Poetics of Female Eroticism." In *The Female Body in Western Culture*, ed. Susan Suleiman. Cambridge: Harvard University Press, pp. 7–29.

7

Foucault on Power:
A Theory for Women?

Nancy Hartsock

If we begin with a general question about the association of power and gender, the answer would seem to be self-evident: Power is associated firmly with the male and masculinity. Commentators on power have frequently remarked on its connections with virility and masculinity.[1] Yet, efforts to change the subordinate status of women require a consideration of the nature of power. In order to change the relations of domination which structure society and define our subordination, we must understand how power works, and thus we need a usable theory of power. Where is it to be found? How is it to be developed? Are relations of power between the sexes comparable to other kinds of power relations? Or are gender relations unique, and thus must we develop a new theory to account for them? Can theories of power currently being developed in the social sciences make fruitful contributions to the analysis of power relations between the sexes? If not, how could these theories be adapted in such a way that gender relations could be adequately conceptualized?

I believe that while gender relations require specific description, much of what has been written about the relations of domination obtaining between other groups is relevant to the situation of women. One could find much common ground among theories of power which emerge from and respond to experiences of domination and subjugation. I am much less sanguine, however, about the utility of theories of power currently being developed in the social sciences. Not only do I find them not useful or fruitful for women or other oppressed groups, but I also fail to see how

This chapter is a revised version of a paper presented at a conference titled "The Gender of Power," at University of Leiden, September 1987, and published as a part of the conference proceedings. *The Gender of Power*, ed. Monique Lejnaar, Kathy Davis, Claudine Helleman, Jantine Oldersmaa, Dini Vos (Leiden: University of Leiden, 1987).

they might be reconceptualized or otherwise adapted to our needs. I have examined a number of these theories elsewhere, including the structuralist alternative proposed by Lévi-Strauss, and found them wanting.[2] Here, I want to argue that poststructuralist theories such as those put forward by Michel Foucault fail to provide a theory of power for women.

We must note at the outset that power is a peculiar concept, one that must be characterized as "essentially contested." That is, different theories of power rest on different assumptions about both the content of existence and the ways we come to know it. That is, different theories of power rest on differing ontologies and epistemologies, and a feminist rethinking of power requires attention to its epistemological grounding.[3]

I have argued elsewhere that epistemologies grow out of differing material circumstances. We must, then, distinguish between theories of power about women—theories which may include the subjugation of women as yet another variable to be considered, and theories of power for women—theories which begin from the experience and point of view of the dominated. Such theories would give attention not only to the ways women are dominated, but also to their capacities, abilities, and strengths. In particular, such theories would use these capacities as guides for a potential transformation of power relationships—that is, for the empower- ment of women. I should add as a qualification that I refer to the empower- ment of women as a group, not simply a few women "making it." One might make similar cases for other marginalized groups.

But to mention the power of women leads immediately to the problem of what is meant by "women." The problem of differences among women has been very prominent in the United States in recent years. We face the task of developing our understanding of difference as part of the theoretical task of developing a theory of power for women. Issues of difference reminds us as well that many of the factors which divide women also unite some women with men—factors such as racial or cultural differences. Perhaps theories of power for women will also be theories of power for other groups as well. We need to develop our understanding of difference by creating a situation in which hitherto marginalized groups can name themselves, speak for themselves, and participate in defining the terms of interaction, a situation in which we can construct an understanding of the world that is sensitive to difference.

What might such a theory look like? Can we develop a general theory, or should we abandon the search for such a theory in favor of making space for a number of heterogeneous voices to be heard? What kinds of common claims can be made about the situations of women and men of color? About those of white women and women and men of color? About the situations of Western peoples and those they have colonized? For example, is it ever legitimate to say "women" without qualification? These kinds of questions make it apparent that the situation we face involves not only substantive claims about the world, but also raises questions about how we come to know the world, about what we can claim for our theories and ultimately about who "we" are. I want to ask what kinds of knowledge claims are required for grounding political action by different groups. Should theories produced by "minorities" rest on different epistemologies than those of the "majority?" Given the fact that the search for theory has been called into question in majority discourse and has been denounced as totalizing, do we want to ask similar questions of minority proposals or set similar standards?

In our efforts to find ways to include the voices of marginalized groups, one might expect helpful guidance from those who have argued against totalizing and universalistic theories such as those of the Enlightenment. Many radical intellectuals have been attracted to a compilation of diverse writings ranging from literary criticism to the social sciences, generally termed postmodern. The writers, among them figures such as Foucault, Derrida, Rorty, and Lyotard, argue against the faith in a universal reason we have inherited from Enlightenment European philosophy. They reject stories that claim to encompass all of human history: As Lyotard puts it, "let us wage war on totality."[4] In its place they propose a social criticism that is *ad hoc,* contextual, plural, and limited. A number of feminist theorists have joined in the criticism of modernity put forward by these writers. They have endorsed their claims about what can and cannot be known or said or read into/from texts.

Despite their apparent congruence with the project I am proposing, I will argue these theories would hinder rather than help its accomplishment. Despite their own desire to avoid universal claims and despite their stated opposition to these claims, some universalistic assumptions creep back into their work. Thus, postmodernism, despite its stated efforts to avoid the problems of European modernism of the eighteenth and nineteenth centuries, at best manages to criticize these theories without putting anything in their place. For those of us who want to understand the world systematically in order to change it, postmodern theories at their best give little guidance. (I should note that I recognize that some postmodernist theorists are committed to ending injustice. But this commitment is not carried through in their theories.) Those of us who are not part of the ruling race, class, or gender, not a part of the minority which controls our world, need to know how it works. Why are we—in all our variousness—systematically excluded and marginalized?[5] What systematic changes would be required to create a more just society? At worst, postmodernist theories can recapitulate the effects of Enlightenment theories which deny the right to participate in defining the terms of interaction. Thus, I contend, in broad terms, that postmodernism represents a dangerous approach for any marginalized group to adopt.

The Construction of the Colonized Other

In thinking about how to think about these issues, I found that the work of Albert Memmi in *The Colonizer and the Colonized* was very useful as a metaphor for understanding both our situation with regard to postmodernist theorists and the situation of some postmodernist theorists themselves: Those of us who have been marginalized enter the discussion from a position analogous to that which the colonized holds in relation to the colonizer. Most fundamentally, I want to argue that the philosophical and historical creation of a devalued "Other" was the necessary precondition for the creation of the transcendental rational subject outside of time and space, the subject who is the speaker in Enlightenment philosophy. Simone de Beauvoir has described the essence of the process in a quite different context: "Evil is necessary to Good, Matter to Idea, and Darkness to Light."[6] While this subject is clearest in the work of bourgeois philosophers such as Kant, one can find echoes of this mode of thought in some of Marx's claims about the proletariat as the universal subject of history.

Memmi described the bond that creates both the colonizer and the colonized as one which destroys both parties, although in different ways. As he draws a portrait of the Other as described by the colonizer, the colonized emerges as the image of everything the colonizer is not. Every negative quality is projected onto her/him. The colonized is said to be lazy, and the colonizer becomes practically lyrical about it. Moreover, the colonized is both wicked and backward, a being who is in some important ways not fully human.[7] As he describes the image of the colonized, feminist readers of de Beauvoir's *Second Sex* cannot avoid a sense of familiarity. We recognize a great deal of this description.[8]

Memmi points to several conclusions drawn about this artificially created Other. First, the Other is always seen as "Not," as a lack, a void, as lacking in the valued qualities of the society, whatever those qualities may be.[9] Second, the humanity of the Other becomes "opaque." Colonizers can frequently be heard making statements such as "you never know what they think. Do they think? Or do they instead operate according to intuition?" (Feminist readers may be reminded of some of the arguments about whether women had souls, or whether they were capable of reason or of learning Latin.) Memmi remarks ironically that the colonized must indeed be very strange, if he remains so mysterious and opaque after years of living with the colonizer. Third, the Others are not seen as fellow individual members of the human community, but rather as part of a chaotic, disorganized, and anonymous collectivity. They carry, Memmi states, "the mark of the plural."[10] In more colloquial terms, they all look alike.

I want to stress once again that I am not claiming that women are a unitary group or that Western white women have the same experiences as women or men of color or as colonized peoples. Rather, I am pointing to a way of looking at the world characteristic of the dominant white, male, Eurocentric ruling class, a way of dividing up the world that puts an omnipotent subject at the center and constructs marginal Others as sets of negative qualities.

What is left of the Other after this effort to dehumanize her or him? She/he is pushed toward becoming an object. As an end, in the colonizer's supreme ambition, she/he should exist only as a function of the needs of the colonizer, that is, be transformed into a pure colonized. An object for himself or herself as well as for the colonizer.[11] The colonized ceases to be a subject of history and becomes only what the colonizer is not. After having shut the colonized out of history and having forbidden him all development, the colonizer asserts his fundamental immobility.[12] Confronted with this image as it is imposed by every institution and in every human contact, the colonized cannot be indifferent to this picture. Its accusations worry the colonized even more because she/he admires and fears the powerful colonizing accuser.

We can expand our understanding of the way this process works by looking briefly at Edward Said's account of the European construction of the Orient. He makes the political dimensions of this ideological move very clear: Said describes the creation of the Orient as an outgrowth of a will to power. "Orientalism," he states, "is a Western style for dominating, restructuring, and having authority over the Orient."[13]

Interestingly enough, in the construction of these power relations, the Orient is often feminized. There is, however, the creation—out of this same process of the opposite of the colonized, the opposite of the Oriental, the opposite of women—of a being who sees himself as located at the center and possessed of all the qualities valued in his society (I use the masculine pronoun here purposely). Memmi describes this process eloquently:

> . . . the colonialist stresses those things that keep him separate rather than emphasizing that which might contribute to the foundation of a joint community. In those differences, the colonized is always degraded and the colonialist finds justification for rejecting his subjectivity. But perhaps the most important thing is that once the behavioral feature or historical or geographical factor which characterizes the colonialist and contrasts him with the colonized has been isolated, this gap must be

> kept from being filled. The colonialist removes the factor from history, time and therefore possible evolution. What is actually a sociological point becomes labeled as being biological, or preferably, metaphysical. It is attached to the colonized's basic nature. Immediately the colonial relationship between colonized and colonizer, founded on the essential outlook of the two protagonists, becomes a definitive category. It is what it is because they are what they are, and neither one nor the other will ever change.[10]

Said points to something very similar. He argues that "European culture gained in strength and identity by setting itself off against the Orient as a sort of surrogate and even underground self."[15] Orientalism is part of the European identity that defines "us" versus the nonEuropeans. To go further, the studied object becomes another being with regard to whom the studying subject becomes transcendent. Why? Because, unlike the Oriental, the European observer is a true human being.[16]

But what does all this have to do with theory and the search for a theory of power for women? I want to suggest that in each of these cases—and the examples could be multiplied—what we see is the construction of the social relations, the power relations, which form the basis of the transcendent subject of Enlightenment theories—he (and I mean *he*) who theorizes. Put slightly differently, the political and social as well as ideological/intellectual creation of the devalued Other was at the same time the creation of the universalizing and totalizing voice postmodernists denounce as the voice of theory.

These social relations and the totalizing voice they constitute are memorialized as well in the rules of formal logic. As Nancy Jay points out, the rules of logic we have chosen to inherit must be seen as principles of order. She calls attention to the principle of identity (if anything is A it is A), the principle of contradiction (nothing can be both A and not-A), and the principle of the excluded middle (anything and everything must be either A or not-A). She notes: "These principles are not representative of the empirical world; they are principles of order. In the empirical world, almost everything is in a process of transition: growing, decaying, ice turning to water and vice versa."[17]

These logical principles of order underlie the pattern of thought I have been describing, a pattern which divides the world into A and not-A. The not-A side is regularly associated with disorder, irrationality, chance, error, impurity. Not-A is necessarily impure, a random catchall kind of category. The clue, Jay notes, is the presence of only one positive term. Thus, men/women/children is one form of categorizing the world, while men/women-and-children is quite different in implication.[18] Radical dichotomy, then, functions to maintain order. The questions posed eloquently in the literature I have been examining are these: In whose interest is it to preserve dichotomies? Who experiences change as disorder?[19] The central point I want to make is that the creation of the Other is simultaneously the creation of the transcendent and omnipotent theorizer who can persuade himself that he exists outside time and space and power relations.

The social relations which express and form a material base for these theoretical notions have been rejected on a world scale over the last several decades. Decolonization struggles, movements of young people, women's movements, racial liberation movements—all these represent the diverse and disorderly Others beginning to demand to be heard and beginning to chip away at the social and political power of the theorizer. These movements have two fundamental intellectual theoretical tasks—one of critique and the other of construction. We who have not been allowed to be subjects of history, who have not been allowed to make our history, are beginning to reclaim our pasts and remake our futures on our own terms.

One of our first tasks is the construction of the subjectivities of the Others, subjectivities which will be both multiple and specific. Nationalism and separatism are important features of this phase of construction. Bernice Reagon (civil rights movement activist, feminist, singer with the band Sweet Honey in the Rock, and social historian with the Smithsonian) describes the process and its problems eloquently:

> [Sometimes] it gets too hard to stay out in that society all the time. And that's when you find a place, and you try to bar the door and check all the people who come in. You come together to see what you can do about shouldering up all of your energies so that you and your kind can survive . . . [T]hat space should be a nurturing space where you sift out what people are saying about you and decide who you really are. And you take the time to try to construct within yourself and within your community who you would be if you were running society . . . [This is] nurturing, but it is also nationalism. At a certain stage, nationalism is crucial to a people if you are ever going to impact as a group in your own interest.[2]

Somehow it seems highly suspicious that it is at the precise moment when so many groups have been engaged in "nationalisms" which involve redefinitions of the marginalized Others that suspicions emerge about the nature of the "subject," about the possibilities for a general theory which can describe the world, about historical "progress." Why is it that just at the moment when so many of us who have been silenced begin to demand the right to name ourselves, to act as subjects rather than objects of history, that just then the concept of subjecthood becomes problematic? Just when we are forming our own theories about the world, uncertainty emerges about whether the world can be theorized. Just when we are talking about the changes we want, ideas of progress and the possibility of systematically and rationally organizing human society become dubious and suspect. Why is it only now that critiques are made of the will to power inherent in the effort to create theory? I contend that these intellectual moves are no accident (but no conspiracy either). They represent the transcendental voice of the Enlightenment attempting to come to grips with the social and historical changes of the middle-to-late twentieth century.

However, the particular forms its efforts have taken indicate a failure of imagination and reflect the fact that dominant modes of thought are imprisoned within Enlightenment paradigms and values. But these are simply questions. Let us look more closely at one effort to describe the tasks we are told to engage in if we adopt the postmodernist project.

Foucault's Resistance and Refusal

Foucault represents one of the several figures in Memmi's landscape. I have so far spoken only of the colonizer and the colonized, and these are indeed the basic structural positions. But Memmi makes an important distinction between the colonizer who accepts and the colonizer who refuses. If, as a group, modernist theories represent the views of the colonizer who accepts, postmodernist ideas can be divided between those who, like Richard Rorty, ignore the power relations involved, and those, like Foucault, who resist these relations. Foucault, I would argue, represents Memmi's colonizer who refuses and thus exists in a painful ambiguity. He is, therefore, a figure who also fails to provide an epistemology which is usable for the task of revolutionalizing, creating, and constructing.[21]

Memmi states that as a Jewish Tunisian he knew the colonizer as well as the colonized, and so "understood only too well (the difficulty of the colonizer who refuses) their inevitable ambiguity and the resulting isolation; more serious still, their inability to act."[22] He notes that it is difficult to escape from a concrete situation and to refuse its ideology while continuing to live in the midst of the concrete relations of a culture. The colonizer who attempts it is a traitor, but he is still not the colonized.[23] The political ineffectiveness of the Left Colonizer comes from the nature of his position in the colony. Has one, Memmi asks, ever seen a serious political demand which did not rest on concrete supports of people or money or force? The colonizer who refuses to become a part of his group fellow citizens faces the difficult political question of who might he be.[24]

This lack of certainty and power infuses Foucault's work most profoundly in his methodological texts. He is clearly rejecting any form of totalizing discourse: Reason, he argues, must be seen as born from chaos, truth as simply an error hardened into unalterable form in the long process of history. He argues for a glance that disperses and shatters the unity of man's being through which he sought to extend his sovereignty.[25] That is, Foucault appears to endorse a rejection of modernity. Moreover, he has engaged in social activism around prisons. His sympathies are obviously with those over whom power is exercised, and he suggests that many struggles can be seen as linked to the revolutionary working-class movement.

In addition, his empirical critiques in works such as *Discipline and Punish* powerfully unmask coercive power. Yet, they do so on the one hand by making use of the values of humanism that he claims to be rejecting: That is, as Nancy Fraser points out, the project gets its political force from "the reader's familiarity with and commitment to modern ideals of autonomy, dignity, and human rights.[26] Moreover, Foucault explicitly attempts to limit the power of his critique by arguing that unmasking power can have only destabilizing rather than transformative effects.[27] But the sense of powerlessness and the isolation of the colonial intellectual resurfaces again and again. Thus, Foucault argues that:

> Humanity does not gradually progress from combat to combat until it arrives at universal reciprocity, where the rule of law finally replaces warfare; humanity installs each of its violences in a system of rules and thus proceeds from domination to domination.[28]

Moreover, Foucault sees intellectuals as working only alongside rather than as those who struggle for power, working locally and regionally. Finally, in opposition to modernity, he calls for a history that is parodic, dissociative, and satirical. These must be seen as positive steps. Foucault is attempting to oppose the establishment of the relations of the colonizer to the colonized. But what is the positive result?

Foucault is a complex thinker whose situation as a colonizer who resists imposes even more complexity and ambiguity on his ideas. I do not pretend to present a comprehensive account of his work here, but rather to make just two arguments. First, despite his obvious sympathy for those who are subjugated in various ways, he writes from the perspective of the dominator, "the self-proclaimed majority." Second and related, perhaps in part because power relations are less visible to those who are in a position to dominate others, systematically unequal relations of power ultimately vanish from Foucault's account of power—a strange and ironic charge to make against someone who is attempting to illuminate power relations.

Before I make these arguments I should insert some qualifications. It should be noted that Foucault himself may recognize that he is in the position of the colonizer who resists. He recognizes that the last ten to fifteen years have changed some features of the intellectual landscape. He notes that the most recent period has been characterized by a variety of dispersed and discontinuous offensives and an "insurrection of subjugated knowledges."[29] He adds that what has emerged is a sense of

> . . . the increasing vulnerability to criticism of things, institutions, practices, discourses. A certain fragility has been discovered in the very bedrock of existence . . . even . . . [those] aspects of it that are most familiar, most solid, and most intimately related to our bodies and to our everyday behavior.[3]

At another point in the essay cited, he refers to contemporary intellectuals as "fragile inheritors." Thus, one might argue that Foucault himself recognizes the effects of decolonization and the revolt of many dominated groups. All this can only make my argument, that he does not offer a theory of power adequate to the analysis of gender, more difficult to support.

I will go even further and note that Foucault makes a number of important contributions to our understanding of contemporary social relations. One can cite his accounts of the development of the confession as a means of producing power by requiring those who are to be dominated to take the initiative. One can note as well his substitution of domination/subjugation for the traditional problem of sovereignty/obedience. In addition, his development of the concept of disciplinary power, a power which possesses, in a sense, the same possibilities for expansion as capital itself, marks a major advance. One might continue to enumerate his contributions, but I will leave that to his disciples. Instead, what I want to argue here is that Foucault reproduces in his work the situation of the colonizer who resists [and in so doing renders his work inadequate and even irrelevant to the needs of the colonized or the dominated]. So, let me return to the two central points I want to make.

Foucault's Perspective

In sum, reading Foucault persuades me that Foucault's world is not my world but is instead a world in which I feel profoundly alien. Indeed, when he argues that this is our world, I am reminded of a joke told about two U.S. comic book figures—the Lone Ranger and Tonto, "his faithful Indian companion" (and subordinate). As the story goes, the two are chased and then surrounded by hostile Indians. As he comes to recognize their danger, the Long Ranger turns to Tonto and asks, "What do we do now?" To which Tonto replies, "What do you mean, 'we,' white boy?"

Foucault's is a world in which things move, rather than people, a world in which subjects become obliterated or, rather, recreated as passive objects, a world in which passivity or refusal represent the only possible choices. Thus, Foucault writes, the confession "detached itself" from religion and "emigrated" toward pedagogy,[31] or he notes that "hypotheses offer themselves."[32] Moreover, he argues that subjects not only cease to be sovereign but also that external forces such as power are given access even to the body and thus are the forces which constitute the subject as a kind of effect.[33]

One commentator has argued that one's concept of power is importantly shaped by the reason why one wishes to think about power in the first place. He goes on to set several possibilities. First, you might imagine what you could do if you had power. Second, you might speculate about what you would imagine if you had power. Third, you might want to assess what power you would need to initiate a new order. Or, fourth, you might want to postulate a range of things outside any form of power we presently understand. Foucault, he argues correctly, is attracted by the first two. Thus, Foucault's imagination of power is "with" rather than "against" power.[34] Said gives no "textual" evidence to support his assertions. But I believe there are a number of indications that Foucault is "with power," that is, understands the world from the perspective of the ruling group. First, from the perspective of the ruling group, other "knowledges" would appear to be illegitimate or "not allowed to function within official knowledge," as Foucault himself says of workers' knowledge.[35] They would appear to be, as Foucault has variously categorized them, "insurrectionary," "disordered," "fragmentary," lacking "autonomous life."[36] To simply characterize the variety of "counter-discourses" or "antisciences" as nonsystematic negates the fact that they rest on organized and indeed material bases.[37] Second, and related, Foucault calls only for resistance and exposure of the system of power relations. Moreover, he is often vague about what exactly this means. Thus, he argues only that one should "entertain the claims" of subjugated knowledges or bring them "into play."[38] Specifically, he argues that the task for intellectuals is less to become part of movements for fundamental change and more to struggle against the forms of power that can transform these movements into instruments of domination.

Perhaps this stress on resistance rather than transformation is due to Foucault's profound pessimism. Power appears to him as ever expanding and invading. It may even attempt to "annex" the counter-discourses that have developed.[39] The dangers of going beyond resistance to power are nowhere more clearly stated than in Foucault's response to one interviewer who asked what might replace the present system. He responded that to even imagine another system is to extend our participation in the present system. Even more sinister, he added that perhaps this is what happened in the Soviet Union, thus suggesting that Stalinism might be the most likely outcome of efforts at social transformation.[40] Foucault's insistence on simply resisting power is carried even further in his arguments that one must avoid claims to scientific knowledge. In particular, one should not claim Marxism as a science because to do so would invest it with the harmful effects of the power of science in modern culture.[41] Foucault then, despite his stated aims of producing an account of power which will enable and facilitate resistance and opposition, instead adopts the position of what he has termed official knowledge with regard to the knowledge of the dominated and reinforces the relations of domination in our society by insisting that those of us who have been marginalized remain at the margins.

The Evanescence of Power

Despite Foucault's efforts to develop an account of power, and precisely because of his perspective as the colonizer who resists, systematic power relations ultimately vanish in his work. This may be related to my first point: Domination, viewed from above, is more likely to appear as equality. Foucault has a great deal to say about what exactly he means by power. Power

> must be understood in the first instance as the multiplicity of force relations immanent in the sphere in which they operate and which constitute their own organization; as the process which, through cease-less struggles and confrontations, transforms, strengthens, or reverses them; or on the contrary, the disjunctions and contradictions which isolate them from one another; and lastly, as the strategies in which they effect.[42]

(A very complicated definition.) He goes on to argue that power is "perma-nent, repetitious, and self reproducing. It is not a thing acquired but rather exists in its exercise. Moreover, power relations are not separate from other relations but are contained within them." At the same time (and perhaps contradictorily) power relations are both intentional and subjec-tive, although Foucault is careful to point out that there is no headquarters which sets the direction.[43] His account of power is perhaps unique in that he argues that wherever there is power, there is resistance.

Much of what Foucault has to say about power stresses the systemic nature of power and its presence in multiple social relations. At the same time, however, his stress on heterogeneity and the specificity of each situation leads him to lose track of social structures and instead to focus on how individuals experience and exercise power. Individuals, he argues, circulate among the threads of power. They "are always in the position of simultaneously undergoing and exercising this power."[44] Individuals are to be seen not as an atom which power strikes, but rather the fact that certain bodies and discourses are constituted as individuals is an effect of power. Thus, power must not be seen as either a single individual dominating others or as one group or class dominating others.[45]

With this move Foucault has made it very difficult to locate domination, including domination in gender relations. He has on the one hand claimed that individuals are constituted by power relations, but he has argued against their constitution by relations such as the domination of one group by another. That is, his account makes room only for abstract individuals, not women, men, or workers.

Foucault takes yet another step toward making power disappear when he proposes the image of a net as a way to understand power. For example, he argues that the nineteenth-century family should be understood as a "network of pleasures and powers linked together at multiple points," a formulation which fails to take account of the important power differentials within the family.[46] The image of the net ironically allows (even facilitates) his ignoring of power relations while claiming to elucidate them. Thus, he argues that power is exercised generally through a "net-like organization" and that individuals "circulate between its threads."[47] Domination is not a part of this image; rather, the image of a network in which we all participate carries implications of equality and agency rather than the systematic domination of the many by the few. Moreover, at times Foucault seems to suggest that not only are we equals but that those of us at the bottom are in some sense responsible for our situations: Power, he argues, comes from below. There is no binary opposition between rulers and ruled, but rather manifold relations of force that take shape in the machinery of production, or families, and so forth, and then become the basis for "wide ranging effects of cleavage that run through the social body as a whole."[48] Certainly in the analysis of power, Foucault argues that rather than begin from the center or the top—the sovereignty— one should conduct an ascending analysis of power, starting from the "infinitesimal mechanisms" which each have their own history. One can then see how these have been colonized and transformed into more global forms of domination. It is certainly true that dominated groups participate in their own domination. But rather than stop with the fact of participation, we would learn a great deal more by focusing on the means by which this participation is exacted. Foucault's argument for an "ascending analysis" of power could lead us to engage in a version of blaming the victim.

Finally, Foucault asserts that power must be understood as "capillary," that it must be analyzed at its extremities.[49] He gives the example of locating power not in sovereignty but in local material institutions, such as torture and imprisonment. But the image of capillary power is one which points to the conclusion that power is everywhere. After all, in physical terms, where do we not have capillaries? Indeed, Foucault frequently uses language which argues that power "pervades the entire social body," or is "omnipresent."[50] Thus, all of social life comes to be a network of power relations—relations which should be analyzed not at the level of large-scale social structures but rather at very local, individual levels. Moreover, Foucault notes important resemblances between such diverse things as schools and prisons, or the development of sexuality in the family and the institutions of "perversion." The whole thing comes to look very homogeneous. Power is everywhere, and so ultimately nowhere.

In the end, Foucault appears to endorse a one-sided wholesale rejection of modernity and to do so without a conception of what is to replace it. Indeed, some have argued persuasively that because Foucault refuses both the ground of foundationalism and the "ungrounded hope" endorsed by liberals such as Rorty, he stands on no ground at all and thus fails to give any reasons for resistance. Foucault suggests that if our resistance succeeded, we would simply be changing one discursive identity for another and in the process create new oppressions.[51]

The "majority" and those like Foucault who adopt the perspective of the "majority" or the powerful can probably perform the greatest possible political service by resisting and by refusing the overconfidence of the past. But the message we get from them is either that we should abandon the project of modernity and substitute a conversation (as Richard Rorty suggests) or that we should simply take up a posture of resistance as the only strategy open to us. But if we are not to abandon the project of creating a new and more just society, neither of these options will work for us.

Toward Theories for Women

Those of us who have been marginalized by the transcendental voice of universalizing theory need to do something other than ignore power relations as Rorty does or resist them as figures such as Foucault and Lyotard suggest. We need to transform them, and to do so, we need a revised and reconstructed theory (indebted to Marx among others) with several important features.

First, rather than getting rid of subjectivity or notions of the subject, as Foucault does and substituting his notion of the individual as an effect of power relations, we need to engage in the historical, political, and theoretical process of constituting ourselves as subjects as well as objects of history. We need to recognize that we can be the makers of history as well as the objects of those who have made history. Our nonbeing was the condition of being of the One, the center, the taken-for-granted ability of one small segment of the population to speak for all; our various efforts to constitute ourselves as subjects (through struggles for colonial independence, racial and sexual liberation struggles, and so on) were fundamental to creating the preconditions for the current questioning of universalist claims. But, I believe, we need to sort out who we really are. Put differently, we need to dissolve the false "we" I have been using into its real multiplicity and variety and out of this concrete multiplicity build an account of the world as seen from the margins, an account which can expose the falseness of the view from the top and can transform the margins as well as the center. The point is to develop an account of the world which treats our perspectives not as subjugated or disruptive knowledges, but as primary and constitutive of a different world.

It may be objected that I am calling for the construction of another totalizing and falsely universal discourse. But that is to be imprisoned by the alternatives imposed by Enlightenment thought and postmodernism: Either one must adopt the perspective of the transcendental and disembodied voice of "reason" or one must abandon the goal of accurate and systematic knowledge of the world. Other possibilities exist and must be (perhaps can only be) developed by hitherto marginalized voices. Moreover, our history of marginalization will work against creating a totalizing discourse. This is not to argue that oppression creates "better" people: On the contrary, the experience of domination and marginalization leaves many scars. Rather, it is to note that marginalized groups are far less likely to mistake themselves for the universal "man." We are well aware that we are not the universal man who can assume his experience of the world is the experience of all. But even if we will not make the mistake of assuming our experience of the world is the experience of all, we still need to name and describe our diverse experiences. What are our commonalities? What are our differences? How can we transform our imposed Otherness into a self-defined specificity?

Second, we must do our work on an epistemological base that indicates that knowledge is possible—not just conversation or a discourse on how it is that power relations work. Conversation as a goal is fine; understanding how power works in oppressive societies is important. But if we are to construct a new society, we need to be assured that some systematic knowledge about our world and ourselves is possible. Those (simply) critical of modernity can call into question whether we ever really knew the world (and a good case can be made that "they" at least did not). They are in fact right that they have not known the world as it is rather than as they wished and needed it to be; they created their world not only in their own image but in the image of their fantasies. To create a world that expresses our own various and diverse images, we need to understand how it works.

Third, we need a theory of power that recognizes that our practical daily activity contains an understanding of the world—subjugated perhaps, but present. Here I am reaffirming Gramsci's argument that everyone is an intellectual and that each of us has an epistemology. The point, then, for "minority" theories is to "read out" the epistemologies in our various practices. I have argued elsewhere for a "standpoint" epistemology—an account of the world with great similarities to Marx's fundamental stance. While I would modify some of what I argued there, I would still insist that we must not give up the claim that material life (class position in Marxist theory) not only structures but sets limits on the understanding of social relations, and that, in systems of domination, the vision available to the rulers will be both partial and will reverse the real order of things.

Fourth, our understanding of power needs to recognize the difficulty of creating alternatives. The ruling class, race, and gender actively structure the material-social relations in which all the parties are forced to participate; their vision, therefore, cannot be dismissed as simply false or misguided. In consequence, the oppressed groups must struggle for their own understandings which will represent achievements requiring both theorizing and the education which grows from political struggle.

Fifth, as an engaged vision, the understanding of the oppressed exposes the relations among people as inhuman and thus contains a call to political action. That is, a theory of power for women, for the oppressed, is not one that leads to a turning away from engagement but rather one that is a call for change and participation in altering power relations.

The critical steps are, first, using what we know about our lives as a basis for critique of the dominant culture and, second, creating alternatives. When the various "minority" experiences have been described and when the significance of these experiences as a ground for critique of the dominant institutions and ideologies of society is better recognized, we will have at least the tools to begin to construct an account of the world sensitive to the realities of race and gender as well as class. To paraphrase Marx, the point is to change the world, not simply to redescribe ourselves or reinterpret the world yet again.

Notes

1. See, for example, David Bell, *Power, Influence, and Authority* (New York: Oxford University Press, 1975), p. 8.

2. See my book *Money, Sex, and Power: Toward a Feminist Historical Materialism* (New York: Longman, 1983; Boston: Northeastern University Press, 1984).

3. My point here is similar to W. B. Gallie's argument that power is an "essentially contested" concept. Power can be categorized as such a concept because it is internally complex, open, and used both aggressively and defensively. Gallie, however, seems not to recognize the epistemological implications of his position.

4. Jean-François Lyotard, *The Post-Modern Condition: A Report on Knowledge,* (Minneapolis: University of Minnesota Press, 1984), p. 81.

5. My language requires that I insert qualification and clarification: I will be using a we/they language. But while it is clear that "they" represent the ruling race, class, and gender, the "we" refers to a "we" who are not and will never be a unitary group, a "we" artificially constructed by the totalizing, Eurocentric, masculine discourse of the Enlightenment. I do not mean to suggest that white Western women share the material situation of the colonized peoples, but rather to argue that we share similar positions in the ideology of the Enlightenment.

6. Simone de Beauvoir, *The Second Sex,* trans. H. M. Parshley (New York: Knopf, 1953), p. 72.

7. Albert Memmi, *The Colonizer and the Colonized* (Boston: Beacon Press, 1967), p. 82.

8. For example, compare de Beauvoir's statement that "at the moment when man asserts himself as subject and free being, the idea of the other arises." (de Beauvoir, 1953, p. 73).

9. Memmi, *The Colonizer and the Colonized,* p. 83.

10. Ibid., p. 85.

11. Ibid., p. 86.

12. Ibid., pp. 92, 95, 113.

13. Edward Said, *Orientalism* (New York: Vintage Press, 1978), p. 3.

14. Memmi, *The Colonizer and the Colonized,* pp. 71–72.

15. Edward Said, *Orientalism,* pp. 3–8.

16. Ibid., pp. 97, 108. See also the reference to the tyrannical observer.

17. Nancy Jay, "Gender and Dichotomy," *Feminist Studies,* Vol. 7, No. 1, Spring 1981, p. 42.

18. Ibid., p. 47.

19. This is Jay's question which I have made my own.

20. Bernice Reagon, "Coalition Politics: Turning the Century," *Home Girls,* ed. Barbara Smith (New York: Kitchen Table Women of Color Press, 1983), p. 359.

21. My argument about Foucault comes from a much more lengthy chapter on him in my forthcoming publication, *Post-Modernism and Political Chance.*

22. Memmi, *The Colonizer and the Colonized,* pp. xiv–xv.

23. Ibid., pp. 20–21.

24. Ibid., p. 41.

25. Michel Foucault, *The Archaeology of Knowledge* (Harper & Row, 1972), pp. 139–164.

26. Nancy Fraser, "Foucault's Body Language: A Post-Humanist Political Rhetoric?" *Salmagundi*, Vol. 61, Fall 1983, p. 59.

27. Charles Taylor, "Foucault on Freedom and Truth," *Political Theory*, Vol. 12, May 1984, pp. 175–176.

28. Michel Foucault, *Language, Counter-Memory, Practice: Selected Essays and Interviews*, ed. Donald Bouchard (Ithaca, NY: Cornell University Press, 1977), p. 151.

29. Michel Foucault, *Power/Knowledge* (New York: Pantheon, 1980), pp. 79, 81.

30. Foucault, *Power/Knowledge* p. 80.

31. Michel Foucault, *The History of Sexuality: An Introduction* (New York: Pantheon, 1978), p. 68.

32. Foucault, *Power/Knowledge*, p. 91.

33. Foucault, *The History of Sexuality*, pp. 142–143.

34. Edward Said, "Foucault and the Imagination of Power," *Foucault: A Critical Reader*, ed. David Hoy (New York: Pantheon, 1986), p. 151.

35. Foucault, *Language, Counter-Memory, Practice*, p. 219.

36. Foucault, *Power/Knowledge*, pp. 81, 85–86.

37. Said, "Foucault and the Imagination of Power," p. 154.

38. Foucault, *Power/Knowledge*, pp. 83, 85.

39. Ibid., p. 88.

40. Foucault, *Language Counter-Memory, Practice*, p. 230.

41. Foucault, *Power/Knowledge*, pp. 84–85.

42. Foucault, *The History of Sexuality*, pp. 92–93.

43. Foucault, *Power/Knowledge*, p. 97.

44. Ibid., p. 98.

45. Ibid.

46. Foucault, *The History of Sexuality*, p. 45.

47. Foucault, *Power/Knowledge*, p. 98.

48. Foucault, *The History of Sexuality*, p. 94.

49. Foucault, *Power/Knowledge*, p. 95.

50. Foucault, *The History of Sexuality*, pp. 92–93.

51. Gad Horowitz, "The Foucaultian Impasse: No Sex, No Self, No Revolution," *Political Theory*, Vol. 16, No. 1, February 1987, pp. 63–64.

References

de Beauvoir, Simone. 1953. *The Second Sex*. Translated by H. M. Parshley. New York: Knopf.

Foucault, Michel. 1972. *The Archaeology of Knowledge*. New York: Harper & Row.

———. 1978, *The History of Sexuality: An Introduction*. New York: Pantheon.

———. 1987. *Language, Counter-Memory, Practice: Selected Essays and Interviews*. Edited by Donald Bouchard. Ithaca: Cornell University Press.

———. 1980. *Power/Knowledge*. Edited by Colin Gordon. New York: Pantheon.

Fraser, Nancy. 1983. "Foucault's Body Language: A Post-Humanist Political Rhetoric?" *Salmagundi:* 61: 55–70.

Gallie, W. B. 1955–1956. "Essentially Contested Concepts." *Proceedings of the Artistotelian Society* 56: 167–198.

Hartsock, Nancy. 1983. "Difference and Domination in the Women's Movement: The Dialect of Theory and Practice." *Class, Race, and Sex: The Dynamics of Control*. Edited by Amy Swerdlow and Hanna Lesinger. Boston: G.K. Hall.

———. 1984. *Money, Sex, and Power: Toward a Feminist Historical Materialism*. New York: Longman.(Boston: Northeastern University Press, 1983).

Hooks, Bell. 1982. *Ain't I a Woman?* Boston: South End Press.

Horowitz, Gad. 1987. "The Foucaultian Impasse: No Sex, No Self, No Revolution." *Political Theory* 15: 61–81.

Jay, Nancy. 1981. "Gender and Dichotomy." *Feminist Studies* 7: 38–56.

Lyotard, Jean-François. 1984. *The Post-Modern Condition: a Report on Knowledge*. Minneapolis: University of Minnesota Press.

Memmi, Albert. 1967. *The Colonizer and the Colonized*. Boston: Beacon Press.

Reagon, Bernice. 1983. "Coalition Politics: Turning the Century." *Home Girls*. Edited by Barbara Smith. New York: Kitchen Table Women of Color Press.

Said, Edward. 1978. *Orientalism*. New York: Vintage Press.

———. 1986. "Foucault and the Imagination of Power." *Foucault: A Critical Reader*. Edited by David Hoy. New York: Pantheon.

Taylor, Charles. 1984. "Foucault on Freedom and Truth." *Political Theory* 12: 152–183.

8

Travels in the Postmodern:
Making Sense of the Local

Elspeth Probyn

In thinking through the concept of the local and how it might be of use to feminist theory despite or because of its various postmodern articulations, an article by Adrienne Rich (1986) comes to mind. In her "Notes toward a Politics of Location" Rich describes a girlhood game, or practice, of addressing letters to her friend which began with the street address and ended via continent, nation, and hemisphere with the postal area of the universe. Being an "army brat," the mid-atlantic product of the "fatherland" (England), a colony (Canada), and sporadically at home in the residual culture of Wales, this was, for me, a game that came naturally. I suppose that the changes of schools and countries could in some small part be controlled through this spatial game of ordering the world. In some ways it was a counterpoint to the early and constant reminder that being from "everywhere" meant that on the playground you were no one (no one's cousin or niece or neighbor since birth). The construction of a wider unity and global possibilities served to displace a rather isolated local.

Rich's description of the pastime, however, places more emphasis on the centrality of the local: "your own house as a tiny fleck on an ever-widening landscape, or as the center of it all from which the circles expanded into the infinite unknown" (p. 212). Further on in the same article, Rich problematizes this memory as she asks: "At the center of what?" (p. 212). In her elegant manner, Rich raises here one of the crucial questions now facing feminism and, more generally, Western thought; in creating our own centers and our own locals, we tend to forget that our centers displace others into the peripheries of our making.

For Rich, this center becomes undone before the demands of "the

---

My thanks to Marty Allor and Larry Grossberg for their invaluable comments and conversations on these subjects.

infinite unknown" and that unknown, in turn, demands a little modesty in the place of an assured mastery. This is to realize that certain claims of solidarity ("As a woman my country is the whole world," (p. 212) come perilously close to colonizing others' experiences. It becomes increasingly difficult to think of the world ordered from the vantage point of one (white) woman. In another register, the ontological conceit of the Western subject becomes untenable.

Against this totalizing gaze, Rich points out that we need to replace the assumption of universalism and construct a feminist theory that starts from the fragments of one's own body. It is important to emphasize that, following Rich, it is "my body" and not "the body" which becomes the site and "the grounds from which to speak *as* women" (p. 213). The body here is definitely not a mythic every-body, and the impulse within Rich's project is to combine the specificity of individual female bodies with a larger feminist politics. Furthermore, the body of which Rich speaks is markedly her own and the contours that she explores (of being a white Jewish lesbian) are not projected onto a universal female body. Thus, Rich differs from an earlier feminist phase which heralded womanhood above the differences of class, race, age, and sexual preference. The white middle-class face of feminism is now at least acknowledged. The idea that anyone could speak for one Woman and all women has become increasingly transparent, but how to speak without the comfort of a preliminary gesture toward the shared ground of women's common oppressions is, however, unresolved.

In this chapter I want to explore a central problematic within feminist cultural theory: Whether the subaltern can speak.[1] I see this problematic composed of a number of intersecting critical questions: the epistemological constitution of knowledge, the ontology of the questioning subject, and the conjunctural question of where and how we may speak. I will organize this exploration around three current metaphors: locale, location, and local. In taking up these often bandied about terms, and in arranging them together, I want to focus on the ground they circle over. Again and again we have heard (and also uttered) the need for specificity, as yet another postmodernist publication ends with a cry for the "local." As Marxists of different shades move into the postmodern, it seems that an unspecified local becomes the site for an unnamed politics.[2] As such, local, locale, and location become abstract terms, cut off from a signifying ground and serving as signposts with no indication of direction. However, a feminist reworking of these metaphors may bring them down to earth; doing so may even bring us to consider both the construction of sites and the methods of researching sites. In differentiating the concepts of locale, location, and local, I want to draw attention to the different levels at which the articulation of theory and practice may proceed. In stressing that these concepts indicate different levels of abstraction, I want to emphasize that theoretical constructs allow for different forms of practice; the "ground" of practice is, after all, not an empirically knowable entity but lies in our ways of thinking. Following Meaghan Morris, I'll emphasize both the spatial and temporal significance of how we come to know. The triad of local, locale, and location thus raises epistemological questions of what constitutes knowledge: of where we speak from and which voices are sanctioned. The ways in which women's practices and experiences have been historically dismissed as local requires that we look at what Morris (1988) calls the "gendering of the spatio-temporal operations (movement/ placement) . . . " (p. 2).

In this vein, the concept of "locale" will be used to designate a place that is the setting for a particular event. I take this "place" as both a discursive and nondiscursive arrangement which holds a gendered event, the home being the most obvious example. In distinction, "local" is that directly issuing from or related to a particular time. Without falling into the romanticism of authenticity, I think that we can identify feminist practices which are directly stitched into the place and time which give rise to them. Finally, by "location" I refer to the methods by which one comes to locate sites of research. Through location knowledges are ordered into sequences which are congruent with previously established categories of knowledge. Location, then, delineates what we may hold as knowable and, following Foucault, renders certain experiences "true" and "scientific" while excluding others. Thus, the epistemology that this suggests most often works to fix the subaltern outside the sanctified boundaries of knowledge, determining the knowledge of the subaltern as peripheral and inconsequential (not fitting in with prearranged sequences). I want, therefore, to question the hierarchical ordering of knowledge.

The temporal-spatial mode I propose here sees theory and practice as intercalated and lateral and as such invokes Jean-François Lyotard's (1986) anaclitic mode of theorizing. His notion of *un procès en ana-* refutes modernist dichotomies and emphasizes the way in which concepts, practices, and fragments rest upon and lean on each other (p. 126). While certain postmodern tenets run through this chapter, I also wish to retain a positive tension between postmodern assumptions and feminist politics. Indeed, it could be argued that what has been labeled as the postmodern dilemma was precipitated not by the supposed passing of modernism but by the questions feminists brought to diverse modernist disciplines. My aim here, however, is not to quibble about who was doing postmodernism first[3] but rather to use various postmodernist arguments critically, watching for holes that could swallow feminism. In this movement we may discover other strategies that allow selves and others to articulate together around new questions.

Living in Locale

It is by now axiomatic that feminism is concerned with the specificities of women's existence. The modes of inquiry may be quite divergent, but there is an underlying feeling that women are the subject of study. Of course, feminist theory goes beyond this and deconstructs what, in fact, it means to say "the subject of study." It also raises the issue of the historical conditions necessary for this formulation to be made. In the most interesting work, women are both the researched and the researcher, implicitly questioning this relationship. As Rosalind Coward (1985) candidly puts it in her book *Female Desires:*

> My fieldwork has been on myself and on my friends and family, whom I have submitted to incessant interrogation about their private lives, their hopes and dreams. Quite deliberately these essays aim at no more than understanding how the representions directed at women enmesh with our actual lives (p. 15).

In Coward's case the mode of analysis may vary widely—from high *Screen* theory to looking at how women live the fragmentary narratives of soap operas, family dinners, and advice columns—all the while examining the construction of "being a woman." In the same book, Coward explores the ways in which:

> Feminine positions are produced as responses to the pleasures offered to us; our subjectivity and identity are formed in definitions of desire which encircle us. These are the experiences which make change such a difficult and daunting task, for female desire is constantly lured by discourses which sustain male privilege (p. 16).

In thinking about how women live with representations of their desire, Coward acknowledges that at some level we invest in these desires. We cannot live outside representations of ideal pleasures, and there is no clear dividing line between an authentic feminine experience and one that along the way may have been "man-made." In other words, we are always negotiating various locales; the ideal articulation of place and event recedes before us. The family dinners consumed can never exactly match the happy ideal, and the makeup used is never quite the way it was supposed to look. In Coward's analysis of female desires, we can't ever quite escape the knowledge that it's never exactly the way "it should be."

The recognition that our lives never quite match up with the representation has been with us for quite some time. Against Coward's implicit "so what," early feminist thinking saw it differently. In *The Feminine Mystique*

Betty Friedan (1963) raised "the problem that has no name" (p. 11). As Friedan described it:

> Each suburban wife struggled with it alone. As she made the beds, shopped for groceries, matched slip cover material, ate peanut butter sandwiches with her children . . . lay beside her husband at night— she was afraid to ask even of herself the silent question—"Is this all?" (p. 11).

Here we see the willing construction of place, the perfect home is all set up and yet the woman asks herself when it's going to start. Friedan's "problem with no name" is actually the question that can't be asked. However, this feeling of all dressed up and nowhere to go, "the silent question [of] is this all?" recognizes the disjuncture between place and event. This was precisely the importance of Friedan's book—that in some way the women who read it recognized themselves. On another level, however, Friedan's description of the entrapment of locale doesn't quite give women the credit of understanding their situation. Women's locale (the suburban home) is ineluctably enticing and within it women were "free to chose automobiles, clothes, appliances, supermarkets; she had everything that women ever dreamed of" (p. 13). The home, therefore, is the locale built up around women, a locale of their own design. Within Friedan's analysis this locale is the defining feature of women's existence. Unfortunately, by ignoring the historical discourses that come to define women's existence as such, Friedan collapses the place (home) with the event (the family). In the *Second Stage* (1981) she defends the locale of family and home as:

> the symbol of that last area where one had any hope of control over one's destiny, of meeting one's most basic human needs, of nourishing that core of personhood threatened by vast impersonal institutions and uncontrollable corporate and government bureaucracies (in Barrett and McIntosh, 1982, p. 17).

Here the locale of home is defined and must be defended against others; it becomes the women's "natural" domain. In true humanist fashion, Friedan wants to replay the private/public dichotomy as she places the family outside of ideology.

In contrast to Friedan's construction of the family as private locale, Michele Barrett and Mary McIntosh directly address the "two-fold character of 'the family' " (p. 8). While they recognize the subjective experience and pleasures that the place of the family may offer, they are quick to point out the ways in which the family serves to reproduce patriarchal structures of power. This separation of the family into place and event allows Barrett and McIntosh to recognize "the powerful appeal of the family, to acknowledge the real satisfactions that it can offer . . . (p. 9). These satisfactions are undoubtedly contradictory (cooking the Sunday dinner may be pleasurable but it's still unpaid). Indeed, it is in raising the contradictions of the family that Barrett and McIntosh denaturalize its satisfactions. Much like Coward's analysis of female pleasures, both the affective lure of place and the ideological working of event are captured here. This two-pronged analysis then allows for the recognition of lived contrarieties; we may invest in these structures while remaining aware of our ideological positioning. In this way the family as locale indicates a certain reflexivity and moves us away from Friedan's formulation of women as domestic dupes, only able to silently wonder about "the problem that has no name."

While Barrett and McIntosh's account of domestic practice certainly moves beyond Friedan's alienated and anonymous housewives, the crucial fact of women's investment in oppressive events is not fully dealt with. Their book, *The Anti-social Family* (1982), is a thorough materialist analysis of the workings of the family as event, as a major part of capitalist machinery. The affectivity of this machine is acknowledged but not fully developed. In other words, we see how the family works to reproduce the conditions of a fundamentally unjust society (we understand the reasons why the event is taking place), but there is little indication of why women would invest in this story (there is no pull of place). To rephrase this in Althusserian terms, Barrett and McIntosh are concerned with how women are "hailed" by the discursive apparatus of the family; it may be in multiple and contradictory ways, but they are nonetheless "interpellated." In contrast to this line of analysis, Valerie Walkerdine (1986) proposes the notion of "positive recognition" to describe "what places the subject in the historical moment" (p. 191). Walkerdine's formulation works against Althusser's conception of "mis-recognition" which for her carries "negative connotations for the study of the ideological (i.e., always-already distorting) interpellation" (p. 191). Against the poststructuralist assertion that we are "always-already positioned," Walkerdine wants to introduce a more fluid model of subject formation. In thinking through how we are positioned by gender, class, and race, she questions the ways in which (subculture) researchers tend to take "discourse at face value" (p. 192). We can no longer take the meanings of discourses for granted and must turn to the ways in which individuals may be differently positioned by them. Gendered practices (within the home, at school, the use of media, and so forth) can therefore not be read off the surface; their meanings to individual women and possible political articulations are never completely guaranteed. Furthermore, the concept of recognition brings together two crucial problematics: First, it rearticulates "the positivity of how domestic relations are lived" (p. 192), and second, it demands that the position of the researcher *vis-à-vis* the researched be denaturalized. The veil of objectivity, which in a scientific model works to erase the researcher's physical and institutional presence from the scene to be studied, must be pulled down. The researcher herself recognizes the affectivity, or the pull of the ideological relations she is studying. As Walkerdine realized: "Often when interviewing the participants I felt that 'I knew what they meant', that I recognized how the practices were regulated or that I understood what it was like to be a participant" (p. 192).

In recognizing a locale we see both the regulation of practices and why those practices in themselves might also be the source of mixed pleasures. This model does not seek to reify those practices; on the contrary in Walkerdine's formulation, it is to question "how we struggle to become subjects and how we resist provided subjectivities in relation to the regulative power of modern social apparatuses" (p. 194). This is also to remember that we negotiate our locales and that we are continuously working to make sense of and articulate both place and event. Moreover, as we approach others' locales we must keep in mind that women are never simply fixed within locale. We may live within patriarchy but at different levels, and in different ways the struggle to rearticulate locale continues. Thus, as Janice Radway has recently pointed out, "we share with others in our everywhere-mediated society the point of view of the active, producing bricoleur . . . (Radway, 1987).

Circumventing Location

In this formulation the bricoleur actively pieces together different signs and produces new (and sometimes unsanctioned) meanings; the bricoleur is always in the process of fashioning her various locales. The concept of "locale" then serves to emphasize the lived contradictions of place and event. In acknowledging that we are daily involved in the reproduction of patriarchy we can nonetheless temper a vision of strict interpellation with the recognition that discourses are negotiated. Individuals live in complex places and differentiate the pull of events. However, if we are to take seriously these relations of place and event, we have to consider the knowledges produced in their interaction.

Living with contradictions does not necessarily enable one to speak of them, and in fact for concrete reasons, it may be dangerous to do so. The recognition that the subaltern works across her positioning does not immediately entail a form of free agency. Whether the subaltern can speak is still in doubt. Gayatri Spivak (1988) sees the question in itself as deficient: Why indeed should the subaltern speak when she will only be rendered "a native informant for first-world intellectuals interested in the voice of the Other" (p. 284). Spivak's response is that "the subaltern women will be as mute as ever" (p. 295). The question of whether the subaltern can speak cannot, for Spivak, be asked. Indeed, Spivak sees the issue as grounded in a form of "epistemic violence" (pp. 281–283). The question of whether the subaltern can speak is in fact an historical subterfuge that "renders the place of the investigator transparent" (p. 284). The ontology of the Western subject necessitates and creates the other: the silent subaltern. Spivak thus reminds us that questions are never innocent even when spoken by well-meaning individuals. The researcher, male or female, is never outside the cultural, political, and economic conditions that allow for only certain questions to be formulated. Spivak's observation that ". . . epistemic violence is the remotely orchestrated, far-flung and heterogeneous project to constitute the colonial subject as Other" is central to the process I've called location.

One of the common-sense meanings of "location" refers to a set constructed outside of a movie studio. While this is not one of the principle ways in which I'll be using this term, it does figure prominently in some postmodernist projects. In Jean Baudrillard's work (the problematic of) the construction of other is erased through a denial of representation. It is rendered as an impossible idea; the masses are impossible, unrepresentable, and therefore silent (1983). In case they are not sufficiently muted by his epistemological violence, Baudrillard (1986) has taken to traveling: "Rouler est une forme spectaculaire d'amnésie. Tout à decouvrir, tout à éfacer" (p. 25). Here we find that if the intellectual moves quick enough, any stray voices will be "erased," lost in the "amnesia" of travel. Through the movement of location, any part of the world can be recreated or made to stand in for another. Moreover, it is seldom questioned whether the set is an accurate portrayal of a particular site. Thus, the cover of his book Amérique (1986) has Montreal standing in for the generic expanse of middle America; it's just like in the movies as Canadian locals are dressed up in American location. As Morris (1988) has said of Baudrillard (as one of the theorists of travel):

> In the world of the third-order simulacra, the encroaching pseudo-places finally merge to eliminate places entirely. This merger is a founding event: once it has taken place, the true (like the real) begins to be reproduced in the image of the pseudo, which begins to become the true (p. 5).

For Baudrillard, then, others disappear because they are impossible and places become simulacra: postcards without people. If, however, there are no subjects (other than simulated ones) in Baudrillard's travel plans, a different form of subjectivity has emerged in other postmodern accounts.

The "nomad" has recently appeared as the model of the Western subject wandering through various locations. For Lawrence Grossberg (1987), the postmodern requires a nomadic subjectivity. What he is describing here seems to run parallel to my discussion of locale: "individuality functions as, and is articulated out of, a nomadic wandering through ever-changing positions and apparatuses" (p. 38). Although Grossberg wants to argue against a Baudrillardian evacuation of subjectivity, the metaphor of the nomad unfortunately recalls some of the more unsalubrious aspects of tourism. The nomad or the tourist is posed as unthreatening, merely passing through; however, his person has questionable effects. Just as economically the benefits of tourism return to the first world, the tourist and the nomad camouflage the theoretical problematic of the ontological implications of Western subjecthood. In Spivak's terms, the epistemic violence continues.

Location, then, can be seen as explicitly articulating epistemological and ontological concerns. I am concerned here with the idea of location as both locating or determining sites and as the process of rendering sites into sequences. Through this process of siting and sequencing, location describes epistemological maneuvers whereby categories of knowledge are established and fixed into sequences. It is also that process which determines what we experience as knowledge and what we know as experience. In Spivak's argument:

> the whole hierarchical taxonomy of concrete experience which has been regarded as completely valid for so long is exactly what has to be got under. At the same time one cannot use that as a terrorism on the people who were obliged to cathect the place of the other, those whose experiences were not quite 'experience' (in McRobbie, 1985 p. 9).

In its hierarchical movement, location insists on a taxonomy of experience. One doesn't have to scratch the surface very deeply to find that class, race, and gender have a lot to do with whose experiences are on top. The classification of experience, moreover, is indivisible from what came before and which knowledges stand as previously sanctioned. Location, then, also depends on a constructed chronology. What can count as knowledge is partially determined by its relationship to previously sanctioned equations. To my mind, it was the early work of Michel Foucault that most forcefully revealed the historical construction of knowledges.[4] Thus, Foucault, (1973) pointed out that we can "rediscover on what basis knowledge and theory became possible; within what space of order knowledge was constituted; on the basis of what historical 'a priori,' and in the element of what possitivity, ideas could appear . . . " (p. xxii).

For Foucault, then, it is what governs statements and the ways in which they govern each other that is of importance. It is therefore through a process of location, of fixing statements in relation to other established statements, that knowledge comes to be ordered. It is through this process that the knowledges produced in locale are denigrated as local, subaltern, and other. Foucault's complex model of power suggests that these subaltern knowledges are not directly oppressed but are merely occluded; they are not brought to light and silently circulate as women's intuition, ritual, and even, instinct. Thus, these experiences are rendered outside of the "true" and the "scientific."

In taking its itinerary from Foucault, some recent feminist work has traveled through unsanctioned histories, resulting in "happy discoveries." Typically, the method of research tends to take the form of random searches; after all, how does one look for silences? An example of this can be found in Judith Brown's account of a seventeenth-century lesbian nun (1986). Here Brown stumbles across a description of Sister Benedette Carlini which causes her to wonder: "What had this nun done to merit such harsh words from the twentieth-century archivist who had read and inventoried the document" (p. 4). From this seventeenth-century nun's life, Brown is able to pull out some "hitherto unexplored areas of women's sexual lives as well as Renaissance views of female sexuality" (p. 4). This type of research is important because it allows us insight into what Foucault called the "historical present." It therefore denaturalizes notions of sexuality as it reveals the historical and ideological process of location. Moreover, this particular example is one instance of working across location; the twentieth-century archivist's judgment and disavowal of the nun is what draws Brown to her. This mode of working between and among sanctioned categories of knowledge jostles the sequencing of location. Both seventeenth- and twentieth-century categories are reworked here, rendering possible the emergence of submerged knowledges. As Angela McRobbie (1984) has pointed out, other knowledges became possible in "working with a consciously loose rather than tight relation in mind. . . . Instead of seeking direct causal links or chains, the emphasis is place on establishing loose sets of relations, capillary actions and movements, spilling out among and between different fields . . . (p. 142).

Making Sense of the Local

Postmodernists of various inclinations have pointed out that the world is a confusing place to live in right now, that it "is marked by a series of events which challenged our ability to make sense of our world and

186 / Elspeth Probyn

ourselves, to normality and the future" (Grossberg, 1987, p. 44). While it's probably not a great deal worse than other times and places, the omnipresence of everyday cruelties hits home with a seemingly increased frequency. Against the apparently unending range of complexities, it is tempting to go the route of Baudrillard and others and treat life as simulation and live out the local in abstraction. However, as I have argued, there are differences involved in how we describe and think about the postmodern and difficult questions that cannot be answered by the panacea of locality. The idea that a politics is inscribed on some abstraction we call the local and that it can be read by some far-off critic is both ludicrous and problematic. As Spivak has cogently put it: "The real critic is not so much interested in distancing him or herself, as in being vigilant. To universalize the local is a very dangerous thing and no good practice comes of it" (in McRobbie, 1985, p. 8).

This is not to give up on the local but rather to work more deeply in and against it. Instead of collapsing the local we have to open it up, to work at different levels. At one level we see the articulation of place and event within what I've called locale. Here we are directed to the struggle between being positioned within patriarchal practices and the intertwined pleasures that we may experience in our day-to-day living. At the level of location, however, we are brought to consider how those experiences may be denied and ordered into the periphery. Interwoven through these concerns is the very immediate question of whether the subaltern can speak. This question requires that we be continually vigilant to the necessity of bringing to the light the submerged conditions that silence others and the other of ourselves. The subaltern's situation is not that of the exotic to be saved. Rather, her position is "naturalized" and reinscribed over and over again through the practices of locale and location. In order for her to ask questions, the ground constructed by these practices must be rearranged.

The surface of social life is indeed complex, articulated as it is by historical complexities. Instead of imploding the historical and the situational into a simulated issue, we have to look at the construction of locale: what event is being reproduced in what place and how individuated knowledge and experience of locale is circumscribed through the process of location. To concretize this, I'll take one local example. At the time of writing, the entire abortion law has been declared unconstitutional in Canada. This was brought about by a series of very local occurrences. Pro-choice groups in Toronto backed Dr. Henry Morgentaler through a string of court cases which ended with the Supreme Court decision that the law against abortion was illegal. This occurrence was a local one although it happened across Canada and applies to all Canadian women. However, the recognition of the law's unconstitutionality points to the fact of locale: the relation of place (women's bodies) to event (reproduction). Effectively what the decision said was that this locale belonged to women and that no one could force the event if she did not want it. Finally, this decision has set in motion demands for location from various anti-abortion groups—that the government set limits and order that a sequence be followed through. Through location, scientific categories of knowledge are to be fixed upon the woman's body: Conception equals life; after the first trimester life occurs, and so forth. Now what we can see here is that this one practice is complexly articulated and embedded in a particular situation. The ways in which the abortion law were fought by groups of individuals shows the situatedness of any struggle. The tactics were different in Montréal than they were in Winnipeg or Toronto. The locale varied enormously as well; the requirements for abortion were very different in differing parts of Canada although abortion fell under federal jurisdiction. This rendering of women's bodies into location will again be contested by local groups in situated ways.

At the end of these scattered travels, it would be tempting to offer a map of the local, something that would point out "you are here," with arrows to indicate the path to be followed. But if anything is clear after these theoretical meanderings, it is that the local exists nowhere in a pure state. The local is only a fragmented set of possibilities that can be articulated into a momentary politics of time and place. Against the postmodernist gesture of local, feminism can render the local into something workable, somewhere to be worked upon. This is to take the local not as the end point, but as the start. This is not to idealize the local as the real, but to look at the ways in which injustices are naturalized in the name of the immediate. In conceiving of the local as a nodal point, we can begin to deconstruct its movements and its meanings. Thus, in thinking of how locale is inscribed on our bodies, in our homes, and on the streets, we can begin to loosen its ideological affects. In uncoupling the event of patriarchy from its site, we move beyond the silent agony of "the problem that has no name." In looking at how location disqualifies certain experiences, we begin to realize that the knowledge of locale is important and powerful. In rearticulating the ground that is locally built around us, we give feminist answers that show up the ideological conditions of certain postmodernist questions.

Notes

1. My use here of the term *subaltern* should be taken in its general sense of "subordinate." It obviously owes much to Spivak's (1986, 1988) usage

of *subaltern* as "excluded" and "not legitimized." Given the Lacanian psychoanalytic overtones of the Other, I prefer, where possible, to refer to those excluded from the multiple levels of empowerment as subaltern. In addition, the etymology of this word reveals the historical articulations of its militaristic and colonial heritage and thus is a reminder of numerous nuances of oppression.

2. For discussion of this tendency, see *Communication* (1988), and *Marxism and the Interpretation of Culture* ed. Cary Nelson and Lawrence Grossberg (1988). Elspeth Probyn (1987) offers a brief critique of the confusion of politics within postmodernism.

3. For one critique of some of the ways in which postmodernists have appropriated feminist work, see Elspeth Probyn (1987).

4. I emphasize that I am taking from Foucault's early work. Spivak formulates an interesting critique of Foucault's inscription of the "Sovereign Subject" (Spivak, 1988).

References

Barrett, Michele and Mary McIntosh. 1982. *The Anti-social Family*. London: Verso.

Brown, Judith C. 1986. *Immodest Acts: The Life of a Lesbian Nun in Renaissance Italy*. New York: Oxford University Press.

Baudrillard, Jean. 1983. *In the Shadow of the Silent Majorities . . . Or the End of the Social*. Translated by Paul Foss, Paul Patton, and John Johnston. New York: Semiotext(e).

———.1986. *Amérique*. Paris: Bernard Grasset.

———.1988. "Between Marxism and Postmodernism." *Communication* 10.

Coward, Rosalind. 1985. *Female Desires: How They Are Sought, Bought and Packaged*. New York: Grove Press.

Friedan, Betty. 1963. *The Feminine Mystique*. New York: Dell Books.

Foucault, Michel. 1973. *The Order of Things: An Archaeology of the Human Sciences*. New York: Vintage Books.

Grossberg, Lawrence. 1987. "The In-Difference of Television." *Screen* 28 (2): 28–48.

Lyotard, Jean-François. 1986. *Le postmoderne expliqué aux enfants*. Paris: Editions Galilee.

McRobbie, Angela. 1984. "Dance and Social Fantasy." *Gender and Generation*. Edited by A. McRobbie and M. Nava. London: Macmillan.

———.1985. "Strategies of Vigilance: An Interview with Gayatri Chakravorti Spivak." *Block 10:* 5–9.

Morris, Meaghan. 1988. "At Henry Parkes Motel," *Cultural Studies* 2 (1): 1–16.

Nelson, Cary and Lawrence Grossberg, eds. 1988. *Marxism and the Interpretation of Culture*. Urbana, IL: University of Illinois Press.

Radway, Janice. "Reception Study, Ethnography and the Problems of Dispersed Audiences and Nomadic Subjects," Paper presented at the International Communications Association Annual Conference, May 1987, Montreal Quebec.

Rich, Adrienne. 1986. *Blood, Bread, and Poetry: Selected Prose 1979–1985*. New York: W. W. Norton & Company.

Probyn, Elspeth. 1987. "Bodies and Anti-bodies: Feminism in the Postmodern," *Cultural Studies* 1 (3): 349–360.

———.1988. "Memories and Past Politics of Postmodernism," *Communication* 10: 305–310.

Spivak, Gayatri Chakravorty. 1988. "Can the Subaltern Speak?" Edited by Cary Nelson and Lawrence Grossberg. *Marxism and the Interpretation of Culture*. Urbana, IL: University of Illinois Press.

———.1986. "Imperialism and Sexual Difference," *Oxford Literary Review*. 8:225–240.

Walkerdine, Valerie. 1986. "Video Replay: Families, Films and Fantasy." *Formations of Fantasy*. Edited by Victor Burgin, James Donald and Cora Kaplan. London: Methuen.

9

A Manifesto for Cyborgs:
Science, Technology, and
Socialist Feminism in the 1980s

Donna Haraway

An Ironic Dream of a Common Language
for Women in the Integrated Circuit

This chapter is an effort to build an ironic political myth faithful to
feminism, socialism, and materialism. Perhaps more faithful as blasphemy
is faithful, than as reverent worship and identification. Blasphemy has
always seemed to require taking things very seriously. I know no better
stance to adopt from within the secular-religious, evangelical traditions of
U.S. politics, including the politics of socialist feminism. Blasphemy
protects one from the Moral Majority within, while still insisting on the
need for community. Blasphemy is not apostasy. Irony is about contradictions that do not resolve into larger wholes, even dialectically, about the
tension of holding incompatible things together because both or all are
necessary and true. Irony is about humor and serious play. It is also a
rhetorical strategy and a political method, one I would like to see more

---

This article was first published in *Socialist Review*, No. 80, 1985. The essay originated
as a response to a call for political thinking about the 1980s from socialist-feminist points
of view, in hopes of deepening our political and cultural debates in order to renew
commitments to fundamental social change in the face of the Reagan years. The cyborg
manifesto tried to find a feminist place for connected thinking and acting in profoundly
contradictory worlds. Since its publication, this bit of cyborgian writing has had a surprising
half life. It has proved impossible to rewrite the cyborg. Cyborg's daughter will have to
find its own matrix in another essay, starting from the proposition that the immune system
is the biotechnical body's chief system of differences in late capitalism, where feminists
might find provocative extraterrestrial maps of the networks of embodied power marked
by race, sex, and class. This chapter is substantially the same as the 1985 version, with
minor revisions and correction of notes.

honored within socialist feminism. At the center of my ironic faith, my blasphemy, is the image of the cyborg.

A cyborg is a cybernetic organism, a hybrid of machine and organism, a creature of social reality as well as a creature of fiction. Social reality is lived social relations, our most important political construction, a world-changing fiction. The international women's movements have constructed "women's experience," as well as uncovered or discovered this crucial collective object. This experience is a fiction and fact of the most crucial, political kind. Liberation rests on the construction of the consciousness, the imaginative apprehension, of oppression, and so of possibility. The cyborg is a matter of fiction and lived experience that changes what counts as women's experience in the late twentieth century. This is a struggle over life and death, but the boundary between science fiction and social reality is an optical illusion.

Contemporary science fiction is full of cyborgs—creatures simultaneously animal and machine, who populate worlds ambiguously natural and crafted. Modern medicine is also full of cyborgs, of couplings between organism and machine, each conceived as coded devices, in an intimacy and with a power that was not generated in the history of sexuality. Cyborg "sex" restores some of the lovely replicative baroque of ferns and invertebrates (such nice organic prophylactics against heterosexism). Cyborg replication is uncoupled from organic reproduction. Modern production seems like a dream of cyborg colonization of work, a dream that makes the nightmare of Taylorism seem idyllic. Modern war is a cyborg orgy, coded by C^3I, command-control-communication-intelligence, an $84 billion item in 1984's U.S. defense budget. I am making an argument for the cyborg as a fiction mapping our social and bodily reality and as an imaginative resource suggesting some very fruitful couplings. Foucault's biopolitics is a flaccid premonition of cyborg politics, a very open field.

By the late twentieth century, our time, a mythic time, we are all chimeras, theorized and fabricated hybrids of machine and organism; in short, we are cyborgs. The cyborg is our ontology; it gives us our politics. The cyborg is a condensed image of both imagination and material reality, the two joined centers structuring any possibility of historical transformation. In the traditions of Western science and politics—the tradition of racist, male-dominant capitalism; the tradition of progress; the tradition of the appropriation of nature as resource for the productions of culture; the tradition of reproduction of the self from the reflections of the other— the relation between organism and machine has been a border war. The stakes in the border war have been the territories of production, reproduction, and imagination. This chapter is an argument for pleasure in the confusion of boundaries and for responsibility in their construction. It is also an effort to contribute to socialist-feminist culture and theory in a postmodernist, nonnaturalist mode and in the utopian tradition of imagining a world without gender, which is perhaps a world without genesis, but maybe also a world without end. The cyborg incarnation is outside salvation history. Nor does it mark time on an Oedipal calendar, attempting to heal the terrible cleavages of gender in oral symbiotic utopia or post-Oedipal apocalypse. As Zoe Sofoulis argues in her unpublished manuscript on Lacan, Klein, and nuclear culture, *Lacklein,* the most terrible and perhaps the most promising monsters in cyborg worlds are embodied in non-Oedipal narratives with a different logic of repression, which we need to understand for our survival.

The cyborg is a creature in a postgender world; it has no truck with bisexuality, pre-Oedipal symbiosis, unalienated labor, or other seductions to organic wholeness through a final appropriation of all the powers of the parts into a higher unity. In a sense, the cyborg has no origin story in the Western sense; a "final" irony since the cyborg is also the awful apocalyptic telos of the West's escalating dominations of abstract individuation, an ultimate self untied at last from all dependency, a man in space. An origin story in the Western humanist sense depends on the myth of original unity, fullness, bliss, and terror, represented by the phallic mother from whom all humans must separate, the task of individual development and of history, the twin potent myths inscribed most powerfully for us in psychoanalysis and Marxism. Hilary Klein has argued that both Marxism and psychoanalysis, in their concepts of labor and of individuation and gender formation, depend on the plot of original unity out of which difference must be produced and enlisted in a drama of escalating domination of woman/nature. The cyborg skips the step of original unity, of identification with nature in the Western sense. This is its illegitimate promise that might lead to subversion of its teleology as Star Wars.

The cyborg is resolutely committed to partiality, irony, intimacy, and perversity. It is oppositional, utopian, and completely without innocence. No longer structured by the polarity of public and private, the cyborg defines a technological polis based partly on a revolution of social relations in the oikos, the household. Nature and culture are reworked; the one can no longer be the resource for appropriation or incorporation by the other. The relationships for forming wholes from parts, including those of polarity and hierarchical domination, are at issue in the cyborg world. Unlike the hopes of Frankenstein's monster, the cyborg does not expect its father to save it through a restoration of the garden, that is, through the fabrication of a heterosexual mate, through its completion in a finished whole, a city and cosmos. The cyborg does not dream of community on the model of the organic family, this time without the Oedipal project. The cyborg would not recognize the Garden of Eden; it is not made of mud and cannot dream of returning to dust. Perhaps that is why I want to see if cyborgs can subvert the apocalypse of returning to nuclear dust in the manic compulsion to name the Enemy. Cyborgs are not reverent; they do not remember the cosmos. They are wary of holism, but needy for connection—they seem to have a natural feel for united front politics, but without the vanguard party. The main trouble with cyborgs, of course, is that they are the illegitimate offspring of militarism and patriarchal capitalism, not to mention state socialism. But illegitimate offspring are often exceedingly unfaithful to their origins. Their fathers, after all, are inessential.

I will return to the science fiction of cyborgs at the end of the chapter, but now I want to signal three crucial boundary breakdowns that make the following political fictional (political scientific) analysis possible. By the late twentieth century in United States, scientific culture, the boundary between human and animal, is thoroughly breached. The last beachheads of uniqueness have been polluted, if not turned into amusement parks—language, tool use, social behavior, mental events. Nothing really convincingly settles the separation of human and animal. Many people no longer feel the need of such a separation; indeed, many branches of feminist culture affirm the pleasure of connection with human and other living creatures. Movements for animal rights are not irrational denials of human uniqueness; they are clear-sighted recognition of connection across the discredited breach of nature and culture. Biology and evolutionary theory over the last two centuries have simultaneously produced modern organisms as objects of knowledge and reduced the line between humans and animals to a faint trace re-etched in ideological struggle or professional disputes between life and social sciences. Within this framework, teaching modern Christian creationism should be fought as a form of child abuse.

Biological-determinist ideology is only one position opened up in scientific culture for arguing the meanings of human animality. There is much room for radical political people to contest for the meanings of the breached boundary.[1] The cyborg appears in myth precisely where the boundary between human and animal is transgressed. Far from signaling a walling off of people from other living things, cyborgs signal disturbingly and pleasurably tight coupling. Bestiality has a new status in this cycle of marriage exchange.

The second leaky distinction is between animal-human (organism) and machine. Pre-cybernetic machines could be haunted; there was always the specter of the ghost in the machine. This dualism structured the dialogue between materialism and idealism that was settled by a dialectical progeny called spirit or history, according to taste. But basically machines were not self-moving, self-designing, autonomous. They could not achieve man's dream, only mock it. They were not man, an author of himself, but only a caricature of that masculinist reproductive dream. To think they were otherwise was paranoid. Now we are not so sure. Late twentieth-

century machines have made thoroughly ambiguous the difference between natural and artificial, mind and body, self-developing and externally
designed, and many other distinctions that used to apply to organisms
and machines. Our machines are disturbingly lively, and we ourselves
frighteningly inert.

Technological determinism is only one ideological space opened up.
by the reconceptions of machine and organism as coded texts through
which we engage in the play of writing and reading the world.[2]
"Textualization" of everything in poststructuralist, postmodernist theory
has been damned by Marxists and socialist feminists for its utopian
disregard for lived relations of domination that ground the "play" of
arbitrary reading.[3]* It is certainly true that postmodernist strategies,
like my cyborg myth, subvert myriad organic wholes (e.g., the poem,
the primitive culture, the biological organism). In short, the certainty
of what counts as nature—a source of insight and a promise of
innocence—is undermined, probably fatally. The transcendent authorization of interpretation is lost and with it the ontology grounding Western
epistemology. But the alternative is not cynicism or faithlessness, that
is, some version of abstract existence, like the accounts of technological
determinism destroying "man" by the "machine" or "meaningful political
action" by the "text." Who cyborgs will be is a radical question; the

---

*A provocative, comprehensive argument about the politics and theories of postmodern-
ism is made by Fredric Jameson, who argues that postmodernism is not an option, a style
among others, but a cultural dominant requiring radical reinvention of left politics from
within; there is no longer any place from without that gives meaning to the comforting
fiction of critical distance. Jameson also makes clear why one cannot be for or against
postmodernism, an essentially moralist move. My position is that feminists (and others)
need continuous cultural reinvention, postmodernist critique, and historical materialism;
only a cyborg would have a chance. The old dominations of white capitalist patriarchy
seem nostalgically innocent now: They normalized heterogeneity, e.g., into man and
woman, white and black. "Advanced capitalism" and postmodernism release heterogeneity
without a norm, and we are flattened, without subjectivity, which requires depth, even
unfriendly and drowning depths. It is time to write *The Death of the Clinic*. The clinic's
methods required bodies and works; we have texts and surfaces. Our dominations don't
work by medicalization and normalization anymore; they work by networking, communications redesign, stress management. Normalization gives way to automation, utter redundancy. Michel Foucault's *Birth of the Clinic, History of Sexuality,* and *Discipline and
Punish* name a form of power at its moment of implosion. The discourse of biopolitics
gives way to technobabble, the language of the spliced substantive; no noun is left whole
by the multinationals. These are their names, listed from one issue of *Science:* Tech-
Knowledge, Genentech, Allergen, Hybritech, Compupro, Genen-cor, Syntex, Allelix,
Agrigenetics Corp., Syntro, Codon, Repligen; Micro-Angelo from Scion Corp., Percom
Data, Inter Systems, Cyborg Corp., Statcom Corp., Intertec. If we are imprisoned by
language, then escape from that prison-house requires language poets, a kind of cultural
restriction enzyme to cut the code; cyborg heteroglossia is one form of radical culture
politics.

answers are a matter of survival. Both chimpanzees and artifacts have politics, so why shouldn't we?[4]

The third distinction is a subset of the second: The boundary between physical and nonphysical is very imprecise for us. Pop physics books on the consequences of quantum theory and the indeterminacy principle are a kind of popular scientific equivalent to the Harlequin romances as a marker of radical change in American white heterosexuality: They get it wrong, but they are on the right subject. Modern machines are quintessentially microelectronic devices: They are everywhere and they are invisible. Modern machinery is an irreverent upstart god, mocking the Father's ubiquity and spirituality. The silicon chip is a surface for writing; it is etched in molecular scales disturbed only by atomic noise, the ultimate interference for nuclear scores. Writing, power, and technology are old partners in Western stories of the origin of civilization, but miniaturization has changed our experience of mechanism. Miniaturization has turned out to be about power; small is not so much beautiful as preeminently dangerous, as in Cruise missiles. Contrast the TV sets of the 1950s or the news cameras of the 1970s with the TV wristbands or hand-sized video cameras now advertised. Our best machines are made of sunshine; they are all light and clean because they are nothing but signals, electromagnetic waves, a section of a spectrum. These machines are eminently portable, mobile— a matter of immense human pain in Detroit and Singapore. People are nowhere near so fluid, being both material and opaque. Cyborgs are ether, quintessence.

The ubiquity and invisibility of cyborgs is precisely why these Sunshine Belt machines are so deadly. They are as hard to see politically as materially. They are about consciousness—or its simulation.[5] They are floating signifiers moving in pickup trucks across Europe, blocked more effectively by the witch-weavings of the displaced and so unnatural Greenham women, who read the cyborg webs of power very well, than by the militant labor of older masculinist politics, whose natural constituency needs defense jobs. Ultimately, the "hardest" science is about the realm of greatest boundary confusion, the realm of pure number, pure spirit, C^3I, cryptography, and the preservation of potent secrets. The new machines are so clean and light. Their engineers are sun worshipers mediating a new scientific revolution associated with the night dream of post industrial society. The diseases evoked by these clean machines are "no more" than the minuscule coding changes of an antigen in the immune system, "no more" than the experience of stress. The "nimble" fingers of "Oriental" women, the old fascination of little Anglo-Saxon Victorian girls with dollhouses, and women's enforced attention to the small take on quite new dimensions in this world. There might be a cyborg Alice taking account of these new dimensions. Ironically, it might be the unnatural cyborg women making chips in Asia and spiral dancing in Santa Rita jail after an antinuclear action whose constructed unities will guide effective oppositional strategies.

So my cyborg myth is about transgressed boundaries, potent fusions, and dangerous possibilities which progressive people might explore as one part of needed political work. One of my premises is that most American socialists and feminists see deepened dualisms of mind and body, animal and machine, idealism and materialism in the social practices, symbolic formulations, and physical artifacts associated with high technology and scientific culture. From *One-Dimensional Man* to *The Death of Nature*,[6] the analytic resources developed by progressives have insisted on the necessary domination of technics and recalled us to an imagined organic body to integrate our resistance. Another of my premises is that the need for unity of people trying to resist worldwide intensification of domination has never been more acute. But a slightly perverse shift of perspective might better enable us to contest for meanings, as well as for other forms of power and pleasure in technologically mediated societies.

From one perspective, a cyborg world is about the final imposition of a grid of control on the planet, about the final abstraction embodied in a Star Wars apocalypse waged in the name of defense, about the final appropriation of women's bodies in a masculinist orgy of war.[7] From another perspective, a cyborg world might be about lived social and bodily realities in which people are not afraid of their joint kinship with animals and machines, not afraid of permanently partial identities and contradictory standpoints. The political struggle is to see from both perspectives at once because each reveals both dominations and possibilities unimaginable from the other vantage point. Single vision produces worse illusions than double vision or many-headed monsters. Cyborg unities are monstrous and illegitimate; in our present political circumstances, we could hardly hope for more potent myths for resistance and recoupling. I like to imagine the Livermore Action Group, LAG, as a kind of cyborg society, dedicated to realistically converting the laboratories that most fiercely embody and spew out the tools of technological apocalypse, and committed to building a political form that actually manages to hold together witches, engineers, elders, perverts, Christians, mothers, and Leninists long enough to disarm the state. Fission Impossible is the name of the affinity group in my town. (Affinity: related not by blood but by choice, the appeal of one chemical nuclear group for another, avidity.)[8]

Fractured Identities

It has become difficult to name one's feminism by a single adjective— or even to insist in every circumstance upon the noun. Consciousness of exclusion through naming is acute. Identities seem contradictory, partial, and strategic. With the hard-won recognition of their social and historical constitution, gender, race, and class cannot provide the basis for belief in "essential" unity. There is nothing about being "female" that naturally binds women. There is not even such a state as "being" female, itself a highly complex category constructed in contested sexual scientific discourses and other social practices. Gender, race, or class consciousness is an achievement forced on us by the terrible historical experience of the contradictory social realities of patriarchy, colonialism, racism and capitalism. Who counts as "us" in my own rhetoric? Which identities are available to ground such a potent political myth called "us," and what could motivate enlistment in this collectivity? Painful fragmentation among feminists (not to mention among women) along every possible fault line has made the concept of woman elusive, an excuse for the matrix of women's dominations of each other. For me—and for many who share a similar historical location in white, professional, middle-class, female, radical, North American, mid-adult bodies—the sources of a crisis in political identity are legion. The recent history for much of the U.S. Left and the U.S. feminism has been a response to this kind of crisis by endless splitting and searches for a new essential unity. But there has also been a growing recognition of another response through coalition—affinity, not identity.[9]

Chela Sandoval, from a consideration of specific historical moments in the formation of the new political voice called women of color, has theorized a hopeful model of political identity called "oppositional consciousness," born of the skills for reading webs of power by those refused stable membership in the social categories of race, sex, or class.[10] "Women of color," a name contested at its origins by those whom it would incorporate, as well as a historical consciousness marking systematic breakdown of all the signs of Man in Western traditions, constructs a king of postmodernist identity out of otherness, difference, and specificity. This postmodernist identity is fully political, whatever might be said about other possible postmodernisms. Sandoval's oppositional consciousness is about contradictory locations and heterochronic calendars, not about relativisms and pluralisms.

Sandoval emphasizes the lack of any essential criterion for identifying who is a woman of color. She notes that the definition of the group has been by conscious appropriation of negation. For example, a chicana or a U.S. black woman has not been able to speak as a woman or as a black person or as a chicano. Thus, she was at the bottom of a cascade of negative identities, left out of even the "privileged" oppressed authorial categories called "women and blacks," who claimed to make the important revolutions. The category "woman" negated all nonwhite women; "black" negated all nonblack people, as well as all black women. But there was also no "she," no singularity, but a sea of differences among U.S. women who have affirmed their historical identity as U.S. women of color. This identity marks out a self-consciously constructed space that cannot affirm the capacity to act on the basis of natural identification, but only on the basis of conscious coalition, of affinity, of political kinship.[11] Unlike the "woman" of some streams of the white women's movement in the United States, there is no naturalization of the matrix, or at least this is what Sandoval argues is uniquely available through the power of oppositional consciousness.

Sandoval's argument has to be seen as one potent formulation for feminists out of the worldwide development of anti-colonialist discourse, that is, discourse dissolving the West and its highest product—the one who is not animal, barbarian, or woman: that is, man, the author of a cosmos called history. As Orientalism is deconstructed politically and semiotically, the identities of the Occident destabilize, including those of its feminists.[12] Sandoval argues that "women of color" have a chance to build an effective unity that does not replicate the imperializing, totalizing revolutionary subjects of previous Marxisms and feminisms which had not faced the consequences of the disorderly polyphony emerging from decolonization.

Katie King has emphasized the limits of identification and the political/ poetic mechanics of identification built into reading "the poem," that generative core of cultural feminism. King criticizes the persistent tendency among contemporary feminists from different "moments" or "conversations" in feminist practice to taxonomize the women's movement to make one's own political tendencies appear to be the telos of the whole. These taxonomies tend to remake feminist history to appear to be an ideological struggle among coherent types persisting over time, especially those typical units called radical, liberal, and socialist feminism. Literally, all other feminisms are either incorporated or marginalized, usually by building an explicit ontology and epistemology.[13] Taxonomies of feminism produce epistemologies to police deviation from official women's experience. Of course, "women's culture," like women of color, is consciously created by mechanisms inducing affinity. The rituals of poetry, music, and certain forms of academic practice have been preeminent. The politics of race and culture in the U.S. women's movements are intimately interwoven. The common achievement of King and Sandoval is learning how to craft a poetic/political unity without relying on a logic of appropriation, incorporation, and taxonomic identification.

The theoretical and practical struggle against unity-through-domination or unity-through-incorporation ironically not only undermines the justifications for patriarchy, colonialism, humanism, positivism, essentialism, scientism, and other unlamented -isms, but all claims for an organic or natural standpoint. I think that radical and socialist/Marxist feminisms have also undermined their/our own epistemological strategies and that this is a crucially valuable step in imagining possible unities. It remains to be seen whether all epistemologies as Western political people have known them fail us in the task to build effective affinities.

It is important to note that the effort to construct revolutionary standpoints, epistemologies as achievements of people committed to changing the world, has been part of the process showing the limits of identification. The acid tools of postmodernist theory and the constructive tools of ontological discourse about revolutionary subjects might be seen as ironic allies in dissolving Western selves in the interests of survival. We are excruciatingly conscious of what it means to have a historically constituted body. But with the loss of innocence in our origin, there is no expulsion from the Garden either. Our politics lose the indulgence of guilt with the *naïveté* of innocence. But what would another political myth for socialist feminism look like? What kind of politics could embrace partial, contradictory, permanently unclosed constructions of personal and collective selves and still be faithful, effective—and, ironically, socialist feminist?

I do not know of any other time in history when there was greater need for political unity to confront effectively the dominations of race, gender, sexuality, and class. I also do not know of any other time when the kind of unity we might help build could have been possible. None of "us" have any longer the symbolic or material capability of dictating the shape of reality to any of "them." Or at least "we" cannot claim innocence from practicing such dominations. White women, including Euroamerican socialist feminists, discovered (i.e., were forced kicking and screaming to notice) the noninnocence of the category "woman." That consciousness changes the configuration of all previous categories; it denatures them as heat denatures a fragile protein. Cyborg feminists have to argue that "we" do not want any more natural matrix of unity and that no construction is whole. Innocence, and the corollary insistence on victimhood as the only ground for insight, has done enough damage. But the constructed revolutionary subject must give late twentieth-century people pause as well. In the fraying of identities and in the reflexive strategies for constructing them, the possibility opens up for weaving something other than a shroud for the day after the apocalypse that so prophetically ends salvation history.

But Marxist/socialist feminisms and radical feminisms have simultaneously naturalized and denatured the category "woman" and consciousness of the social lives of "women." Perhaps a schematic caricature can highlight both kinds of moves. Marxian socialism is rooted in an analysis of wage labor which reveals class structure. The consequence of the wage relationship is systematic alienation, as the worker is dissociated from his [sic] product. Abstraction and illusion rule in knowledge; domination rules in practice. Labor is the preeminently privileged category enabling the Marxist to overcome illusion and find that point of view which is necessary for changing the world. Labor is the humanizing activity that makes man; labor is an ontological category permitting the knowledge of a subject, and so the knowledge of subjugation and alienation.

In faithful filiation, socialist feminism advanced by allying itself with the basic analytic strategies of this Marxism. The main achievement of both Marxist feminists and socialist feminists was to expand the category of labor to accommodate what (some) women did, even when the wage relation was subordinated to a more comprehensive view of labor under capitalist patriarchy. In particular, women's labor in the household and women's activity as mothers generally, that is, reproduction in the socialist feminist sense, entered theory on the authority of analogy to the Marxian concept of labor. The unity of women here rests on an epistemology based on the ontological structure of "labor." Marxist/socialist feminism does not "naturalize" unity; it is a possible achievement based on a possible standpoint rooted in social relations. The essentializing move is in the ontological structure of labor or of its analogue, women's activity.[14]* The inheritance of Marxian humanism, with its preeminently Western self, is the difficulty for me. The contribution from these formulations has been the emphasis on the daily responsibility of real women to *build* unities, rather than to naturalize them.

Catherine MacKinnon's version of radical feminism is itself a caricature of the appropriating, incorporating, totalizing tendencies of Western theories of identity grounding action.[15] It is factually and politically wrong to assimilate all of the diverse "moments" or "conversations" in recent women's politics named radical feminism to MacKinnon's version. But the teleological logic of her theory shows how an epistemology and ontology—including their negations—erase or police difference. Only one of the effects of MacKinnon's theory is the rewriting of the history of the polymorphous field called radical feminism. The major effect is the production of a theory of experience, of women's identity, that is a kind of apocalypse for all revolutionary standpoints. That is, the totalization built into this tale of radical feminism achieves its end—the unity of women—by enforcing the experience of and testimony to radical nonbeing. As for the Marxist/socialist feminist, consciousness is an achieve-

---

*The central role of object-relations versions of psychoanalysis and related strong universalizing moves in discussing reproduction, caring work, and mothering in many approaches to epistemology underline their authors' resistance to what I am calling postmodernism. For me, both the universalizing moves and these versions of psychoanalysis make analysis of "women's place in the integrated circuit" difficult and lead to systematic difficulties in accounting for or even seeing major aspects of the construction of gender and gendered social life.

teleological theory/logic > polices difference
production of z theory of experience
the experience of znd testimony to rzdiccl nonbeing

ment, not a natural fact. MacKinnon's theory eliminates some of the difficulties built into humanist revolutionary subjects, but at the cost of radical reductionism.

MacKinnon argues that feminism necessarily adopted a different analytical strategy from Marxism, looking first not at the structure of class, but at the structure of sex/gender and its generative relationship, men's constitution and appropriation of women sexually. Ironically, MacKinnon's "ontology" constructs a nonsubject, a nonbeing. Another's desire, not the self's labor, is the origin of "woman." She therefore develops a theory of consciousness that enforces what can count as "women's" experience—anything that names sexual violation, indeed, sex itself as far as "women" can be concerned. Feminist practice is the construction of this form of consciousness; that is, the self-knowledge of a self-who-is-not.

Perversely, sexual appropriation in this feminism still has the epistemological status of labor, that is, the point from which analysis able to contribute to changing the world must flow. But sexual objectification, not alienation, is the consequence of the structure of sex/gender. In the realm of knowledge, the result of sexual objectification is illusion and abstraction. However, a woman is not simply alienated from her product, but in a deep sense she does not exist as a subject, or even potential subject, since she owes her existence as a woman to sexual appropriation. To be constituted by another's desire is not the same thing as to be alienated in the violent separation of the laborer from his product.

MacKinnon's radical theory of experience is totalizing in the extreme; it does not so much marginalize as obliterate the authority of any other women's political speech and action. It is a totalization producing what Western patriarchy itself never succeeded in doing—feminists' consciousness of the nonexistence of women, except as products of men's desire. I think MacKinnon correctly argues that no Marxian version of identity can firmly ground women's unity. But in solving the problem of the contradictions of any Western revolutionary subject for feminist purposes, she develops an even more authoritarian doctrine of experience. If my complaint about socialist/Marxian standpoints is their unintended erasure of polyvocal, unassimilable, radical difference made visible in anti-colonial discourse and practice, MacKinnon's intentional erasure of all difference through the device of the "essential" nonexistence of women is not reassuring.

In my taxonomy, which like any other taxonomy is a reinscription of history, radical feminism can accommodate all the activities of women named by socialist feminists as forms of labor only if the activity can somehow be sexualized. Reproduction had different tones of meanings for the two tendencies, one rooted in labor, one in sex, both calling the consequences of domination and ignorance of social and personal reality "false consciousness."

Beyond either the difficulties or the contributions in the argument of any one author, neither Marxist nor radical-feminist points of view have tended to embrace the status of a partial explanation; both were regularly constituted as totalities. Western explanation has demanded as much; how else could the Western author incorporate its others? Each tried to annex other forms of domination by expanding its basic categories through analogy, simple listing, or addition. Embarrassed silence about race among white radical and socialist feminists was one major, devastating political consequence. History and polyvocality disappear into political taxonomies that try to establish genealogies. There was no structural room for race (or for much else) in theory claiming to reveal the construction of the category "woman" and social group "women" as a unified or totalizable whole. The structure of my caricature looks like this:

Socialist Feminism—
 structure of class//wage labor//alienation
 labor, by analogy reproduction, by extension sex, by addition race
Radical Feminism—
 structure of gender//sexual appropriation//objectification
 sex, by analogy labor, by extension reproduction, by addition race

In another context, the French theorist Julia Kristeva claimed women appeared as a historical group after World War II, along with groups like youth. Her dates are doubtful, but we are now accustomed to remembering that as objects of knowledge and as historical actors, "race" did not always exist, "class" has a historical genesis, and "homosexuals" are quite junior. It is no accident that the symbolic system of the family of man—and so the essence of woman—breaks up at the same moment that networks of connection among people on the planet are unprecedentedly multiple, pregnant, and complex. "Advanced capitalism" is inadequate to convey the structure of this historical moment. In the Western sense, the end of man is at stake. It is no accident that woman disintegrates into women in our time. Perhaps socialist feminists were not substantially guilty of producing essentialist theory that suppressed women's particularity and contradictory interests. I think we have been, at least through unreflective participation in the logics, languages, and practices of white humanism and through searching for a single ground of domination to secure our revolutionary voice. Now we have less excuse. But in the consciousness of our failures, we risk lapsing into boundless difference and giving up on the confusing task of making partial, real connection. Some differences

are playful; some are poles of world historical systems of domination. ✓
Epistemology is about knowing the difference.

The Informatics of Domination

In this attempt at an epistemological and political position, I would like
to sketch a picture of possible unity, a picture indebted to socialist and
feminist principles of design. The frame for my sketch is set by the extent
and importance of rearrangements in worldwide social relations tied to
science and technology. I argue for a politics rooted in claims about
fundamental changes in the nature of class, race, and gender in an emerging system of world order analogous in its novelty and scope to that created
by industrial capitalism; we are living through a movement from an
organic, industrial society to a polymorphous, information system—from
all work to all play, a deadly game. Simultaneously material and ideological, the dichotomies may be expressed in the following chart of transitions
from the comfortable old hierarchical dominations to the scary new networks I have called the informatics of domination:

Representation	Simulation
Bourgeois novel, realism	Science fiction, postmodernism
Organism	Biotic component
Depth, integrity	Surface, boundary
Heat	Noise
Biology as clinical practice	Biology as inscription
Physiology	Communications engineering
Small group	Subsystem
Perfection	Optimization
Eugenics	Population Control
Decadence, *Magic Mountain*	Obsolescence, *Future Shock*
Hygiene	Stress management
Microbiology, tuberculosis	Immunology, AIDS
Organic division of labor	Ergonomics/cybernetics of labor
Functional specialization	Modular construction
Reproduction	Replication
Organic sex role specialization	Optimal genetic strategies
Biological determinism	Evolutionary inertia, constraints
Community ecology	Ecosystem
Racial chain of being	Neo-imperialism, United Nations humanism
Scientific management in home/factory	Global factory/electronic cottage
Family/market/factory	Women in the integrated circuit
Family wage	Comparable worth
Public/private	Cyborg citizenship
Nature/culture	Fields of difference
Cooperation	Communications enhancement

Freud	Lacan
Sex	Genetic engineering
Labor	Robotics
Mind	Artificial intelligence
World War II	Star Wars
White capitalist patriarchy	Informatics of domination

This list suggests several interesting things.[16] First, the objects on the right-hand side cannot be coded as "natural," a realization that subverts naturalistic coding for the left-hand side as well. We cannot go back ideologically or materially. It's not just that "god" is dead; so is the "goddess." Or both are revivified in the worlds charged with microelectronic and biotechnological politics. In relation to objects like biotic components, one must think not in terms of essential properties, but in terms of design, boundary constraints, rates of flows, systems logics, costs of lowering constraints. Sexual reproduction is one kind of reproductive strategy among many, with costs and benefits as a function of the system environment. Ideologies of sexual reproduction can no longer reasonably call on notions of sex and sex role as organic aspects in natural objects like organisms and families. Such reasoning will be unmasked as irrational, and ironically corporate executives reading *Playboy* and anti-porn radical feminists will make strange bedfellows in jointly unmasking the irrationalism.

Likewise for race, racist and anti-racist ideologies about human diversity have to be formulated in terms of frequencies of parameters. It is "irrational" to invoke concepts like primitive and civilized. For liberals and radicals, the search for integrated social systems gives way to a new practice called "experimental ethnography" in which an organic object dissipates in attention to the play of writing. At the level of ideology, we see translations of racism and colonialism into languages of development and underdevelopment, rates and constraints of modernization. Any objects or persons can be "reasonably" thought of in terms of disassembly and reassembly; no "natural" architectures constrain system design. The financial districts in all the world's cities, as well as the export-processing and free-trade zones, proclaim this elementary fact of "late capitalism." The entire universe of objects that can be known scientifically must be formulated as problems in communications engineering (for the managers) or theories of the text (for those who would resist). Both are cyborg semiologies.

One should expect control strategies to concentrate on boundary conditions and interfaces, on rates of flow across boundaries—and not on the integrity of natural objects. "Integrity" or "sincerity" of the Western self gives way to decision procedures and expert systems. For example, control strategies applied to women's capacities to give birth to new human beings will be developed in the languages of population control and maximization of goal achievement for individual decisionmakers. Control strategies will be formulated in terms of rates, costs of constraints, degrees of freedom. Human beings, like any other component or subsystem, must be localized in a system architecture whose basic modes of operation are probabilistic, statistical. No objects, spaces, or bodies are sacred in themselves; any component can be interfaced with any other if the proper standard, the proper code, can be constructed for processing signals in a common language. Exchange in this world transcends the universal translation effected by capitalist markets that Marx analyzed so well. The privileged pathology affecting all kinds of components in this universe is stress—communications breakdown.[17] The cyborg is not subject to Foucault's biopolitics; the cyborg simulates politics, a much more potent field of operations. Discursive constructions are no joke.

This kind of analysis of scientific and cultural objects of knowledge which have appeared historically since World War II prepares us to notice some important inadequacies in feminist analysis which has proceeded as if the organic, hierarchical dualism ordering discourse in the West since Aristotle still ruled. They have been cannibalized, or as Zoe Sofia (Sofoulis) might put it, they have been "techno-digested." The dichotomies between mind and body, animal and human, organism and machine, public and private, nature and culture, men and women, primitive and civilized are all in question ideologically. The actual situation of women is their integration/exploitation into a world system of production/reproduction and communication called the informatics of domination. The home, work place, market, public arena, the body itself—all can be dispersed and interfaced in nearly infinite, polymorphous ways, with large consequences for women and others—consequences that themselves are very different for different people and which make potent oppositional international movements difficult to imagine and essential for survival. One important route for reconstructing socialist-feminist politics is through theory and practice addressed to the social relations of science and technology, including crucially the systems of myth and meanings structuring our imaginations. The cyborg is a kind of disassembled and reassembled, postmodern collective and personal self. This is the self feminists must code.

Communications technologies and biotechnologies are the crucial tools recrafting our bodies. These tools embody and enforce new social relations for women worldwide. Technologies and scientific discourses can be partially understood as formalizations, that is, as frozen moments, of the fluid social interactions constituting them, but they should also be viewed as instruments for enforcing meanings. The boundary is permeable between tool and myth, instrument and concept, historical systems of social relations and historical anatomies of possible bodies, including objects of knowledge. Indeed, myth and tool mutually constitute each other.

Furthermore, communications sciences and modern biologies are constructed by a common move—the translation of the world into a problem of coding, a search for a common language in which all resistance to instrumental control disappears and all heterogeneity can be submitted to disassembly, reassembly, investment, and exchange.

In communications sciences, the translation of the world into a problem in coding can be illustrated by looking at cybernetic (feedback controlled) systems theories applied to telephone technology, computer design, weapons deployment, or data-base construction and maintenance. In each case, solution to the key questions rests on a theory of language and control; the key operation is determining the rates, directions, and probabilities of flow of a quantity called information. The world is subdivided by boundaries differentially permeable to information. Information is just that kind of quantifiable element (unit, basis of unity) which allows universal translation and so unhindered instrumental power (called effective communication). The biggest threat to such power is interruption of communication. Any system breakdown is a function of stress. The fundamentals of this technology can be condensed into the metaphor C^3I, command-control-communication-intelligence, the military's symbol for its operations theory.

In modern biologies, the translation of the world into a problem in coding can be illustrated by molecular genetics, ecology, sociobiological evolutionary theory, and immunobiology. The organism has been translated into problems of genetic coding and read-out. Biotechnology, a writing technology, informs research broadly.[18] In a sense, organisms have ceased to exist as objects of knowledge, giving way to biotic components, that is, special kinds of information-processing devices. The analogous moves in ecology could be examined by probing the history and utility of the concept of the ecosystem. Immunobiology and associated medical practices are rich exemplars of the privilege of coding and recognition systems as objects of knowledge, as constructions of bodily reality for us. Biology here is a king of cryptography. Research is necessarily a kind of intelligence activity. Ironies abound. A stressed system goes awry; its communication processes break down; it fails to recognize the difference between self and other. Human babies with baboon hearts evoke national ethical perplexity—for animal-rights activists at least as much as for the guardians of human purity. In the United States gay men and intravenous drug users are the most "privileged" victims of an awful immune-system disease that marks (inscribes on the body) confusion of boundaries and moral pollution.[19]

But these excursions into communications sciences and biology have been at a rarefied level; there is a mundane, largely economic reality to support my claim that these sciences and technologies indicate fundamental transformations in the structure of the world for us. Communications technologies depend on electronics. Modern states, multinational corporations, military power, welfare-state apparatuses, satellite systems, political processes, fabrication of our imaginations, labor-control systems, medical constructions of our bodies, commercial pornography, the international division of labor, and religious evangelism depend intimately upon electronics. Microelectronics is the technical basis of simulacra, that is, of copies without originals.

Microelectronics mediates the translations of labor into robotics and word processing, sex into genetic engineering and reproductive technologies, and mind into artificial intelligence and decision procedures. The new biotechnologies concern more than human reproduction. Biology as a powerful engineering science for redesigning materials and processes has revolutionary implications for industry, perhaps most obvious today in areas of fermentation, agriculture, and energy. Communications sciences and biology are constructions of natural-technical objects of knowledge in which the difference between machine and organism is thoroughly blurred; mind, body, and tool are on very intimate terms. The "multinational" material organization of the production and reproduction of daily life and the symbolic organization of the production and reproduction of culture and imagination seem equally implicated. The boundary-maintaining images of base and superstructure, public and private, or material and ideal never seemed more feeble.

I have used Rachel Grossman's image of women in the integrated circuit to name the situation of women in a world so intimately restructured through the social relations of science and technology.[20] I use the odd circumlocution, "the social relations of science and technology," to indicate that we are not dealing with a technological determinism, but with a historical system depending upon structured relations among people. But the phrase should also indicate that science and technology provide fresh sources of power, that we need fresh sources of analysis and political action.[21] Some of the rearrangements of race, sex, and class rooted in high-tech-facilitated social relations can make socialist feminism more relevant to effective progressive politics.

The Homework Economy

The "New Industrial Revolution" is producing a new worldwide working class, as well as new sexualities and ethnicities. The extreme mobility of capital and the emerging international division of labor are intertwined with the emergence of new collectivities and the weakening of familiar groupings. These developments are neither gender- nor race-neutral. White men in advanced industrial societies have become newly vulnerable to permanent job loss, and women are not disappearing from the job rolls at the same rates as men. It is not simply that women in third-world countries are the preferred labor force for the science-based multinationals in the export-processing sectors, particularly in electronics. The picture is more systematic and involves reproduction, sexuality, culture, consumption, and production. In the prototypical Silicon Valley, many women's lives have been structured around employment in electronics-dependent jobs, and their intimate realities include serial heterosexual monogamy, negotiating child care, distance from extended kin or most other forms of traditional community, a high likelihood of loneliness and extreme economic vulnerability as they age. The ethnic and racial diversity of women in Silicon Valley structures a microcosm of conflicting differences in culture, family, religion, education, and language.

Richard Gordon has called this new situation the homework economy.[22] Although he includes the phenomenon of literal homework emerging in connection with electronics assembly, Gordon intends "homework economy" to name a restructuring of work that broadly has the characteristics formerly ascribed to female jobs, jobs literally done only by women. Work is being redefined as both literally female and feminized, whether performed by men or women. To be feminized means to be made extremely vulnerable; able to be disassembled, reassembled, exploited as a reserve labor force; seen less as workers than as servers; subjected to time arrangements on and off the paid job that make a mockery of a limited work day; leading an existence that always borders on being obscene, out of place, and reducible to sex. De-skilling is an old strategy newly applicable to formerly privileged workers. However, the homework economy does not refer only to large-scale de-skilling, nor does it deny that new areas of high skill are emerging, even for women and men previously excluded from skilled employment. Rather, the concept indicates that factory, home, and market are integrated on a new scale and that the places of women are crucial—and need to be analyzed for differences among women and for meanings for relations between men and women in various situations.

The homework economy as a world capitalist organizational structure is made possible by (not caused by) the new technologies. The success of the attack on relatively privileged, mostly white men's unionized jobs is tied to the power of the new communications technologies to integrate and control labor despite extensive dispersion and decentralization. The consequences of the new technologies are felt by women both in the loss of the family (male) wage (if they ever had access to this white privilege) and in the character of their own jobs, which are becoming capital-intensive, for example, office work and nursing.

The new economic and technological arrangements are also related to the collapsing welfare state and the ensuing intensification of demands on women to sustain daily life for themselves as well as for men, children, and old people. The feminization of poverty—generated by dismantling the welfare state, by the homework economy where stable jobs become the exception, and sustained by the expectation that women's wage will not be matched by a male income for the support of children—has become an urgent focus. The causes of various women-headed households are a function of race, class, or sexuality; but their increasing generality is a ground for coalitions of women on many issues. That women regularly sustain daily life partly as a function of their enforced status as mothers is hardly new; the kind of integration with the overall capitalist and progressively war-based economy is new. The particular pressure, for example, on U.S. black women, who have achieved an escape from (barely) paid domestic service and who now hold clerical and similar jobs in large numbers, has large implications for continued enforced black poverty with employment. Teenage women in industrializing areas of the third world increasingly find themselves the sole or major source of a cash wage for their families, while access to land is ever more problematic. These developments must have major consequences in the psychodynamics and politics of gender and race.

Within the narrative framework of three major stages of capitalism (commercial/early industrial, monopoly, multinational)—tied to nationalism, imperialism, and multinationalism, and related to Jameson's three dominant aesthetic periods of realism, modernism, and postmodernism—I would argue that specific forms of families dialectically relate to forms of capital and to its political and cultural concomitants. Although lived problematically and unequally, ideal forms of these families might be schematized as (1) the patriarchal nuclear family, structured by the dichotomy between public and private and accompanied by the white bourgeois ideology of separate spheres and nineteenth-century Anglo-American bourgeois feminism; (2) the modern family mediated (or enforced) by the welfare state and institutions like the family wage, with a flowering of a-feminist heterosexual ideologies, including their radical versions represented in Greenwich Village around World War I; and (3) the "family" of the homework economy with its oxymoronic structure of women-headed households and its explosion of feminisms and the paradoxical intensification and erosion of gender itself.

This is the context in which the projections for worldwide structural unemployment stemming from the new technologies are part of the picture of the homework economy. As robotics and related technologies put men out of work in "developed" countries and exacerbate failure to generate male jobs in third-world "development" and as the automated office becomes the rule even in labor-surplus countries, the feminization of work intensifies. Black women in the United States have long known what it looks like to face the structural underemployment ("feminization") of black men, as well as their own highly vulnerable position in the wage economy. It is no longer a secret that sexuality, reproduction, family, and community life are interwoven with this economic structure in myriad ways which have also differentiated the situations of white and black women. Many more women and men will contend with similar situations, which will make cross-gender and race alliances on issues of basic life support (with or without jobs) necessary, not just nice.

The new technologies also have a profound effect on hunger and on food production for subsistence worldwide. Rae Lessor Blumberg estimates that women produce about 50 percent of the world's subsistence food.[23]* Women are excluded generally from benefiting from the increased high-tech commodification of food and energy crops, their days are made more arduous because their responsibilities to provide food do not diminish, and their reproductive situations are made more complex. Green Revolution technologies interact with other high-tech industrial production to alter gender divisions of labor and differential gender migration patterns.

The new technologies seem deeply involved in the forms of "privatization" that Ros Petchesky has analyzed, in which militarization, right-wing family ideologies and policies, and intensified definitions of corporate (and state) property as private synergistically interact.[24] The new communications technologies are fundamental to the eradication of "public life" for everyone. This facilitates the mushrooming of a permanent high-tech military establishment at the cultural and economic expense of most people, but especially of women. Technologies like video games and highly miniaturized television seem crucial to production of modern forms of "private life." The culture of video games is heavily oriented to individual competition and extraterrestrial warfare. High-tech, gendered imagina-

---

*The conjunction of the Green Revolution's social relations with biotechnologies like plant genetic engineering makes the pressures on the land in the third world increasingly intense. The Agency for International Development's estimates (*New York Times* October 14, 1984) used at the 1984 World Food Day are that in Africa, women produce about 90 percent of rural food supplies, about 60 to 80 percent in Asia, and provide 40 percent of agricultural labor in the Near East and Latin America. Blumberg charges that world organizations' agricultural politics, as well as those of multinationals and national governments in the third world, generally ignore fundamental issues in the sexual division of labor. The present tragedy of famine in Africa might owe as much to male supremacy as to capitalism, colonialism, and rain patterns. More accurately, capitalism and racism are usually structurally male dominant.

tions are produced here, imaginations that can contemplate destruction of the planet and a sci-fi escape from its consequences. More than our imaginations is militarized, and the other realities of electronic and nuclear warfare are inescapable. These are the technologies that promise ultimate mobility and perfect exchange—and incidentally enable tourism, that perfect practice of mobility and exchange, to emerge as one of the world's largest single industries.

The new technologies affect the social relations of both sexuality and reproduction, and not always in the same ways. The close ties of sexuality and instrumentality, of views of the body as a kind of private satisfaction- and utility-maximizing machine, are described nicely in sociobiological origin stories that stress a genetic calculus and explain the inevitable dialectic of domination of male and female gender roles.[25] These sociobiological stories depend on a high-tech view of the body as a biotic component or cybernetic communications system. Among the many transformations of reproductive situations is the medical one, where women's bodies have boundaries newly permeable to both "visualization" and "intervention." Of course, who controls the interpretation of bodily boundaries in medical hermeneutics is a major feminist issue. The speculum served as an icon of women's claiming their bodies in the 1970s; that handcrafted tool is inadequate to express our needed body politics in the negotiation of reality in the practices of cyborg reproduction. Self-help is not enough. The technologies of visualization recall the important cultural practice of hunting with the camera and the deeply predatory nature of a photographic consciousness.[26] Sex, sexuality, and reproduction are central actors in high-tech myth systems structuring our imaginations of personal and social possibility.

Another critical aspect of the social relations of the new technologies is the reformulation of expectations, culture, work, and reproduction for the large scientific and technical work force. A major social and political danger is the formation of a strongly bimodal social structure, with masses of women and men of all ethnic groups, but especially people of color, confined to a homework economy, illiteracy of several varieties, and general redundancy and impotence, controlled by high-tech repressive apparatuses ranging from entertainment to surveillance and disappearance. An adequate socialist-feminist politics should address women in the privileged occupational categories and particularly in the production of science and technology that constructs scientific-technical discourse, processes, and objects.[27]

This issue is only one aspect of inquiry into the possibility of a feminist science, but it is important. What kind of constitutive role in the production of knowledge, imagination, and practice can new groups doing science have? How can these groups be allied with progressive social and political movements? What kind of political accountability can be constructed to tie women together across the scientific-technical hierarchies separating us? Might there be ways of developing feminist science/technology politics in alliance with anti-military science facility conversion action groups? Many scientific and technical workers in Silicon Valley, the high-tech cowboys included, do not want to work on military science.[28] Can these personal preferences and cultural tendencies be welded into progressive politics among this professional middle class in which women, including women of color, are coming to be fairly numerous?

Women in the Integrated Circuit

Let me summarize the picture of women's historical locations in advanced industrial societies, as these positions have been restructured partly through the social relations of science and technology. If it was ever possible ideologically to characterize women's lives by the distinction of public and private domains—suggested by images of the division of working-class life into factory and home, of bourgeois life into market and home, and of gender existence into personal and political realms—it is now a totally misleading ideology, even to show how both terms of these dichotomies construct each other in practice and in theory. I prefer a network ideological image, suggesting the profusion of spaces and identities and the permeability of boundaries in the personal body and in the body politic. "Networking" is both a feminist practice and a multinational corporate strategy—weaving is for oppositional cyborgs.

So let me return to the earlier image of the informatics of domination and trace one vision of women's "place" in the integrated circuit, touching only a few idealized social locations seen primarily from the point of view of advanced capitalist societies: Home, Market, Paid Work Place, State, School, Clinic-Hospital, and Church. Each of these idealized spaces is logically and practically implied in every other locus, perhaps analogous to a holographic photograph. I want to suggest the impact of the social relations mediated and enforced by the new technologies in order to help formulate needed analysis and practical work. However, there is no "place" for women in these networks, only geometries of difference and contradiction crucial to women's cyborg identities. If we learn how to read these webs of power and social life, we might learn new couplings, new coalitions. There is no way to read the following list from a standpoint of "identification," of a unitary self. The issue is dispersion. The task is to survive in diaspora.

Home: Women-headed households, serial monogamy, flight of men, old women alone, technology of domestic work, paid home work, reemergence of home sweatshops, home-based businesses and telecommuting, electronic cottage, urban homelessness, migration, module architecture, reinforced (simulated) nuclear family, intense domestic violence.

Market: Women's continuing consumption work, newly targeted to buy the profusion of new production from the new technologies (especially as the competitive race among industrialized and industrializing nations to avoid dangerous mass unemployment necessitates finding ever bigger new markets for ever less clearly needed commodities); bimodal buying power, coupled with advertising targeting of the numerous affluent groups and neglect of the previous mass markets; growing importance of informal markets in labor and commodities parallel to high-tech, affluent market structures; surveillance systems through electronic funds transfer; intensified market abstraction (commodification) of experience, resulting in ineffective utopian or equivalent cynical theories of community; extreme mobility (abstraction) of marketing/financing systems; interpenetration of sexual and labor markets; intensified sexualization of abstracted and alienated consumption.

Paid Work Place: Continued intense sexual and racial division of labor, but considerable growth of membership in privileged occupational categories for many white women and people of color; impact of new technologies on women's work in clerical, service, manufacturing (especially textiles), agriculture, electronics; international restructuring of the working classes; development of new time arrangements to facilitate the homework economy (flex time, part time, overtime, no time); homework and out work; increased pressures for two-tiered wage structures; significant numbers of people in cash-dependent populations worldwide with no experience or no further hope of stable employment; most labor "marginal" or "feminized."

State: Continued erosion of the welfare state; decentralizations with increased surveillance and control; citizenship by telematics; imperialism and political power broadly in the form of information-rich/information-poor differentiation; increased high-tech militarization increasingly opposed by many social groups; reduction of civil service jobs as a result of the growing capital intensification of office work, with implications for occupational mobility for women of color; growing privatization of material and ideological life and culture; close integration of privatization and militarization, the high-tech forms of bourgeois capitalist personal and public life; invisibility of different social groups to each other, linked to psychological mechanisms of belief in abstract enemies.

School: Deepening coupling of high-tech capital needs and public education at all levels, differentiated by race, class, and gender; managerial classes involved in educational reform and refunding at the cost of remaining progressive educational democratic structures for children and teachers; education for mass ignorance and repression in technocratic and militarized culture; growing anti-science mystery cults in dissenting and radical political movements; continued relative scientific illiteracy among white women and people of color; growing industrial direction of education (especially higher education) by science-based multinationals (particularly in electronics- and biotechnology-dependent companies); highly educated, numerous elites in a progressively bimodal society.

Clinic-Hospital: Intensified machine-body relations; renegotiations of public metaphors which channel personal experience of the body, particularly in relation to reproduction, immune system functions, and "stress" phenomena; intensification of reproductive politics in response to world historical implications of women's unrealized, potential control of their relation to reproduction; emergence of new historically specific diseases; struggles over meanings and means of health in environments pervaded by high-technology products and processes; continuing feminization of health work; intensified struggle over state responsibility for health; continued ideological role of popular health movements as a major form of American politics.

Church: Electronic fundamentalist "super-saver" preachers solemnizing the union of electronic capital and automated fetish gods; intensified importance of churches in resisting the militarized state; central struggle over women's meanings and authority in religion; continued relevance of spirituality, intertwined with sex and health, in political struggle.

The only way to characterize the informatics of domination is as a massive intensification of insecurity and cultural impoverishment, with common failure of subsistence networks for the most vulnerable. Since much of this picture interweaves with the social relations of science and technology, the urgency of a socialist-feminist politics addressed to science and technology is plain. There is much now being done, and the grounds for political work are rich. For example, the efforts to develop forms of collective struggle for women in paid work, like District 925 of the SEIU (Service Employees International Union) should be a high priority for all of us. These efforts are profoundly tied to technical restructuring of labor processes and reformations of working classes. These efforts also are providing understanding of a more comprehensive kind of labor organization, involving community, sexuality, and family issues never privileged in the largely white male industrial unions.

The structural rearrangements related to the social relations of science and technology evoke strong ambivalence. But it is not necessary to be ultimately depressed by the implications of late twentieth-century women's relation to all aspects of work, culture, production of knowledge, sexuality, and reproduction. For excellent reasons, most Marxisms see domination best and have trouble understanding what can only look like false consciousness and people's complicity in their own domination in late capitalism. It is crucial to remember that what is lost, perhaps especially from women's points of view, is often virulent forms of oppression, nostalgically naturalized in the face of current violation. Ambivalence toward the disrupted unities mediated by high-tech culture requires not sorting consciousness into categories of "clear-sighted critique grounding a solid political epistemology" versus "manipulated false consciousness," but subtle understanding of emerging pleasures, experiences, and powers with serious potential for changing the rules of the game.

There are grounds for hope in the emerging bases for new kinds of unity across race, gender, and class, as these elementary units of socialist-feminist analysis themselves suffer protean transformations. Intensifications of hardship experienced worldwide in connection with the social relations of science and technology are severe. But what people are experiencing is not transparently clear, and we lack sufficiently subtle connections for collectively building effective theories of experience. Present efforts—Marxist, psychoanalytic, feminist, anthropological—to clarify even "our" experience are rudimentary.

I am conscious of the odd perspective provided by my historical position—a Ph.D. in biology for an Irish Catholic girl was made possible by Sputnik's impact on U.S. national science-education policy. I have a body and mind as much constructed by the post–World War II arms race and cold war as by the women's movements. There are more grounds for hope by focusing on the contradictory effects of politics designed to produce loyal American technocrats, which as well produced large numbers of dissidents, rather than by focusing on the present defeats.

The permanent partiality of feminist points of view has consequences for our expectations of forms of political organization and participation. We do not need a totality in order to work well. The feminist dream of a common language, like all dreams for a perfectly true language, of a perfectly faithful naming of experience, is a totalizing and imperialist one. In that sense, dialectics too is a dream language, longing to resolve contradiction. Perhaps, ironically, we can learn from our fusions with animals and machines how not to be Man, the embodiment of Western logos. From the point of view of pleasure in these potent and taboo fusions, made inevitable by the social relations of science and technology, there might indeed be a feminist science.

Cyborgs: A Myth of Political Identity

I want to conclude with a myth about identity and boundaries which might inform late twentieth-century political imaginations. I am indebted in this story to writers like Joanna Russ, Samuel Delany, John Varley, James Tiptree, Jr., Octavia Butler, and Vonda McIntyre.[29] These are our storytellers exploring what it means to be embodied in high-tech worlds. They are theorists for cyborgs. Exploring conceptions of bodily boundaries and social order, the anthropologist Mary Douglas should be credited with helping us to consciousness about how fundamental body imagery is to world view and so to political language.[30] French feminists like Luce Irigaray and Monique Wittig, for all their differences, know how to write the body, how to weave eroticism, cosmology, and politics from imagery of embodiment, and especially for Wittig, from imagery of fragmentation and reconstitution of bodies.[31]

American radical feminists like Susan Griffin, Audre Lorde, and Adrienne Rich have profoundly affected our political imaginations—and perhaps restricted too much what we allow as a friendly body and political language.[32] They insist on the organic, opposing it to the technological. But their symbolic systems and the related positions of eco-feminism and feminist paganism, replete with organicisms, can only be understood in Sandoval's terms as oppositional ideologies fitting the late twentieth century. They would simply bewilder anyone not preoccupied with the machines and consciousness of late capitalism. In that sense they are part of the cyborg world. But there are also great riches for feminists in explicitly embracing the possibilities inherent in the breakdown of clean distinctions between organism and machine and similar distinctions structuring the Western self. It is the simultaneity of breakdowns that cracks the matrices of domination and opens geometric possibilities. What might be learned from personal and political "technological" pollution? I will look briefly at two overlapping groups of texts for their insight into the construction of a potentially helpful cyborg myth: constructions of women of color and monstrous selves in feminist science fiction.

Earlier I suggested that "women of color" might be understood as a cyborg identity, a potent subjectivity synthesized from fusions of outsider identities and in the complex political-historical layerings of Audre Lorde's "biomythography," *Zami*.[33] There are material and cultural grids mapping this potential. Lorde captures the tone in the title of her book *Sister Outsider*. In my political myth, Sister Outsider is the offshore woman, whom U.S. workers, female and feminized, are supposed to regard as the enemy preventing their solidarity, threatening their security. Onshore, inside the boundary of the United States, Sister Outsider is a potential amid the races and ethnic identities of women manipulated for division, competition, and exploitation in the same industries. "Women of color" are the preferred labor force for the science-based industries, the real women for whom the worldwide sexual market, labor market, and politics of reproduction kaleidoscope into daily life. Young Korean women hired in the sex industry and in electronics assembly are recruited from high schools, educated for the integrated circuit. Literacy, especially in English, distinguishes the "cheap" female labor so attractive to the multinationals.

Contrary to Orientalist stereotypes of the "oral primitive," literacy is a special mark of women of color, acquired by U.S. black women as well as men through a history of risking death to learn and to teach reading and writing. Writing has a special significance for all colonized groups. Writing has been crucial to the Western myth of the distinction of oral and written cultures, primitive and civilized mentalities, and more recently to the erosion of that distinction in postmodernist theories attacking the phallogocentrism of the West, with its worship of the monotheistic, phallic, authoritative, and singular work, the unique and perfect name.[34] Contests for the meanings of writing are a major form of contemporary political struggle. Releasing the play of writing is deadly serious. The poetry and stories of U.S. women of color are repeatedly about writing, about access to the power to signify, but this time that power must be neither phallic nor innocent. Cyborg writing must not be about the Fall, the imagination of a once-upon-a-time wholeness before language, before writing, before Man. Cyborg writing is about the power to survive not on the basis of original innocence, but on the basis of seizing the tools to mark the world that marked them as other.

The tools are often stories, retold stories, versions that reverse and displace the hierarchical dualisms of naturalized identities. In retelling origin stories, cyborg authors subvert the central myths of origin of Western culture. We have all been colonized by those origin myths, with their longing for fulfillment in apocalypse. The phallogocentric origin stories most crucial for feminist cyborgs are built into the literal technologies—technologies that write the world, biotechnology and microelectronics—that have recently textualized our bodies as code problems on the grid of C^3I. Feminist cyborg stories have the task of recoding communication and intelligence to subvert command and control.

Figuratively and literally, language politics pervade the struggles of women of color, and stories about language have a special power in the rich contemporary writing by U.S. women of color. For example, retellings of the story of the indigenous woman Malinche, mother of the mestizo "bastard" race of the new world, master of languages, and mistress of Cortés, carry special meaning for Chicana constructions of identity. Cherríe Moraga in *Loving in the War Years* explores the themes of identity when one never possessed the original language, never told the original story, never resided in the harmony of legitimate heterosexuality in the garden of culture, and so cannot base identity on a myth or a fall from innocence and right to natural names, mother's or father's.[35] Moraga's writing, her superb literacy, is presented in her poetry as the same kind of violation as Malinche's mastery of the conqueror's language—a violation, an illegitimate production, that allows survival. Moraga's language is not "whole"; it is self-consciously spliced, a chimera of English and Spanish, both conqueror's languages. But it is this chimeric monster, without claim to an original language before violation, that crafts the erotic, competent, potent identities of women of color. Sister Outsider hints at the possibility of world survival not because of her innocence, but because of her ability to live on the boundaries, to write without the founding myth of original wholeness, with its inescapable apocalypse of final return to a deathly oneness that Man has imagined to be the innocent and all-powerful Mother, freed at the End from another spiral of appropriation by her son. Writing marks Moraga's body, affirms it as the body of a woman of color, against the possibility of passing into the unmarked category of the Anglo father or into the Orientalist myth of "original illiteracy" of a mother that never was. Malinche was mother here, not Eve before eating the forbidden fruit. Writing affirms Sister Outsider, not the Woman-before-the-Fall-into-Writing needed by the phallogocentric Family of Man.

Writing is preeminently the technology of cyborgs, etched surfaces of the late twentieth century. Cyborg politics is the struggle for language and the struggle against perfect communication, against the one code that translates all meaning perfectly, the central dogma of phallogocentrism. That is why cyborg politics insist on noise and advocate pollution, rejoicing in the illegitimate fusions of animal and machine. These are the couplings which make Man and Woman so problematic, subverting the structure of desire, the force imagined to generate language and gender, and so subverting the structure and modes of reproduction of Western identity, of nature and culture, of mirror and eye, slave and master, body and mind. "We" did not originally choose to be cyborgs, but choice grounds a liberal politics and epistemology that imagines the reproduction of individuals before the wider replications of "texts."

From the perspective of cyborgs, freed of the need to ground politics in "our" privileged position of the oppression that incorporates all other dominations, the innocence of the merely violated, the ground of those closer to nature, we can see powerful possibilities. Feminisms and Marxisms have run aground of Western epistemological imperatives to construct a revolutionary subject from the perspective of a hierarchy of oppressions and a latent position of moral superiority, innocence, and greater closeness to nature. With no available original dream of a common language or original symbiosis promising protection from hostile "masculine" separation, but written into the play of a text that has no finally privileged reading or salvation history, to recognize "oneself" as fully implicated in the world, frees us of the need to root politics in identification, vanguard parties, purity, and mothering. Stripped of identity, the bastard race teaches about the power of the margins and the importance of a mother like Malinche. Women of color have transformed her from the evil mother of masculinist fear into the originally literate mother who teaches survival.

This is not just deconstruction but liminal transformation. Every story that begins with original innocence and privileges the return to wholeness imagines the drama of life to be individuation, separation, the birth of the self, the tragedy of autonomy, the fall into writing, alienation; that is, war, tempered by imaginary respite in the bosom of the Other. These plots are ruled by a reproductive politics—rebirth without flaw, perfection, abstraction. In this plot women are imagined either better or worse off, but all agree they have less selfhood, weaker individuation, more fusion to the oral, to Mother, less at stake in masculine autonomy. But there is another route to having less at stake in masculine autonomy, a route that does not pass through Woman, Primitive, Zero, the Mirror Stage and its imaginary. It passes through women and other present-tense, illegitimate cyborgs, not of Woman born, who refuse the ideological resources of victimization so as to have a real life. These cyborgs are the people who refuse to disappear on cue, no matter how many times a Western commentator remarks on the sad passing of another primitive, another organic group done in by Western technology, by writing.[36] These real-life cyborgs, for example, the Southeast Asian village women workers in Japanese and U.S. electronics firms described by Aihwa Ong, are actively rewriting the texts of their bodies and societies. Survival is the stakes in this play of readings.

To recapitulate, certain dualisms have been persistent in Western traditions; they have all been systemic to the logics and practices of domination of women, people of color, nature, workers, animals—in short, domination of all constituted as others, whose task is to mirror the self. Chief among these troubling dualisms are self/other, mind/body, culture/nature, male/female, civilized/primitive, reality/appearance, whole/part, agent/resource, maker/made, active/passive, right/wrong, truth/illusion, total/partial, God/man. The self is the One who is not dominated, who knows that by the service of the other; the other is the one who holds the future, who knows that by the experience of domination, which gives the lie to the autonomy of the self. To be One is to be autonomous, to be powerful, to be God; but to be One is to be an illusion and so to be involved in a dialectic of apocalypse with the other. Yet, to be other is to be multiple, without clear boundaries, frayed, insubstantial. One is too few, but two are too many.

High-tech culture challenges these dualisms in intriguing ways. It is not clear who makes and who is made in the relation between human and machine. It is not clear what is mind and what is body in machines that resolve into coding practices. Insofar as we know ourselves in both formal discourse (e.g., biology) and in daily practice, (e.g., the homework economy in the integrated circuit), we find ourselves to be cyborgs, hybrids, mosaics, chimeras. Biological organisms have become biotic systems, communications devices like others. There is no fundamental, ontological separation in our formal knowledge of machine and organism, of technical and organic. The replicant Rachel in the film *Blade Runner* stands as the image of a cyborg culture's fear, love, and confusion.

One consequence is that our sense of connection to our tools is heightened. The trance state experienced by many computer users has become a staple of science-fiction film and cultural jokes. Perhaps paraplegics and other severely handicapped people can (and sometimes do) have the most intense experiences of complex hybridization with other communication devices.[37] Anne McCaffrey's prefeminist *The Ship Who Sang* explored the consciousness of a cyborg, hybrid of girl's brain and complex machinery, formed after the birth of a severely handicapped child. Gender, sexuality, embodiment, skill: All were reconstituted in the story. Why should our bodies end at the skin or include at best other beings encapsulated by skin? From the seventeenth century till now, machines could be animated— given ghostly souls to make them speak or move or to account for their orderly development and mental capacities. Or organisms could be mechanized—reduced to body understood as resource of mind. These machine/organism relationships are obsolete, unnecessary. For us, in imagination and in other practice, machines can be prosthetic devices, intimate components, friendly selves. We don't need organic holism to give impermeable wholeness, the total woman and her feminist variants (mutants?). Let me conclude this point by a very partial reading of the logic of the cyborg monsters of my second group of texts, feminist science fiction.

The cyborgs populating feminist science fiction make very problematic the statuses of man or woman, human, artifact, member of a race, individual identity, or body. Katie King clarifies how pleasure in reading these fictions is not largely based on identification. Students facing Joanna Russ for the first time, students who have learned to take modernist writers like James Joyce or Virginia Woolf without flinching, do not know what to make of *The Adventures of Alyx of The Female Man*, where characters refuse the reader's search for innocent wholeness while granting the wish for heroic quests, exuberant eroticism, and serious politics. *The Female Man* is the story of four versions of one genotype, all of whom meet, but even taken together do not make a whole, resolve the dilemmas of violent moral action, nor remove the growing scandal of gender. The feminist science fiction of Samuel Delany, especially *Tales of Neverÿon*, mocks stories of origin by redoing the neolithic revolution, replaying the founding moves of Western civilization to subvert their plausibility. James Tiptree, Jr., an author whose fiction was regarded as particularly manly until her "true" gender was revealed, tells tales of reproduction based on nonmammalian technologies like alternation of generations or male brood pouches and male nurturing. John Varley constructs a supreme cyborg in his archfeminist exploration of Gaea, a mad goddess-planet-trickster-old-woman-technological device on whose surface an extraordinary array of post cyborg symbioses are spawned. Octavia Butler writes of an African sorceress pitting her powers of transformation against the genetic manipulations of her rival (*Wild Seed*), of time warps that bring a modern U.S. black woman into slavery where her actions in relation to her white master-ancestor determine the possibility of her own birth (*Kindred*), and of the illegitimate insights into identity and community of an adopted cross-species child who came to know the enemy as self (*Survivor*). In her recent novel, *Dawn* (1987), the first installment of a series called *Xenogenesis*, Butler tells the story of Lilith Iyapo, whose personal name recalls Adam's first and repudiated wife and whose family name marks her status as the widow of the son of Nigerian immigrants to the United States. A black woman and a mother whose child is dead, Lilith mediates the transformation of humanity through genetic exchange with extraterrestrial lovers/rescuers/destroyers/genetic engineers, who reform earth's habitats after the nuclear holocaust and coerce surviving humans into intimate fusion with them. It is a novel that interrogates reproductive, linguistic, and nuclear politics in a mythic field structured by late twentieth-century race and gender.

Because it is particularly rich in boundary transgressions, Vonda McIntyre's *Superluminal* can close this truncated catalogue of promising and dangerous monsters who help redefine the pleasures and politics of embodiment and feminist writing. In a fiction where no character is "simply" human, human status is highly problematic. Orca, a genetically altered diver, can speak with killer whales and survive deep ocean conditions, but she longs to explore space as a pilot, necessitating bionic implants jeopardizing her kinship with the divers and cetaceans. Transformations are effected by virus vectors carrying a new developmental code, by transplant surgery, by implants of microelectronic devices, by analogue doubles, and by other means. Laenea becomes a pilot by accepting a heart implant and a host of other alterations allowing survival in transit at speeds exceeding that of light. Radu Dracul survives a virus-caused plague on his outerworld planet to find himself with a time sense that changes the boundaries of spatial perception for the whole species. All the characters explore the limits of language, the dream of communicating experience, and the necessity of limitation, partiality, and intimacy even in this world of protean transformation and connection. *Superluminal* stands also for the defining contradictions of a cyborg world in another sense; it embodies textually the intersection of feminist theory and colonial discourse in the science fiction I have alluded to in this essay. This is a conjunction with a long history that many first world feminists have tried to repress, including myself in my readings of *Superluminal* before being called to account by Zoe Soufoulis, whose different location in the world system's informatics of domination made her acutely alert to the imperialist moment of all science-fiction cultures, including women's science fiction. From an Australian feminist sensitivity, Sofoulis remembered more readily McIntyre's role as writer of the adventures of Captain Kirk and Spock in "Star Trek" than her rewriting the romance in *Superluminal*.

Monsters have always defined the limits of community in Western imaginations. The centaurs and Amazons of ancient Greece established the limits of the centered polis of the Greek male human by their disruption of marriage and boundary pollutions of the warrior with animality and woman. Unseparated twins and hermaphrodites were the confused human material in early modern France who grounded discourse on the natural and supernatural, medical and legal, portents and diseases—all crucial to establishing modern identity.[38] The evolutionary and behavioral sciences of monkeys and apes have marked the multiple boundaries of late twentieth-century industrial identities. Cyborg monsters in feminist science fiction define quite different political possibilities and limits from those proposed by the mundane fiction of Man and Woman.

There are several consequences to taking seriously the imagery of cyborgs as other than our enemies. Our bodies, ourselves—bodies are maps of power and identity. Cyborgs are no exceptions. A cyborg body is not innocent; it was not born in a garden; it does not seek unitary identity and so generates antagonistic dualisms without end (or until the world ends); it takes irony for granted. One is too few, and two is only one possibility. Intense pleasure in skill, machine skill, ceases to be a sin, but an aspect of embodiment. The machine is not an it to be animated, worshiped, and dominated. The machine is us, our processes, an aspect of our embodiment. We can be responsible for machines; they do not dominate or threaten us. We are responsible for boundaries; we are they. Up till now (once upon a time), female embodiment seemed to be given, organic, necessary; female embodiment seemed to mean skill in mothering and its metaphoric extensions. Only by being out of place could we take intense pleasure in machines and then with excuses that this was organic activity after all, appropriate to females. Cyborgs might consider more seriously the partial, fluid, sometimes aspect of sex and sexual embodiment. Gender might not be global identity after all, even if it has profound historical breadth and depth.

The ideologically charged question of what counts as daily activity, as experience, can be approached by exploiting the cyborg image. Feminists have recently claimed that women are given to dailiness, that women more than men somehow sustain daily life, and so have a privileged epistemological position potentially. There is a compelling aspect to this claim, one that makes visible unvalued female activity and names it as the ground of life. But the ground of life? What about all the ignorance of women, all the exclusions and failures of knowledge and skill? What about men's access to daily competence, to knowing how to build things, to take them apart, to play? What about other embodiments? Cyborg gender is a local possibility taking a global vengeance. Race, gender, and capital require a cyborg theory of wholes and parts. There is no drive in cyborgs to produce total theory, but there is an intimate experience of boundaries, their construction and deconstruction. There is a myth system waiting to become a political language to ground one way of looking at science and technology and challenging the informatics of domination— in order to act potently.

One last image: organisms and organismic, holistic politics depend on metaphors of rebirth and invariably call on the resources of reproductive sex. I would suggest that cyborgs have more to do with regeneration and are suspicious of the reproductive matrix and of most birthing. For salamanders, regeneration after injury, such as the loss of a limb, involves regrowth of structure and restoration of function with the constant possibility of twinning or other odd topographical productions at the site of former injury. The regrown limb can be monstrous, duplicated, potent. We have all been injured, profoundly. We require regeneration, not rebirth, and the possibilities for our reconstitution include the utopian dream of the hope for a monstrous world without gender.

Cyborg imagery can help express two crucial arguments in this essay: (1) the production of universal, totalizing theory is a major mistake that misses most of reality, probably always, but certainly now; (2) taking responsibility for the social relations of science and technology means refusing an anti-science metaphysics, a demonology of technology, and so means embracing the skillful task of reconstructing the boundaries of daily life, in partial connection with others, in communication with all of our parts. It is not just that science and technology are possible means of great human satisfaction, as well as a matrix of complex dominations. Cyborg imagery can suggest a way out of the maze of dualisms in which we have explained our bodies and our tools to ourselves. This is a dream not of a common language, but of a powerful infidel heteroglossia. It is an imagination of a feminist speaking in tongues to strike fear into the circuits of the super savers of the New Right. It means both building and destroying machines, identities, categories, relationships, spaces, stories. Although both are bound in the spiral dance, I would rather be a cyborg than a goddess.

Acknowledgments

Research was funded by an Academic Senate Faculty Research Grant from the University of California, Santa Cruz. An earlier version of this chapter, on genetic engineering, appeared as "Lieber Kyborg als Göttin: Für eine sozialistisch-feministische Unterwanderung der Gentechnologie," in Bernd-Peter Lange and Anna Marie Stuby, eds., (Berlin: Argument-Sonderband 105, 1984), pp. 66–84. The cyborg manifesto grew from "New Machines, New Bodies, New Communities: Political Dilemmas of a Cyborg Feminist," The Scholar and the Feminist X: The Question of Technology Conference, April 1983.

The people associated with the History of Consciousness Board of University of California, Santa Cruz, have had an enormous influence on this essay, so that it feels collectively authored more than most, although those I cite may not recognize their ideas. In particular, members of graduate and undergraduate feminist theory, science and politics, and theory and methods courses have contributed to the cyborg manifesto. Particular debts here are due Hilary Klein ("Marxism, Psychoanalysis, and Mother Nature"); Paul Edwards ("Border Wars: The Science and Politics of Artificial Intelligence"); Lisa Lowe ("Julia Kristeva's *Des Chinoises:* Representing Cultural and Sexual Others"); Jim Clifford, "On Ethnographic Allegory," in James Clifford and George E. Marcus, eds., *Writing Culture, the Poetics and Politics of Ethnography* (University of California Press, 1985), pp. 98–121.

Parts of the chapter were my contribution to a collectively developed session, Poetic Tools and Political Bodies: Feminist Approaches to High Technology Culture, 1984 California American Studies Association, with History of Consciousness graduate students Zoe Soufoulis, "Jupiter Space"; Katie King, "The Pleasures of Repetition and the Limits of Identification in Feminist Science Fiction: Reimaginations of the Body after the Cyborg"; and Chela Sandoval, "The Construction of Subjectivity and Oppositional Consciousness in Feminist Film and Video." Sandoval's theory of oppositional consciousness was published as "Women Respond to Rascism: A Report on the National Women's Studies Association Conference," Center for Third World Organizing, Oakland, California, n.d. For Sofoulis's semiotic-psychoanalytic readings of nuclear culture, see Z. Sofia, "Exterminating Fetuses: Abortion, Disarmament and the Sexo-Semiotics of Extraterrestrialism," Nuclear Criticism issue, *Diacritics,* Vol 14, No. 2, 1984, pp. 47–59. King's manuscripts ("Questioning Tradition: Canon Formation and the Veiling of Power"; "Gender and Genre: Reading the Science Fiction of Joanna Russ"; "Varley's Titan and Wizard: Feminist Parodies of Nature, Culture, and Hardware") deeply inform the cyborg manifesto.

Barbara Epstein, Jeff Escoffier, Rusten Hogness, and Jaye Miler gave extensive discussion and editorial help. Members of the Silicon Valley Research Project of the University of California, Santa Cruz and participants in conferences and workshops sponsored by SVRP (Silicone Valley Research Project) have been very important, especially Rick Gordon, Linda Kimball, Nancy Snyder, Langdon Winner, Judith Stacey, Linda Lim, Patricia Fernandez-Kelly, and Judith Gregory. Finally, I want to thank Nancy Hartsock for years of friendship and discussion on feminist theory and feminist science fiction. I also thank Elizabeth Bird for my favorite political button: Cyborgs for Earthly Survival.

Notes

1. Useful references to left and/or feminist radical science movements and theory and to biological/biotechnological issues include Ruth Bleier, *Science and Gender: A Critique of Biology and Its Themes on Women* (New York: Pergamon, 1984); Ruth Bleier, ed., *Feminist Approaches to Science* (New York: Pergamon, 1986); Sandra Harding, *The Science Question in Feminism* (Ithaca, NY: Cornell University Press, 1986); Anne Fausto-Sterling, *Myths of Gender* (New York: Basic Books, 1985): Stephen J. Gould, *Mismeasure of Man* (New York: Norton, 1981); Ruth Hubbard, Mary Sue Henifin, Barbara Fried, eds., *Biological Woman, the Convenient Myth* (Cambridge, MA: Schenkman, 1982); Evelyn Fox Keller, *Reflections on Gender and Science* (New Haven, CT: Yale University Press, 1985); R. C. Lewontin, Steve Rose, and Leon Kamin, *Not in Our Genes* (New York: Pantheon, 1984); *Radical Science Journal* (from 1987, *Science as Culture*), 26 Freegrove Road, London N7 9RQ; *Science for the People,* 897 Main St., Cambridge, MA 02139.

2. Starting points for left and/or feminist approaches to technology and politics include Ruth Schwartz Cowan, *More Work for Mother: The Ironies of Household Technology from the Open Hearth to the Microwave* (New York: Basic Books, 1983); Joan Rothschild, *Machina ex Dea: Feminist Perspectives on Technology* (New York: Pergamon, 1983); Sharon Traweek, *Beantimes and Lifetimes: The World of High Energy Physics* (Cambridge, MA: Harvard University Press, 1988); R. M. Young and Les Levidov, eds., *Science, Technology, and the Labour Process,* Vols. 1–3 (London: CSE Books); Joseph Weizenbaum, *Computer Power and Human Reason* (San Francisco: Freeman, 1976); Langdon Winner, *Autonomous Technology: Technics Out of Control as a Theme in Political Thought* (Cambridge, MA: MIT Press, 1977); Langdon Winner, *The Whale and the Reactor* (Chicago: Chicago University Press, 1986); Jan Zimmerman, ed., *The Technological Woman: Interfacing with Tomorrow* (New York: Praeger, 1983); Tom Athanasiou, "High-tech Politics. The Case of Artificial Intelligence," *Socialist Review,* No. 92, 1987, pp. 7–35; Carol Cohn, "Nuclear Language and How We Learned to Pat the Bomb," *Bulletin of*

Atomic Scientists, June 1987, pp. 17–24; Terry Winograd and Fernando Flores, *Understanding Computers and Cognition: A New Foundation for Design* (New Jersey: Ablex, 1986); Paul Edwards, "Border Wars: The Politics of Artificial Intelligence," *Radical America,* Vol. 19, No. 6, 1985, pp. 39–52; *Global Electronics Newsletter,* 867 West Dana St., #204, Mountain View, CA 94041; *Processed World,* 55 Sutter St., San Francisco, CA 94104; *ISIS,* Women's International Information and Communication Service, P.O. Box 50 (Cornavin), 1211 Geneva 2, Switzerland, and Via Santa Maria dell'Anima 30, 00186 Rome, Italy. Fundamental approaches to modern social studies of science that do not continue the liberal mystification that it all started with Thomas Kuhn, include: Karin Knorr-Cetina, *The Manufacture of Knowledge* (Oxford: Pergamon, 1981); K. D. Knorr-Cetina and Michael Mulkay, eds., *Science Observed: Perspectives on the Social Study of Science* (Beverly Hills, CA: Sage, 1983); Bruno Latour and Steve Woolgar, *Laboratory Life: The Social Construction of Scientific Facts* (Beverly Hills, CA: Sage, 1979); Robert M. Young, "Interpreting the Production of Science," *New Scientist,* Vol. 29, March 1979, pp. 1026–1028. More is claimed than is known about room for contesting productions of science in the mythic/material space of "the laboratory"; the 1984 Directory of the Network for the Ethnographic Study of Science, Technology, and Organizations lists a wide range of people and projects crucial to better radical analysis; available from NESSTO, P.O. Box 11442, Stanford, CA 94305.

3.   Fredric Jameson, "Post Modernism, or the Cultural Logic of Late Capitalism," *New Left Review,* July/August 1984, pp. 53–94. See Marjorie Perloff, " 'Dirty' Language and Scramble Systems," *Sulfur* Vol 2, 1984, pp. 178–183; Kathleen Fraser, *Something (Even Human Voices) in the Foreground, a Lake* (Berkeley, CA: Kelsey St. Press, 1984). For feminist modernist/postmodernist cyborg writing, see *How(ever),* 871 Corbett Ave., San Francisco, CA 94131.

4.   Frans de Waal, *Chimpanzee Politics: Power and Sex among the Apes* (New York: Harper & Row, 1982); Langdon Winner, "Do artifacts have politics?" *Daedalus* (Winter 1980): 121–136.

5.   Jean Baudrillard, *Simulations,* trans. P. Foss, P. Patton, P. Beitchman (New York: Semiotext(e), 1983). Jameson ("Postmodernism," p. 66) points out that Plato's definition of the simulacrum is the copy for which there is no original, i.e., the world of advanced capitalism, of pure exchange. See *Discourse 9,* Spring/Summer 1987, for a special issue on technology (Cybernetics, Ecology, and the Postmodern Imagination).

6.   Herbert Marcuse, *One-Dimensional Man* (Boston: Beacon Press, 1964); Carolyn Merchant, *Death of Nature* (San Francisco: Harper & Row, 1980).

7.   Zoe Sofia, "Exterminating Fetuses," *Diacritics,* Vol. 14, No. 2, Summer 1984, pp. 47–59, and "Jupiter Space" (Pomona, CA: American Studies Association, 1984).

8.   For ethnographic accounts and political evaluations, see Barbara Epstein,

"The Politics of Prefigurative Community: The Non-Violent Direction Action Movement," *The Year Left,* forthcoming, and Noel Sturgeon, qualifying essay on feminism, anarchism, and nonviolent direct-action politics, University of California, Santa Cruz, 1986. Without explicit irony, adopting the spaceship earth/whole earth logo of the planet photographed from space, set off by the slogan "Love Your Mother," the May 1987 Mothers and Others Day action at the nuclear weapons testing facility in Nevada nonetheless took account of the tragic contradictions of views of the earth. Demonstrators applied for official permits to be on the land from officers of the Western Shoshone tribe, whose territory was invaded by the U.S. government when it built the nuclear weapons test ground in the 1950s. Arrested for trespassing, the demonstrators argued that the police and weapons facility personnel, without authorization from the proper officials, were the trespassers. One affinity group at the women's action called themselves the Surrogate Others, and in solidarity with the creatures forced to tunnel in the same ground with the bomb, they enacted a cyborgian emergence from the constructed body of a large, nonheterosexual desert worm.

9. Powerful developments of coalition politics emerge from "third world" speakers, speaking from nowhere, the displaced center of the universe, earth: "We live on the third planet from the sun"—*Sun Poem* by Jamaican writer Edward Kamau Braithwaite, review by Nathaniel Mackey, *Sulfur,* Vol. 2, 1984, pp. 200–205. *Home Girls,* ed. Barbara Smith (New York: Kitchen Table Women of Color Press, 1983), ironically subverts naturalized identities precisely while constructing a place from which to speak called home. See Bernice Reagan, "Coalition Politics, Turning the Century," pp. 356–368. Trinh T. Minh-ha, ed., "She, the Inappropriate/d Other," *Discourse* Vol. 8, Fall/Winter 1986–1987.

10. Chela Sandoval, "Dis-Illusionment and the Poetry of the Future: The Making of Oppositional Consciousness," Ph.D. qualifying essay, University of California, Santa Cruz, 1984.

11. Bell Hooks, *Ain't I a Woman?* (Boston: South End Press, 1981); Bell Hooks, *Feminist Theory: From Margin to Center* (Boston: South End Press, 1984); Gloria Hull, Patricia Bell Scott, and Barbara Smith, eds., *All the Women Are White, All the Men Are Black, But Some of Us Are Brave: Black Women's Studies* (Old Westbury, NY: Feminist Press, 1982). Toni Cade Bambara, *The Salt Eaters* (New York: Vintage/Random House, 1981), writes an extraordinary postmodernist novel, in which the women of color theater group, The Seven Sisters, explores a form of unity. Elliott Butler-Evans, *Race, Gender, and Desire: Narrative Strategies and the Production of Ideology in the Fiction of Toni Cade Bambara, Toni Morrison and Alice Walker,* Ph.D. Dissertation, University of California, Santa Cruz, 1987.

12. On Orientalism in feminist works and elsewhere, see Lisa Lowe, "Orientation: Representations of Cultural and Sexual 'Others,'" Ph.D. thesis, University of California, Santa Cruz; Edward Said, *Orientalism* (New York:

228 / Donna Haraway

Pantheon, 1978). Chandra Talpade Mohanty, "Under Western Eyes: Feminist Scholarship and Colonial Discourse," *Boundry* Vol. 2, No. 12, and Vol 3, No. 13, 1984, pp. 333–357; "Many Voices, One Chant: Black Feminist Perspectives," *Feminist Review*, Vol. 17, Autumn 1984.

13. Katie King has developed a theoretically sensitive treatment of the workings of feminist taxonomies as genealogies of power in feminist ideology and polemic: Katie King, "Canons without Innocence," Ph.D. thesis, University of California, Santa Cruz, 1987, and "The Situation of Lesbianism as Feminism's Magical Sign: Contests for Meaning in the U.S. Women's Movement, 1968–72," *Communication* Vol. 9, No. 1, 1985, pp. 65–91. King examines an intelligent, problematic example of taxonomizing feminisms to make a little machine producing the desired final position; Alison Jaggar, *Feminist Politics and Human Nature* (Totowa, NJ: Rowman & Allanheld, 1983). My caricature here of socialist and radical feminism is also an example.

14. The feminist standpoint argument has been developed by Jane Flax, "Political Philosophy and the Patriarchal Unconsciousness," *Discovering Reality*, ed. Sandra Harding and Merill Hintikka, (Dordrecht: Reidel, 1983); Sandra Harding, "The Contradictions and Ambivalence of a Feminist Science," ms.; Harding and Hintikka, *Discovering Reality*; Nancy Hartsock, *Money, Sex and Power* (New York: Longman, 1983) and "The Feminist Standpoint: Developing the Ground for a Specifically Feminist Historical Materialism," *Discovering Reality*, ed. S. Harding and M. Hintikka; Mary O'Brien, *The Politics of Reproduction* (New York: Routledge & Kegan Paul, 1981); Hilary Rose, "Hand, Brain, and Heart: A Feminist Epistemology for the Natural Sciences," *Signs*, Vol. 9, No. I, 1983, pp. 73–90; Dorothy Smith, "Women's Perspective as a Radical Critique of Sociology," Sociological Inquiry Vol 44, 1974, and "A Sociology of Women," *The Prism of Sex*, ed. J. Sherman and E. T. Beck, Madison, WI: University of Wisconsin Press, 1979). For rethinking theories of feminist materialism and feminist standpoint in response to criticism, see Chapter 7 in Harding, *The Science Question in Feminism,* op. cit. (note 1); Nancy Hartsock, "Rethinking Modernism: Minority vs. Majority Theories," *Cultural Critique* 7 (1987): 187–206; Hilary Rose, "Women's Work: Women's Knowledge," *What is Feminism? A Re-examination*, ed. Juliet Mitchell and Ann Oakley (New York: Pantheon, 1986), pp. 161–83.

15. Catherine MacKinnon, "Feminism, Marxism, Method, and the State: An Agenda for Theory," *Signs*, Vol. 7, No. 3, Spring 1982, pp. 515–544. See also MacKinnon, *Feminism Unmodified* (Cambridge, MA: Harvard University Press, 1987). I make a category error in "modifying" MacKinnon's positions with the qualifier "radical," thereby generating my own reductive critique of extremely heterogeneous writing, which does explicitly use that label, by my taxonomically interested argument about writing which does not use the modifier and which brooks no limits and thereby adds to the various dreams of a common, in the sense of univocal, language for feminism. My category error was occasioned by an assignment to write

from a particular taxonomic position which itself has a heterogeneous history, socialist feminism, for *Socialist Review*. A critique indebted to MacKinnon, but without the reductionism and with an elegant feminist account of Foucault's paradoxical conservatism on sexual violence (rape), is Teresa de Lauretis, "The Violence of Rhetoric: Considerations on Representation and Gender," *Semiotica*, Vol. 54, 1985, pp. 11–31, and Teresa de Lauretis, ed., *Feminist Studies/Critical Studies* (Bloomington: Indiana University Press, 1986). A theoretically elegant feminist social-historical examination of family violence, that insists on women's, men's, and children's complex agency without losing sight of the material structures of male domination, race, and class, is Linda Gordon, *Heroes of their own Lives* (New York: Viking, 1988).

16. My previous efforts to understand biology as a cybernetic command-control discourse and organisms as "natural-technical objects of knowledge" are "The High Cost of Information in Post-World War II Evolutionary Biology," *Philosophical Forum*, Vol. 13, Nos. 2–3, 1979, pp. 206–237; "Signs of Dominance: From a Physiology to a Cybernetics of Primate Society," *Studies in History of Biology*, Vol. 6, 1983, pp. 129–219; "Class, Race, Sex, Scientific Objects of Knowledge: A Socialist-Feminist Perspective on the Social Construction of Productive Knowledge and Some Political Consequences," *Women in Scientific and Engineering Professions*, ed. Violet Haas and Carolyn Perucci (Ann Arbor, MI: University of Michigan Press, 1984), pp. 212–229.

17. E. Rusten Hogness, "Why Stress? A Look at the Making of Stress, 1936–1956," available from the author, 4437 Mill Creek Rd., Healdsburg, CA 95448.

18. A left entry to the biotechnology debate: *Genewatch*, a Bulletin of the Committee for Responsible Genetics, 5 Doane St., 4th floor, Boston, MA 02109; Susan Wright, "Recombinant DNA Technology and Its Social Transformation, 1972–82," *Osiris*, 2nd series, Vol. 2, 1986, pp. 303–360 and "Recombinant DNA: The Status of Hazards and Controls," *Environment*, July/August 1982; Edward Yoxen, *The Gene Business* (New York: Harper & Row, 1983).

19. Paula Treichler, "AIDS, Homophobia, and Biomedical Discourse: An Epidemic of Signification," forthcoming in *Cultural Studies*.

20. Starting references for "women in the integrated circuit": *Scientific-Technological Change and the Role of Women in Development*, ed. Pamela D'Onofrio-Flores and Sheila M. Pfafflin (Boulder, CO: Westview Press, 1982); Maria Patricia Fernandez-Kelly, *For We Are Sold, I and My People* (Albany, NY: SUNY Press, 1983); Annette Fuentes and Barbara Ehrenreich, *Women in the Global Factory* (Boston: South End Press, 1983), with an especially useful list of resources and organizations; Rachael Grossman, "Women's Place in the Integrated Circuit," *Radical America*, Vol. 14, No. I, 1980, pp. 29–50; *Women and Men and the International Division of Labor*, ed. June Nash and M. P. Fernandez-Kelly (Albany, NY: SUNY

Press, 1983); Aihwa Ong, "Japanese Factories, Malay Workers: Industrialization and the Cultural Construction of Gender in West Malaysia, *Power and Difference,* ed. Shelly Errington and Jane Atkinson (Palo Alto, CA: Stanford University Press, forthcoming); Aihwa Ong, *Spirits of Resistance and Capitalist Discipline: Factory Workers in Malaysia* (Albany, SUNY Press, 1987); *Science Policy Research Unity, Microelectronics and Women's Employment in Britain* (University of Sussex, 1982).

21. The best example is Bruno Latour, *Les Microbes: Guerre et Paix, suivi de Irréductions* (Paris: Métailié, 1984).

22. For the homework economy and some related arguments: Richard Gordon, "The Computerization of Daily Life, the Sexual Division of Labor, and the Homework Economy," paper delivered at the Silicon Valley Workshop Group conference, 1983; Richard Gordon and Linda Kimball, "High-Technology, Employment and the Challenges of Education," *SVRG Working Paper,* No. 1, July 1985; Judith Stacey, "Sexism by a Subtler Name? Postindustrial Conditions and Postfeminist Consciousness in the Silicon Valley," *Socialist Review,* no. 96, 1987, pp. 7–30; Women's Work, Men's Work, ed. Barbara F. Reskin and Heidi Hartmann (Washington, DC: National Academy of Sciences Press, 1986); *Signs,* Vol. 10, No. 2, 1984, special issue on women and poverty; Stephen Rose, *The American Profile Poster: Who Owns What, Who Makes How Much, Who Works Where, and Who Lives With Whom?* (New York: Pantheon, 1986); Patricia Hill Collins, "Third World Women in America," and Sara G. Burr, "Women and Work," ed. Barbara K. Haber, *The Women's Annual,* 1981 (Boston: G. K. Hall, 1982); Judith Gregory and Karen Nussbaum, "Race against Time: Automation of the Office," *Office: Technology and People,* Vol. 1, 1982, pp. 197–236; Frances Fox Piven and Richard Cloward, *The New Class War: Reagan's Attack on the Welfare State and Its Consequences* (New York: Pantheon, 1982); Microelectronics Group, *Microelectronics: Capitalist Technology and the Working Class* (London: CSE, 1980); Karin Stallard, Barbara Ehrenreich, and Holly Sklar, *Poverty in the American Dream* (Boston: South End Press, 1983) including a useful organization and resource list.

23. Rae Lessor Blumberg, "A General Theory of Sex Stratification and Its Application to the Position of Women in Today's World Economy," paper delivered to Sociology Board, University of California, Santa Cruz, February 1983. Also R. L. Blumberg, *Stratification: Socioeconomic and Sexual Inequality* (Boston: Brown, 1981). See also Sally Hacker, "Doing It the Hard Way: Ethnographic Studies in the Agribusiness and Engineering Classroom," California American Studies Association, Pomona, 1984, forthcoming in *Humanity and Society*; S. Hacker and Lisa Bovit, Agriculture to Agribusiness: Technical Imperatives and Changing Roles" *Proceedings of the Society for the History of Technology, Milwaukee,* 1981; Lawrence Busch and William Lacy, *Science, Agriculture, and the Politics of Research* (Boulder, CO: Westview Press, 1983); Denis Wilfred, "Capital and Agriculture, a Review of Marxian Problematics," *Studies in Political Economy,*

No. 7, 1982, pp. 127–154; Carolyn Sachs, *The Invisible Farmers: Women in Agricultural Production* (Totowa, NJ: Rowman & Allanheld, 1983). International Fund for Agricultural Development, IFAD Experience Relating to Rural Women, 1977–84 (Rome: IFAD, 1985), 37 pp. Thanks to Elizabeth Bird, "Green Revolution Imperialism," I & II, ms. University of California, Santa Cruz, 1984.

24. Cynthia Enloe, "Women Textile Workers in the Militarization of Southeast Asia," *Women and Men*, ed. Nash and Fernandez-Kelly; Rosalind Petchesky, "Abortion, Anti-Feminism, and the Rise of the New Right," *Feminist Studies*, Vol. 7, No. 2, 1981. Cynthia Enloe, *Does Khaki Become You? The Militarization of Women's Lives* (Boston: South End Press, 1983).

25. For a feminist version of this logic, see Sarah Blaffer Hrdy, *The Woman That Never Evolved* (Cambridge, MA: Harvard University Press, 1981). For an analysis of scientific women's story-telling practices, especially in relation to sociobiology, in evolutionary debates around child abuse and infanticide, see Donna Haraway, "The Contest for Primate Nature: Daughters of Man the Hunter in the Field, 1960–80," *The Future of American Democracy*, ed. Mark Kann (Philadelphia: Temple University Press, 1983), pp. 175–208. See also D. Haraway, *Primate Visions: Gender, Race, and Nature in the World of Modern Science* (New York: Routledge, 1989).

26. For the moment of transition of hunting with guns to hunting with cameras in the construction of popular meanings of nature for an American urban immigrant public, see Donna Haraway, "Teddy Bear Patriarchy," *Social Text*, No. 11, Winter 1984–1985, pp. 20–64; Roderick Nash, "The Exporting and Importing of Nature: Nature-Appreciation as a Commodity, 1850–1980," *Perspectives in American History*, Vol. 3, 1979, pp. 517–560; Susan Sontag, *On Photography* (New York: Dell, 1977); and Douglas Preston, "Shooting in Paradise," *Natural History*, Vol. 93, No. 12, December 1984, pp. 14–19.

27. For crucial guidance for thinking about the political/cultural implications of the history of women doing science in the United States see *Women in Scientific and Engineering Professions*, ed. Violet Haas and Carolyn Perucci (Ann Arbor, MI: University of Michigan Press, 1984); Sally Hacker, "The Culture of Engineering: Women, Workplace, and Machine," *Women's Studies International Quarterly*, Vol. 4, No. 3, 1981, pp. 341–353; Evelyn Fox Keller, *A Feeling for the Organism* (San Francisco: Freeman, 1983); National Science Foundation, *Women and Minorities in Science and Engineering* (Washington, DC: NSF, 1988); Margaret Rossiter, *Women Scientists in America* (Baltimore, MD: Johns Hopkins University Press, 1982); Londa Schiebinger, "The History and Philosophy of Women in Science: A Review Essay," *Signs*, Vol. 12, No. 2, 1987, pp. 305–332.

28. John Markoff and Lenny Siegel, "Military Micros," University of California, Santa Cruz, Silicon Valley Research Project conference, 1983. High Technology Professionals for Peace and Computer Professionals for Social Responsibility are promising organizations.

29. Katie King, "The Pleasure of Repetition and the Limits of Identification in Feminist Science Fiction: Reimaginations of the Body after the Cyborg," California American Studies Association, Pomona, 1984. An abbreviated list of feminist science fiction underlying themes of this essay: Octavia Bulter, *Wild Seed, Mind of My Mind, Kindred, Survivor;* Suzy McKee Charnas, *Motherlines;* Samuel Delany, *Tales of Neverÿon;* Anne McCaffery, *The Ship Who Sang, Dinosaur Planet;* Vonda McIntyre, *Superluminal, Dreamsnake;* Joanna Russ, *Adventures of Alyx, The Female Man;* James Tiptree, Jr., *Star Songs of an Old Primate, Up the Walls of the World;* John Varley, *Titan, Wizard, Demon.*

30. Mary Douglas, *Purity and Danger* (London: Routledge & Kegan Paul, 1966), *Natural Symbols* (London: Cresset Press, 1970).

31. French feminisms contribute to cyborg heteroglossia. Carolyn Burke, "Irigaray through the Looking Glass," *Feminist Studies,* Vol. 7, No. 2, Summer 1981, pp. 288–306; Luce Irigaray, *Ce sexe qui n'en est pas un* (Paris: Minuit, 1977); L. Irigaray, *Et l'une ne bouge pas sans l'autre* (Paris: Minuit, 1979); *New French Feminisms,* ed. Elaine Marks and Isabelle de Courtivron (Amherst, MA: University of Massachusetts Press, 1980); *Signs,* Vol. 7, No. I, Autumn 1981, special issue on French feminism; Monique Wittig, *The Lesbian Body,* trans. David LeVay (New York: Avon, 1975; *Le corps lesbien,* 1973). See especially *Feminist Issues: A Journal of Feminist Social and Political Theory,* 1 (1980), and Claire Duchen, *Feminism in France: From May '68 to Mitterand* (London: Routledge Kegan & Paul, 1986).

32. But all these poets are very complex, not least in treatment of themes of lying and erotic, decentered collective and personal identities. Susan Griffin, *Women and Nature: The Roaring Inside Her* (New York: Harper & Row, 1978); Audre Lorde, *Sister Outsider* (Trumansburg, NY: Crossing Press, 1984); Adrienne Rich, *The Dream of a Common Language* (New York: Norton, 1978).

33. Audre Lorde, *Zami, a New Spelling of my Name* (Trumansburg, NY: Crossing Press, 1983); Katie King, "Audre Lorde: Layering History/Constructing Poetry," Canons without Innocence, Ph.D. thesis, University of California, Santa Cruz, 1987.

34. Jacques Derrida, *Of Grammatology,* trans. and introd. G. C. Spivak (Baltimore, MD: Johns Hopkins University Press, 1976), especially part II, "Nature, Culture, Writing"; Claude Lévi-Strauss, *Tristes Tropiques,* trans. John Russell (New York: Criterion Books, 1961), especially "The Writing Lesson"; Henry Louis Gates, "Writing 'Race' and the Difference It Makes," in "Race," Writing and Difference, special issue of *Critical Inquiry,* Vol. 12, No. 1, Autumn 1985, pp. 1–20; *Cultures in Contention,* ed. Douglas Kahn and Diane Neumaier, (Seattle: Real Comet Press, 1985); Walter Ong, *Orality and Literacy: The Technologizing of the Word* (New York: Methuen, 1982); Cheris Kramarae and Paula Treichler, *A Feminist Dictionary* (Boston: Pandora, 1985).

35. Cherrie Moraga, *Loving in the War Years* (Boston: South End Press, 1983). The sharp relation of women of color to writing as theme and politics can be approached through "The Black Woman and the Diaspora: Hidden Connections and Extended Acknowledgments," An International Literacy Conference, Michigan State University, October 1985; *Black Women Writers: A Critical Evaluation,* ed. Mari Evans (Garden City, NY: Doubleday/ Anchor, 1984); Barbara Christian, *Black Feminist Criticism* (New York: Pergamon, 1985); *The Third Woman: Minority Women Writers of the United States,* ed. Dexter Fisher (Boston: Houghton Mifflin, 1980); several issues of *Frontiers,* especially vol. 5, 1980, "Chicanas en el Ambiente Nacional" and Vol. 7, 1983, "Feminisms in the Non-Western World"; Maxine Hong Kingston, *China Men* (New York: Knopf, 1977); *Black Women in White America: A Documentary History,* ed. Gerda Lerner (New York: Vintage, 1973); Paula Giddings, *When and Where I Enter: The Impact of Black Women on Race and Sex in America* (Toronto: Bantam, 1985); *This Bridge Called My Back: Writings by Radical Women of Color,* ed. Cherrie Moraga and Gloria Anzaldua (Watertown, MA: Persephone, 1981); *Sisterhood Is Global,* ed. Robin Morgan (Garden City, NY: Anchor/Doubleday, 1984). The writing of white women has had similar meanings: Sandra Gilbert and Susan Gubar, *The Madwoman in the Attic* (New Haven, CT: Yale University Press, 1979); Joanna Russ, *How to Suppress Women's Writing* (Austin, TX: University of Texas Press, 1983).

36. James Clifford argues persuasively for recognition of continuous cultural reinvention, the stubborn nondisappearance of those "marked" by Western imperializing practices; see "On Ethnographic Allegory" Clifford and Marcus, *op. cit.* (acknowledgments), and "On Ethnographic Authority," *Representations,* Vol. I, No. 2 (1983), pp. 118–146.

37. The convention of ideologically taming militarized high technology by publicizing its applications to speech and motion problems of the disabled-differently abled takes on a special irony in monotheistic, patriarchal, and frequently anti-Semitic culture when computer-generated speech allows a boy with no voice to chant the Haftorah at his bar mitzvah. See Vic Sussman, "Personal Technology Lends a Hand," *Washington Post Magazine,* Nov. 9, 1986, pp. 45–46. Making the always context-relative social definitions of "abledness" particularly clear, military high-tech has a way of making human beings disabled by definition, a perverse aspect of much automated battlefield and Star Wars R&D. See John Noble Welford, "Pilot's Helmet Helps Interpret High Speed World," *New York Times,* July 1, 1986, pp. 21, 24.

38. Page DuBois, *Centaurs and Amazons* (Ann Arbor, MI: University of Michigan Press, 1982); Lorraine Daston and Katharine Park, "Hermaphrodites in Renaissance France," ms., n.d.; Katharine Park and Lorraine Daston, "Unnatural Conceptions: The Study of Monsters in 16th and 17th Century France and England," *Past and Present,* No. 92, August 1981, pp. 20–54. The word *monster* shares its root with the verb *to demonstrate*.

10

Mapping the Postmodern

Andreas Huyssen

Time and again postmodernism has been denounced and ridiculed in recent debates, both by neoconservatives and the cultural Left in the United States. If such ridicule were all that could be said about postmodernism (apart from the equally vocal celebrations of the postmodern which do not hold much interest for me either), then it would not be worth the trouble of taking up the subject at all. I might just as well stop right here and join the formidable chorus of those who lament the loss of quality and proclaim the decline of the arts since the 1960s. My argument, however, will be a different one. While the recent media hype about postmodernism in architecture and the arts has propelled the phenomenon into the limelight, it has also tended to obscure its long and complex history. Much of my ensuing argument will be based on the premise that what appears on one level as the latest fad, advertising pitch, and hollow spectacle, is part of a slowly emerging cultural transformation in Western societies, a change in sensibility for which the term *postmodernism* is actually, at least for now, wholly adequate. The nature and depth of that transformation are debatable, but transformation it is. I don't want to be misunderstood as claiming that there is a wholesale paradigm shift of the cultural, social and economic orders;[1] any such claim clearly would be overblown. But in an important sector of our culture there is a noticeable shift in sensibility, practices and discourse formations which distinguishes a postmodern set of assumptions, experiences, and propositions from that of a preceding period. What needs further exploration is whether this transformation has

This essay was first published in a slightly longer version in *New German Critique*, Vol. 33, Fall 1984, pp. 5–52. It was also published in Andreas Huyssen, *After the Great Divide: Modernism, Mass Culture, Postmodernism*, (Bloomington, IN: Indiana University Press, 1986).

generated genuinely new aesthetic forms in the various arts or whether it mainly recycles techniques and strategies of modernism itself, reinscribing them into an altered cultural context. Of course, there are good reasons why any attempt to take the postmodern seriously in its own terms meets with so much resistance. It is indeed tempting to dismiss many of the current manifestations of postmodernism as a fraud perpetrated on a gullible public by the New York art market in which reputations are built and gobbled up faster than painters can paint: witness the frenzied brushwork of the new expressionists. It is also easy to argue that much of the contemporary inter-arts, mixed-media and performance culture, which once seemed so vital, is now spinning its wheels and speaking in tongues, relishing, as it were, the eternal recurrence of the *déjà vu*. With good reason we may remain skeptical toward the revival of the Wagnerian *Gesamtkunstwerk* as postmodern spectacle in Syberberg or Robert Wilson. The current Wagner cult may indeed by a symptom of a happy collusion between the megalomania of the postmodern and that of the premodern on the edge of modernism. The search for the grail, it seems, is on.

But it is almost too easy to ridicule the postmodernism of the current New York art scene or of Documenta 7. Such total rejection will blind us to postmodernism's critical potential which, I believe, also exists, even though it may be difficult to identify.[2] The notion of the art work as critique actually informs some of the more thoughtful condemnations of postmodernism, which is accused of having abandoned the critical stance that once characterized modernism. However, the familiar ideas of what constitutes a critical art (*Parteilichkeit* and vanguardism, *l'art engagé*, critical realism or the aesthetic of negativity, the refusal of representation, abstraction, reflexiveness) have lost much of their explanatory and normative power in recent decades. This is precisely the dilemma of art in a postmodern age. Nevertheless, I see no reason to jettison the notion of a critical art altogether. The pressures to do so are not new; they have been formidable in capitalist culture ever since romanticism, and if our postmodernity makes it exceedingly difficult to hold on to an older notion of art as critique, then the task is to redefine the possibilities of critique in postmodern terms rather than relegating it to oblivion. If the postmodern is discussed as a historical condition rather than only as style it becomes possible and indeed important to unlock the critical moment in postmodernism itself and to sharpen its cutting edge, however blunt it may seem at first sight. What will no longer do is either to eulogize or to ridicule postmodernism *en bloc*. The postmodern must be salvaged from its champions and from its detractors. This essay is meant to contribute to that project.

In much of the postmodernism debate, a very conventional thought pattern has asserted itself. Either it is said that postmodernism is continuous with modernism, in which case the whole debate opposing the two is specious; or, it is claimed that there is a radical rupture, a break with modernism, which is then evaluated in either positive or negative terms. But the question of historical continuity or discontinuity simply cannot be adequately discussed in terms of such an either/or dichotomy. To have questioned the validity of such dichotomous thought patterns is of course one of the major achievements of Derridean deconstruction. But the poststructuralist notion of endless textuality ultimately cripples any meaningful historical reflection on temporal units shorter than, say, the long wave of metaphysics from Plato to Heidegger or the spread of *modernité* from the mid-nineteenth century to the present. The problem with such historical macro-schemes, in relation to postmodernism, is that they prevent the phenomenon from even coming into focus.

I will therefore take a different route. I will not attempt here to define what postmodernism *is*. The term *postmodernism* itself should guard us against such an approach as it positions the phenomenon as relational. Modernism as that from which postmodernism is breaking away remains inscribed into the very word with which we describe our distance from modernism. Thus, keeping in mind postmodernism's relational nature, I will simply start from the *Selbstverständnis* of the postmodern as it has shaped various discourses since the 1960's. What I hope to provide in this essay is something like a large-scale map of the postmodern which surveys several territories and on which the various postmodern artistic and critical practices could find their aesthetic and political place. Within the trajectory of the postmodern in the United States I will distinguish several phases and directions. My primary aim is to emphasize some of the historical contingencies and pressures that have shaped recent aesthetic and cultural debates but have either been ignored or systematically blocked out in critical theory *à l'américaine*. While drawing on developments in architecture, literature and the visual arts, my focus will be primarily on the critical discourse about the postmodern: postmodernism in relation to, respectively, modernism, the avantgarde, neo-conservatism and poststructuralism. Each of these constellations represents a somewhat separate layer of the postmodern and will be presented as such. And, finally, central elements of the *Begriffsgeschichte* of the term will be discussed in relation to a broader set of questions that have arisen in recent debates about modernism, modernity and the historical avantgarde.[3] A crucial question for me concerns the extent to which modernism and the avantgarde as forms of an adversary culture were nevertheless conceptually and practically bound up with capitalist modernization and/or with communist vanguardism, that modernization's twin brother. As I hope this essay will show, postmodernism's critical dimension lies precisely in its radical questioning of those presuppositions which linked modernism and the avantgarde to the mindset of modernization.

The Exhaustion of the Modernist Movement

Let me begin, then, with some brief remarks about the trajectory and migrations of the term *postmodernism*. In literary criticism it goes back as far as the late 1950s when it was used by Irving Howe and Harry Levin to lament the levelling off of the modernist movement. Howe and Levin were looking back nostalgically to what already seemed like a richer past. Postmodernism was first used emphatically in the 1960s by literary critics such as Leslie Fiedler and Ihab Hassan who held widely divergent views of what a postmodern literature was. It was only during the early and mid-1970s that the term gained a much wider currency, encompassing first architecture, then dance, theater, painting, film and music. While the postmodern break with classical modernism was fairly visible in architecture and the visual arts, the notion of a postmodern rupture in literature has been much harder to ascertain. At some point in the late 1970s, postmodernism, not without American prodding, migrated to Europe via Paris and Frankfurt. Kristeva and Lyotard took it up in France, Habermas in Germany. In the United States, meanwhile, critics had begun to discuss the interface of postmodernism with French poststructuralism in its peculiar American adaptation, often simply on the assumption that the avantgarde in theory somehow had to be homologous to the avantgarde in literature and the arts. While skepticism about the feasibility of an artistic avantgarde was on the rise in the 1970s, the vitality of theory, despite its many enemies, never seemed in serious doubt. To some, indeed, it appeared as if the cultural energies that had fueled the art movements of the 1960s were flowing during the 1970s into the body of theory, leaving the artistic enterprise high and dry. While such an observation is at best of impressionistic value and also not quite fair to the arts, it does seem reasonable to say that, with postmodernism's big-bang logic of expansion irreversible, the maze of the postmodern became ever more impenetrable. By the early 1980s the modernism/postmodernism constellation in the arts and the modernity/postmodernity constellation in social theory had become one of the most contested terrains in the intellectual life of Western societies. And the terrain is contested precisely because there is so much more at stake than the existence or non-existence of a new artistic style, so much more also than just the "correct" theoretical line.

Nowhere does the break with modernism seem more obvious than in recent American architecture. Nothing could be further from Mies van der Rohe's functionalist glass curtain walls than the gesture of random historical citation which prevails on so many postmodern façades. Take, for example, Philip Johnson's AT&T highrise, which is appropriately broken up into a neoclassical mid-section, Roman colonnades at the street level and a Chippendale pediment at the top. Indeed, a growing nostalgia for various life forms of the past seems to be a strong undercurrent in the culture of the 1970s and 1980s. And it is tempting to dismiss this historical eclecticism, found not only in architecture, but in the arts, in film, in literature and in the mass culture of recent years, as the cultural equivalent of the neoconservative nostalgia for the good old days and as a manifest sign of the declining rate of creativity in late capitalism. But is this nostalgia for the past, the often frenzied and exploitative search for usable traditions, and the growing fascination with pre-modern and primitive cultures—is all of this rooted only in the cultural institutions' perpetual need for spectacle and frill, and thus perfectly compatible with the status quo? Or does it perhaps also express some genuine and legitimate dissatisfaction with modernity and the unquestioned belief in the perpetual modernization of art? If the latter is the case, which I believe it is, then how can the search for alternative traditions, whether emergent or residual, be made culturally productive without yielding to the pressures of conservatism which, with a vise-like grip, lays claim to the very concept of tradition? I am not arguing here that all manifestations of the postmodern recuperation of the past are to be welcomed because somehow they are in tune with the *Zeitgeist*. I also don't want to be misunderstood as arguing that postmodernism's fashionable repudiation of the high modernist aesthetic and its boredom with the propositions of Marx and Freud, Picasso and Brecht, Kafka and Joyce, Schönberg and Stravinsky are somehow marks of a major cultural advance. Where postmodernism simply jettisons modernism it just yields to the cultural apparatus' demands that it legitimize itself as radically new, and it revives the philistine prejudices modernism faced in its own time.

But even if postmodernism's own propositions don't seem convincing—as embodied, for example, in the buildings by Philip Johnson, Michael Graves and others—that does not mean that continued adherence to an older set of modernist propositions would guarantee the emergence of more convincing buildings or works of art. The recent neoconservative attempt to reinstate a domesticated version of modernism as the only worthwhile truth of twentieth-century culture—manifest for instance in the 1984 Beckmann exhibit in Berlin and in many articles in Hilton Kramer's *New Criterion*—is a strategy aimed at burying the political and aesthetic critiques of certain forms of modernism which have gained ground since the 1960s. But the problem with modernism is not just the fact that it can be integrated into a conservative ideology of art. After all, that already happened once on a major scale in the 1950s.[4] The larger problem we recognize today, it seems to me, is the closeness of various forms of modernism in its own time to the mindset of modernization, whether in its capitalist or communist version. Of course, modernism was never a monolithic phenomenon, and it contained *both* the modernization euphoria of futurism, constructivism and Neue Sachlichkeit and some of the starkest critiques of modernization in the various modern forms of "romantic anti-capitalism."[5] The problem I address in this essay is not what modernism *really was*, but rather how it was perceived retrospectively, what dominant values and knowledge it carried, and how it functioned ideologically and culturally after World War II. It is a specific image of modernism that has become the bone of contention for the postmoderns, and that image has to be reconstructed if we want to understand postmodernism's problematic relationship to the modernist tradition and its claims to difference.

Architecture gives us the most palpable example of the issues at stake. The modernist utopia embodied in the building programs of the Bauhaus, of Mies, Gropius and Le Corbusier, was part of a heroic attempt after the Great War and the Russian Revolution to rebuild a war-ravaged Europe in the image of the new, and to make building a vital part of the envisioned renewal of society. A new Enlightenment demanded rational design for a rational society, but the new rationality was overlayed with a utopian fervor which ultimately made it veer back into myth—the myth of modernization. Ruthless denial of the past was as much an essential component of the modern movement as its call for modernization through standardization and rationalization. It is well-known how the modernist utopia shipwrecked on its own internal contradictions and, more importantly, on politics and history.[6] Gropius, Mies and others were forced into exile, Albert Speer took their place in Germany. After 1945, modernist architecture was largely deprived of its social vision and became increasingly an architecture of power and representation. Rather than standing as harbingers and promises of the new life, modernist housing projects became symbols of alienation and dehumanization, a fate they shared with the assembly line, that other agent of the new which had been greeted with exuberant enthusiasm in the 1920s by Leninists and Fordists alike.

Charles Jencks, one of the most well-known popularizing chroniclers of the agony of the modern movement and spokesman for a postmodern architecture, dates modern architecture's symbolic demise July 15, 1972, at 3:32 p.m. At that time several slab blocks of St. Louis' Pruitt-Igoe Housing (built by Minoru Yamasaki in the 1950s) were dynamited, and the collapse was dramatically displayed on the evening news. The modern machine for living, as Le Corbusier had called it with the technological euphoria so typical of the 1920s, had become unlivable, the modernist experiment, so it seemed, obsolete. Jencks takes pains to distinguish the initial vision of the modern movement from the sins committed in its name later on. And yet, on balance he agrees with those who, since the 1960s, have argued against modernism's hidden dependence on the machine metaphor and the production paradigm, and against its taking the factory as the primary model for all buildings. It has become commonplace in postmodernist circles to favor a reintroduction of multivalent symbolic dimensions into architecture, a mixing of codes, an appropriation of local vernaculars and regional traditions.[7] Thus Jencks suggests that architects look two ways simultaneously, "towards the traditional slow-changing codes and particular ethnic meanings of a neighborhood, and towards the fast-changing codes of architectural fashion and professionalism."[8] Such schizophrenia, Jencks holds, is symptomatic of the postmodern moment in architecture; and one might well ask whether it does not apply to contemporary culture at large, which increasingly seems to privilege what Bloch called *Ungleichzeitigkeiten* (non-synchronisms),[9] rather than favoring only what Adorno, the theorist of modernism par excellence, described as *der fortgeschrittenste Materialstand der Kunst* (the most advanced state of artistic material). Where such postmodern schizophrenia is creative tension resulting in ambitious and successful buildings, and where, conversely, it veers off into an incoherent and arbitrary shuffling of styles, will remain a matter of debate. We should also not forget that the mixing of codes, the appropriation of regional traditions and the uses of symbolic dimensions other than the machine were never entirely unknown to the architects of the International Style. In order to arrive at his postmodernism, Jencks ironically had to exacerbate the very view of modernist architecture which he persistently attacks.

One of the most telling documents of the break of postmodernism with the modernist dogma is a book coauthored by Robert Venturi, Denise Scott-Brown and Steven Izenour and entitled *Learning from Las Vegas*. Rereading this book and earlier writings by Venturi from the 1960s today,[10] one is struck by the proximity of Venturi's strategies and solutions to the pop sensibility of those years. Time and again the authors use pop art's break with the austere canon of high modernist painting and pop's uncritical espousal of the commercial vernacular of consumer culture as an inspiration for their work. What Madison Avenue was for Andy Warhol, what the comics and the Western were for Leslie Fiedler, the landscape of Las Vegas was for Venturi and his group. The rhetoric of *Learning from Las Vegas* is predicated on the glorification of the billboard strip and of the ruthless shlock of casino culture. In Kenneth Frampton's ironic words, it offers a reading of Las Vegas as "an authentic outburst of popular phantasy."[11] I think it would be gratuitous to ridicule such odd notions of cultural populism today. While there is something patently absurd about such propositions, we have to acknowledge the power they mustered to explode the reified dogmas òf modernism and to reopen a set of questions which the modernism gospel of the 1940s and 1950s had largely blocked from view: questions of ornament and metaphor in architecture, of figuration and realism in painting, of story and representation in literature, of the body in music and theater. Pop in the broadest sense was the context in which a notion of the postmodern first took shape, and from the beginning until today, the most significant trends within postmodernism have challenged modernism's relentless hostility to mass culture.

Postmodernism in the 1960s: An American Avantgarde?

I will now suggest a historical distinction between the postmodernism of the 1960s and that of the 1970s and early 1980s. My argument will roughly be this: 1960s' and 1970s' postmodernism both rejected or criticized a certain version of modernism. Against the codified high modernism of the preceding decades, the postmodernism of the 1960s tried to revitalize the heritage of the European avantgarde and to give it an American form along what one could call in short-hand the Duchamp-Cage-Warhol axis. By the 1970s, this avantgardist postmodernism of the 1960s had in turn exhausted its potential, even though some of its manifestations continued well into the new decade. What was new in the 1970s was, on the one hand, the emergence of a culture of eclecticism, a largely affirmative postmodernism which had abandoned any claim to critique, transgression or negation; and, on the other hand, an alternative postmodernism in which resistance, critique and negation of the status quo were redefined in non-modernist and non-avantgardist terms, terms which match the political developments in contemporary culture more effectively than the older theories of modernism. Let me elaborate.

What were the connotations of the term postmodernism in the 1960s? Roughly since the mid-1950s literature and the arts witnessed a rebellion of a new generation of artists such as Rauschenberg and Jasper Johns, Kerouac, Ginsberg and the Beats, Burroughs and Barthelme against the dominance of abstract expressionism, serial music and classical literary modernism.[12] The rebellion of the artists was soon joined by critics such as Susan Sontag, Leslie Fiedler and Ihab Hassan who all vigorously though in very different ways and to a different degree, argued for the postmodern. Sontag advocated camp and a new sensibility, Fiedler sang the praise of popular literature and genital enlightenment, and Hassan—closer than the others to the moderns—advocated a literature of silence, trying to mediate between the "tradition of the new" and post-war literary developments. By that time, modernism had of course been safely established as the canon in the academy, the museums and the gallery network. In that canon the New York School of abstract expressionism represented the epitome of that long trajectory of the modern which had begun in Paris in the 1850s and 1860s and which had inexorably led to New York—the American victory in culture following on the heels of the victory on the battlefields of World War II. By the 1960s artists and critics alike shared a sense of a fundamentally new situation. The assumed postmodern rupture with the past was felt as a loss: art and literature's claims to truth and human value seemed exhausted, the belief in the constitutive power of the modern imagination just another delusion. Or it was felt as a breakthrough toward an ultimate liberation of instinct and consciousness, into the global village of McLuhanacy, the new Eden of polymorphous perversity, Paradise Now, as the Living Theater proclaimed it on stage. Thus critics of post-modernism such as Gerald Graff have correctly identified two strains of the postmodern culture of the 1960s: the apocalyptic desperate strain and the visionary celebratory strain, both of which, Graff claims, already existed within modernism.[13] While this is certainly true, it misses an important point. The ire of the postmodernists was directed not so much against modernism as such, but rather against a certain austere image of 'high modernism,' as advanced by the New Critics and other custodians of modernist culture. Such a view, which avoids the false dichotomy of choosing either continuity or discontinuity, is supported by a retrospective essay by John Barth. In a 1980 piece in *The Atlantic*, entitled "The Literature of Replenishment," Barth criticizes his own 1968 essay "The Literature of Exhaustion," which seemed at the time to offer an adequate summary of the apocalyptic strain. Barth now suggests that what his earlier piece was really about "was the effective 'exhaustion' not of language or of literature but of the aesthetic of high modernism."[14] And he goes on to describe Beckett's *Stories and Texts for Nothing* and Nabokov's *Pale Fire* as late modernist marvels, distinct from such postmodernist writers as Italo Calvino and Gabriel Marquez. Cultural critics like Daniel Bell, on the other hand, would simply claim that the postmodernism of the 1960s was the "logical culmination of modernist intentions,"[15] a view which rephrases Lionel Trilling's despairing observation that the demonstrators of the 1960s were practicing modernism in the streets. But my point here is precisely that high modernism had never seen fit to be in the streets in the first place, that its earlier undeniably adversary role was superseded in the 1960s by a very different culture of confrontation in the streets *and* in art works, and that this culture of confrontation transformed inherited ideological notions of style, form and creativity, artistic autonomy and the imagination to which modernism had by then succumbed. Critics like Bell and Graff saw the rebellion of the late 1950s and the 1960s as continuous with modernism's earlier nihilistic and anarchic strain; rather than seeing it as a postmodernist revolt against classical modernism, they interpreted it as a profusion of modernist impulses into everyday life. And in some sense they were absolutely right, except that this "success" of modernism fundamentally altered the terms of how modernist culture was to be perceived. Again, my argument here is that the revolt of the 1960s was never a rejection of modernism *per se*, but rather a revolt against that version of modernism which had been domesticated in the 1950s, become part of the liberal-conservative consensus of the times, and which had even been turned into a propaganda weapon in the cultural-political arsenal of Cold War anti-communism. The modernism against which artists rebelled was no longer felt to be an adversary culture. It no longer opposed a dominant class and its world view, nor had it maintained its programmatic purity from contamination by the culture industry. In other words, the revolt sprang precisely from the success of modernism, from the fact that in the United States, as in West Germany and France, for that matter, modernism had been perverted into a form of affirmative culture.

I would go on to argue that the global view which sees the 1960s as part of the modern movement extending from Manet and Baudelaire, if not from romanticism, to the present is not able to account for the specifically American character of postmodernism. After all, the term accrued its emphatic connotations in the United States, not in Europe. I would even claim that it could not have been invented in Europe at the time. For a variety of reasons, it would not have made any sense there. West Germany was still busy rediscovering its own moderns who had been burnt and banned during the Third Reich. If anything, the 1960s in West Germany produced a major shift in evaluation and interest from one set of moderns to another: from Benn, Kafka and Thomas Mann to Brecht, the left expressionists and the political writers of the 1920s, from Heidegger and Jaspers to Adorno and Benjamin, from Schönberg and Webern to Eisler, from Kirchner and Beckmann to Grosz and Heartfield. It was a search for alternative cultural traditions within modernity and as such directed against the politics of a depoliticized version of modernism, which had come to provide much needed cultural legitimation for the Adenauer restoration. During the 1950s, the myths of "the golden twenties," the "conservative revolution," and universal existentialist *Angst*, all helped block out and suppress the realities of the fascist past. From the depths of barbarism and the rubble of its cities, West Germany was trying to reclaim a civilized modernity and to find a cultural identity tuned to international modernism which would make others forget Germany's past as predator and pariah of the modern world. Given this context, neither the variations on modernism of the 1950s nor the struggle of the 1960s for alternative democratic and socialist cultural traditions could have possibly been construed as *postmodern*. The very notion of postmodernism has emerged in Germany only since the late 1970s and then not in relation to the culture of the 1960s, but narrowly in relation to recent architectural developments and, perhaps more importantly, in the context of the new social movements and their radical critique of modernity.[16]

In France, too, the 1960s witnessed a return to modernism rather than a step beyond it, even though for different reasons than in Germany, some of which I will discuss in the later section on poststructuralism. In the context of French intellectual life, the term *postmodernism* was simply not around in the 1960s, and even today it does not seem to imply a major break with modernism as it does in the U.S.

I would now like to sketch four major characteristics of the early phase of postmodernism which all point to postmodernism's continuity with the international tradition of the modern, yes, but which—and this is my point—also establish American postmodernism as a movement *sui generis*.[17]

First, the postmodernism of the 1960s was characterized by a temporal imagination which displayed a powerful sense of the future and of new frontiers, of rupture and discontinuity, of crisis and generational conflict, an imagination reminiscent of earlier continental avantgarde movements such as Dada and surrealism rather than of high modernism. Thus the revival of Marcel Duchamp as godfather of 1960s postmodernism is no historical accident. And yet, the historical constellation in which the postmodernism of the 1960s played itself out (from the Bay of Pigs and the civil rights movement to the campus revolts, the anti-war movements and the counter-culture) makes this avantgarde specifically American, even where its vocabulary of aesthetic form and techniques was not radically new.

Secondly, the early phase of postmodernism included an iconoclastic attack on what Peter Bürger has tried to capture theoretically as the "institution art." By that term Bürger refers first and foremost to the ways in which art's role in society is perceived and defined, and, secondly, to ways in which art is produced, marketed, distributed and consumed. In his book *Theory of the Avantgarde* Bürger has argued that the major goal of the historical European avantgarde (Dada, early surrealism, the postrevolutionary Russian avantgarde[18]) was to undermine, attack and transform the bourgeois institution art and its ideology of autonomy rather than only changing artistic and literary modes of representation. Bürger's approach to the question of art as institution in bourgeois society goes a long way toward suggesting useful distinctions between modernism and the avantgarde, distinctions which in turn can help us place the American avantgarde of the 1960s. In Bürgers account the European avantgarde was primarily an attack on the highness of high art and on art's separateness from everyday life as it had evolved in nineteenth-century aestheticism and its repudiation of realism. Bürger argues that the avantgarde attempted to reintegrate art and life or, to use his Hegelian-Marxist formula, to sublate art into life, and he sees this reintegration attempt, I think correctly, as a major break with the aestheticist tradition of the later nineteenth century. The value of Bürger's account for contemporary American debates is that it permits us to distinguish different stages and different projects within the trajectory of the modern. The usual equation of the avantgarde with modernism can indeed no longer be maintained. Contrary to the avantgarde's intention to merge art and life, modernism always remained bound up with the more traditional notion of the autonomous art work, with the construction of form and meaning (however estranged or ambiguous, displaced or undecidable such meaning might be), and with the specialized status of the aesthetic.[19] The politically important point of Bürger's account for my argument about the 1960s is this: The historical avantgarde's iconoclastic attack on cultural institutions and on traditional modes of representation presupposed a society in which high art played an essential role in legitimizing hegemony, or, to put it in more neutral terms, to support a cultural establishment and its claims to aesthetic knowledge. It had been the achievement of the historical avantgarde to demystify and to undermine the legitimizing discourse of high art in European society. The various modernisms of this century, on the other hand, have either maintained or restored versions of high culture, a task which was certainly facilitated by the ultimate and perhaps unavoidable failure of the historical avantgarde to reintegrate art and life. And yet, I would suggest that it was this specific radicalism of the avantgarde, directed against the institutionalization of high art as a discourse of hegemony, that recommended itself as a source of energy and inspiration to the American postmodernists of the 1960s. Perhaps for the first time in American culture an avantgardist revolt against a tradition of high art and what was perceived as its hegemonic role made political sense. High art had indeed become institutionalized in the burgeoning museum, gallery, concert, record and paperback culture of the 1950s. Modernism itself had entered the mainstream via mass reproduction and the culture industry. And during the Kennedy years, high culture even began to take on functions of political representation with Robert Frost and Pablo Casals, Malraux and Stravinsky at the White House. The irony in all of this is that the first time the U.S. had something resembling an "institution art" in the emphatic European sense, it was modernism itself, the kind of art whose purpose had always been to resist institutionalization. In the form of happenings, pop vernacular, psychedelic art, acid rock, alternative and street theater, the postmodernism of the 1960s was groping to recapture the adversary ethos which had nourished modern art in its earlier stages, but which it seemed no longer able to sustain. Of course, the "success" of the pop avantgarde, which itself had sprung full-blown from advertising in the first place, immediately made it profitable and thus sucked it into a more highly developed culture industry than the earlier European avantgarde ever had to contend with. But despite such cooption through commodification the pop avantgarde retained a certain cutting edge in its proximity to the 1960s culture of confrontation.[20] No matter how deluded about its potential effectiveness, the attack on the institution art was always also an attack on hegemonic social institutions, and the raging battles of the 1960s over whether or not pop was legitimate art prove the point.

Thirdly, many of the early advocates of postmodernism shared the technological optimism of segments of the 1920s avantgarde. What photography and film had been to Vertov and Tretyakov, Brecht, Heartfield and Benjamin in that period, television, video and the computer were for the prophets of a technological aesthetic in the 1960s. McLuhan's cybernetic and technocratic media eschatology and Hassan's praise for "runaway technology," the "boundless dispersal by media," "the computer as substitute consciousness"—all of this combined easily with euphoric visions of a postindustrial society. Even if compared to the equally exuberant technological optimism of the 1920s, it is striking to see in retrospect how uncritically media technology and the cybernetic paradigm were espoused in the 1960s by conservatives, liberals and leftists alike.[21]

The enthusiasm for the new media leads me to the fourth trend within early postmodernism. There emerged a vigorous, though again largely uncritical attempt to validate popular culture as a challenge to the canon of high art, modernist or traditional. This "populist" trend of the 1960s with its celebration of rock 'n roll and folk music, of the imagery of everyday life and of the multiple forms of popular literature gained much of its energy in the context of the counter-culture and by a next to total abandonment of an earlier American tradition of a critique of modern mass culture. Leslie Fiedler's incantation of the prefix "post" in his essay "The New Mutants" had an exhilarating effect at the time.[22] The postmodern harbored the promise of a "post-white," "post-male," "post-humanist," "post-Puritan" world. It is easy to see how all of Fielder's adjectives aim at the modernist dogma and at the cultural establishment's notion of what Western Civilization was all about. Susan Sontag's camp aesthetic did much the same. Even though it was less populist, it certainly was as hostile to high modernism. There is a curious contradiction in all this. Fiedler's populism reiterates precisely that adversarial relationship between high art and mass culture which, in the accounts of Clement Greenberg and Theodor W. Adorno, was one of the pillars of the modernist dogma Fiedler had set out to undermine. Fiedler just takes his position on the other shore, opposite Greenberg and Adorno, as it were, validating the popular and pounding away at "elitism." And yet, Fiedler's call to cross the border and close the gap between high art and mass culture as well as his implied political critique of what later came to be called "eurocentrism" and "logocentrism" can serve as an important marker for subsequent developments within postmodernism. A new creative relationship between high art and certain forms of mass culture is, to my mind, indeed one of the major marks of difference between high modernism and the art and literature which followed it in the 1970s and 1980s both in Europe and the

United States. And it is precisely the recent self-assertion of minority cultures and their emergence into public consciousness which has undermined the modernist belief that high and low culture have to be categorically kept apart; such rigorous segregation simply does not make much sense *within* a given minority culture which has always existed outside in the shadow of the dominant high culture.

In conclusion, I would say that from an American perspective the postmodernism of the 1960s had some of the makings of a genuine avantgarde movement, even if the overall political situation of 1960s' America was in no way comparable to that of Berlin or Moscow in the early 1920s when the tenuous and short-lived alliance between avantgardism and vanguard politics was forged. For a number of historical reasons the ethos of artistic avantgardism as iconoclasm, as probing reflection upon the ontological status of art in modern society, as an attempt to forge another life was culturally not yet as exhausted in the U.S. of the 1960s as it was in Europe at the same time. From a European perspective, therefore, it all looked like the endgame of the historical avantgarde rather than like the breakthrough to new frontiers it claimed to be. My point here is that American postmodernism of the 1960s was both: an American avantgarde *and* the endgame of international avantgardism. And I would go on to argue that it is indeed important for the cultural historian to analyze such *Ungleichzeitigkeiten* within modernity and to relate them to the very specific constellations and contexts of national and regional cultures and histories. The view that the culture of modernity is essentially internationalist—with its cutting edge moving in space and time from Paris in the later nineteenth and early twentieth centuries to Moscow and Berlin in the 1920s and to New York in the 1940s—is a view tied to a teleology of modern art whose unspoken subtext is the ideology of modernization. It is precisely this teleology and ideology of modernization which has become increasingly problematic in our postmodern age, problematic not so much perhaps in its descriptive powers relating to past events, but certainly in its normative claims.

Postmodernism in the 1970s and 1980s

In some sense, I might argue that what I have mapped so far is really the prehistory of the postmodern. After all, the term *postmodernism* only gained wide currency in the 1970s while much of the language used to describe the art, architecture and literature of the 1960s was still derived—and plausibly so—from the rhetoric of avantgardism and from what I have called the ideology of modernization. The cultural developments of the 1970s, however, are sufficiently different to warrant a separate description. One of the major differences, indeed, seems to be that the rhetoric of avantgardism has faded fast in the 1970s so that one can speak perhaps only now of a genuinely post-modern and post-avantgarde culture. Even if, with the benefit of hindsight, future historians of culture were to opt for such a usage of the term, I would still argue that the adversary and critical element in the notion of postmodernism can only be fully grasped if one takes the late 1950s as the starting point of a mapping of the postmodern. If we were to focus only on the 1970s, the adversary moment of the postmodern would be much harder to work out precisely because of the shift within the trajectory of postmodernism that lies somewhere in the fault lines between "the '60s" and "the '70s."

By the mid-1970s, certain basic assumptions of the preceding decade had either vanished or been transformed. The sense of a "futurist revolt" (Fiedler) was gone. The iconoclastic gestures of the pop, rock and sex avantgardes seemed exhausted since their increasingly commercialized circulation had deprived them of their avantgardist status. The earlier optimism about technology, media and popular culture had given way to more sober and critical assessments: television as pollution rather than panacea. In the years of Watergate and the drawn-out agony of the Vietnam war, of the oil-shock and the dire predictions of the Club of Rome, it was indeed difficult to maintain the confidence and exuberance of the 1960s. Counter-culture, New Left and anti-war movement were ever more frequently denounced as infantile aberrations of American history. It was easy to see that the 1960s were over. But it is more difficult to describe the emerging cultural scene which seemed much more amorphous and scattered than that of the 1960s. One might begin by saying that the battle against the normative pressures of high modernism waged during the 1960s had been successful—too successful, some would argue. While the 1960s could still be discussed in terms of a logical sequence of styles (Pop, Op, Kinetic,Minimal, Concept) or in equally modernist terms of art versus anti-art and non-art, such distinctions have increasingly lost ground in the 1970s.

The situation in the 1970s seems to be characterized rather by an ever wider dispersal and dissemination of artistic practices all working out of the ruins of the modernist edifice, raiding it for ideas, plundering its vocabulary and supplementing it with randomly chosen images and motifs from pre-modern and non-modern cultures as well as from contemporary mass culture. Modernist styles have actually not been abolished, but, as one art critic recently observed, continue "to enjoy a kind of half-life in mass culture,"[23] for instance in advertising, record cover design, furniture and household items, science fiction illustration, window displays, etc. Yet another way of putting it would be to say that all modernist and avantgardist techniques, forms and images are now stored for instant recall in the computerized memory banks of our culture. But the same memory also stores all of pre-modernist art as well as the genres, codes and image worlds of popular cultures and modern mass culture. How precisely these enormously expanded capacities for information storage, processing and recall have affected artists and their work remains to be analyzed. But one thing seems clear: the great divide that separated high modernism from mass culture and that was codified in the various classical accounts of modernism no longer seems relevant to postmodern artistic or critical sensibilities.

Since the categorical demand for the uncompromising segregation of high and low has lost much of its persuasive power, we may be in a better position now to understand the political pressures and historical contingencies which shaped such accounts in the first place. I would suggest that the primary place of what I am calling the great divide was the age of Stalin and Hitler when the threat of totalitarian control over all culture forged a variety of defensive strategies meant to protect high culture in general, not just modernism. Thus conservative culture critics such as Ortega Y Gasset argued that high culture needed to be protected from the "revolt of the masses." Left critics like Adorno insisted that genuine art resist its incorporation into the capitalist culture industry which he defined as the total administration of culture from above. And even Lukács, the left critic of modernism *par excellence*, developed his theory of high bourgeois realism not in unison with but in antagonism to the Zhdanovist dogma of socialist realism and its deadly practice of censorship.

It is surely no coincidence that the Western codification of modernism as canon of the twentieth century took place during the 1940s and 1950s, preceding and during the Cold War. I am not reducing the great modernist works, by way of a simple ideology critique of their function, to a ploy in the cultural strategies of the Cold War. What I am suggesting, however, is that the age of Hitler, Stalin and the Cold War produced specific accounts of modernism, such as those of Clement Greenberg and Adorno,[24] whose aesthetic categories cannot be totally divorced from the pressures of that era. And it is in this sense, I would argue, that the logic of modernism advocated by those critics has become an aesthetic dead end to the extent that it has been upheld as rigid guideline for further artistic profusion and critical evaluation. As against such dogma, the postmodern has indeed opened up new directions and new visions. As the confrontation between "bad" socialist realism and the "good" art of the free world began to lose its ideological momentum in an age of *détente*, the whole relationship between modernism and mass culture as well as the problem of realism could be reassessed in less reified terms. While the issue was already raised in the 1960s, e.g., in pop art and various forms of documentary literature, it was only in the 1970s that artists increasingly drew on popular or mass cultural forms and genres, overlaying them with modernist and/ or avantgardist strategies. A major body of work representing this tendency is the New German Cinema, and here especially the firms of Rainer Werner Fassbinder, whose success in the United States can be explained precisely in those terms. It is also no coincidence that the diversity of mass culture was now recognized and analyzed by critics who increasingly began to work themselves out from under the modernist dogma that all mass culture is monolithic Kitsch, psychologically regressive and mind-destroying. The possibilities for experimental meshing and mixing of mass culture and modernism seemed promising and produced some of the most successful and ambitious art and literature of the 1970s. Needless to say, it also produced aesthetic failures and fiascos, but then modernism itself did not only produce masterworks.

It was especially the art, writing, film making and criticism of women and minority artists with their recuperation of buried and mutilated traditions, their emphasis on exploring forms of gender- and race-based subjectivity in aesthetic productions and experiences, and their refusal to be limited to standard canonizations, which added a whole new dimension to the critique of high modernism and to the emergence of alternative forms of culture. Thus, we have come to see modernism's imaginary relationship to African and Oriental art as deeply problematic, and will approach, say, contemporary Latin American writers other than by praising them for being good modernists, who, naturally, learned their craft in Paris. Women's criticism has shed some new light on the modernist canon itself from a variety of different feminist perspectives. Without succumbing to the kind of feminine essentialism which is one of the more problematic sides of the feminist enterprise, it just seems obvious that were it not for the critical gaze of feminist criticism, the male determinations and obsessions of Italian futurism, Vorticism, Russian constructivism, Neue Sachlichkeit or surrealism would probably still be blocked from our view; and the writings of Marie Luise Fleisser and Ingeborg Bachmann, the paintings of Frida Kahlo would still be known only to a handful of specialists. Of course such new insights can be interpreted in multiple ways, and the debate about gender and sexuality, male and female authorship and reader/spectatorship in literature and the arts is far from over, its implications for a new image of modernism not yet fully elaborated.

In light of these developments it is somewhat baffling that feminist criticism has so far largely stayed away from the postmodernism debate which is considered not to be pertinent to feminist concerns. The fact that to date only male critics have addressed the problem of modernity/ postmodernity, however, does not mean that it does not concern women. I would argue—and here I am in full agreement with Craig Owens[25]— that women's art, literature and criticism are an important part of the postmodern culture of the 1970s and 1980s and indeed a measure of the vitality and energy of that culture. Actually, the suspicion is in order that the conservative turn of these past years has indeed something to do with the sociologically significant emergence of various forms of "otherness" in the cultural sphere, all of which are perceived as a threat to the stability and sanctity of canon and tradition. Current attempts to restore a 1950s version of high modernism for the 1980s certainly point in that direction. And it is in this context that the question of neo-conservatism becomes politically central to the debate about the postmodern.

Habermas and the Question of Neo-Conservatism

Both in Europe and the U.S., the waning of the 1960s was accompanied by the rise of neo-conservatism and soon enough there emerged a new constellation characterized by the terms postmodernism and neo-conservatism. Even though their relationship was never fully elaborated, the Left took them to be compatible with each other or even identical, arguing that postmodernism was the kind of affirmative art that could happily coexist with political and cultural neo-conservatism. Until very recently, the question of the postmodern was simply not taken seriously on the Left,[26] not to speak of those traditionalists in the academy or the museum for whom there is still nothing new and worthwhile under the sun since the advent of modernism. The Left's ridiculing of postmodernism was of a piece with its often haughty and dogmatic critique of the counter-cultural impulses of the 1960s. During much of the 1970s, after all, the thrashing of the 1960s was as much a pastime of the Left as it was the gospel according to Daniel Bell.

Now, there is no doubt that much of what went under the label of postmodernism in the 1970s is indeed affirmative, not critical, in nature, and often, especially in literature, remarkably similar to tendencies of modernism which it so vocally repudiates. But not all of it is simply affirmative, and the wholesale writing off of postmodernism as a symptom of capitalist culture in decline is reductive, unhistorical and all too reminiscent of Lukács' attacks on modernism in the 1930s. Can one really make such clear-cut distinctions as to uphold modernism, today, as the only valid form of twentieth-century "realism",[27] an art that is adequate to the *condition moderne*, while simultaneously reserving all the old epitheta— inferior, decadent, pathological—to postmodernism? And isn't it ironic that many of the same critics who will insist on this distinction are the first ones to declare emphatically that modernism already had it all and that there is really nothing new in postmodernism. . .

I would instead argue that in order not to become the Lukács of the postmodern by opposing, today, a "good" modernism to a "bad" postmodernism, we try to salvage the postmodern from its assumed total collusion with neo-conservatism wherever possible; and that we explore the question whether postmodernism might not harbor productive contradictions, perhaps even a critical and oppositional potential. If the postmodern is indeed a historical and cultural condition (however transitional or incipient), then oppositional culture practices and strategies must be located *within* postmodernism, not necessarily in its gleaming facades, to be sure, but neither in some outside ghetto of a properly 'progressive' or a correctly 'aesthetic' art. Just as Marx analyzed the culture of modernity dialectically as bringing both progress and destruction,[28] the culture of postmodernity, too, must be grasped in its gains as well as in its losses, in its promises as well as in its deprivations; and yet, it may be precisely one of the characteristics of the postmodern that the relationship between progress and destruction of cultural forms between tradition and modernity can no longer be understood today the same way Marx understood it at the dawn of modernist culture.

It was, of course, Jürgen Habermas' intervention which, for the first time, raised the question of postmodernism's relationship to neo-conservatism in a theoretically and historically complex way. Ironically, however, the effect of Habermas' argument, which identified the postmodern with various forms of conservatism, was to reinforce leftist cultural stereotypes rather than challenge them. In his 1980 Adorno-prize lecture,[29] which has become a focal point for the debate, Habermas criticized both conservatism (old, neo and young) and postmodernism for not coming to terms either with the exigencies of culture in late capitalism or with the successes and failures of modernism itself. Significantly, Habermas' notion of modernity—the modernity he wishes to see continued and completed—is purged of modernism's nihilistic and anarchic strain just as his opponents', e.g., Lyotard's,[30] notion of an aesthetic (post)modernism is determined to liquidate any trace of the enlightened modernity inherited from the 18th century which provides the basis for Habermas' notion of modern culture. Rather than rehearsing the theoretical differences between Habermas and Lyotard one more time—a task which Martin Jay has performed admirably in a recent article on "Habermas and Modernism"[31]—I want to point to the German context of Habermas' reflections which is too readily forgotten in American debates, since Habermas himself refers to it only marginally.

Habermas' attack on postmodern conservatisms took place on the heels of the political *Tendenzwende* of the mid-1970s, the conservative backlash which has affected several Western countries. He could cite an analysis of American neo-conservatism without even having to belabor the point that the neo-conservative strategies to regain cultural hegemony and to wipe out the effect of the 1960s in political and cultural life are very similar in the FRG. But the national contingencies of Habermas' argument are at least as important. He was writing at the tail end of a major thrust of modernization of German cultural and political life which seemed to have gone awry sometime during the 1970s, producing high levels of disillusionment both with the utopian hopes and the pragmatic promises of 1968/69. Against the growing cynicism, which has since then been brilliantly diagnosed and criticized in Peter Sloterdijk's *Kritik der zynischen Vernunft* as a form of "enlightened false consciousness,"[32] Habermas tries to salvage the emancipatory potential of enlightened reason which to him is the *sine qua non* of political democracy. Habermas defends a substantive notion of communicative rationality, especially against those who will collapse reason with domination, believing that by abandoning reason they free themselves from domination. Of course Habermas' whole project of a critical social theory revolves around a defense of enlightened modernity, which is not identical with the aesthetic modernism of literary critics and art historians. It is directed simultaneously against political conservatism (neo or old) and against what he perceives, not unlike Adorno, as the cultural irrationality of a post-Nietzschean aestheticism embodied in surrealism and subsequently in much of contemporary French theory. The defense of enlightenment in Germany is and remains an attempt to fend off the reaction from the Right.

During the 1970s, Habermas could observe how German art and literature abandoned the explicit political commitments of the 1960s, a decade often described in Germany as a "second enlightenment"; how autobiography and *Erfahrungstexte* replaced the documentary experiments in prose and drama of the preceding decade; how political poetry and art made way for a new subjectivity, a new romanticism, a new mythology; how a new generation of students and young intellectuals became increasingly weary of theory, left politics and social science, preferring instead to flock toward the revelations of ethnology and myth. Even though Habermas does not address the art and literature of the 1970s directly—with the exception of the late work of Peter Weiss, which is itself an exception—it seems not too much to assume that he interpreted this cultural shift in light of the political *Tendenzwende*. Perhaps his labelling of Foucault and Derrida as young conservatives is as much a response to German cultural developments as it is to the French theorists themselves. Such a speculation may draw plausibility from the fact that since the late 1970s certain forms of French theory have been quite influential, especially in the subcultures of Berlin and Frankfurt, among those of the younger generation who have turned away from critical theory made in Germany.

It would be only a small step, then, for Habermas to conclude that a post-modern, post-avantgarde art indeed fits in all too smoothly with various forms of conservatism, and is predicated on abandoning the emancipatory project of modernity. But to me, there remains the question of whether these aspects of the 1970s—despite their occasionally high levels of self-indulgence, narcissism and false immediacy—do not also represent a deepening and a constructive displacement of the emancipatory impulses of the 1960s. But one does not have to share Habermas' positions on modernity and modernism to see that he did indeed raise the most important issues at stake in a form that avoided the usual apologies and facile polemics about modernity and postmodernity.

His questions were these: How does postmodernism relate to modernism? How are political conservatism, cultural eclecticism or pluralism, tradition, modernity and anti-modernity interrelated in contemporary Western culture? To what extent can the cultural and social formation of the 1970s be characterized as postmodern? And, further, to what extent is postmodernism a revolt against reason and enlightenment, and at what point do such revolts become reactionary—a question heavily loaded with the weight of recent German history? In comparison, the standard American accounts of postmodernism too often remain entirely tied to questions of aesthetic style or poetics; the occasional nod toward theories of a postindustrial society is usually intended as a reminder that any form of Marxist of neo-Marxist thought is simply obsolete. In the American debate, three positions can be schematically outlined. Postmodernism is dismissed outright as a fraud and modernism held up as the universal truth, a view which reflects the thinking of the 1950s. Or modernism is condemned as elitist and postmodernism praised as populist, a view which reflects the thinking of the 1960s. Or there is the truly 1970s proposition that "anything goes," which is consumer capitalism's cynical version of "nothing works," but which at least recognizes that the older dichotomies no longer work. Needless to say, none of these positions ever reached the level of Habermas' interrogation.

However, there were problems not so much with the questions Habermas raised, as with some of the answers he suggested. Thus his attack on Foucault and Derrida as young conservatives drew immediate fire from poststructuralist quarters, where the reproach was turned around and Habermas himself was labelled a conservative. At this point, the debate was quickly reduced to the silly question: "Mirror, mirror on the wall, who is the least conservative of us all?" And yet, the battle between "Frankfurters and French fries," as Rainer Nägele once referred to it, is instructive because it highlights two fundamentally different visions of modernity. The French vision of modernity begins with Nietzsche and Mallarmé and is thus quite close to what literary criticism describes as modernism. Modernity for the French is primarily—though by no means exclusively— an aesthetic question relating to the energies released by the deliberate destruction of language and other forms of representation. For Habermas, on the other hand, modernity goes back to the best traditions of the Enlightenment, which he tries to salvage and to reinscribe into the present philosophical discourse in a new form. In this, Habermas differs radically from an earlier generation of Frankfurt School critics, Adorno and Horkheimer who, in *The Dialectic of Enlightenment*, developed a view of modernity which seems to be much closer in sensibility to current French theory than to Habermas. But even though Adorno and Horkheimer's assessment of the enlightenment was so much more pessimistic than Habermas',[33] they also held on to a substantive notion of reason and subjectivity which much of French theory has abandoned. It seems that in the context of the French discourse, enlightenment is simply identified with a history of terror and incarceration that reaches from the Jacobins via the *métarécits* of Hegel and Marx to the Soviet Gulag. I think Habermas is right in rejecting that view as too limited and as politically dangerous. Auschwitz, after all, did not result from too much enlightened reason—even though it was organized as a perfectly rationalized death factory—but from a violent anti-enlighten-ment and anti-modernity affect, which exploited modernity ruthlessly for its own purposes. At the same time, Habermas' turn against the French post-Nietzschean vision of *modernité* as simply anti-modern or, as it were, postmodern, itself implies too limited an account of modernity, at least as far as aesthetic modernity is concerned.

In the uproar over Habermas' attack on the French poststructuralists, the American and European neo-conservatives were all but forgotten, but I think we should at least take cognizance of what cultural neo-conservatives actually say about postmodernism. The answer is fairly simple and straightforward: they reject it and they think it is dangerous. Two exam-ples: Daniel Bell, whose book on the postindustural society has been quoted time and again as supporting sociological evidence by advocates of postmodernism, actually rejects postmodernism as a dangerous popular-ization of the modernist aesthetic. Bell's modernism only aims at aesthetic pleasure, immediate gratification and intensity of experience, all of which, to him, promote hedonism and anarchy. It is easy to see how such a jaundiced view of modernism is quite under the spell of those " terrible" 1960s and cannot at all be reconciled with the austere high modernism of a Kafka, a Schönberg or a T.S. Eliot. At any rate, Bell sees modernism as something like an earlier society's chemical waste deposits which, during the 1960s, began to spill over, not unlike Love Canal, into the mainstrean of culture, polluting it to the core. Ultimately, Bell argues in the *The Cultural Contradictions of Capitalism*, modernism and postmod-ernism together are responsible for the crisis of contemporary capitalism.[34] Bell—a postmodernist? Certainly not in the aesthetic sense, for Bell actually shares Habermas' rejection of the nihilistic and aestheticist trend within modernist/postmodernist culture. But Habermas may have been right in the broader political sense. For Bell's critique of contemporary capitalist culture is energized by a vision of a society in which the values and norms of everyday life would no longer be infected by aesthetic modernism, a society which, within Bell's framework, one might have to call post-modern. But any such reflection on neo-conservatism as a form of anti-liberal, anti-progressive postmodernity remains beside the point. Given the aesthetic force-field of the term postmodernism, no neo-conservative today would dream of identifying the neo-conservative project as postmodern.

On the contrary, cultural neo-conservatives often appear as the last-ditch defenders and champions of modernism. Thus in the editorial to the first issue of *The New Criterion* and in an accompanying essay entitled "Postmodern: Art and Culture in the 1980s,"[35] Hilton Kramer rejects the postmodern and counters it with a nostalgic call for the restoration of modernist standards of quality. Differences between Bell's and Kramer's accounts of modernism notwithstanding, their assessment of postmodernism is identical. In the culture of the 1970s, they will only see loss of quality, dissolution of the imagination, decline of standards and values, and the triumph of nihilism. But their agenda is not art history. Their agenda is political. Bell argues that postmodernism "undermines the social structure itself by striking at the motivational and psychic-reward system which has sustained it."[36] Kramer attacks the politicization of culture which, in his view, the 1970s have inherited from the 1960s, that "insidious assault on the mind." And like Rudi Fuchs and the 1982 Documenta, he goes on to shove art back into the closet of autonomy and high seriousness where it is supposed to uphold the new criterion of truth. Hilton Kramer—a postmodernist? No, Habermas was simply wrong, it seems, in his linkage of the postmodern with neo-conservatism. But again the situation is more complex than it seems. For Habermas, modernity means critique, enlightenment and human emancipation, and he is not willing to jettison this political impulse because doing so would terminate left politics once and for all. Contrary to Habermas, the neo-conservative resorts to an established tradition of standards and values which are immune to criticism and change. To Habermas, even Hilton Kramer's neo-conservative defense of a modernism deprived of its adversary cutting edge would have to appear as post-modern, post-modern in the sense of anti-modern. The question in all of this is absolutely not whether the classics of modernism are or are not great works of art. Only a fool could deny that they are. But a problem does surface when their greatness is used as unsurpassable model and appealed to in order to stifle contemporary artistic production. Where that happens, modernism itself is pressed into the service of anti-modern resentment, a figure of discourse which has a long history in the multiple *querelles des anciens et des modernes.*

The only place where Habermas could rest assured of neo-conservative applause, however, is in his attack on Foucault and Derrida. Any such applause, however, would carry the proviso that neither Foucault nor Derrida be associated with conservatism. And yet, Habermas was right, in a sense, to connect the postmodernism problematic with poststructuralism. Roughly since the late 1970s, debates about aesthetic postmodernism and poststructuralist criticism have intersected in the U.S. The relentless hostility of neo-conservatives to both poststructuralism and postmodernism may not prove the point, but it is certainly suggestive. Thus the February 1984 issue of *The New Criterion* contains a report by Hilton Kramer on the Modern Language Association's centennial convention last December in New York, and the report is polemically entitled "The MLA Centennial Follies." The major target of the polemic is precisely French poststructuralism and its American appropriation. But the point is not the quality or the lack thereof in certain presentations at the convention. Again, the real issue is a political one. Deconstruction, feminist criticism, Marxist criticism, all lumped together as undesirable aliens, are said to have subverted American intellectual life via the academy. Reading Kramer, the cultural apocalypse seems near, and there would be no reason for surprise if *The New Criterion* were soon to call for an import quota on foreign theory.

What, then, can one conclude from these ideological skirmishes for a mapping of postmodernism in the 1970s aand 1980s? First, Habermas was both right and wrong about the collusion of conservatism and postmodernism, depending on whether the issue is the neo-conservative political vision of a post-modern society freed from all aesthetic, i.e., hedonistic, modernist and postmodernist subversions, or whether the issue is aesthetic postmodernism. Secondly, Habermas and the neo-conservatives are right in insisting that postmodernism is not so much a question of style as it is a question of politics and culture at large. The neo-conservative lament about the politicization of culture since the 1960s is only ironic in this context since they themselves have a thoroughly political notion of culture. Thirdly, the neo-conservatives are also right in suggesting that there are continuities between the oppositional culture of the 1960s and that of the 1970s. But their obsessive fixation on the 1960s, which they try to purge from the history books, blinds them to what is different and new in the cultural developments of the 1970s. And, fourthly, the attack on poststructuralism by Habermas and the American neo-conservatives raises the question of what to make of that fascinating interweaving and intersecting of poststructuralism with postmodernism, a phenomenon that is much more relevant in the U.S. than in France. It is to this question that I will now turn in my discussion of the critical discourse of American postmodernism in the 1970s and 1980s.

Poststructuralism: Modern or postmodern?

The neo-conservative hostility toward both is not really enough to establish a substantive link between postmodernism and poststructuralism; and it may indeed be more difficult to establish such a link than it would seem at first. Certainly, since the late 1970s we have seen a consensus emerge in the U.S. that if postmodernism represents the contemporary "avantgarde" in the arts, poststructuralism must be its equivalent in "critical theory."[37] Such a parallelization is itself favored by theories and practices of textuality and intertextuality which blur the boundaries between the literary and the critical text, and thus it is not surprising that the names of the French *maîtres penseurs* of our time occur with striking regularity in the discourse on the postmodern.[38] On a superficial level, the parallels seem indeed obvious. Just as postmodern art and literature have taken the place of an earlier modernism as the major trend of our times, poststructuralist criticism has decisively passed beyond the tenets of its major predecessor, the New Criticism. And just as the New Critics championed modernism, so the story goes, poststructuralism—as one of the most vital forces of the intellectual life of the 1970s—must somehow be allied with the art and literature of its own time, i.e., with postmodernism.[39] Actually, such thinking, which is quite prevalent if not always made explicit, gives us a first indication of how American postmodernism still lives in the shadow of the moderns. For there is no theoretical or historical reason to elevate the synchronism of the New Criticism with high modernism into norm or dogma. Mere simultaneity of critical and artistic discourse formations does not *per se* mean that they have to overlap, unless, of course, the boundaries between them are intentionally dismantled, as they are in modernist and postmodernist literature as well as in poststructuralist discourse.

And yet, however much postmodernism and poststructuralism in the U.S. may overlap and mesh, they are far from identical or even homologous. I do not question that the theoretical discourse of the 1970s has had a profound impact on the work of a considerable number of artists both in Europe and in the U.S. What I do question, however, is the way in which this impact is automatically evaluated in the U.S. as postmodern and thus sucked into the orbit of the kind of critical discourse that emphasizes radical rupture and discontinuity. Actually, both in France and in the U.S. poststructuralism is much closer to modernism than is usually assumed by the advocates of postmodernism. The distance that does exist between the critical discourses of the New Criticism and poststructuralism (a constellation which is only pertinent in the U.S., not in France) is not identical with the differences between modernism and postmodernism. I will argue that poststructuralism is primarily a discourse of and about modernism,[40] and that if we are to locate the postmodern in poststructuralism it will have to be found in the ways various forms of poststructuralism have opened up new problematics in modernism and have reinscribed modernism into the discourse formations of our own time.

Let me elaborate my view that poststructuralism can be perceived, to a significant degree, as a theory of modernism. I will limit myself here to certain points that relate back to my discussion of the modernism/postmodernism constellation in the 1960s and 1970s: the questions of aestheticism and mass culture, subjectivity and gender.

If it is true that postmodernity is a historical condition making it sufficiently unique and different from modernity, then it is striking to see how deeply the poststructuralist critical discourse—in its obsession with *écriture* and writing, allegory and rhetoric, and in its displacement of revolution and politics to the aesthetic—is embedded in that very modernist tradition which, at least in American eyes, it presumably transcends. What we find time and again is that American poststructuralist writers and critics emphatically privilege aesthetic innovation and experiment; that they call for self-reflexiveness, not, to be sure, of the author-subject, but of the text; that they purge life, reality, history, society from the work of art and its reception, and construct a new autonomy, based on a pristine notion of textuality, a new art for art's sake which is presumably the only kind possible after the failure of all and any commitment. The insight that the subject is constituted in language and the notion that there is nothing outside the text have led to the privileging of the aesthetic and the linguistic which aestheticism has always promoted to justify its imperial claims. The list of 'no longer possibles' (realism, representation, subjectivity, history, etc.,etc.) is as long in poststructuralism as it used to be in modernism, and it is very similar indeed.

Much recent writing has challenged the American domestication of French poststructuralism.[41] But it is not enough to claim that in the transfer to the U.S. French theory lost the political edge it has in France. The fact is that even in France the political implications of certain forms of poststructuralism are hotly debated and in doubt.[42] It is not just the institutional pressures of American literary criticism which have depoliticized French theory; the aestheticist trend *within* poststructuralism itself has facilitated the peculiar American reception. Thus it is no coincidence that the politically weakest body of French writing (Derrida and the late Barthes) has been privileged in American literature departments over the more politically intended projects of Foucault and the early Baudrillard, Kristeva and Lyotard. But even in the more politically conscious and self-conscious theoretical writing in France, the tradition of modernist aestheticism—mediated through an extremely selective reading of Nietzsche—is so powerful a presence that the notion of a radical rupture between the modern and the postmodern cannot possibly make much sense. It is furthermore striking that despite the considerable differences between the various poststructuralist projects, none of them seems formed in any substantial way by postmodernist works of art. Rarely, if ever, do they even address postmodernist works. In itself, this does not vitiate the power of the theory. But it does make for a kind of dubbing where the poststructuralist language is not in sync with the lips and movements of the postmodern body. There is no doubt that center stage in critical theory is held by the classical modernists: Flaubert, Proust and Bataille in Barthes; Nietzsche and Heidegger, Mallarmé and Artaud in Derrida; Nietzsche, Magritte and Bataille in Foucault; Mallarmé and Lautréamont, Joyce and Artaud in Kristeva; Freud in Lacan; Brecht in Althusser and Macherey, and so on *ad infinitum*. The enemies still are realism and representation, mass culture and standardization, grammar, communication and the presumably all-powerful homogenizing pressures of the modern State.

I think we must begin to entertain the notion that rather than offering a *theory of postmodernity* and developing an analysis of contemporary culture, French theory provides us primarily with an *archeology of modernity*, a theory of modernism at the stage of its exhaustion. It is as if the creative powers of modernism had migrated into theory and come to full self-consciousness in the poststructuralist text—the owl of Minerva spreading its wings at the fall of dusk. Poststructuralism offers a theory of modernism characterized by *Nachträglichkeit*, both in the psychoanalytic and the historical sense. Despite its ties to the tradition of modernist aestheticism, it offers a reading of modernism which differs substantially from those offered by the New Critics, by Adorno or by Greenberg. It is no longer the modernism of "the age of anxiety," the ascetic and tortured modernism of a Kafka, a modernism of negativity and alienation, ambiguity and abstraction, the modernism of the closed and finished work of art. Rather, it is a modernism of playful transgression, of an unlimited weaving of textuality, a modernism all confident in its rejection of representation and reality, in its denial of the subject, of history, and of the subject of history; a modernism quite dogmatic in its rejection of presence and in its unending praise of lacks and absences, deferrals and traces which produce, presumably, not anxiety but, in Roland Barthes' terms, *jouissance*, bliss.[43]

But if poststructuralism can be seen as the *revenant* of modernism in the guise of theory, then that would also be precisely what makes it postmodern. It is a postmodernism that works itself out not as a rejection of modernism, but rather as a retrospective reading which, in some cases, is fully aware of modernism's limitations and failed political ambitions. The dilemma of modernism had been its inability, despite the best intentions, to mount an effective critique of bourgeois modernity and modernization. The fate of the historical avantgarde especially had proven how modern art, even where it ventured beyond art for art's sake, was ultimately forced back into the aesthetic realm. Thus the gesture of poststructuralism, to the extent that it abandons all pretense to a critique that would go beyond language games, beyond epistemology and the aesthetic, seems at least plausible and logical. It certainly frees art and literature from that overload of responsibilities—to change life, change society, change the world—on which the historical avantgarde shipwrecked, and which lived on in France through the 1950s and 1960s embodied in the figure of Jean Paul Sartre. Seen in this light, poststructuralism seems to seal the fate of the modernist project which, even where it limited itself to the aesthetic sphere, always upheld a vision of a redemption of modern life through culture. That such visions are no longer possible to sustain may be at the heart of the postmodern condition, and it may ultimately vitiate the poststructuralist attempt to salvage aesthetic modernism for the late twentieth century. At any rate, it all begins to ring false when poststructuralism presents itself, as it frequently does in American writings, as the latest "avantgarde" in criticism, thus ironically assuming, in its institutional *Selbstverständnis*, the kind of teleological posturing which poststructuralism itself has done so much to criticize.

But even where such pretense to academic avantgardism is not the issue, one may well ask whether the theoretically sustained self-limitation to language and textuality has not been too high a price to pay; and whether it is not this self-limitation (with all it entails) which makes this poststructuralist modernism look like the atrophy of an earlier aestheticism rather than its innovative transformation. I say atrophy because the turn-of-the-century European aestheticism could still hope to establish a realm of beauty in opposition to what it perceived as the vulgarities of everyday bourgeois life, an artificial paradise thoroughly hostile to official politics and the kind of jingoism known in Germany as *Hurrapatriotismus*. Such an adversary function of aestheticism, however, can hardly be maintained at a time when capital itself has taken the aesthetic straight into the commodity in the form of styling, advertising and packaging. In an age of commodity aesthetics, aestheticism itself has become questionable either as an adversary or as a hibernating strategy. To insist on the adversary function of *écriture* and of breaking linguistic codes when every second ad bristles with domesticated avantgardist and modernist strategies strikes me as caught precisely in that very overestimation of art's transformative function for society which is the signature of an earlier, modernist, age. Unless, of course,*écriture* is merely practiced as a glass bead game

262 / Andreas Huyssen

in happy, resigned, or cynical isolation from the realm the uninitiated keep calling reality.

Take the later Roland Barthes.[44] His *The Pleasure of the Text* has become a major, almost canonical formulation of the postmodern for many American literary critics who may not want to remember that already twenty years ago Susan Sontag had called for an erotics of art intended to replace the stuffy and stifling project of academic interpretation. Whatever the differences between Barthes' *jouissance* and Sontag's erotics (the rigors of New Criticism and structuralism being the respective *Feindbilder*), Sontag's gesture, at the time, was a relatively radical one precisely in that it insisted on presence, on a sensual experience of cultural artifacts; in that it attacked rather than legitimized a socially sanctioned canon whose prime values were objectivity and distance, coolness and irony; and in that it licensed the flight from the lofty horizons of high culture into the netherlands of pop and camp.

Barthes, on the other hand, positions himself safely within high culture and the modernist canon, maintaining equal distance from the reactionary Right which champions anti-intellectual pleasures and the pleasure of anti-intellectualism, and the boring Left which favors knowledge, commitment, combat, and disdains hedonism. The Left may indeed have forgotten, as Barthes claims, the cigars of Marx and Brecht.[45] But however convincing cigars may or may not be as signifiers of hedonism, Barthes himself certainly forgets Brecht's constant and purposeful immersion in popular and mass culture. Barthes' very un-Brechtian distinction between *plaisir* and *jouissance*—which he simultaneously makes and unmakes[46]— reiterates one of the most tired topoi of the modernist aesthetic and of bourgeois culture at large: there are the lower pleasures for the rabble, i.e., mass culture, and then there is the *nouvelle cuisine* of the pleasure of the text, of *jouissance*. Barthes himself describes *jouissance* as a "mandarin praxis,"[47] as a conscious retreat, and he describes modern mass culture in the most simplistic terms as petit-bourgeois. Thus his appraisal of *jouissance* depends on the adoption of that traditional view of mass culture that the Right and the Left, both of which he so emphatically rejects, have shared over the decades.

This becomes even more explicit in *The Pleasure of the Text* where we read: "The bastard form of mass culture is humiliated repetition: content, ideological schema, the blurring of contradictions—these are repeated, but the superficial forms are varied: always new books, new programs, new films, news items, but always the same meaning."[48] Word for word, such sentences could have been written by Adorno in the 1940s. But, then, everybody knows that Adorno's was a theory of modernism, not of postmodernism. Or was it? Given the ravenous eclecticism of postmodernism, it has recently become fashionable to include even Adorno and

Benjamin into the canon of postmodernists *avant la lettre*—truly a case of the critical text writing itself without the interference of any historical consciousness whatsoever. Yet the closeness of some of Barthes' basic propositions to the modernist aesthetic could make such a rapprochement plausible. But then one might want to stop talking of postmodernism altogether, and take Barthes' writing for what it is: a theory of modernism which manages to turn the dung of post-68 political disillusionment into the gold of aesthetic bliss. The melancholy science of Critical Theory has been transformed miraculously into a new "gay science," but it still is, essentially, a theory of modernist literature.

Barthes and his American fans ostensibly reject the modernist notion of negativity replacing it with play, bliss, *jouissance*, i.e., with a critical form of affirmation. But the very distinction between the *jouissance* provided by the modernist, "writerly" text and the mere pleasure (*plaisir*) provided by " the text that contents, fills, grants euphoria,"[49] reintroduces, through the back door, the same high culture/low culture divide and the same type of evaluations which were constitutive of classical modernism. The negativity of Adorno's aesthetic was predicated on the consciousness of the mental and sensual depravations of modern mass culture and on his relentless hostility to a society which needs such depravation to reproduce itself. The euphoric American appropriation of Barthes' *jouissance* is predicated on ignoring such problems and on enjoying, not unlike the 1984 yuppies, the pleasures of writerly connoisseurism and textual gentrification. That, indeed, may be a reason why Barthes has hit a nerve in the American academy of the Reagan years, making him the favorite son who has finally abandoned his earlier radicalism and come to embrace the finer pleasures of life, pardon, the text.[50] But the problems with the older theories of a modernism of negativity are not solved by somersaulting from anxiety and alienation into the bliss of *jouissance*. Such a leap diminishes the wrenching experiences of modernity articulated in modernist art and literature; it remains bound to the modernist paradigm by way of simple reversal; and it does very little to elucidate the problem of the postmodern.

Just as Barthes' theoretical distinctions between *plaisir* and *jouissance*, the readerly and the writerly text, remain within the orbit of modernist aesthetics, so the predominant poststructuralist notions about authorship and subjectivity reiterate propositions known from modernism itself. A few brief comments will have to suffice.

In a discussion of Flaubert and the writerly, i.e., modernist, text Barthes writes: "He (Flaubert) does not stop the play of codes (or stops it only partially), so that (and this is indubitably the proof of writing) *one never knows if he is responsible for what he writes* (if there is a subject *behind* his language); for the very being of writing (the meaning of the labor that constitutes it) is to keep the question Who is speaking? from ever being answered."⁵¹ A similarly prescriptive denial of authorial subjectivity underlies Foucault's discourse analysis. Thus Foucault ends his influential essay "What Is an Author?" by asking rhetorically "What matter who's speaking?" Foucault's "murmur of indifference"⁵² affects both the writing and speaking subject, and the argument assumes its full polemical force with the much broader anti-humanist proposition, inherited from structuralism, of the "death of the subject." But none of this is more than a further elaboration of the modernist critique of traditional idealist and romantic notions of authorship and authenticity, originality and intentionality, self-centered subjectivity and personal identity. More importantly, it seems to me that as a postmodern, having gone through the modernist purgatory, I would ask different questions. Isn't the "death of the subject/author" position tied by mere reversal to the very ideology that invariably glorifies the artist as genius, whether for marketing purposes or out of conviction and habit? Hasn't capitalist modernization itself fragmented and dissolved bourgeois subjectivity and authorship, thus making attacks on such notions somewhat quixotic? And, finally, doesn't poststructuralism, where it simply denies the subject altogether, jettison the chance of challenging the *ideology of the subject* (as male, white, and middle-class) by developing alternative and different notions of subjectivity?

To reject the validity of the question Who is writing? or Who is speaking? is simply no longer a radical position in 1984. It merely duplicates on the level of aesthetics and theory what capitalism as a system of exchange relations produces tendentially in everyday life: the denial of subjectivity in the very process of its construction. Poststructuralism thus attacks the appearance of capitalist culture—individualism writ large—but misses its essence; like modernism, it is always also in sync with rather than opposed to the real processes of modernization.

The postmoderns have recognized this dilemma. They counter the modernist litany of the death of the subject by working toward new theories and practices of speaking, writing and acting subjects.⁵³ The question of how codes, texts, images and other cultural artifacts constitute subjectivity is increasingly being raised as an always already historical question. And to raise the question of subjectivity at all no longer carries the stigma of being caught in the trap of bourgeois or petit-bourgeois ideology; the discourse of subjectivity has been cut loose from its moorings in bourgeois individualism. It is certainly no accident that questions of subjectivity and authorship have resurfaced with a vengeance in the postmodern text. After all, it does matter who is speaking or writing.

Summing up, then, we face the paradox that a body of theories of modernism and modernity, developed in France since the 1960s, has come to be viewed, in the U.S., as the embodiment of the postmodern in theory. In a certain sense, this development is perfectly logical. Poststructuralism's readings of modernism are new and exciting enough to be considered somehow beyond modernism as it has been perceived before; in this way poststructuralist criticism in the U.S. yields to the very real pressures of the postmodern. But against any facile conflation of poststructuralism with the postmodern, we must insist on the fundamental non-identity of the two phenomena. In America, too, poststructuralism offers a theory of modernism, not a theory of the postmodern.

As to the French theorists themselves, they rarely speak of the postmodern. Lyotard's *La Condition Postmoderne*, we must remember, is the exception, not the rule.[54] What the French explicitly analyze and reflect upon is *le texte moderne* and *la modernité*. Where they talk about the postmodern at all, as in the cases of Lyotard and Kristeva,[55] the question seems to have been prompted by American friends, and the discussion almost immediately and invariably turns back to problems of the modernist aesthetic. For Kristeva, the question of postmodernism is the question of how anything can be written in the twentieth century and how we can talk about this writing. She goes on to say that postmodernism is "that literature which writes itself with the more or less conscious intention of expanding the signifiable and thus the human realm."[56] With the Bataillean formulation of writing-as-experience of limits, she sees the major writing since Mallarmé and Joyce, Artaud and Burroughs as the "exploration of the typical imaginary relationship, that to the mother, through the most radical and problematic aspect of this relationship, language."[57] Kristeva's is a fascinating and novel approach to the question of modernist literature, and one that understands itself as a political intervention. But it does not yield much for an exploration of the differences between modernity and postmodernity. Thus it cannot surprise that Kristeva still shares with Barthes and the classical theorists of modernism an aversion to the media whose function, she claims, is to collectivize all systems of signs thus enforcing contemporary society's general tendency toward uniformity.

Lyotard, who like Kristeva and unlike the deconstructionists is a political thinker, defines the postmodern, in his essay "Answering the Question: What is Postmodernism?," as a recurring stage within the modern itself. He turns to the Kantian sublime for a theory of the non-representable essential to modern art and literature. Paramount are his interest in rejecting representation, which is linked to terror and totalitarianism, and his demand for radical experimentation in the arts. At first sight, the turn to Kant seems plausible in the sense that Kant's autonomy aesthetic and notion of "disinterested pleasure" stands at the threshold of a modernist aesthetic, at a crucial juncture of that differentiation of spheres which has been so important in social thought from Weber to Habermas. And yet, the turn to Kant's sublime forgets that the eighteenth century fascination with the sublime of the universe, the cosmos, expresses precisely that very desire of totality and representation which Lyotard so abhors and persistently criticizes in Habermas' work.[58] Perhaps Lyotard's text says more here than it means to. If historically the notion of the sublime harbors a secret desire for totality, then perhaps Lyotard's sublime can be read as an attempt to totalize the aesthetic realm by fusing it with all other spheres of life, thus wiping out the differentiations between the aesthetic realm and the life-world on which Kant did after all insist. At any rate, it is no coincidence that the first moderns in Germany, the Jena romantics, built their aesthetic strategies of the fragment precisely on a rejection of the sublime which to them had become a sign of the falseness of bourgeois accommodation to absolutist culture. Even today the sublime has not lost its link to terror which, in Lyotard's reading, it opposes. For what would be more sublime and unrepresentable than the nuclear holocaust, the bomb being the signifier of an ultimate sublime. But apart from the question whether or not the sublime is an adequate aesthetic category to theorize contemporary art and literature, it is clear that in Lyotard's essay the postmodern as aesthetic phenomenon is not seen as distinct from modernism. The crucial historical distinction which Lyotard offers in *La Condition Postmoderne* is that between the *métarécits* of liberation (the French tradition of enlightened modernity) and of totality (the German Hegelian/ Marxist tradition) on the one hand, and the modernist experimental discourse of language games on the other. Enlightened modernity and its presumable consequences are pitted against aesthetic modernism. The irony in all of this, as Fred Jameson has remarked,[59] is that Lyotard's commitment to radical experimentation is politically "very closely related to the conception of the revolutionary nature of high modernism that Habermas faithfully inherited from the Frankfurt School."

No doubt, there are historically and intellectually specific reasons for the French resistance to acknowledging the problem of the postmodern as a historical problem of the late twentieth century. At the same time, the force of the French rereading of modernism proper is itself shaped by the pressures of the 1960s and 1970s, and it has thus raised many of the key questions pertinent to the culture of our own time. But it still has done very little toward illuminating an emerging postmodern culture, and it has largely remained blind to or uninterested in many of the most promising artistic endeavors today. French theory of the 1960s and 1970s has offered us exhilarating fireworks which illuminate a crucial segment of the trajectory of modernism, but, as appropriate with fireworks, after dusk has fallen. This view is borne out by none less that Michel Foucault who, in the late 1970s, criticized his own earlier fascination with language and epistemology as a limited project of an earlier decade: "The whole relentless theorization of writing which we saw in the 1960s was doubtless only a swansong."[60] Swansong of modernism, indeed; but as such already a moment of the postmodern. Foucault's view of the intellectual movement of the 1960s as a swansong, it seems to me, is closer to the truth than its American rewriting, during the 1970s, as the latest avantgarde.

Whither Postmodernism?

The cultural history of the 1970s still has to be written, and the various postmodernisms in art, literature, dance, theater, architecture, film, video, and music will have to be discussed separately and in detail. All I want to do now is to offer a framework for relating some recent cultural and political changes to postmodernism, changes which already lie outside the conceptual network of "modernism/avantgardism" and have so far rarely been included in the postmodernism debate.[61]

I would argue that the contemporary arts—in the widest possible sense, whether they call themselves postmodernist or reject that label—can no longer be regarded as just another phase in the sequence of modernist and avantgardist movements which began in Paris in the 1850s and 1860s and which maintained an ethos of cultural progress and vanguardism through the 1960s. On this level, postmodernism cannot be regarded simply as a sequel to modernism, as the latest step in the neverending revolt of modernism against itself. The postmodern sensibility of our time is different from both modernism and avantgardism precisely in that it raises the question of cultural tradition and conservation in the most fundamental way as an aesthetic and a political issue. It doesn't always do it successfully, and it often does it exploitatively. And yet, my main point about contemporary postmodernism is that it operates in a field of tension between tradition and innovation, conservation and renewal, mass culture and high art, in which the second terms are no longer automatically privileged over the first; a field of tension which can no longer be grasped in categories such as progress vs. reaction, Left vs. Right, present vs. past, modernism vs. realism, abstraction vs. representation, avantgarde vs. Kitsch. The fact that such dichotomies, which after all are central to the classical accounts of modernism, have broken down is part of the shift in the following terms: Modernism and the avantgarde were always closely related to social and industrial modernization. They were related to it as an adversary culture, yes, but they drew their energies, not unlike Poe's *Man of the Crowd*, from their proximity to the crises brought about by modernization and progress. Modernization—such was the widely held belief, even when the word was not around—had to be traversed. There was a vision of emerging on the other side. The modern was a world-scale drama played out on the European and American stage, with mythic modern man as its hero and with modern art as a driving force, just as Saint-Simon had envisioned it already in 1825. Such heroic visions of modernity and of art as a force of social change (or, for that matter, resistance to undesired change) are a thing of the past, admirable for sure, but no longer in tune with current sensibilities, except perhaps with an emerging apocalyptic sensibility as the flip side of modernist heroism.

Seen in this light, postmodernism at its deepest level represents not just another crisis within the perpetual cycle of boom and bust, exhaustion and renewal, which has characterized the trajectory of modernist culture. It rather represents a new type of crisis of that modernist culture itself. Of course, this claim has been made before, and fascism indeed was a formidable crisis of modernist culture. But fascism was never the alternative to modernity it pretended to be, and our situation today is very different from that of the Weimar Republic in its agony. It was only in the 1970s that the historical limits of modernism, modernity and modernization came into sharp focus. The growing sense that we are not bound to *complete* the project of modernity (Habermas' phrase) and still do not necessarily have to lapse into irrationality or into apocalyptic frenzy, the sense that art is not exclusively pursuing some telos of abstraction, non-representation and sublimity—all of this has opened up a host of possibilities for creative endeavors today. And in certain ways it has altered our views of modernism itself. Rather than being bound to a one-way history of modernism which interprets it as a logical unfolding toward some imaginary goal, and which thus is based on a whole series of exclusions, we are beginning to explore its contradictions and contingencies, its tensions and internal resistances to its own "forward" movement. Postmodernism is far from making modernism obsolete. On the contrary, it casts a new light on it and appropriates many of its aesthetic strategies and techniques inserting them and making them work in new constellations. What has become obsolete, however, are those codifications of modernism in critical discourse which, however subliminally, are based on a teleological view of progress and modernization. Ironically, these normative and often reductive codifications have actually prepared the ground for that repudiation of modernism which goes by the name of the postmodern. Confronted with the critic who argues that this or that novel is not up to the latest in narrative technique, that it is regressive, behind the times and thus uninteresting, the postmodernist is right in rejecting modernism. But such rejection affects only that trend within modernism which has been codified into a narrow dogma, not modernism as such. In some ways, the story of modernism and postmodernism is like the story of the hedgehog and the hare: the hare could not win because there always was more than just one hedgehog. But the hare was still the better runner. . .

The crisis of modernism is more that just a crisis of those trends within it which tie it to the ideology of modernization. In the age of late capitalism, it is also a new crisis of art's relationship to society. At their most emphatic, modernism and avantgardism attributed to art a privileged status in the processes of social change. Even the aestheticist withdrawal from the concern of social change is still bound to it by virtue of its denial of the status quo and the construction of an artificial paradise of exquisite beauty. When social change seemed beyond grasp or took an undesired turn, art was still privileged as the only authentic voice of critique and protest, even when it seemed to withdraw into itself. The classical accounts of high modernism attest to that fact. To admit that these were heroic illusions—perhaps even necessary illusions in art's struggle to survive in dignity in a capitalist society—is not to deny the importance of art in social life.

But modernism's running feud with mass society and mass culture as well as the avantgarde's attack on high art as a support system of cultural hegemony always took place on the pedestal of high art itself. And certainly that is where the avantgarde has been installed after its failure, in the 1920s, to create a more encompassing space for art in social life. To continue to demand today that high art leave the pedestal and relocate elsewhere (wherever that might be) is to pose the problem in obsolete terms. The pedestal of high art and high culture no longer occupies the privileged space it used to, just as the cohesion of the class which erected its monuments on that pedestal is a thing of the past; recent conservative attempts in a number of Western countries to restore the dignity of the classics of Western Civilization, from Plato via Adam Smith to the high modernists, and to send students back to the basics, prove the point. I am not saying here that the pedestal of high art does not exist any more. Of course it does, but it is not what it used to be. Since the 1960s, artistic activities have become much more diffuse and harder to contain in safe categories or stable institutions such as the academy, the museum or even the established gallery network. To some, this dispersal of cultural and artistic practices and activities will involve a sense of loss and disorientation; others will experience it as a new freedom, a cultural liberation. Neither may be entirely wrong, but we should recognize that it was not only recent theory or criticism that deprived the univalent, exclusive and totalizing accounts of modernism of their hegemonic role. It was the activities of artists, writers, film makers, architects, and performers that have propelled us beyond a narrow vision of modernism and given us a new lease on modernism itself.

In political terms, the erosion of the triple dogma modernism/modernity/avantgardism can be contextually related to the emergence of the problematic of "otherness," which has asserted itself in the socio-political sphere as much as in the cultural sphere. I cannot discuss here the various and multiple forms of otherness as they emerge from differences in subjectivity, gender and sexuality, race and class, temporal *Ungleichzeitigkeiten* and spatial geographic locations and dislocations. But I want to mention at least four recent phenomena which, in my mind, are and will remain constitutive of postmodern culture for some time to come.

Despite all its noble aspirations and achievements, we have come to recognize that the culture of enlightened modernity has also always (though by no means exclusively) been a culture of inner and outer imperialism, a reading already offered by Adorno and Horkheimer in the 1940s and an insight not unfamiliar to those of our ancestors involved in the multitude of struggles against rampant modernization. Such imperialism, which works inside and outside, on the micro and macro levels, no longer goes unchallenged either politically, economically or culturally. Whether these challenges will usher in a more habitable, less violent and more democratic world remains to be seen, and it is easy to be skeptical. But enlightened cynicism is as insufficient an answer as blue-eyed enthusiasm for peace and nature.

The women's movement has led to some significant changes in social structure and cultural attitudes which must be sustained even in the face of the recent grotesque revival of American machismo. Directly and indirectly, the women's movement has nourished the emergence of women as a self-confident and creative force in the arts, in literature, film and criticism. The ways in which we now raise questions of gender and sexuality, reading and writing, subjectivity and enunciation, voice and performance are unthinkable without the impact of feminism, even though many of these activities may take place on the margin or even outside the movement proper. Feminist critics have also contributed substantially to revisions of the history of modernism, not just by unearthing forgotten artists, but also by approaching the male modernists in novel ways. This is true also of the "new French feminists" and their theorization of the feminine in modernist writing, even though they often insist on maintaining a polemical distance from an American-type feminism.[62]

During the 1970s, questions of ecology and environment have deepened from single-issue politics to a broad critique of modernity and modernization, a trend which is politically and culturally much stronger in West Germany than in the U.S. A new ecological sensibility manifests itself not only in political and regional subcultures, in alternative life-styles and the new social movements in Europe, but it also affects art and literature in a variety of ways: the work of Joseph Beuys, certain land art projects, Christo's California running fence, the new nature poetry, the return to local traditions, dialects, and so on. It was especially due to the growing ecological sensibility that the link between certain forms of modernism and technological modernization has come under critical scrutiny.

There is a growing awareness that other cultures, non-European, non-

Western cultures must be met by means other than conquest or domination, as Paul Ricoeur put it more than twenty years ago, and that the erotic and aesthetic fascination with "the Orient"—so prominent in Western culture, including modernism—is deeply problematic. This awareness will have to translate into a type of intellectual work different from that of the modernist intellectual who typically spoke with the confidence of standing at the cutting edge of time and of being able to speak for others. Foucault's notion of the local and specific intellectual as opposed to the "universal" intellectual of modernity may provide a way out of the dilemma of being locked into our own culture and traditions while simultaneously recognizing their limitations.

In conclusion, it is easy to see that a postmodernist culture emerging from these political, social and cultural constellations will have to be a postmodernism of resistance, including resistance to that easy postmodernism of the "anything goes" variety. Resistance will always have to be specific and contingent upon the cultural field within which it operates. It cannot be defined simply in terms of negativity or non-identity à la Adorno, nor will the litanies of a totalizing, collective project suffice. At the same time, the very notion of resistance may itself be problematic in its simple opposition to affirmation. After all, there are affirmative forms of resistance and resisting forms of affirmation. But this may be more a semantic problem than a problem of practice. And it should not keep us from making judgments. How such resistance can be articulated in art works in ways that would satisfy the needs of the political and those of the aesthetic, of the producers and of the recipients, cannot be prescribed, and it will remain open to trial, error and debate. But it is time to abandon that dead-end dichotomy of politics and aesthetics which for too long has dominated accounts of modernism, including the aestheticist trend within poststructuralism. The point is not to eliminate the productive tension between the political and the aesthetic, between history and the text, between engagement and the mission of art. The point is to heighten that tension, even to rediscover it and to bring it back into focus in the arts as well as in criticism. No matter how troubling it may be, the landscape of the postmodern surrounds us. It simultaneously delimits and opens our horizons. It's our problem and our hope.

Notes

1. On this question see Fredric Jameson, "Postmodernism or the Cultural Logic of Capitalism," *New Left Review*, Vol. 146, July–August 1984, pp. 53–92, whose attempt to identify postmodernism with a new stage in the developmental logic of capital, I feel, overstates the case.
2. For a distinction between a critical and an affirmative postmodernism, see

Hal Foster's inroduction to *The Anti-Aesthetic* (Port Townsend, Washington: Bay Press, 1984). Foster's new essay in this issue, however, indicates a change of mind with regard to the critical potential of postmodernism.

3. For an earlier attempt to give a *Begriffsgeschichte* of postmodernism in literature, see the various essays in *Amerikastudien*, 22:1 (1977), 9–46 (includes a valuable bibliography). Cf. also Ihab Hassan, *The Dismemberment of Orpheus*, second edition (Madison: University of Wisconsin Press, 1982), especially the new "Postface 1982: Toward a Concept of Postmodernism," pp. 259–271.—The debate about modernity and modernization in history and the social sciences is too broad to document here; for an excellent survey of the pertinent literature, see Hans-Ulrich Wehlder, *Modernisierungstheorie und Geschichte* (Göttingen: Vandenhoeck & Ruprecht, 1975).—On the question of modernity and the arts, see Matei Calinescu, *Faces of Modernity* (Bloomington: Indiana University Press, 1977); Marshal Berman, *All That Is Solid Melts Into Air: The Experience of Modernity* (New York: Simon and Schuster, 1982); Eugene Lunn, *Marxism and Modernism* (Berkeley and Los Angeles: University of California Press, 1982); Peter Bürger, *Theory of the Avantgarde* (Minneapolis: University of Minnesota Press, 1984). Also important for this debate is the recent work by cultural historians on specific cities and their culture, e.g., Carl Schorske's and Robert Waissenberger's work on fin-de-siècle Vienna, Peter Gay's and John Willett's work on the Weimar Republic, and, for a discussion of American anti-modernism at the turn of the century, T.J. Jackson Lears' *No Place of Grace* (New York: Pantheon, 1981).

4. On the ideological and political function of modernism in the 1950s cf. Jost Hermand, "Modernism Restored: West German Painting in the 1950s," *NGC*, 32 (Spring/Summer 1984); and Serge Guilbaut, *How New York Stole the Idea of Modern Art* (Chicago: Chicago University Press, 1983).

5. For a thorough discussion of this concept, see Robert Sayre and Michel Löwy, "Figures of Romantic Anti-Capitalism," *NGC*, 32 (Spring/Summer 1984).

6. For an excellent discussion of the politics of architecture in the Weimar Republic see the exhibition catalogue *Wem gehört die Welt: Kunst und Gesellschaft in der Weimarer Republik* (Berlin: Neue Gesellschaft für bildende Kunst, 1977), pp. 38–157. Cf. also Robert Hughes, "Trouble in Utopia," in *The Shock of the New* (New York: Alfred A. Knopf, 1981), pp. 164–211.

7. The fact that such strategies can cut different ways politically is shown by Kenneth Frampton in his essay "Towards a Critical Regionalism," in *The Anti-Aesthetic*, pp. 23–38.

8. Charles A. Jencks, *The Language of Postmodern Architecture* (New York: Rizzoli, 1977), p. 97.

9. For Bloch's concept of *Ungleichzeitigkeit*, see Ernst Bloch, "Non-Synchronism and the Obligation to its Dialectics," and Anson Rabinbach's "Ernst

Blochs's *Heritage of our Times* and Facism," in *NGC*, 11 (Spring 1977), 5–38.

10. Robert Venturi, Denise Scott Brown, Steven Izenour, *Learning from Las Vegas* (Cambridge: MIT Press, 1972). Cf. also the earlier study by Venturi, *Complexity and Contradiction in Architecture* (New York: Museum of Modern Art, 1966).

11. Kenneth Frampton, *Modern Architecture: A Critical History* (New York: and Toronto: Oxford University Press, 1980), p. 290.

12. I am mainly concerned here with the *Selbstverständnis* of the artists, not with the question of whether their work really went beyond modernism or whether it was in all cases politically "progressive." On the politics of the Beat rebellion see Barbara Ehrenreich, *The Hearts of Men* (New York: Doubleday, 1984), esp. pp. 52–67.

13. Gerald Graff, "The Myth of the Postmodern Breakthrough," in *Literature Against Itself* (Chicago: Chicago University Press, 1979), pp. 31–62.

14. John Barth, "The Literature of Replenishment: Postmodernist Fiction," *Atlantic Monthly*, 245:1 (January 1980), 65–71.

15. Daniel Bell, *The Cultural Contradictions of Capitalism* (New York: Basic Books, 1976), p. 51.

16. The specific connotations the notion of postmodernity has taken on in the German peace and anti-nuke movements as well as within the Green Party will not be discussed here, as this article is primarily concerned with the American debate.—In German intellectual life, the work of Peter Sloterdijk is eminently relevant for these issues, although Sloterdijk does not use the word "postmodern"; Peter Sloterdijk, *Critique of Cynical Reason* (Minn.: University of Minnesota Press, 1987). Equally pertinent is the peculiar German reception of French theory, especially of Foucault, Baudrillard, and Lyotard; see for example *Der Tod der Moderne, Eine Diskussion* (Tübingen: Konkursbuchverlag, 1983). On the apocalyptic shading of the postmodern in Germany see Ulrich Horstmann, *Das Untier. Konturen einer Philosophie der Menschenflucht* (Wien-Berlin: Medusa, 1983).

17. The following section will draw on arguments developed less fully in my earlier article entitled "The Search for Tradition: Avantgarde and Postmodernism in the 1970s," *NGC*, 22 (Winter, 1981), 23–40. Also in Huyssen, *After the Great Divide* (Bloomington: Indiana University Press, 1986).

18. Peter Bürger, *Theory of the Avantgarde* (Minneapolis: University of Minnesota Press, 1984).The fact that Bürger reserves the term avantgarde for mainly these three movements may strike the American reader as idiosyncratic or as unnecessarily limited unless the place of the argument within the tradition of twentieth-century German aesthetic thought from Brecht and Benjamin to Adorno is understood.

19. This difference between modernism and the avantgarde was one of the pivotal points of disagreement between Benjamin and Adorno in the 1930s, a debate to which Bürger owes a lot. Confronted with the successful

fusion of aesthetics, politics and everyday life in fascist Germany, Adorno condemned the avantgarde's intention to merge art with life and continued to insist, in best modernist fashion, on the autonomy of art; Benjamin on the other hand, looking backward to the radical experiments in Paris, Moscow and Berlin in the 1920s, found a messianic promise in the avant-garde, especially in surrealism, a fact which may help explain Benjamin's strange (and, I think, mistaken) appropriation in the U.S. as a postmodern critic *avant la lettre*.

20. Cf. my essay "The Cultural Politics of Pop," *New German Critique*, 4 (Winter 1975), 77–97. Also in Huyssen, *After the Great Divide*.

21. The Left's fascination with the media was perhaps more pronounced in Germany that it was in the U.S. Those were the years when Brecht's radio theory and Benjamin's "The Work of Art in the Age of Mechanical Reproduction" almost became cult texts. See, for example, Hans Magnus Enzensberger, "Baukasten zu einer Theorie der Medien," *Kursbuch*, 20 (March 1970), 159–186. Reprinted in H.M.E., *Palaver* (Frankfurt am Main: Suhrkamp, 1974). The old belief in the democratizing potential of the media is also intimated on the last pages of Lyotard's *The Postmodern Condition*, not in relation to radio, film or television, but in relation to computers.

22. Leslie Fiedler, "The New Mutants" (1965), *A Fiedler Reader* (New York: Stein and Day, 1977), pp. 189–210.

23. Edward Lucie-Smith, *Art in the Seventies* (Ithaca: Cornell University Press, 1980), p. 11.

24. For a lucid discussion of Greenberg's theory of modern art in its historical context see T.J. Clark, "Clement Greenberg's Theory of Art," *Critical Inquiry*, 9:1 (September 1982), 139–156. For a different view of Greenberg see Ingeborg Hoesterey, "Die Moderne am Ende? Zu den ästhetischen Positionen von Jürgen Habermas und Clement Greenberg," *Zeitschrift für Ästhetik und allgemeine Kunstwissenschaft*, 29:2 (1984). On Adorno's theory of modernism see Eugene Lunn, *Marxism and Modernism* (Berkeley and Los Angeles: University of California Press, 1982); Peter Bürger, *Vermittlung—Rezeption—Funktion* (Frankfurt am Main: Suhrkamp, 1980). Cf. also my essay "Adorno in Reverse: From Hollywood to Richard Wagner," *NGC*, 29 (Spring-Summer 1983), 8–38. Also in Huyssen, *After the Great Divide*.

25. See Craig Owens, "The Discourse of Others," in Hal Foster, ed., *The Anti-Aesthetic* pp. 65–90.

26. It is with the recent publications by Fred Jameson and Hal Foster's *The Anti-Aesthetic* that things have begun to change.

27. Of course, those who hold this view will not utter the word "realism" as it is tarnished by its traditionally close association with the notions of "reflection," "representation," and a transparent reality; but the persuasive power of the modernist doctrine owes much to the underlying idea that only modernist art and literature are somehow adequate to our time.

28. For a work that remains very much in the orbit of Marx's notion of modernity and tied to the political and cultural impulses of the American 1960s see Marshall Berman, *All That Is Solid Melts Into Air: the Experience of Modernity* (New York: Simon and Schuster, 1982). For a critique of Berman see David Bathrick's review essay in this issue.

29. Jürgen Habermas, "Modernity versus Postmodernity," *NGC*, 22 (Winter 1981), 3–14. (Reprinted in Foster, ed., *The Anti-Aesthetic*.)

30. Jean-François Lyotard, "Answering the Question: What Is Postmodernism?" in *The Postmodern Condition* (Minneapolis: University of Minnesota Press, 1984), pp. 71–82.

31. Martin Jay, "Habermas and Modernism," *Praxis International*, 4:1 (April 1984), 1–14. Cf. in the same issue Richard Rorty, "Habermas and Lyotard on Postmodernity," 32–44.

32. Peter Sloterdijk, *Critique of Cynical Reason*. Sloterdijk himself tries to salvage the emancipatory potential of reason in ways fundamentally different from Habermas', ways which could indeed be called postmodern. For a brief, but incisive discussion in English of Sloterdijk's work see Leslie A. Adelson, "Against the Enlightenment: A Theory with Teeth for the 1980s," *German Quarterly*, 57:4 (Fall 1984), 625–631.

33. Cf. Jürgen Habermas, "The Entwinement of Myth and Enlightenment Re-reading *Dialectic of Enlightenment*," *NGC*, 26 (Spring-Summer 1982), 13–30. Also in Habermas, *The Philosophical Discourse of Modernity* (Cambridge: MIT Press, 1987).

34. Of course there is another line of argument in the book which *does* link the crisis of capitalist culture to economic developments. But I think that as a rendering of Bell's polemical stance the above description is valid.

35. The Editors, "A Note on *The New Criterion*," *The New Criterion*, 1:1 (September 1982), 1–5. Hilton Kramer, "Postmodern: Art and Culture in the 1980s," *ibid*, 36–42.

36. Bell, *The Cultural Contradictions of Capitalism*, p. 54.

37. I follow the current usage in which the term "critical theory" refers to a multitude of recent theoretical and interdisciplinary endeavors in the humanities. Originally, Critical Theory was a much focused term that referred to the theory developed by the Frankfurt School since the 1930s. Today, however, the critical theory of the Frankfurt School is itself only a part of an expanded field of critical theories, and this may ultimately benefit its reinscription in contemporary critical discourse.

38. The same is not always true the other way round, however. Thus American practitioners of deconstruction usually are not very eager to address the problem of the postmodern. Actually, American deconstruction, such as practiced by the late Paul de Man, seems altogether unwilling to grant a distinction between the modern and the postmodern at all. Where de Man addresses the problem of modernity directly, as in his seminal essay "Literary History and Literary Modernity" in *Blindness and Insight*, he projects

characteristics and insights of modernism back into the past so that ultimately all literature becomes, in a sense, essentially modernist.

39. A cautionary note may be in order here. The term poststructuralism is by
now about as amorphous as 'postmodernism,' and it encompasses a variety
of quite different theoretical endeavors. For the purposes of my discussion,
however, the differences can be bracketed temporarily in order to approach
certain similarities between different poststructuralist projects.

40. This part of the argument draws on the work about Foucault by John
Rajchman, "Foucault, or the Ends of Modernism," *October*, 24 (Spring
1983), 37–62, and on the discussion of Derrida as a theorist of modernism
in Jochen Schulte-Sasse's introduction to Peter Bürger, *Theory of the
Avantgarde*.

41. Jonathan Arac, Wlad Godzich, Wallace Martin, eds., *The Yale Critics:
Deconstruction in America* (Minneapolis: University of Minnesota Press,
1983).

42. See Nancy Fraser's article in *New German Critique*, No. 33. 1984.

43. 'Bliss' is an inadequate rendering of *jouissance* as the English term lacks
the crucial bodily and hedonistic connotations of the French word.

44. My intention is not to reduce Barthes to the positions taken in his later
work. The American success of this work, however, makes it permissible
to treat it as a symptom, or, if you will, as a *"mythologie."*

45. Roland Barthes, *The Pleasure of the Text* (New York: Hill and Wang,
1975), p. 22.

46. See Tania Modleski, "The Terror of Pleasure: The Contemporary Horror
Film and Postmodern Theory," in Modleski, ed., *Studies in Entertainment*
(Bloomington: Indiana University Press, 1986), pp. 155–166.

47. Barthes, p. 38.

48. Barthes, p. 41 f.

49. Barthes, p. 14.

50. Thus the fate of pleasure according to Barthes was extensively discussed at
a forum of the 1983 MLA while an hour later, in a session on the future of
literary criticism, various speakers extolled the emergence of a new historical criticism. This, it seems to me, marks an important line of conflict and
tension in the current litcrit scene in the U.S.

51. Roland Barthes, *S/Z* (New York: Hill and Wang, 1974), p. 140.

52. Michel Foucault, "What Is an Author?" in *Language, counter-memory,
practice* (Ithaca: Cornell University Press, 1977), p. 138.

53. This shift in interest back to questions of subjectivity is actually also present
in some of the later poststructuralist writings, for instance in Kristeva's
work on the symbolic and the semiotic and in Foucault's work on sexuality.
On Foucault see Biddy Martin, "Feminism, Criticism, and Foucault," *NGC*,
27 (Fall 1982), 3–30. On the relevance of Kristeva's work for the American

context see Alice Jardine, "Theories of the Feminine," *Enclitic*, 4:2 (Fall 1980), 5–15; and "Pre-Texts for the Transatlantic Feminist," *Yale French Studies*, 62 (1981), 222-236. Cf. also Teresa de Lauretis, *Alice Doesn't: Feminism, Semiotics, Cinema* (Bloomington: Indiana University Press, 1984), especially ch. 6 "Semiotics and Experience."

54. Jean-François Lyotard, *La Condition Postmoderne* (Paris: Minuit, 1979). English translation *The Postmodern Condition* (Minneapolis: University of Minnesota Press, 1984).

55. The English translation of *La Condition Postmoderne* includes the essay, important for the aesthetic debate, "Answering the Question: What is Postmodernism?" For Kristeva's statement on the postmodern see "Postmodernism?" *Bucknell Review*, 25:11 (1980), 136–141.

56. Kristeva, "Postmodernism?" 137.

57. *Ibid*, 139 f.

58. In fact, *The Postmodern Condition* is a sustained attack on the intellectual and political traditions of the Enlightenment embodied for Lyotard in the work of Jürgen Habermas.

59. Fredric Jameson, "Foreword" to Lyotard, *The Postmodern Condition*, p. XVI.

60. Michel Foucault, "Truth and Power," in *Power/Knowledge* (New York: Pantheon, 1980), p. 127.

61. The major exception is Craig Owens, "The Discourse of Others," in Hal Foster, ed., *The Anti-Aesthetic*, p. 65–98.

62. Cf. Elaine Marks and Isabelle de Courtivon, eds., *New French Feminisms* (Amherst: University of Massachusetts Press, 1980). For a critical view of French theories of the feminine cf. the work by Alice Jardine cited in Footnote 56 and her essay "Gynesis," *diacritics*, 12:2 (Summer 1982), 54–65.

Part III

Identity and Differentiation

11

A Feminist Theory of Social Differentiation

Anna Yeatman

Feminist social scientists have two identities: feminist and social scientist. Naively, I have thought these identities to be mutually required. The idea of the social is the core orienting ("ultimate") value of both feminism and social science, or so I thought. By the idea of social I mean the distinctively modern self-conception where we comprehend ourselves as a community of agents whose agency constructs the world in which we live. A society is any self-interpreting community of agents, and an agent is one who participates in the communicative structures of self-interpretation and legitimation. If a feminist could be assumed to be oriented by the purpose of transcending the inequality and patriarchy built into the modern gender division of labor, this purpose could be forwarded only by, first, revealing the conventional or agentic character of that gender division of labor and, second, by inquiring as to what equality of status as agents may mean for restructuring relations between males and females and insuring that any social division of labor is congruent with that equality of status. In short a post-patriarchal order would require the de-constitution of the mutually exclusive cultural categories "men" and "women," and the re-situation of all as social actors, units of social agency. None of this seemed to make any sense without the idea of the social.

Similarly, it seemed to me that social scientists in general, and sociologists in particular, would be excited by the challenges which the feminist project of a post-patriarchal complex society demanded of their theoretical understanding of the idea of the social. Specifically, I was struck by the promise of the feminist challenge for the idea of social differentiation which Durkheim, Parsons, Luhmann, and others have developed to connote the nature of the complexity of an industrialized, "modern" society. Both Parsons and Luhmann have developed this idea to show how the various subsystems of a modern society—for example, the polity, the occupational system, the educational system, family life, and so forth— are "differentiated" as distinct but mutually dependent functional parts of the whole. This is a structural-functionalism which has considerable merit for the self-interpretation of a modern society since it shows the necessity of the relative autonomy of each of these functional spheres, and in this way espouses a sociological pluralism which indicates the nature of the connection between the complexity of this multisphered modern society and a cultural orientation to democratic values. A democratic respect for plural viewpoints can be only underlined by an appreciation of the plurality of life spheres.

In particular, a theory of social differentiation promises a more adequate and consistent elaboration of the idea of the social as this connotes the requirements of an agentic community than is available in "older" theoretical accounts of "society." For example, the Aristotelian account of society *qua* polis is an account of the genetic progression from a procreative human couple united with their progeny and slaves (the household) to a community of households (the village) to an association of villages (the polis). The freedom of the polis depends on a hierarchical ordering of relationships where the least inclusive (the household) are the most natural, and where the freedom of the most inclusive (the polis) depends on a freedom from the natural exigencies (needs) which determine the substance of household relationships. Agency is a barely emergent value in this account, and the hierarchy differentiating different types of humans (free men, women, children, slaves) differentiates those who are more or less capable of agency. The modern theories of social differentiation, on the other hand, display a metaphor of horizontal (lateral) integration, the implication being that, since all functional spheres are equally necessary to the life of the social system, they are equally social and, thus, equally participant in an agentic order. Accordingly, when Parsons (Parsons and Bales, 1955: 16) declares that "It is because the *human* personality is not 'born' but must be 'made' through the socialization process that in the first instances families are necessary" he appears to be drawing family life into the agentic order by according it the functions of primary socialization of individual agents and of ongoing recognition of their uniqueness and integrity as individual agents. In this perspective the family is not more natural than the polity but represents a different order of requirements for a culture of agency to operate.

We might have expected this theoretical orientation to social differentiation to have welcomed contemporary feminist development of the idea of social differentiation. Feminists have argued that, if social differentiation is to operate equitably, and if all individual agents are to be equally developed in the requirements of an agentic culture, then social differentiation must be restructured so that it becomes a feature of every individual agent's life. Instead of the "primitive" version of social differentiation where social functions (parenting, for example) are delegated to particular classes of agents, all agents are to participate in the several life spheres of their society. This means that the differentiation between these spheres—between "work" and "family," for example—must be restructured so as to permit individual agents to participate in all of them and to ensure that the patterns of participation in any one sphere or across all of them do not advantage or disadvantage particular groups of agents. The corollary of this is that the identity of individual agents develops a complexity consonant with their participation in all of the life spheres of a modern society. This must mean that they all develop a more adequate understanding of the kind of policies required for the effective intercalation of the differentiated spheres and for their relatively independent operation as distinct spheres.[1] Altogether this is a more consistent and mature account of the idea of social differentiation than can be found in the prefeminist exponents of the idea.

These being the types of assumptions I made, I began to work on the project of developing a feminist or post-patriarchal theory of social differentiation. The project has foundered on several shoals. These can be reduced to three central problems. First, social science in general and sociology in particular are proving refractory to the paradigm challenge which post-patriarchal values represent. Second, contemporary feminist theory is having to come to terms with its affinity with postmodernism, and it is therefore confronted with issues of how to situate its own value commitments in relation to the relativistic implications of a postmodern pluralism. Third, it is not clear that the demands of a postmodern discursive universe permit, in the sense of giving legitimacy to, "grand theorizing" of the type that any systems theory involves. In short, there are methodological as well as substantive issues posed by the postmodern situation of feminist theorizing.

In this paper I want to examine these three hindrances to proceeding with a post-patriarchal theory of social differentiation, and see where they leave such a project. Since I sense myself cutting loose from old moorings, I assume my conclusions will have a highly provisional character. In this exercise, however, I have the comfort of knowing that other feminist (social) theorists are confronting similar issues and asking similar questions.

Is Modern Social Science Inherently Patriarchal?

As posed the question is tautological. This is because it is clear now that the social sciences, including sociology, are structured by a modernist perspective. It is precisely the postmodern features of feminist theorizing which enable its perception of a "paradigm" difference between itself and modern social science, although it must be said that feminism lies on the cusp of a paradigm revolution and the features of the alternative emergent paradigm are not yet clear.[2]

There is a note of what may be described only as bewilderment in two feminist-sociologist examinations of why sociology seems to have proved so resistant to feminist challenge (see Stacey and Thorne, 1985; Yeatman, 1986). Indeed Stacey and Thorne (1985: 302) conclude that "feminist sociologists—especially when compared with our counterparts in anthropology, history, and literature—have been less successful in moving to the next stage of reconstructing basic paradigms of the discipline." The bewilderment exists precisely because it would seem that the core premise, or presupposition, of sociology—the idea of the social—provides a ready accommodation of sociological to feminist agendas. For example, in my own discussion (1986: 162) of "Women, Domestic Life and Sociology," I carefully prepared the ground for this statement:

> In principle, then, we can say that sociology as a theoretical enterprise offers a welcome to a feminist agenda. However, the actual history of sociology indicates this theoretical friendliness is contradicted and, often overcome, by persisting masculinist bias. If the promise of sociology in respect of the feminist agenda is to be realized, it is important to track and reject this bias. At the same time, this will be to develop and strengthen the general theoretical enterprise that characterizes sociology. In the light of what I have argued above to be the current phase of the feminist agenda, I will track this masculinist bias of sociology as it is expressed in failure to incorporate domestic or personal life in how social life is conceived.

The phrase "masculinist bias" indicates that I was not willing to entertain the idea that the fundamental theoretical structures of sociology are masculinist. In retrospect it seems obvious that my own argument indicates that it is not an issue of a flaw that can be corrected but an issue of a paradigm revolution.

In relation to the other social sciences—anthropology, social psychology, political economy, social history—it is sociology which has had the distinctive mission of elaborating the core or axial value of social science: the idea of the social. Allied to this mission is the identification of sociology with the reflexive, self-interpretive conventions of a self-styled "modern" society. Accordingly if it should turn out that the idea of the social is a distinctively modernist idea then, clearly, sociology must prove more vulnerable and therefore more resistant to the paradigm challenge which postmodernist feminism represents.

Like all other "disciplines" in a highly professionalized world of expanded higher education, sociology is subject to all the features which make them disciplines in the Foucauldian sense of that word. That is, like other disciplines, sociology is a specific set of institutionalized intellectual practices which involve rigorously maintained gatekeeping procedures that police what have come to be institutionalized as the substantive and methodological canons of the discipline (see Foucault, 1984). Moreover, the high degree of professionalization and specialization of knowledge production means that, like other knowledge disciplines, sociology has become identified both with a highly technical discourse and with routinized knowledge production. Such features keep sociology segregated from widely shared issues of cultural significance. Tied to this increasingly esoteric quality of sociology is the virtual impossibility of staging generic theoretical debates found to be of relevance for most participants in the discipline. When such debates appear to occur, their segregation within what is now a sub-discipline—sociological theory—underlines their status as a doxology constructed in relation to the "founding" debates of the discipline, the ones inaugurated by those who have been appropriated within the genealogy of the discipline as its classicists: Marx, Weber, Durkheim. Inevitably the contemporary echoes of these original voices lack their vigor and vitality.

If, however, it is merely a phase of routinization which has obstructed sociology's openness to new challenges like feminism, perhaps we can take comfort from Weber's (1949: 112) proposal of some kind of cyclical progression of any rationalized knowledge through charismatic stages of renewal and openness and routinized stages of theoretical closure:

> All research in the cultural sciences in an age of specialization once it is oriented towards a given subject matter through particular settings of problems and has established its methodological principles, will consider the analysis of the data as an end in itself. It will discontinue assessing the value of the individual facts in terms of their relationship to ultimate value-ideas. Instead it will lose its awareness of its ultimate rootedness in the value-ideas in general. And it is well that should be so. But there comes a moment when the atmosphere changes. The significance of the unreflectively utilized viewpoints become uncertain and the road is lost in the twilight. The light of the great cultural problems moves on. Then science too prepares to change its standpoint and its analytical apparatus and to view the streams of events from the heights of thought.

"The light of the great cultural problems" has moved on, but it is not clear that there is any automaticity in the extent to which sociology is prepared to follow suit. Sociology is an intellectual enterprise structured by the dualisms of the modernist perspective. Its own particular versions of these dualisms—for example, structure/agency, social structure/culture, social/psychological, family/society—are logically derivative of the basic dualistic structure of the modernist consciousness: individual/society; subjective/objective; reason/emotion, and so forth. Sociology cannot change this modernist framework of reference which has governed it as a specific intellectual enterprise without abandoning its whole tradition and approach, without, that is, becoming something other than itself. Yet it is precisely the nature of the contemporary feminist challenge to require sociology, as all expressions of modern science, to move beyond this dualistic ordering of reality in the direction of integrating what have been regarded hitherto as opposing terms.

When the challenge is such as to implicate the very identity of sociology as an intellectual and professional enterprise, we would expect there to be sustained resistance from those whose identities and careers are bound up with this enterprise. Thus, even though all theoretically sophisticated sociologists acknowledge the conventional and increasingly anachronistic quality of the dualisms which structure their intellectual enterprise, there is a tacit consent to abide by the conventional structures of the discipline. In this way they are stabilized as an orthodoxy, and institutional and professional authority is used to keep the feminist challenge at bay and the increasing theoretical impoverishment of the professional enterprise hidden from view. This is the primary reason for the discipline becoming more and more like a discipline in the Foucauldian sense. Any discipline which is at a stage of defending itself against paradigm challenge perforcedly draws ranks and assumes a stance of closure, where large substantive questions are precluded as irrelevant and where canonical precision and technical perfection are rewarded.

It makes sense also that this resistance is deepest and most sustained in those disciplines which are assigned roles in the essential gatekeeping of modernist conventions. The disciplines of sociology, economics, psychology and political science have been each assigned specific roles in a division of such gatekeeping labor, where their specific version of the modernist dualisms supplies a necessary variant of this logical structure, such that taken together they constituted a universe rather than parts of one. In short it is these disciplines which supply the synchronics of the dualistic ordering of reality.[3] History, literature, and anthropology are discursively rather than strategically related to the modernist conventions, which is why they may be more susceptible to the feminist challenge, as Stacey and Thorne claim. The latter may have the discursive space to admit a plurality of conventions and perspectives that the former lack, although it should not be supposed that this means that literature, history, and anthropology can genuinely accommodate a post-dualistic perspective. Their pluralism shields a modernist structure of mind precisely because it is a boundless and fully relativized type of pluralism. I will have more to say on this issue in the next section where I discuss relativist tendencies in postmodernism.

The place of sociology in this strategic gatekeeping of modernist conventions is an interesting one. Charged with the role of elaborating the idea of the social, the central dualistic convention in sociology is that which counterposes the terms "social" and "natural." While sociologists elaborate the value of "social" to cover all aspects of human existence, and thereby to bring them within a systemic domain of agency, and interagency, they do so in such a way as to presuppose the "natural" as a logical residual and limiting term. This enables sociology to maintain the ruling modernist fiction—the contraposition of the values "individual" and "society"—by identifying the "natural" aspects of human actors with their individual aspects.[4] The consequence is that the idea of the social is identified with trans-individual, nonindividual, and, even, anti-individual values. This is why the modern idea of the social cannot assimilate the feminist challenge nor provide intellectual direction for it.

Finally, it is necessary to say something of the structure of power which is constituted by the modernist dualistic ordering of reality. This feature becomes evident when we reflect on the dualisms which are inscribed in the basic structures of modern authority relations: men and women; parents and children; management and workers. These dualisms are articulated in relation to each other within the governing model of what it means to be an individual in the modernist sense of that term. An individual is one who "heads" and "manages" a unit of household and/or productive economy, where the historical conventions of a preindustrial, patriarchal household economy are maintained and mediated under new conditions. Thus to be an individual one has to both command a unit of domestic economy (a consumption-oriented family) *and* command effective market capacity as a private proprietor, even if the property concerned in this context is one's own capacity to labor. To be sure, in the marketplace some are more effective individuals than others, that is to say, own more property or wealth, and it is this hierarchy of effective market capacity which locates these individuals in the hierarchical relationship of management and worker.

The point is that the central motif of the modernist model of individuality is private property: individuality resides in ownership of private property, in what Macpherson (1962) called "possessive individualism." Under the conditions of household economy wives, children, and household servants were located within the private property of masculine individuals (see Yeatman, 1984). This patriarchalist character of modern private property has been mediated rather than eroded by the increasing tendency since the

Married Women's Property Acts of the mid to late nineteenth century to locate wives and children in the formal status of being persons in their own right.

The dualistic ordering of reality follows from as much as it constitutes the structures of modern patriarchalist individuality. For an individuality which inheres in private property, the values of private and public, individual and social must be always dichotomously arraigned. Patriarchalist individuals establish their individuality *via* the medium of subjective mastery over (1) others and things placed within what is conceived as the domain of objects (the modern connotation of "nature") and (2) themselves (self-mastery). Perforcedly this is an individuality which limits freedom, that is to say, freedom *qua* subjective mastery, to one term of a whole series of oppositions or dichotomies: subject/object; reason/nature; mind/body; science/intuition; impersonal/personal; masculine/feminine; adult/child; independence/dependence; public/private; individual/society; market/state. The dichotomous operation of terms means that individual freedom can slip from one term to its opposite, and back again: thus, there is a sense in which this dichotomous ordering of reality is set up as a series of alibis, all designed to secure the mastery of his world by a possessive individual. It becomes clear that this individual's freedom *qua* mastery is predicated on the existence of a whole host of quasi-individual actors to whom the task of representing the "other" term of the dichotomies may be delegated. Thus, if the patriarchal individual is to appear reasonable and impartial, there must be an other so placed as to represent nonreasonable and partial viewpoints or values; or, indeed, the other represents the restrictive and routinized character of a domesticated rationality, and the nonreasonable and partial stance is re-framed so as to seem the epitome of an untamed (undomesticated) and rugged individualism.

For another to be so placed they must fall within the possessive individual's jurisdiction; and, for there to be a normative order which both restrains, and secures, possessive individualism, a culture of possessive individualism is required which articulates the private jurisdictions of possessive individuals within a general structure of modern patriarchalist domination. This mode of domination asserts itself as a monovocal and monological legal-rational order, one which appears as an impersonal, objective, and impartial authority. This appearance is necessary because (1) possessive individuals relinquish their private mastery only on condition that the authority by which they agree to be bound is not that of any individual;[5] (2) one term in the dichotomous series of terms must subordinate the other term, hence authority is asserted as the reduction of opposition and the triumph of one, superordinate value.

Feminism and Postmodernism

The modernist perspective contains a fundamental contradiction: the individualization of social life, which is developed by the culture of possessive individualism, dissolves and deconstructs the monological, monovocal structures of divine authority and that authority's expression in kinship and kingship institutions. Instead of a divinely sanctioned, consensual moral order, there emerges the decentred world of a plurality of individual agents responsible for their own destinies. At the same time that this order of individualized agency undermines all religious presuppositions and secularizes our reality, the primitive type of individuality involved necessitates that there be a single standard or norm of authority which subordinates the plurality of individualized agency, and renders it so many distinct versions of this sole authoritative voice. Accordingly, the implications of the modernist discovery of the existence of individualized and therefore plural values are contained in the face of the necessity to reduce this plurality to a single standard. Even while the idea is established by such as Locke, Hume, Herder, Vico, and Weber that it is the pragmatics of an individualized agency which lead and orient what actors know and value, the necessity for a monovocal and monological authority sustains, albeit in secular form, the religious idea of a single source, truth, or value. Hence the plurality of individualized agency is reduced to, or contained within, the monovocal structures of *Geist* (Hegel), labor (Marx), and utility (Bentham) or, more vulgarly, within the everyday constructions of "what every reasonable man knows," "what all civilized men regard as," and so forth.

It is postmodernism which has exploded (imploded?) this contradiction of modernism by insisting the plurality is not containable or reducible in these ways, and by showing how the monovocal, monological structures of modern authority have authorized the totalizing tendencies of oppositional forms of modernist discourse (scientific socialism, for example). The postmodern exploration of the pluralistic implications of a universal culture of individualized agency has been forced by the mid- and late-twentieth-century revolts against the monovocal structures of modern patriarchal possessive individualism: the postcolonial movements of self-determination; the various expressions of antiracist and multiculturalist movements within the metropolitan or, more broadly, "developed" societies; and, contemporary feminism. All these movements have disrupted the dichotomous structure of subject and other which underpinned the private property relations of modern patriarchal individualism by disestablishing the "other" as a permissible term. Where status as "other" allowed there to be a metonymic relation between the categories of women, children, savages, natives, and orientals, disestablishment of this status brings all the complexity of admitting the extraordinary wealth of diversity which all these formerly subsumed as other represent. Moreover it requires their participation in constituting their identity (their sense of self, needs, and so on) within a universal culture of individualized agency.

All of this is to make the obvious point, that when the historical task is enjoined as one of integrating all those once consigned to the sphere of private property into what becomes a universal culture of individualized agency, then patriarchalist possessive individualism and its dualistic mode of ordering/mastering reality must go. Instead of an individuality *qua* mastery, we have to conceive an individuality which locates its freedom in processes and relations which integrate all these dichotomous terms. Needless to say, this is an individuality which understands itself in a relational way, that is to say, understands the interactional bases of a self-concept and the kind of interactional culture necessary to foster and support the self-expression and participation of all.

The project of developing the norms and institutions of a universal culture of individualized agency is a coherent project. It is one which situates the plurality of individualized agency within a democratic ethic. In so doing this project will have to explore dialogical and pluri-vocal structures of authority,[6] as it will have to explore participative structures and ways of doing things that are much more attentive to what we currently call "process."

In this respect postmodernism enjoins a new and qualitatively distinct stage of democratization. It is this implication of postmodernism which feminist theories in the 1980s begin to discover and to celebrate. Strathern (1986: 8) argues indeed that "academic feminist scholarship—the way in which its many voices are positioned as speaking to one another—has a postmodern structure."

If postmodernism empowers, as in a sense it is empowered by, feminism and feminist-inspired democratic visions, feminist theorists will have to give up their own "trained" subscription to modernist perspectives which sustain monovocal, monological constructions of authority. As Fraser and Nicholson (1989) have argued this means that feminist theorists must abandon their own versions of the modernist meta-narratives which have inspired the great general theories of modernity.[7] They point out that all the general theories of "the" sexual division of labor are modernist, and that, as grand narratives, they represent the "blow-ups" of historically specific cultural constructions of our own. Thus, Rosaldo's (1974) justly celebrated model (see Yeatman, 1984b) for explaining patriarchal authority as a universal institution generalizes the twentieth-century version of the "cult of domesticity" in falsely imputing to all societies a cultural binary classification of public (the world of men) and domestic (the world of women). Similarly Chodorow (1979), who built on Rosaldo's framework and defined women's universal gender role in terms of "mothering," can be viewed as offering a brilliant theory of how mid-twentieth-century reproduction of gendered personalities (as either masculine or feminine) works in a self-styled modern society, but this is what it is: a reflection on the cultural categories structuring gender in her own society. "Mothering" and "primary parenting" are distinctively late modern ideas and values. They presuppose the development of the idea of childhood, and of the construction of "home" as an affectively oriented relational setting differentiated from the extra-domestic, and thus public, settings of an impersonal market and bureaucratized state. As Fraser and Nicholson (1989: 31) remark, Chodorow "is not the only recent feminist social theorist who has constructed a quasi-metanarrative around a putatively cross-cultural, female-associated activity." They (1989: 31) continue:

> On the contrary, theorists like Ann Ferguson and Nancy Folbre, Nancy Hartsock, and Catherine MacKinnon have built similar theories around notions of sex-affective production, reproduction, and sexuality respectively. Each claims to have identified a basic kind of human practice found in all societies which has cross-cultural explanatory power. In each case, the practice in question is associated with a biological or quasi-biological need and is construed as functionally necessary to the reproduction of society. . . .
>   The difficulty here is that categories like sexuality, mothering, reproduction, and sex-affective production group together phenomena which are not necessarily conjoined in all societies while separating off from one another phenomena which are not necessarily separated. As a matter of fact, it is doubtful whether these categories have any determinate cross-cultural content. Thus for a theorist to use such categories to construct a universalistic social theory is to risk projecting the socially dominant conjunctions and dispersions of her own society onto others, thereby distorting important features of both. Social theorists would do better first to construct genealogies of the *categories* of sexuality, reproduction, and mothering before assuming their universal significance.

It is important to emphasize that if postmodernism means we have to abandon universalistic, general theories and, instead, to explore the multivocal worlds of different societies and cultures, this is *not* the same thing as abandoning the political-ethical project of working out the conditions for a universal pragmatics of individualized agency. The very orientation of postmodernism to the agentic quality and features of our sociocultural worlds underlines the significance of this political-ethical project.

It is at this point that feminists, as others who are committed to developing the democratic implications of postmodernism, need to firmly distinguish their position from those who take postmodernism to imply an anomic relativism. When we examine how relativism is seen to be an implication of postmodernism we discover an entirely different agenda, which is antifeminist in consequence if not by design.

It is precisely in the postmodernist spirit that we come to grasp the metaphoricality of our world, that is to say, it comes to be revealed as constituted by and through specific structures of meaning for which our agency is responsible. It is against this backdrop that we come to appreciate the metaphoricality of the modernist dichotomies. They lose their erstwhile natural appearance and are revealed as factitious, contingent orderings of reality. Many have taken the postmodern emphases on agency and the plurality of its expressions as underlining the factitious and, in their view, arbitrary character of the systems of meaning through which we constitute the realities which exist for us. When the quality of factitiousness assumes the appearance of arbitrariness it is not because this is a logical consequence of our appreciation that it is by the structures of our agency (meaningfully oriented behavior) that we live. There is nothing arbitrary about these in the least, as the hermeneutic recovery of them in their coherence as a *structure* of meaning, gestalt, or "discourse" indicates. They are arbitrary only as they are evaluated in relation to a nostalgic elegy for the erstwhile "essentialist" and "foundationalist" loadstones of modernism: reason, progress, science, objectivity, (Western) civilization, and so on.

Here reference to the work of Foucault is instructive. Foucault appears the prototypical postmodernist in his construction and deconstruction of the modern cultural heritage as a series of discontinuous discursive and disciplinary practices. Yet, counterposed to these "discontinuous practices" of expressed reality (speech, knowledges, and the institutional disciplines they constitute) is the nonexpressible (*désir*). This, lying as it does outside the historicity of discourses, assumes the status of a natural, universal, noumenal order of being. Thus, if Foucault (1987: 127) says "there is no prediscursive providence which disposes the world in our favor," he does not move beyond fixation on the loss of this illusion and he (1984: 127) is necessarily constrained to see "discourse as a violence which we do to things, or in any case as a practice which we impose on them." Shades here of Durkheim's (1964: 13) formulation of "social facts" as "things" which exercise "an external constraint" on "the individual." This position requires Foucault to reduce all claims to legitimation to expressions of power and to assume that it is might which constitutes right. Democracy, freedom, equality, justice become arraigned as so many structures of symbolic expediency which do violence to things (see Wolin, 1986; and Daraki, 1986).

Let us be quite clear as to what is going on here. Foucault turns out to be thoroughly modernist in his dualistic contra-positioning of "discourses" (artifice) and *désir* (nature). It is his postmodernism which leads him to invert the value of the dichotomous terms so that rationalized agency comes to assume a discontinuous and contingent status when set against both the extra-discursive terrain of desire, and all that is cast in the mold of the other by the rationalized discourses of modern society. If his postmodernism appears to remove legitimacy from the rationalized discourses of modernity, Foucault rescues the idea of a monovocal and monological authority by shielding it within the extra-discursive, noumenal world. Like Durkheim, Foucault is entirely unprepared to surrender the monotypical and monovocal qualities of individualized patriarchal authority which is located in this terrain that lies beyond the worlds of discursive agency (see also Chodorow's, 1985, critique of left Freudian "drive theory"). Put differently, by viewing the sociocultural orders of reality as contingent and arbitrary—as "a violence done to things"— Foucault achieves an intellectual "deregulation" of the democratically oriented culture of individualized agency. When the culture of a self-reflexive agency, and all its ethical achievements and demands, is relativized, postmodernist relativism reveals itself as the last-ditch stand of modern patriarchy.

Since it cannot shield itself from the democratic challenges to monotypical, monological, and monovocal structures of authority, it evacuates the ground of issues of legitimation and converts right into might. This is indeed an intellectual deregulation which permits dominant groups to maintain their privileges while evading normative debate over them in relation to principles of equity, justice, and democracy. Sandra Harding (1986: 657), whose article helped me to see this, puts it well:

> It is worth keeping in mind that the articulation of relativism as an intellectual position emerges historically only as an attempt to dissolve challenges to the legitimacy of purportedly universal beliefs and ways of life. It is an objective problem or a solution to a problem, only *from the perspective of the dominating groups*. Reality may indeed appear to have many different structures from the perspective of our different locations in social relations, but some of those appearances are ideologies in the strong sense of the term: they are not only false and "interested" beliefs but also ones that are used to structure social relations for the rest of us. For subjugated groups, a relativist stance expresses a false consciousness. It accepts the dominant group's insistence that their right to hold distorted views (and, of course, to make policy for all of us on the basis of those views) is intellectually legitimate.

It is inevitable that those whose interests underline the cultural loss which postmodernism represents will stress its negative possibilities while those whose interests align them with the democratic promise of postmodernism will emphasize its positive possibilities. Since it is an issue precisely of interpretation this is a political contest. It is critical that feminists join this contest and develop the democratic potential of postmodernism while exposing the patriarchalism of relativist de-regulation. If they are to do this they will have to forswear their own version of patriarchalist nostalgia, namely all feminist essentialist tendencies which function to privilege women (taken as an extra-discursive, or given, category) and the moral authority (also a monovocal one) which these tendencies accord femaleness. There is much less in the maintenance of some form of essentialism going for feminism than for patriarchalist reaction: the former's interest lies clearly with the maintenance and development of democratic discourse. It lies also with the coming to light of precisely how factitious and historical the whole dualistic modern discourse is.

Concluding Remarks

It will be clear that here I have made a decision to opt for the challenges of a postmodern feminist theorizing, where the value commitment is to developing a post-patriarchal, democratic culture of individualized agency or, put differently, to developing universalistic standards of a discursively oriented sociality. I have not abandoned sociology: sociology has abandoned feminism. However, insofar as postmodern perspectives develop out of the contradictions of modernism, I remain thoroughly in debt to the inheritance of modern social science.

But: a feminist theory of social differentiation? I do not think so. A systems approach will not work, not at least in harness to feminist values and standards of cultural significance. Perforcedly a systems approach maintains a monovocal, monotypical, monological orientation to authority.

The task as I see it is to begin discursive and dialogically oriented modes of theorizing. I suspect these have to be tied to modes of intellectual or reflective activity which bridge intellectualistic (theoretical) and practical modes of working to build a post-patriarchal democratic world. This is true of perhaps most feminist theorists, in that they link their intellectualized identities to a practical feminist politics, but I mean more than the standard homily in favor of the unity of theory and practice. There is something peculiar to the conditions of feminist theorizing which MacKinnon (1982: 543) attempts to grasp by claiming, "Feminism is the first [radical] theory to emerge from those whose interest it affirms."[9] What this suggests, I think, is that the normative commitments and theoretical work of feminists are tied to something large, something small, quotidian practices on behalf of the same values, whether these concern refusing to allow a feminist politics to be ghettoized within an academic institution, raising one's children in a dialogical, discursive orientation to authority, or thinking carefully about one's role as a manager with regard to equal opportunity and process issues. My point is that we will understand what it means to develop discursive and dialogically oriented modes of theorizing only as we admit all the people with whom we are connected into trying out and evaluating these ideas in relation to current value questions and practical issues.

In this we need to recognize the political contests of postmodernism and appreciate that patriarchalist reaction has successfully developed de-regulation in a number of contexts. De-regulation permits a narcissistic, socially unaccountable expression of possessive individualism (see Chodorow, 1985). It is this which is defining the central and mainstream political agendas in Australia, New Zealand, Britain, and the United States at the present time. Within these agendas the pluralism of a postmodern democratic politics becomes defined as the crisis of "ungovernability" or—another favored term—as "pluralistic stagnation" (see Marsh, 1983). Those of us who are committed to developing a democratically oriented, postmodern, and post-patriarchal "social science" need to appreciate this as a cultural guerrilla undertaking, where the abandonment of democratic discourse by mainstream "disciplines" and political parties means that it can be revitalized by those in whose interests it is to develop a genuinely democratized sociality. To do this and to develop our theorizing, it is necessary to find ways of effective engagement with a wide variety of audiences and networks which, over time, can build sets of discursive practices which foster a post-patriarchal, democratic world.

Notes

1. I have attempted to specify this post-patriarchal framework of social differentiation more fully in "The Social Differentiation of State, Civil Society and Family Life" (see Yeatman, 1986b).

2. Marilyn Strathern, a feminist social anthropologist with whom I have dialogued, has reached similar conclusions to these: see her (1986b) "The Study of Gender Relations: A Personal Context."

3. As far as I am aware we do not have yet a full account of the respective places of strategic modern discourses in this synchronic structure. There is, however, a literature developing which provides the groundwork for such an account. For example, there is the "school" of social-legal analysts who are showing the dualistic structures of modern legal thought: see Olsen (1983), Kennedy (1982), Horowitz (1982), Klare (1982). There are the beginnings of a similar type of exercise with regard to political theory: see Pateman (1983), Yeatman (1984a). There are several articles of Strathern (1985,

1986a) which indicate her use of both feminism and Melanesian ethnography to surface the deep structures of the modernist perspective. Finally, in the policy studies areas there are some interesting feminist-influenced challenges to the dualism of "social" and "economic" policy (see Dowse, 1983) and the dualism of the "realm of the natural" and the "realm of the artificial" (see Peattie & Rein, 1983).

4. This leads, of course, to an "over-socialized" conception of individual agents. For some elaboration of this argument, see Yeatman (1986b); and for an excellent analysis of how left versions of Freudian social theory have maintained an individual-social dichotomy in such a way as to permit the individual "freedom-from" responsibility for their social connectedness, see Chodorow (1985).

5. Once we understand the political culture of possessive individualism, it becomes clear that Locke and Rousseau cannot be bettered in their understanding of its requirements. Compare Locke's (1690/1963), *The Second Treatise*, par. 87: 367): "And thus all private judgment of every particular Member being excluded, the ["the," monovocal] Community comes to be Umpire, by settled standing Rules, indifferent, and the same to all Parties. . . ." with Rousseau's (1973: 174) conception of the social Contract: "Each man, in giving himself to all, gives himself to nobody; and as there is no associate over which he does not acquire the same right as he yields others over himself, he gains an equivalent for everything he loses, and an increase of force for the preservation of what he has."

6. This is beginning to happen in the work of democratic theorists like William Connolly (see, e.g., Connolly, 1984).

7. Fraser and Nicholson draw on Lyotard's identification of modernism with "grand narratives" and they (1989: 22) comment: "The postmodern condition is one in which 'grand narratives' of legitimation are no longer credible. By 'grand narratives' he [Lyotard] means, in the first instance, overarching philosophies of history like the Enlightenment story of the gradual but steady progress of reason and freedom, Hegel's dialectic of the spirit coming to know itself, and, most importantly, Marx's drama of the forward march of human productive capacities via class conflict culminating in proletarian revolution. . . . The story guarantees that some sciences and some politics have the *right* pragmatics and, so, are the *right* practices."

8. The ambivalence of this (Owens, 1983: 58) masculine evaluation of postmodernism is clear: "Pluralism, however, reduces us [whom does he mean?] to being an other among others [!]; it is not a recognition, but a reduction to difference to absolute indifference, equivalence, interchangeability (what Jean Baudrillard calls 'implosion'). What is at stake, then, is not only the hegemony of Western culture, but also (our sense of) our identity as a culture."

9. MacKinnon's (1982: 543) passage is both suggestive and elusive: "Feminist method is consciousness-raising: the collective critical reconstruction of the meaning of women's social experience, as women live through it. Marxism

and feminism . . . posit a different relation between thought and thing, both in terms of the relationship of the analysis itself to the social life it captures and in terms of the participation of the thought in the social life it analyzes. To the extent that materialism is scientific it posits and refers to a reality outside thought which it considers to have an objective—that is, truly nonsocially perspectival—context. Consciousness-raising, by contrast, inquires into an intrinsically social situation, into that mixture of thought and materiality which is women's sexuality in the most generic sense. It approaches its world through a process that shares its determination: women's consciousness, not as individual or subjective ideas, but as collective social being. . . . Feminism turns theory itself—the pursuit of a true analysis of social life— into the pursuit of consciousness and turns an analysis of inequality into a critical embrace of its own determinants. The process is transformative as well as perceptive, since thought and thing are inextricable and reciprocally constituting of women's oppression. . . . The pursuit of consciousness becomes a form of political practice."

References

Chodorow, N. (1979), *The Reproduction of Mothering: Psychoanalysis and the Sociology of Gender*, Berkeley and Los Angeles: University of California Press.

Chodorow, N. (1985), "Beyond Drive Theory," *Theory and Society*, 14:3: 271– 321.

Connolly, W. E. (1984), "The Politics of Discourse," in M. Shapiro (ed.), *Language and Politics*, New York: New York University Press.

Daraki, M. (1986), "Michael Foucault's Journey to Greece," *Telos*, 67: 87–111.

Dowse, S. (1983), "The Women's Movement Fandango with the State: The Movement's Role in Public Policy Since 1972," in C. Baldock and B. Cass (eds.), *Women, Social Welfare and the State*, Australia, Allen & Unwin.

Durkheim, E. (1964), *The Rules of Sociological Method*, New York: The Free Press.

Foster, H. (1983), "The Discourse of Others: Feminists and Postmodernism," in H. Foster (ed.), *The Anti-Aesthetic: Essays on Postmodern Culture*, Washington, Bay Press.

Foucault, M. (1984), "The Order of Discourse," in M. Shapiro (ed.), *Language and Politics*, New York: New York University Press.

Fraser, N., and Nicholson, L. (1989), "Social Criticism without Philosophy: An Encounter between Feminism and Postmodernism," in this book.

Harding, S. (1986), "The Instability of the Analytical Categories of Feminist Theory," *Signs*, 11:4, 645–65.

Horowitz, M. H. (1982), "The History of the Public/Private Distinction," *University of Pennsylvania Law Review*, vol. 130, 1423–29.

Kennedy, D. (1982), "The Stages of the Decline of the Public/Private Distinction," *University of Pennsylvania Law Review*, vol. 130, 1349–58.

Klare, K. E. (1982), "The Public/Private Distinction in Labor Law," *University of Pennsylvania Law Review*, vol. 130, 1358–1423.

Locke, J. (1965), *Two Treatises of Government* (Laslett edition), New York: Mentor.

MacKinnon, C. A. (1982), "Feminism, Marxism, Method, and the State: An Agenda for Theory," *Signs*, 7:3, 515–45.

Macpherson, C. B. (1962), *The Political Theory of Possessive Individualism*, Oxford: Oxford University Press.

Olsen, F. G. (1983), "The Family and the Market: A Study of Ideology and Legal Reform," *Harvard Law Review*, 96:7, 1497–1579.

Owens, Craig (1983), "The Discourse of Others: Feminists and Postmodernism," in H. Foster (ed.), *The Anti-Aesthetic: Essays on Postmodern Culture*, Washington: Bay Press.

Parson, T., and Bales, R. F. (1955), *Family, Socialization and Interaction Process*, New York: Free Press.

Peattie, L., and Rein, M. (1983), *Women's Claims: A Study in Political Economy*, Oxford: Oxford University Press.

Rosaldo, M. (1974), "Women, Culture, and Society: A Theoretical Overview," in M. Rosaldo & L. Lamphere (eds.), *Women, Culture, and Society*, Stanford: Stanford University Press.

Rousseau, J.-J. (1975), *The Social Contract and Discourses*, London: Dent.

Stacey, J., and Thorne, B. (1985), "The Missing Feminist Revolution in Sociology," *Social Problems*, 32: 4, 301–17.

Strathern, M. (1985), "Dislodging a World View: Challenge and Counter-Challenge in the Relationship between Feminism and Anthropology," *Australian Feminist Studies*, 1: 1–15.

Strathern, M. (1986a), "Out of Context: The Persuasive Fictions of Anthropology," Frazer Lecture, University of Liverpool.

Strathern, M. (1986b), "The Study of Gender Relations: A Personal Context," prepared for *Anthropologie et Sociétés*, issue on "Les rapports hommes-femmes," edited by Deirdre Meintel.

Weber, M. (1949), *The Methodology of the Social Sciences*, New York: The Free Press.

Wolin, R. (1986), "Foucault's Aesthetic Decisionism," *Telos*, No. 67, 71–87.

Yeatman, A. (1984a), "Despotism and Civil Society: The Limits of Patriarchal Citizenship," in J. H. Stiehm (ed.), *Women's Views of the Political World of Men*, New York: Transnational.

Yeatman, A. (1984b), "Gender and the Differentiation of Social Life into Public and Domestic Domains," Special Issue Series, *Social Analysis* ("Gender and Social Life," ed. A. Yeatman) 15: 32–50.

Yeatman, A. (1986a), "Women, Domestic Life and Sociology," in C. Pateman and E. Gross (eds.), *Feminist Challenges: Social and Political Theory*, Sydney, Allen & Unwin.

Yeatman, A. (1986b), "The Social Differentiation of State, Civil Society and Family Life: A Working Model of Post-Patriarchal Structures of Citizenship," Paper presented to 1986 Sociological Association of Australian and New Zealand Conference, Armidale, New England.

12

The Ideal of Community and the Politics of Difference

Iris Marion Young

Prologue

The ideal of community, I suggest in this chapter, privileges unity over difference, immediacy over mediation, sympathy over recognition of the limits of one's understanding of others from their point of view. Community is an understandable dream, expressing a desire for selves that are transparent to one another, relationships of mutual identification, social closeness and comfort. The dream is understandable, but politically problematic, I argue, because those motivated by it will tend to suppress differences among themselves or implicitly to exclude from their political groups persons with whom they do not identify. The vision of small, face-to-face, decentralized units that this ideal promotes, moreover, is an unrealistic vision for transformative politics in mass urban society.

I did not write this essay only with feminists in mind. The commitments and concerns that motivate it, however, derive in large measure from my experience with feminist groups and discussions. On the one hand, feminists have been paradigm exponents of the ideal of community I criticize. On the other hand, feminist discussions of the importance of attending to differences among women are a primary political impetus for my seeking to criticize that ideal.

Dominant strains of feminism have expressed the ideal of community I criticize on two levels. First, we have often expected our political groups to fulfill our desire for community as against the alienation and individualism we find hegemonic in capitalist patriarchal society. Thus, we have looked for mutual identification and mutual affirmation in our feminist groups, finding conflict or respectful distance suspect. We have had understandable reasons for seeking unity and mutual identification in

I am grateful to David Alexander, Ann Ferguson, Roger Gottlieb, Peter Manicas, Peter Onuf, Lucius Outlaw, Michael Ryan, Richard Schmitt, Ruth Smith, Tom Wartenburg, and Hugh Wilder for helpful comments on earlier versions of this chapter.

our groups. For most of us, feminism has been more than just a politics, it has also been a personal and spiritual quest for self-knowledge and cultural affirmation. Insofar as feminist groups have been impelled by a desire for closeness and mutual identification, however, our political effectiveness may have been limited. Deconstruction, which I rely on in this chapter for my critique of community, shows that a desire for unity or wholeness in discourse generates borders, dichotomies, and exclusions. I suggest that the desire for mutual identification in social relations generates exclusions in a similar way. A woman in a feminist group that seeks to affirm mutual identification will feel and be doubly excluded if by virtue of her being different in race, class, culture, or sexuality she does not identify with the others nor they with her. A desire for community in feminist groups, that is, helps reproduce their homogeneity.

Second, on a more general level of political vision, feminists have developed little in the way of models of political organizing that can serve as alternatives to interest group bureaucracy, on the one hand, or the small personalized task group, on the other. Despite our critical attention to much of the male tradition of political theory, many of us have retained uncritically an anarchist, participatory democratic communitarianism to express our vision of the ideal society. Indeed, many of us have assumed that women and feminists can best realize this ideal, because women's culture is less individualistic and less based in competition than men's culture, and because, we claim, women are psychologically and politically more oriented toward care and mutuality. I argue in this chapter that conditions of modern urban mass society require conceiving an alternative vision of the unoppressive society.

This alternative must be a politics of difference. Although I derive the logical and metaphysical critique of the unity of community from postmodernist philosophy, I take the concrete political vision of inexhaustible heterogeneity in large part from feminism. Discussions among us of the oppressive implications of assumptions of the unity of women, and the importance of attending to the specific differences among women, portend the beginnings of a politics beyond community. I imagine the political structure and social relations that have evolved in the National Women's Studies Association to offer glimmers of the openness to unassimilated otherness that in the last section of this chapter I define as a norm for the unoppressive city.

Introduction

Radical theorists and activists often appeal to an ideal of community as an alternative to the oppression and exploitation that they argue, characterizes capitalist patriarchal society. Such appeals often do not explicitly articulate the meaning of the concept of community but rather tend to evoke an affective value. Even more rarely do those who invoke an ideal of community as an alternative to capitalist patriarchal society ask what it presupposes or implies, or what it means concretely to institute a society that embodies community. I raise a number of critical questions about the meaning, presuppositions, implications, and practical import of the ideal of community.

As in all conceptual reflections, in this case there is no universally shared concept of community, only particular articulations that overlap, complement, or sit at acute angles to one another.[1] I will rely on the definitions and expositions of a number of writers for examples of conceptualizations about community as a political ideal. All these writers share a critique of liberal individualist social ontology, and most think democratic socialism is the best principle of social organization. I claim acceptance for my analysis only within this general field of political discourse, although I suspect that much of the conceptual structure I identify applies to an ideal of community that might be appealed to by more conservative or liberal writers.

I criticize the notion of community on both philosophical and practical grounds. I argue that the ideal of community participates in what Derrida calls the metaphysics of presence and Adorno calls the logic of identity, a metaphysics that denies difference. The ideal of community presumes subjects can understand one another as they understand themselves. It thus denies the difference between subjects. The desire for community relies on the same desire for social wholeness and identification that underlies racism and ethnic chauvinism on the one hand and political sectarianism on the other.

Insofar as the ideal of community entails promoting a model of face-to-face relations as best, it devalues and denies difference in the form of temporal and spatial distancing. The ideal of a society consisting of decentralized face-to-face communities is undesirably utopian in several ways. It fails to see that alienation and violence are not only a function of mediation of social relations but also can and do exist in face-to-face relations. It implausibly proposes a society without the city. It fails to address the political question of the relations among face-to-face communities.

The ideal of community, finally, totalizes and detemporalizes its conception of social life by setting up an opposition between authentic and inauthentic social relations. It also detemporalizes its understanding of social change by positing the desired society as the complete negation of existing society. It thus provides no understanding of the move from here to there that would be rooted in an understanding of the contradictions and possibilities of existing society.

I propose that instead of community as the normative ideal of political emancipation, that radicals should develop a politics of difference. A model of the unoppressive city offers an understanding of social relations without domination in which persons live together in relations of mediation among strangers with whom they are not in community.

The Metaphysics of Presence

Western conceptualization, as expressed both in philosophical writing, other theoretical writing, and quite often everyday speech as well, exhibits what Derrida calls a logic of identity.[2] This metaphysics consists in a desire to think things together in a unity, to formulate a representation of a whole, a totality. It seeks the unity of the thinking subject with the object thought, that the object would be a grasping of the real. The urge to unity seeks to think everything that is a whole or to describe some ontological region, such as social life, as a whole, a system. Such totalization need not be restricted to synchronic conceptualization, moreover. The conceptualization of a process teleologically also exhibits the logic of identity, inasmuch as the end conceptually organizes the process into a unity.

The desire to bring things into unity generates a logic of hierarchical opposition. Any move to define an identity, a closed totality, always depends on excluding some elements, separating the pure from the impure. Bringing particular things under a universal essence, for example, depends on determining some attribute of particulars as accidental, lying outside the essence. Any definition or category creates an inside/outside distinction, and the logic of identity seeks to keep those borders firmly drawn. In the history of Western thought the metaphysics of presence has created a vast number of such mutually exclusive oppositions that structure whole philosophies: subject/object; mind/body, culture/nature, male/female. In the metaphysical tradition the first of these is elevated over the second because it designates the unified, the chaotic, unformed, transforming. Metaphysical thinking makes distinctions and formulates accounts by relying on such oppositions, where one side designates the pure, authentic, good, and the other the impure, inauthentic, bad.

The logic of identity also seeks to understand the subject, the person, as a self-identical unity. Beginning with Descartes, modern philosophy is particularly preoccupied with the unity of consciousness and its immediate presence to itself. The tradition of transcendental philosophy from Descartes through Kant to Husserl conceives the subject as a unity and an origin, the self-same starting point of thought and meaning, whose signification is never out of its grasp.

There are two sorts of criticisms Derrida, Adorno, Kristeva, and others make of the metaphysics of presence. First, its effort to bring things into unity is doomed to failure. The claim to totality asserted by this metaphysics is incoherent, because, as I have already discussed, the process of totalizing itself expels some aspects of the entities. Some of the experienced particulars are expelled to an unaccounted-for, "accidental" realm, what Derrida calls the supplement and Adorno calls the addendum. The move to create totality, as the logic of hierarchical opposition shows, creates not one, but two: inside and outside. The identity or essence sought receives its meaning and purity only by its relation to its outside. What Derrida calls the method of deconstruction consists in showing how with a concept or category what it claims to exclude is implicated in it. Dialectical logic, of course, makes a similar claim. The method of deconstruction, or what Adorno calls negative dialectic, however, rejects the Hegelian method of dialectic. For Hegelian dialectic is the ultimate totalizer, bringing the oppositions generated by metaphysical logic into ultimate unity within a totality.

Second, the metaphysics of presence represses or denies difference. This term has come to carry a great deal of meaning in these philosophical accounts. As I understand it, difference means the irreducible particularity of entities, which makes it impossible to reduce them to commonness or bring them into unity without remainder. Such particularity derives from the contextuality of existence, the being of a thing and what is said about it is a function of its contextual relation to other things. Adorno in particular contrasts the logic of identity with entities in their particularity, which for him also means their materiality. Idealism, which Adorno thinks exhibits the logic of identity, withdraws from such particularity and constructs unreal essences.[3]

Derrida defines difference primarily in terms of the functioning of language, expressing the irreducible spatiotemporality of language. The sign signifies, has meaning, by its place in the chain of signs, by differing from other signs. Any moment of signification also defers, holds in abeyance, any completion of its meaning. Any utterance has a multiplicity of meanings and directions of interpretation and development in which it can be taken. For Derrida, the metaphysics of presence seeks to detemporalize and despatialize this signifying process, inventing the illusion of pure present meaning which eliminates the referential relation. This is idealism: conceiving the being and truth of things as lying outside time and change.[4]

Kristeva more often uses the term *heterogeneity* than difference, but like Derrida and Adorno she suggests that a logic of identity represses heterogeneity, which she associates with the body as well as language. She too focuses on language and the process of signification, especially the speaking subject. The subject is never a unity, but always in process, for Kristeva, producing meaning through the play between the literal and figurative, representational and musical aspects that any speech simultaneously carries.[5]

Along with such writers as Anthony Giddens and Fred Dallmayr, I think the critique of the metaphysics of presence and the claim that we need to attend to the irreducibility of difference have important implications for social philosophy and social theory.[6] I will argue that the ideal of community exhibits the desire for unity these writers find in the metaphysics of presence. Community usually appears as one side of a dichotomy in which individualism is the opposite pole, but as with any such opposition, each side is determined by its relation to the other. I argue that the ideal of community exhibits a totalizing impulse and denies difference in two primary ways. First, it denies the difference within and between subjects. Second, in privileging face-to-face relations it seeks a model of social relations that are not mediated by space and time distancing. In radically opposing the inauthentic social relations of alienated society with the authentic social relations of community, moreover, it detemporalizes the process of social change into a static before and after structure.

The Opposition between Individualism and Community

Critics of liberalism frequently invoke a conception of community to project an alternative to the individualism and abstract formalism they attribute to liberalism.[7] This alternative social ontology rejects the image of persons as separate and self-contained atoms, each with the same formal rights, the rights to keep others out, separate. In the idea of community, critics of liberalism find a social ontology which sees the attributes of a person as coeval with the society in which he or she lives.

For such writers, the ideal of community evokes the absence of the self-interested competitiveness of modern society. In this ideal of community, critics of liberalism find an alternative to the abstract, formal methodology of liberalism. Existing in community with others entails more than merely respecting their rights, but rather attending to and sharing in the particularity of their needs and interests.

For example, in his critique of Rawls, Michael Sandel argues that liberalism's emphasis on the primacy of justice presupposes a self as an antecedent unity existing prior to its desires and goals, whole unto itself, separated and bounded. This is an unreal and incoherent conception of the self, he argues, better replaced by a constitutive conception of self as the product of an identity it shares with others, all of whom mutually understand and affirm one another. This constitutive conception of self is expressed by the concept of community.

> And insofar as our constitutive self-understandings comprehend a wider subject than the individual alone, whether a family or a tribe or a city or class or nation or people, to this extent they define a community in the constitutive sense. And what marks such a community is not merely

a spirit of benevolence, or the prevalence of communitarian values, or even certain 'shared final ends' alone, but a common vocabulary of discourse and a background of implicit practices and understandings within which the opacity of persons is reduced if never finally dissolved. Insofar as justice depends for its pre-eminence on the separatedness and boundedness of persons in the cognitive sense, its priority would diminish as that opacity faded and those community values deepened.[8]

In contemporary political discussion, for the most part, the ideal of community arises in this way as a response to the individualism perceived as the prevailing theoretical position, and the alienation and fragmentation perceived as the prevailing condition of society. Community appears, that is, as part of an opposition, individualism/community, separated self/ shared self. In this opposition each term comes to be defined by its negative relation to the other, thus existing in a logical dependency. I suggest that this opposition, however, is integral to modern political theory and is not an alternative to it.

The opposition individualism/community receives one of its expressions in bourgeois culture in the opposition between masculinity and femininity. The culture identifies masculinity with the values associated with individualism—self-sufficiency, competition, separation, the formal equality of rights. The culture identifies femininity, on the other hand, with the values associated with community-affective relations of care, mutual aid, and cooperation.

Carol Gilligan has recently posed this opposition between masculine and feminine in terms of the opposition between two orientations on moral reasoning.[9] The "ethic of rights" that Gilligan takes to be typical of masculine thinking emphasizes the separation of selves and the sense of fair play necessary to mediate the competition among such separated selves. The "ethic of care," on the other hand, which she takes to be typical of feminine thinking, emphasizes relatedness among persons and is an ethic of sympathy and affective attention to particular needs, rather than formal measuring of each according to universal rules. This ethic of care expresses the relatedness of the ideal of community as opposed to the atomistic formalism of liberal individualism.

The opposition between individualism and community, then, is homologous with and often implies the opposition masculine/feminine, public/ private, calculative/affective, instrumental/aesthetic, which are also present in modern political thinking.[10] This thinking has always valued the first side of these oppositions more highly than the second, and it has provided them with a dominant institutional expression in the society. For that reason asserting the value of community over individualism, the feminine over the masculine, the aesthetic over the instrumental, the relational over the competitive, does have some critical force with respect to the dominant ideology and social relations. The oppositions themselves, however, arise from and belong to bourgeois culture, and for that reason merely reversing their valuation does not constitute a genuine alternative to capitalist patriarchal society.

Like most such oppositions, moreover, individualism and community have a common logic underlying their polarity, which makes it possible for them to define each other negatively. Each entails a denial of difference and desire to bring multiplicity and heterogeneity into unity, although in opposing ways. Liberal individualism denies difference by positing the self as a solid, self-sufficient unity, not defined by or in need of anything or anyone other than itself. Its formalistic ethic of rights denies difference by leveling all such separated individuals under a common measure of rights. Community, on the other hand, denies difference by positing fusion rather than separation as the social ideal. Community proponents conceive the social subject as a relation of unity composed by identification and symmetry among individuals within a totality. As Sandel puts it, the opacity of persons tends to dissolve as ends, vocabulary, and practices become identical. This represents an urge to see persons in unity with each other in a shared whole.

As is the case with many dichotomies, in this one the possibilities for social ontology and social relations appear to be exhausted in the two categories. For many writers, the rejection of individualism logically entails asserting community, and conversely any rejection of community entails that one necessarily supports individualism. In their discussion of the debate between Elshtain and Ehrenreich, for example, Sara Evans and Harry Boyte claim that Ehrenreich promotes individualism because she rejects the appeal to community that Elshtain makes.[11] The possibility that there could be other conceptions of social organization does not appear because all possibilities have been reduced to the mutually exclusive opposition between individualism and community.

Ultimately, however, for most radical theorists the hard opposition of individualism and community breaks down. Unlike reactionary appeals to community which consistently assert the subordination of individual aims and values to the collective, most radical theorists assert that community itself consists in the respect for and fulfillment of individual aims and capacities. The neat distinction between individualism and community thus generates a dialectic in which each is a condition for the other.

Denying Difference within and between Subjects

In her interpretation of Marx's ontology, Carol Gould formulates such a dialectical conception of community as the transcended synthesis of sociality and individuality. This ideal society of the future is realized as the third stage of process of social evolution. The first stage is a communal society in which the individual is subjected to the collective, and the second is the individualist society of capitalist alienation.

> The separate subjects who are related to each other only as objects, namely, as beings for another, now recognize themselves in these objects, or recognize these objects as like themselves. Therefore they recognize each other as subjects, and the unity between subjects and objects is reestablished in this recognition. The subjects are then related to each other not as alien external others, but as aspects of a common species subject. The relations are therefore internal, since they are the interrelations within this common or communal subject which is now no longer made up of discrete individuals in external relations, but rather of individuals who are unified in their common subjectivity. . . . The subjects are therefore mutually interdependent and the relations between them are internal because each subject is what it is—a sub-ject—through its relation to the other, namely, through being recog-nized as a subject by the other. These individuals therefore form a communal but differentiated subject that expresses itself in and through each individual. The whole or unity that is reconstituted in these internal relations among the individuals is thus mediated or differentiated by their individuality, but unified by their commonality.[12]

According to Derrida, dialectical logic represses difference not by bringing multiplicity under a simple universal but by putting closure on the process of exteriorization. This closure emerges in the concept of a whole or totality within which opposites, differences, are reconciled and balanced.[13] Like many other expressions of this ideal of community, Gould's conception of community works on and through a totalizing desire to reconcile the differences of subjects.

The communitarian ideal participates in the metaphysics of presence because it conceives that subjects no longer need be exterior to one another. They need no longer outrun one another in directions they do not mutually understand and affirm. The ideal, moreover, extends this mutuality to its conception of the good society as a telos, an end to the conflict and violence of human interaction. Community here is conceived as a totality in two ways. It has no ontological exterior, since it realizes the unity of general will and individual subjectivity. It also has no historical exterior, for there is no further stage to travel.

While she does not specifically speak of her ideal as community, Seyla Benhabib expresses a similar ideal of person relating to one another through reciprocal recognition of subjectivities as a particular standpoint of moral autonomy. Liberalism holds a conception of moral autonomy, what she calls the "standpoint of the generalized other," which abstracts from the difference, desires and feeling among persons, to regard all as sharing a common set of formal rights and duties. In contrast, what Benhabib calls the "standpoint of the concrete other" views each person in his or her concrete individuality.

> In assuming this standpoint, we abstract from what continues our commonality and seek to understand the other as he/she understands himself/herself. We seek to comprehend the needs of the other, their motivations, what they search for and what they desire. Our relation to the other is governed by the norm of *complementary reciprocity:* each is entitled to expect and assume from the other forms of behavior through which the other feels recognized and confirmed as a concrete, individual being with specific needs, talents and capacities. Our differences in this case complement rather than exclude one another.[14]

Benhabib's notion of the standpoint of the concrete other expresses community as the mutual and reciprocal understanding of persons, relating internally, as Gould puts it, rather than externally. Many other writers express a similar ideal of relating to other persons internally, understanding them from their point of view. In the quotation previously cited, Sandel poses the elimination of the opacity of other persons as the ideal for community. Isaac Balbus represents the goal of radical politics and the establishment of community as the overcoming of the "otherness" of other in reciprocal recognition.[15] Roberto Unger articulates the ideal of community as the political alternative to personal love. In community persons relate to one another as concrete individuals who recognize themselves in each other because they have shared purposes. The conflict between the demands of individuality and the demands of sociability disappears in mutual sympathy.[16] Dorothy Allison proposes an ideal of community for feminists that is characterized by a "shared feeling of belonging and merging," with an "ecstatic sense of oneness."[17]

All these formulations seek to understand community as a unification of particular persons through the sharing of subjectivities: Persons will cease to be opaque, other, not understood, and instead become fused, mutually sympathetic, understanding one another as they understand themselves. Such an ideal of shared subjectivity, or the transparency of subjects to one another, denies difference in the sense of the basic asymmetry of subjects. As Hegel first brought to focus and Sartre's analysis deepened, persons necessarily transcend each other because subjectivity is negativity. The regard of the other upon me is always objectifying. Other persons never see the world from my perspective, and I am always faced with an experience of myself I do not have in witnessing the other's objective grasp of my body, actions, and words.

This mutual intersubjective transcendence, of course, makes sharing between us possible, a fact that Sartre notices less than Hegel. The sharing, however, is never complete mutual understanding and reciprocity. Sharing, moreover, is fragile. The other person may at the next moment understand my words differently from the way I meant them or carry my actions to consequences I do not intend. The same difference that makes sharing between us possible also makes misunderstanding, rejection, withdrawal, and conflict always possible conditions of social being.

The notion that each person can understand the other as he or she understands himself or herself, moreover, that persons can know other subjects in their concrete needs and desires, presupposes that a subject can know himself or herself and express that knowledge accurately and unambiguously to others. Such a concept of self-knowledge retains the Cartesian understanding of subjectivity basic to the modern metaphysics of presence. The idea of the self as a unified subject of desire and need and an origin of assertion and action has been powerfully called into question by contemporary philosophers.[18] I will rely on my reading of Julia Kristeva.

Without elaborating the linguistic detail in which she couches her notion of the subject-in-process, I will summarize briefly the general idea. Kristeva relies on a psychoanalytic notion of the unconscious to assert that subjectivity is heterogeneous and decentered. Consciousness, meaning, and intention are only possible because the subject-in-process slips and surpasses its intentions and meanings. Any utterance, for example, not only has a literal meaning, but is laden with ambiguities, embodied in gesture, tone of voice, and rhythm that all contribute to the heterogeneity of its meaning without being intended. So it is with actions and interactions with other persons. What I say and do always has a multiplicity of meanings, ambiguities, plays, and these are not always coherent.[19]

Because the subject is not a unity, it cannot be present to itself and know itself. I do not always know what I mean, need, want, desire, because these do not arise from some ego as origin. Often I express my desire in gesture or tone of voice, without meaning to do so. Consciousness, speech, expressiveness are possible only if the subject always surpasses itself and is thus necessarily unable to comprehend itself. Subjects all have multiple desires that do not cohere; they attach layers of meanings to objects without always being aware of each layer or their connections. Consequently, any individual subject is a play of differences that cannot be comprehended.

If the subject is heterogeneous process, unable to be present to itself, then it follows that subjects cannot make themselves transparent, wholly present to one another. If each subject escapes its own comprehension and for that reason cannot fully express to another its needs and desires, then necessarily each subject also escapes sympathetic comprehension by others. I cannot understand another as he or she understands himself or herself, because he or she does not completely understand himself or herself. Indeed, because other people's expression to me may outrun their own awareness or intention, I may understand certain aspects of them more fully than they.

Gould appeals to such an ideal of "common subjectivity" as an alternative to the commodification of persons she finds characteristic of capitalist domination. Her conceptualization suggests that only if persons understood one another "internally," as she puts it, would such domination be eliminated. While I certainly do not wish to deny that current social relations are full of domination and exploitation, conceiving the elimination of these conditions in terms of an impossible ideal of shared subjectivity can tend to deflect attention from more concrete analysis of the conditions of their elimination.

Not only does this ideal of shared subjectivity express an impossibility, but it has undesirable political implications. Political theorists and activists should distrust this desire for reciprocal recognition and identification with others, I suggest, because it denies difference in the concrete sense of making it difficult for people to respect those with whom they do not identify. I suggest that the desire for mutual understanding and reciprocity underlying the ideal of community is similar to the desire for identification that underlies racial and ethnic chauvinism.

In ordinary speech for most people in the United States, the term *community* refers to the people with whom I identify in a locale. It refers to neighborhood, church, school. It also carries connotations of ethnicity or race. For most people in the United States, insofar as they consider themselves members of communities at all, a community is a group that shares a specific heritage, a common self-identification, a common culture and set of norms. In the United States today, identification as a member of such a community also often occurs as an oppositional differentiation from other groups, who are feared or at best devalued. Persons identify only with some other persons, feel in community only with those, and fear the difference others confront them with because they identify with a different culture, history, and point of view on the world.

Racism, ethnic chauvinism, and class devaluation, I suggest, grow partly from a desire for community, that is, from the desire to understand others as they understand themselves and from the desire to be understood as I understand myself. Practically speaking, such mutual understanding can be approximated only within a homogeneous group that defines itself by common attributes. Such common identification, however, entails reference also to those excluded.[20] In the dynamics of racism and ethnic chauvinism in the United States today, the positive identification of some groups is often achieved by first defining other groups as the other, the devalued semihuman. I do not claim that appeal to the ideal of community is itself racist. Rather, my claim is that such appeals, within the context of a racist and chauvinistic society, can validate the impulses that reproduce racist and ethnically chauvinistic identification.

The striving for mutual identification and shared understanding among those who seek to foster a radical and progressive politics, moreover, can and has led to denying or suppressing differences within political groups or movements. Many feminist groups, for example, have sought to foster relations of equality and reciprocity of understanding in such a way that disagreement, difference, and deviation have been interpreted as a breech of sisterhood, the destruction of personal relatedness and community. There has often been strong pressure within women's groups for members to share the same understanding of the world and the same lifestyle, in addition to distributing tasks equally and rotating leadership. Such pressure has often led to group and even more movement homogeneity—primarily straight, or primarily lesbian, or primarily white, or primarily academic.[21] In recent years feminists, perhaps more seriously than other progressive political groups, have discussed how their organizations and movement might become more heterogeneous and recognize difference. A continuing desire for mutual identification and reciprocity, however, hampers the implementation of a principled call for heterogeneity.

In a racist, sexist, homophobic society that has despised and devalued certain groups, it is necessary and desirable for members of those groups to adhere with one another and celebrate a common culture, heritage, and experience. Even with such separatist movements, however, too strong a desire for unity can lead to repressing the differences within the group or forcing some out: gays and lesbians from black nationalist groups, for example, or feminists from Native American groups, and so on.

Many other progressive political organizations and movements founder on the same desire for community. Too often people in political groups take mutual friendship to be a goal of the group and thus find themselves wanting as a group when they do not achieve such commonality.[22] Such a desire for community often channels energy away from the political goals of the group and also produces a clique atmosphere which keeps groups small and turns potential members away. A more acceptable politics would acknowledge that members of an organization do not understand one another as they understand themselves and would accept this distance without closing it into exclusion.

Denial of Difference as Time and Space Distancing

Many political theorists who put forward an ideal of community specify small-group, face-to-face relations as essential to the realization of that ideal. Peter Manicas expresses a version of the ideal of community that includes this face-to-face specification.

> Consider an association in which persons are in face-to-face contact, but where the relations of persons are not mediated by "authorities," sanctified rules, reified bureaucracies or commodities. Each is prepared to absorb the attitudes, reasoning and ideas of others and each is in a position to do so. Their relations, thus, are open, immediate and reciprocal. Further, the total conditions of their social lives are to be conjointly determined with each having an equal voice and equal power. When these conditions are satisfied and when as a result, the consequences and fruits of their associated and independent activities are perceived and consciously become an object of individual desire and effort, then there is a democratic community.[23]

Roberto Unger argues that community requires face-to-face interaction among members within a plurality of contexts. To understand other people and to be understood by them in our concrete individuality, we must not only work together but play together, take care of children together, grieve together, and so on.[24] Christian Bay envisions the good society as founded upon small face-to-face communities of direct democracy and many-sided interaction.[25] Michael Taylor specifies that in a community, relations among members must be direct and many-sided. Like Manicas, he asserts that relations are direct only when they are unmediated by representatives, leaders, bureaucrats, state institutions, or codes.[26] While Gould does not specify face-to-face relations as necessary, some of her language suggests that community can only be realized in such face-to-face relations. In the institutionalization of democratic socialism, she says, "social combination now becomes the *immediate* subjective relations of mutuality among individuals. The relations, again become *personal* relations as in the precapitalist stage, but no longer relations of domination and no longer mediated, as in the second stage, by external objects."[27]

I take there to be several problems with the privileging of face-to-face relations by theorists of community. It presumes an illusory ideal of unmediated social relations and wrongly identifies mediation with alienation. It denies difference in the sense of time and space distancing. It implies a model of the good society as consisting of decentralized small units, which is both unrealistic and politically undesirable. Finally, it avoids the political question of the relation among the decentralized communities.

All the writers cited previously give primacy to face-to-face presence because they claim that only under those conditions can the social relations be *immediate*. I understand them to mean several things by social relations that are immediate. They are direct, personal relations, in which each

understands the other in her or his individuality. This is an extension of
the ideal of mutual understanding I have criticized in the previous section.
Immediacy also here means relations of co-presence in which persons
experience a simultaneity of speaking and hearing and are in the same
space, that is, have the possibility to move close enough to touch.[28]

This ideal of the immediate presence of subjects to one another, however, is a metaphysical illusion. Even a face-to-face relation between two
people is mediated by voice and gesture, spacing and temporality. As
soon as a third person enters the interaction, the possibility arises of the
relation between the first two being mediated through the third, and so
on. The mediation of relations among persons by speech and actions of
still other persons is a fundamental condition of sociality. The richness,
creativity, diversity, and potential of a society expand with growth in the
scope and means of its media, linking persons across time and distance.
The greater the time and distance, however, the greater the number of
persons who stand between other persons.

The normative privileging of face-to-face relations in the ideal of community seeks to suppress difference in the sense of the time and space
distancing of social processes, which material media facilitate and enlarge.
Such an ideal dematerializes its conception of interaction and institutions.
For all social interaction takes place over time and across space. Social
desire consists in the urge to carry meaning, agency, and the effects of
agency beyond the moment and beyond the place. As laboring subjects
we separate the moment of production from the moment of consumption.
Even societies confined to a limited territory with few institutions and a
small population devise means of their members communicating with one
another over distances, means of maintaining their social relationships
even though they are not face to face. Societies occupy wider and wider
territorial fields and increasingly differentiate their activity in space, time,
and function, a movement that, of course, accelerates and takes on qualitatively specific form in modern industrial societies.[29]

I suggest that there are no conceptual grounds for considering face-to-
face relations more pure, authentic social relations than relations mediated
across time and distance. For both face-to-face and non-face-to-face relations are mediated relations, and in both there is as much the possibility
of separation and violence as there is communication and consensus.
Theorists of community are inclined to privilege face-to-face relations, I
suggest, because they wrongly identify mediation and alienation.

By alienation, I mean a situation in which persons do not have control
either over their actions, the conditions of their action, or the consequences
of their action, due to the intervention of other agents.[30] Social mediation
is a condition for the possibility of alienation in this sense; media make
possible the intervention of agents between the conditions of a subject's

action and the action or between a subject's action and its consequences. Thus, media make domination and exploitation possible. In modern society the primary structures creating alienation and domination are bureaucracy and commodification of all aspects of human activity, including and especially labor. Both bureaucracy and commodification of social relations depend on complex structures of mediation among a large number of persons.

That mediation is a necessary condition of alienation, however, does not entail the reverse implication: That only by eliminating structures of mediation do we eliminate alienation. If temporal and spatial distancing are basic to social processes, and if persons always mediate between other persons to generate social networks, then a society of immediacy is impossible. While mediation may be a necessary condition for alienation, it is not sufficient. Alienation is that specific process of mediation in which the actions of some serve the ends of others without reciprocation and without being explicit, and this requires coercion and domination.

By positing a society of immediate face-to-face relations as ideal, community theorists generate a dichotomy between the "authentic" society of the future and the "inauthentic" society we live in, which is characterized only by alienation, bureaucratization, and degradation. Such a dichotomization between the inauthentic society we have and the authentic society of community, however, detemporalizes our understanding of social change. On this understanding, social change and revolution consist in the complete negation of this society and the establishment of the truly good society. In her scheme of social evolution, Gould conceives of "the society of the future" as the negated sublation of capitalist society. This understands history not as temporal process but as divided into two static structures: the before of alienated society and the after of community.

The projection of the ideal of community as the radical other of existing society denies difference in the sense of the contradictions and ambiguities of social life. Instead of dichotomizing the pure and the impure into two stages of history or two kinds of social relations, a liberating politics should conceive the social process in which we move as a multiplicity of actions and structures which cohere and contradict, some of them exploitative and some of them liberating. The polarization between the impure, inauthentic society we live in and the pure, authentic society we seek to institute detemporalizes the process of change because it fails to articulate how we move from one to the other. If institutional change is possible at all, it must begin from intervening in the contradictions and tensions of existing society. No telos of the final society exists, moreover; society understood as a moving and contradictory process implies that change for the better is always possible and always necessary.

The requirement that genuine community embody face-to-face relations, when taken as a model of the good society, carries a specific vision of social organization. Since the ideal of community demands that relations between members be direct and many-sided, the ideal society is composed of small locales, populated by a small enough number of persons so that each can be personally acquainted with all the others. For most writers, this implies that the ideal social organization is decentralized, with small-scale industry and local markets. Each community aims for economic self-sufficiency, and each democratically makes its own decisions about how to organize its working and playing life.

I do not doubt the desirability of small groups in which individuals have personal acquaintance with one another and interact in a plurality of contexts. Just as the intimacy of living with a few others in the same household has unique dimensions that are humanly valuable, so existing with others in communities of mutual friendship has specific characteristics of warmth and sharing that are humanly valuable. Furthermore, there is no question that capitalist patriarchal society discourages and destroys such communities of mutual friendship, just as it squeezes and fragments families. In our vision of the good society, we surely wish to include institutional arrangements that would nurture the specific experience of mutual friendship, which only relatively small groups interacting in a plurality of contexts can produce. Recognizing the specific value of such face-to-face relations, however, is quite a different matter from proposing them as the organizing principle of a whole society.

Such a model of the good society as composed of decentralized, economically self-sufficient, face-to-face communities functioning as autonomous political entities is both wildly utopian and undesirable. To bring it into being would require dismantling the urban character of modern society, a gargantuan physical overhaul of living space, work places, places of trade and commerce. A model of a transformed better society must in some concrete sense begin from the concrete material structures that are given to us at this time in history, and in the United States these are large-scale industry and urban centers. The model of society composed of small communities is not desirable, at least in the eyes of many. If we take seriously the way many people live their lives today, it appears that people enjoy cities, that is, places where strangers are thrown together.

One final problem arises from the model of face-to-face community taken as a political goal. The model of the good society as usually articulated leaves completely unaddressed the question of how such small communities are to relate to one another. Frequently, the ideal projects a level of self-sufficiency and decentralization which suggests that proponents envision few relations among the decentralized communities except those of friendly visits. But surely it is unrealistic to assume that such decentralized communities need not engage in extensive relations of exchange of resources, goods, and culture. Even if one accepts the notion that a radical restructuring of society in the direction of a just and humane society entails people living in small democratically organized units of work and neighborhood, this has not addressed the important political question: How will the relations among these communities be organized so as to foster justice and prevent domination? When we raise this political question the philosophical and practical importance of mediation re-emerges. Once again, politics must be conceived as a relationship of strangers who do not understand one another in a subjective and immediate sense, relating across time and distance.

City Life and the Politics of Difference

I have claimed that radical politics must begin from historical givens and conceive radical change not as the negation of the given but rather as making something good from many elements of the given. The city, as a vastly populated area with large-scale industry and places of mass assembly, is for us a historical given, and radical politics must begin from the existence of modern urban life. The material surroundings and structures available to us define and presuppose urban relationships. The very size of populations in our society and most other nations of the world, coupled with a continuing sense of national or ethnic identity with millions of other people, all support the conclusion that a vision of dismantling the city is hopelessly utopian.

Starting from the given of modern urban life is not simply necessary, moreover, it is desirable. Even for many of those who decry the alienation, massification, and bureaucratization of capitalist patriarchal society, city life exerts a powerful attraction. Modern literature, art, and film have celebrated city life, its energy, cultural diversity, technological complexity, and the multiplicity of its activities. Even many of the most staunch proponents of decentralized community love to show visiting friends around the Boston or San Francisco or New York in which they live, climbing up towers to see the glitter of lights and sampling the fare at the best ethnic restaurants. For many people deemed deviant in the closeness of the face-to-face community in which they lived, whether "independent" women or socialists or gay men and lesbians, the city has often offered a welcome anonymity and some measure of freedom.[31] To be sure, the liberatory possibilities of capitalist cities have been fraught with ambiguity.

Yet, I suggest that instead of the ideal of community, we begin from our positive experience of city life to form a vision of the good society. Our political ideal is the unoppressive city. In sketching this ideal, I assume some material premises. We will assume a productivity level in the society that can meet everyone's needs, and a physical urban environment that is cleaned up and renovated. We will assume, too, that everyone who can work has meaningful work and those who cannot are provided for with dignity. In sketching this ideal of city life, I am concerned to describe the city as a *kind of relationship* of people to one another, to their own history and one another's history. Thus, by "city" I am not referring only to those huge metropolises that we call cities in the United States. The kinds of relationship I describe obtain also ideally in those places we call towns, where perhaps 10,000 or 20,000 people live.

As a process of people's relating to one another, city life embodies difference in all the senses I have discussed in this chapter. The city obviously exhibits the temporal and spatial distancing and differentiation that I have argued, the ideal of community seeks to collapse. On the face of the city environment lies its history and the history of the individuals and groups that have dwelt within it. Such physical historicity, as well as the functions and groups that live in the city at any given time, create its spatial differentiation. The city as a network and sedimentation of discretely understood places, such as particular buildings, parks, neighborhoods, and as a physical environment offers changes and surprises in transition from one place to another.

The temporal and spatial differentiation that mark the physical environment of the city produce an experience of aesthetic *inexhaustibility*. Buildings, squares, the twists and turns of streets and alleys offer an inexhaustible store of individual spaces and things, each with unique aesthetic characteristics. The juxtaposition of incongruous styles and functions that usually emerge after a long time in city places contribute to this pleasure in detail and surprise. This is an experience of difference in the sense of always being inserted. The modern city is without walls; it is not planned and coherent. Dwelling in the city means always having a sense of beyond, that there is much human life beyond my experience going on in or near these spaces, and I can never grasp the city as a whole.

City life thus also embodies difference as the contrary of the face-to-face ideal expressed by most assertions of community. City life is the "being-together" of strangers. Strangers encounter one another, either face to face or through media, often remaining strangers and yet acknowledging their contiguity in living and the contributions each makes to the others. In such encountering people are not "internally" related, as the community theorists would have it, and do not understand one another from within their own perspective. They are externally related, they experience each other as other, different, from different groups, histories, professions, cultures, which they do not understand.

The public spaces of the city are both an image of the total relationships of city life and a primary way those relationships are enacted and experienced. A public space is a place accessible to anyone, where people engage in activity as individuals or in small groups. In public spaces people are aware of each other's presence and even at times attend to it. In a city there are a multitude of such public spaces: streets, restaurants, concert halls, parks. In such public spaces the diversity of the city's residents come together and dwell side by side, sometimes appreciating one another, entertaining one another, or just chatting, always to go off again as strangers. City parks as we now experience them often have this character.

City life implies a social exhaustibility quite different from the ideal of the face-to-face community in which there is mutual understanding and group identification and loyalty. The city consists in a great diversity of people and groups, with a multitude of subcultures and differentiated activities and functions, whose lives and movements mingle and overlap in public spaces. People belong to distinct groups or cultures and interact in neighborhoods and work places. They venture out from these locales, however, to public places of entertainment, consumption, and politics. They witness one another's cultures and functions in such public interaction, without adopting them as their own. The appreciation of ethnic foods or professional musicians, for example, consists in the recognition that these transcend the familiar everyday world of my life.

In the city strangers live side by side in public places, giving to and receiving from one another social and aesthetic products, often mediated by a huge chain of interactions. This instantiates social relations as difference in the sense of an understanding of groups and cultures that are different, with exchanging and overlapping interactions that do not issue in community, yet which prevent them from being outside of one another. The social differentiation of the city also provides a positive inexhaustibility of human relations. The possibility always exists of becoming acquainted with new and different people, with different cultural and social experiences; the possibility always exists for new groups to form or emerge around specific interests.

The unoppressive city is thus defined as openness to unassimilated otherness. Of course, we do not have such openness to difference in our current social relations. I am asserting an ideal, which consists in a politics of difference. Assuming that group differentiation is a given of social life for us, how can the relationships of group identities embody justice, respect, and the absence of oppression? The relationship among group identities and cultures in our society is blotted by racism, sexism, xenophobia, homophobia, suspicion, and mockery. A politics of difference lays down institutional and ideological means for recognizing and affirming differently identifying groups in two basic senses: giving political representation to group interests and celebrating the distinctive cultures and characteristics of different groups.

Many questions arise in proposing a politics of difference. What defines a group that deserves recognition and celebration? How does one provide representation to group interests that avoids the mere pluralism of liberal interest groups? What are institutional forms by which the mediations of the city and the representations of its groups in decision making can be made democratic? These questions, as well as many others, confront the ideal of the unoppressive city. They are not dissimilar from questions of the relationships that ought to exist among communities. They are questions, however, which appeal to community as the ideal of social life appears to repress or ignore. Some might claim that a politics of difference does express what the ideal of community ought to express, despite the meaning that many writers give the concept of community. Fred Dallmayr, for example, reserves the term *community* for just this openness toward unassimilated otherness, designating the more totalistic understanding of social relations I have criticized as either "communalism" or "movement."

> As opposed to the homogeneity deliberately fostered in the movement, the communitarian mode cultivates diversity—but without encouraging willful segregation or the repressive preponderance of one of the social subsectors. . . . Community may be the only form of social aggregation which reflects upon, and makes room for, otherness or the reverse side of subjectivity (and inter-subjectivity) and thus for the play of difference—the difference between ego and Other and between man and nature.[33]

In the end it may be a matter of stipulation whether one chooses to call such politics as play of difference "community." Because most articulations of the ideal of community carry the urge to unity I have criticized, however, I think it is less confusing to use a term other than community rather than to redefine the term. Whatever the label, the concept of social relations that embody openness to unassimilated otherness with justice and appreciation needs to be developed. Radical politics, moreover, must develop discourse and institutions for bringing differently identified groups together without suppressing or subsuming the differences.

Notes

1. I examine community specifically as a normative ideal designating how social relations ought to be organized. There are various nonnormative uses of the term *community* to which my analysis does not apply. Sociologists engaged in community studies, for example, usually use the term to mean something like "small town" or "neighborhood," and they use the term primarily in a descriptive sense. The questions raised apply to community understood only as a normative model of social organization. See Jessie

Bernard, *The Sociology of Community*, (Glenview, IL: Scott, Foresman and Co., 1973) for a summary of different sociological theories of community in its nonnormative senses.

2. The texts of these authors I am relying on primarily are Jacques Derrida, *Of Grammatology* (Baltimore, MD: Johns Hopkins University Press, 1976); Theodor Adorno, *Negative Dialectics* (New York: Continuum Publishing Company, 1973); Julia Kristeva, *Polylogue* (Paris: Editions du Seuil, 1977). These three writers have a similar critique of Western metaphysics. Several writers have noted similarities between Adorno and Derrida in this regard. See Fred Dallmayr, *Twilight of Subjectivity: Contributions to a Post-Structuralist Theory of Politics* (Amherst, MA: University of Massachusetts Press, 1981), pp. 107–14, 127–36; and Michael Ryan, *Marxism and Deconstruction* (Baltimore, MD: Johns Hopkins University Press, 1982), pp. 73–81. For an account that draws some parallel between Kristeva and Adorno in this respect, see Drucilla Cornell and Adam Thurschwell, "Feminism, Negativity and Intersubjectivity," *Praxis International*, vol. 5, no. 4, 1986, pp. 484–504. My account of metaphysics of presence is based on my reading of these three writers, but I do not claim to be "representing" what they say. Nor in this chapter am I claiming to appropriate all these writers say for social theory. While I do regard the critique of the ideal of community I engage in here loosely as a deconstructive critique along the lines of Derrida's method, I part ways with him and some of the other poststructuralists insofar as I think that it is both possible and necessary to pose alternative conceptualizations. Doing so is, of course, always a positing, and hence excludes and demarks, thus always itself open to the possibility of deconstructive critique.

3. Adorno, *Negative Dialectics*, Part Two, pp. 134–210.

4. Derrida, *Of Grammatology*, pp. 12–87.

5. Kristeva, "Le sujet en procès," "L'expérience et la pratique," "Matière, sense, dialectique," *Polylogue* pp. 55–136, 263–86.

6. Anthony Giddens, *Central Problems in Social Theory* (Berkeley, CA: University of California Press, 1979), pp. 28–40; Dallmayr, *Twilight of Subjectivity*, pp. 107–115.

7. R. P. Wolff, *The Poverty of Liberalism* (Boston: Beacon Press, 1978), Chapter 5.

8. Michael Sandel, *Liberalism and the Limits of Justice* (Cambridge: Cambridge University Press, 1982), pp. 172–173.

9. Carol Gilligan, *In a Different Voice* (Cambridge: Cambridge University Press, 1981).

10. I develop more thoroughly the implications of these oppositions in modern political theory and practice and a practical vision of their unsettling in my paper "Impartiality and the Civic Public: Some Implications of Feminist Critics of Modern Political Theory," *Praxis International*, vol. 5, no. 4, 1986, pp. 381–401.

11. Harry C. Boyte and Sara M. Evans, "Strategies in Search of America: Cultural Radicalism, Populism, and Democratic Culture," *Socialist Review* (May to August 1984), pp. 73–100.

12. Carol Gould, *Marx's Social Ontology* (Cambridge, MA: MIT Press, 1978), p. 9.

13. Ryan, *Marxism and Deconstruction,* pp. 65–71.

14. Seyla Benhabib, "Communicative Ethics and Moral Autonomy," presented at a meeting of the American Philosophical Association, Eastern Division, December 1982; see also "The Generalized and Concrete Other: Toward a Feminist Critique of Substitutionalist Universalism," *Praxis International,* Vol. 5, No. 4, 1986, pp. 402–424.

15. Isaac Balbus, *Marxism and Domination* (Princeton: Princeton University Press, 1983).

16. Roberto Mangabeira Unger, *Knowledge and Politics* (New York: The Free Press, 1975), pp. 220–222.

17. Dorothy Alison, "Weaving the Web of Community," *Quest: A Feminist Quarterly,* vol. 4, 1978, p. 79.

18. Sandel, in *Liberalism and the Limits of Justice,* levels a powerful critique against Rawls by arguing that his theory of justice presupposes a self as separated from and prior to the actions it undertakes as its unified origin. Sandel gives several arguments showing the incoherence of such a conception of the unified self prior to the context of action.

19. Kristeva, "Le sujet en procès," *Polylogue,* pp. 55–106.

20. Sartre's *Critique of Dialectical Reason* is a classic statement on this dynamic of inclusion and exclusion. For another statement referring specifically to the exclusionary aspects of attempts to found communities, see Rosabeth Moss Kantner, *Commitment and Community: Communes and Utopias in Sociological Perspective* (Cambridge, MA: Harvard University Press, 1972), pp. 52–53.

21. Francine Rainone, "Community, Politics and Spirituality," paper presented at a conference on Feminism and Psychology, Boston, MA, February 1984; Jana Sawicki, "Foucault and Feminism: Towards a Politics of Difference," *Hypatia: A Journal of Feminist Philosophy,* vol. 1, no. 2, 1986, pp. 23–36. See also Audre Lorde, essays in *Sister Outsider* (Trumansburg, NY: The Crossing Press, 1984), especially "The Master's Tools Will Never Dismantle the Master's House," and "Age, Race, Class and Sex: Women Redefining Difference."

22. Wini Breines documents this urge to mutual friendship and some of the disappointments that followed from it in the student movement in the 1960s in her book *Community and Organization in the New Left: 1962–68* (South Hadley, MA: J. F. Bergin Publishers, 1982), especially Chapter 4.

23. Peter Manicas, *The Death of the State* (New York: Putnam and Sons, 1974), p. 247.

24. Unger, *Knowledge and Politics*, pp. 262–63.

25. Christian Bay, *Strategies of Political Emancipation* (South Bend, IL: Notre Dame Press, 1981), Chapters 5 and 6.

26. Michael Taylor, *Community, Anarchy and Liberty* (Cambridge: Cambridge University Press, 1982), pp. 27–28.

27. Gould, *Marx's Social Ontology*, p. 26.

28. Derrida discusses the illusory character of this ideal of immediate presence of subjects to one another in community in his discussion of Levi-Strauss and Rousseau. See *Of Grammatology*, pp. 101–140.

29. Anthony Giddens, *Central Problems in Social Theory*, pp. 198–233.

30. For a useful account of alienation, see Richard Schmitt, *Alienation and Class* (Cambridge, MA: Schenkman Publishing Co., 1983), especially Chapter 5. In this book Schmitt, like many other of the writers I have cited, takes community to stand as the negation of the society of alienation. Unlike those writers discussed in this section, however, he does not take face-to-face relations as a condition of community. To the degree that he makes a pure/impure distinction and exhibits the desire for unity I have criticized, however, the critique articulated here applies to Schmitt's appeal to the ideal of community.

31. Marshall Berman presents a fascinating account of the attractions of city life in *All That Is Solid Melts Into Air* (New York: Simon & Schuster, 1982). George Shulman points to the open-endedness of city life as contrasted with the pastoral vision of community in "The Pastoral Idyll of *Democracy*," *Democracy*, vol. 3, 1983, pp. 43–54; for a similar critique, see David Plotke, "Democracy, Modernization, and Democracy," *Socialist Review*, vol. 14, March-April 1984, pp. 31–56.

32. In my previously cited paper, "Impartiality and the Civic Public," I formulate some ideas of a heterogeneous public life; I have developed further some principles of a politics of difference in "Elements of a Politics of Difference," paper presented at the North American Society for Social Philosophy, Colorado Springs, August 1985.

33. Dallmayr, *Twilight of Subjectivity*, pp. 142–143.

13

Gender Trouble, Feminist Theory, and Psychoanalytic Discourse

Judith Butler

Within the terms of feminist theory, it has been quite important to refer to the category of "women" and to know what it is we mean. We tend to agree that women have been written out of the histories of culture and literature that men have written, that women have been silenced or distorted in the texts of philosophy, biology, and physics, and that there is a group of embodied beings socially positioned as "women" who now, under the name of feminism, have something quite different to say. Yet, this question of being a woman is more difficult than it perhaps originally appeared, for we refer not only to women as a social category but also as a felt sense of self, a culturally conditioned or constructed subjective identity. The descriptions of women's oppression, their historical situation or cultural perspective has seemed, to some, to require that women themselves will not only recognize the rightness of feminist claims made in their behalf, but that, together, they will discover a common identity, whether in their relational attitudes, in their embodied resistance to abstract and objectifying modes of thought and experience, their felt sense of their bodies, their capacity for maternal identification or maternal thinking, the nonlinear directionality of their pleasures or the elliptical and plurivocal possibilities of their writing.

But does feminist theory need to rely on a notion of what it is fundamentally or distinctively to be a "woman"? The question becomes a crucial one when we try to answer what it is that characterizes the world of women that is marginalized, distorted, or negated within various masculinist practices. Is there a specific femininity or a specific set of values that have been written

---

My genuine thanks to Joan W. Scott for giving thoughtful response to many versions of this piece. I am grateful to the American Council of Learned Societies and to the Institute for Advanced Study in Princeton for sponsoring this work.

out of various histories and descriptions that can be associated with women as a group? Does the category of woman maintain a meaning separate from the conditions of oppression against which it has been formulated?

For the most part, feminist theory has taken the category of women to be foundational to any further political claims without realizing that the category effects a political closure on the kinds of experiences articulable as part of a feminist discourse. When the category is understood as representing a set of values or dispositions, it becomes normative in character and, hence, exclusionary in principle. This move has created a problem both theoretical and political, namely, that a variety of women from various cultural positions have refused to recognize themselves as "women" in the terms articulated by feminist theory with the result that these women fall outside the category and are left to conclude that (1) either they are not women as they have perhaps previously assumed or (2) the category reflects the restricted location of its theoreticians and, hence, fails to recognize the intersection of gender with race, class, ethnicity, age, sexuality, and other currents which contribute to the formation of cultural (non)identity. In response to the radical exclusion of the category of women from hegemonic cultural formations on the one hand and the internal critique of the exclusionary effects of the category from within feminist discourse on the other, feminist theorists are now confronted with the problem of either redefining and expanding the category of women itself to become more inclusive (which requires also the political matter of settling who gets to make the designation and in the name of whom) or to challenge the place of the category as a part of a feminist normative discourse. Gayatri Spivak has argued that feminists need to rely on an operational essentialism, a false ontology of women as a universal in order to advance a feminist political program.[1] She concedes that the category of women is not fully expressive, that the multiplicity and discontinuity of the signified rebels against the univocity of the sign, but she suggests that we need to use it for strategic purposes. Julia Kristeva suggests something similar, I think, when she recommends that feminists use the category of women as a political tool without attributing ontological integrity to the term, and she adds that, strictly speaking, women cannot be said to exist.[2]

But is it the presumption of ontological integrity that needs to be dispelled, or does the practical redeployment of the category without any ontological commitments also effect a political consolidation of its semantic integrity with serious exclusionary implications? Is there another normative point of departure for feminist theory that does not require the reconstruction or rendering visible of a female subject who fails to represent, much less emancipate, the array of embodied beings culturally positioned as women?

Psychoanalytic theory has occupied an ambiguous position in the feminist quandary over whether the category of women has a rightful place within feminist political discourse. On the one hand, psychoanalysis has sought to identify the developmental moments in which gendered identity is acquired. Yet, those feminist positions which take their departure from the work of Jacques Lacan have sought to underscore the unconscious as the tenuous ground of any and all claims to identity. A work that makes both arguments, Juliet Mitchell's *Psycho-analysis and Feminism* (1974), sought not only to show that gender is constructed rather than biologically necessitated but to identify the precise developmental moments of that construction in the history of gendered subjects. Mitchell further argues on structuralist grounds that the narrative of infantile development enjoyed relative universality and that psychoanalytic theory seemed, therefore, to offer feminists a way to describe a psychological and cultural ground of shared gender identification.[3] In a similar position, Jacqueline Rose asserts: "The force of psychoanalysis is therefore precisely that it gives an account of patriarchal culture as a trans-historical and cross-cultural force. It therefore conforms to the feminist demand for a theory which can explain women's subordination across specific cultures and different historical moments."[4] As much as psychoanalytic theory provided feminist theory with a way to identify and fix gender difference through a metanarrative of shared infantile development, it also helped feminists show how the very notion of the subject is a masculine prerogative within the terms of culture. The paternal law which Lacanian psychoanalysis takes to be the ground of all kinship and all cultural relations not only sanctions male subjects but institutes their very possibility through the denial of the feminine. Hence, far from being subjects, women are, variously, the Other, a mysterious and unknowable lack, a sign of the forbidden and irrecoverable maternal body, or some unsavory mixture of the above.

Elaborating on Lacanian theory, but making significant departures from its presumptions of universal patriarchy, Luce Irigaray maintains that the very construct of an autonomous subject is a masculine cultural prerogative from which women have been excluded. She further claims that the subject is always already masculine, that it bespeaks a refusal of dependency required of male acculturation, understood originally as dependency on the mother, and that its "autonomy" is founded on a repression of its early and true helplessness, need, sexual desire for the mother, even identification with the maternal body. The subject thus becomes a fantasy of autogenesis, the refusal of maternal foundations and, in generalized form, a repudiation of the feminine. For Irigaray, then, it would make no sense to refer to a female subject or to women as subjects, for it is precisely the construct of the subject that necessitates relations of hierarchy, exclusion, and domination. In a word, there can be no subject without an Other.[5]

Irig.

very nice on Irigaray

Psychoanalytic criticism of the epistemological point of departure, beginning with Freud's criticism of Enlightenment views of "man" as a rational being and later echoed in Lacan's critique of Cartesianism, has offered feminist theorists a way of criticizing the disembodied pretensions of the masculine knower and exposing the strategy of domination implicit in that disingenuous epistemological gesture. The destabilization of the subject within feminist criticism becomes a tactic in the exposure of masculine power and, in some French feminist contexts, the death of the subject spells the release or emancipation of the suppressed feminine sphere, the specific libidinal economy of women, the condition of *écriture feminine*.

But clearly, this set of moves raises a political problem: If it is not a female subject who provides the normative model for a feminist emancipatory politics, then what does? If we fail to recuperate the subject in feminist terms, are we not depriving feminist theory of a notion of agency that casts doubt on the viability of feminism as a normative model? Without a unified concept of woman or, minimally, a family resemblance among gender-related terms, it appears that feminist politics has lost the categorial basis of its own normative claims. What constitutes the "who," the subject, for whom feminism seeks emancipation? If there is no subject, who is left to emancipate?

The feminist resistance to the critique of the subject shares some concerns with other critical and emancipatory discourses: If oppression is to be defined in terms of a loss of autonomy by the oppressed, as well as a fragmentation or alienation within the psyche of the oppressed, then a theory which insists upon the inevitable fragmentation of the subject appears to reproduce and valorize the very oppression that must be overcome. We need perhaps to think about a typology of fragmentations or, at least, answer the question of whether oppression ought to be defined in terms of the fragmentation of identity and whether fragmentation *per se* is oppressive. Clearly, the category of women is internally fragmented by class, color, age, and ethnic lines, to name but a few; in this sense, honoring the diversity of the category and insisting upon its definitional nonclosure appears to be a necessary safeguard against substituting a reification of women's experience for the diversity that exists.[6] But how do we know what exists prior to its discursive articulation? Further, the critique of the subject means more than the rehabilitation of a multiple subject whose various "parts" are interrelated within an overriding unity, a coalitional subject, or an internal polity of pluralistically related points of view. Indeed, the political critique of the subject questions whether making a conception of identity into the ground of politics, however internally complicated, prematurely forecloses the possible cultural articulations of the subject-position that a new politics might well generate.

This kind of political position is clearly not in line with the humanist presuppositions of either feminism or related theories on the Left. At least since Marx's *Early Manuscripts,* the normative model of an integrated and unified self has served emancipatory discourses. Socialist feminism has clearly reformulated the doctrine of the integrated subject in opposition to the split between public and private spheres which has concealed domestic exploitation and generally failed to acknowledge the value of women's work, as well as the specific moral and cultural values which originate or are sustained within the private sphere. In a further challenge to the public/private distinction in moral life, Carol Gilligan and others have called for a reintegration of conventional feminine virtues, such as care and other relational attitudes, into conventional moral postures of distance and abstraction, a kind of reintegration of the human personality, conceived as a lost unity in need of restoration. Feminist psychoanalytic theory based in object-relations has similarly called for a restructuring of child-rearing practices which would narrow the schism between gender differences produced by the predominating presence of the mother in the nurturing role. Again, the integration of nurturance and dependency into the masculine sphere and the concomitant assimilation of autonomy into the feminine sphere suggests a normative model of a unified self which tends toward the androgynous solution. Others insist on the deep-seated specificity of the feminine rooted in a primary maternal identification which grounds an alternative feminine subject, who defines herself relationally and contextually and who fails to exhibit the inculcated masculine fear of dependency at the core of the repudiation of the maternal and, subsequently, of the feminine. In this case, the unified self reappears not in the figure of the androgyne but as a specifically feminine subject organized by a founding maternal identification.

The differences between Lacanian and post-Lacanian feminist psychoanalytic theories on the one hand and those steeped in the tradition of object-relations and ego psychology on the other center on the conception of the subject or the ego and its ostensible integrity. Lacanian feminists such as Jacqueline Rose argue that object-relations theorists fail to account for the unconscious and for the radical discontinuities which characterize the psyche prior to the formation of the ego and a distinct and separate sense of self. By claiming certain kinds of identifications are primary, object-relations theorists make the relational life of the infant primary to psychic development itself, conflating the psyche with the ego and relegating the unconscious to a less significant role. Lacanian theorists insist upon the unconscious as a source of discontinuous and chaotic drives or significations, and they claim that the ego is a perpetually unstable phenomenon, resting upon a primary repression of unconscious drives which return perpetually to haunt and undermine the ostensible unity of the ego.[7]

Although these theories tend to destabilize the subject as a construct of coherence, they nevertheless institute gender coherence through the stabilizing metanarrative of infantile development. According to Rose and to Juliet Mitchell, the unconscious is an open libidinal/linguistic field of discontinuities which contest the rigid and hierarchizing codes of sexual difference encoded in language, regulating cultural life. Although the unconscious thus becomes a locus of subversion, it remains unclear what changes the unconscious can provide considering the rigid synchronicity of the structuralist frame. The rules constituting and regulating sexual difference within Lacanian terms evince an immutability which seriously challenges their usefulness for any theory of social and cultural transformation. The failure to historicize the account of the rules governing sexual difference inevitably institutes that difference as the reified foundation of all intelligible culture, with the result that the paternal law becomes the invariant condition of intelligibility, and the variety of contestations not only can never undo that law but, in fact, require the abiding efficacy of that law in order to maintain any meaning at all.

In both sets of psychoanalytic analyses, a narrative of infantile development is constructed which assumes the existence of a primary identification (object-relations) or a primary repression (the *Urverdrangung* which founds the Lacanian male subject and marks off the feminine through exclusion) which instantiates gender specificity and subsequently informs, organizes, and unifies identity. We hear time and again about *the* boy and *the* girl, a tactical distancing from spatial and temporal locations which elevates the narrative to the mythic tense of a reified history. Although object-relations poses an alternative version of the subject based in relational attitudes characteristically feminine and Lacanian (or anti-Lacanian) theories maintain the instability of the subject based in the disruptive potential of the unconscious manifest at the tentative boundaries of the ego; they each offer story lines about gender acquisition which effect a narrative closure on gender experience and a false stabilization of the category of woman. Whether as a linguistic and cultural law which makes itself known as the inevitable organizing principle of sexual difference or as the identity forged through a primary identification that the Oedipal complex requires, gender meanings are circumscribed within a narrative frame which both unifies certain legitimate sexual subjects and excludes from intelligibility sexual identities and discontinuities which challenge the narrative beginnings and closures offered by these competing psychoanalytic explanations.

Whether one begins with Freud's postulation of primary bisexuality (Juliet Mitchell and Jacqueline Rose) or with the primacy of object-relations (Chodorow, Benjamin), one tells a story that constructs a discrete gender identity and discursive location which remains relatively fixed. Such theories do not need to be explicitly essentialist in their arguments in order to be effectively essentialist in their narrative strategies. Indeed, most psychoanalytic feminist theories maintain that gender is constructed, and they view themselves (and Freud) as debunking the claims of essential femininity or essential masculinity. Indeed, this seems to be the case when we consider Freud's claim, for instance, in *The Three Essays on the Theory of Sexuality* that heterosexuality is not a given of biological life but a developmental accomplishment,[8] his theory of primary bisexuality,[9] and his further claim in *New Introductory Lectures on Psychoanalysis* that to become a woman is a laborious construction which takes the repression of primary bisexuality as its premise.[10]

At its most general level of narrative development, the object-relations and Lacanian versions of gender development offer (1) a utopian postulation of an originally predifferentiated state of the sexes which (2) also preexists the postulation of hierarchy, and (3) gets ruined either by the sudden and swift action of the paternal law (Lacanian) or the anthropologically less ambitious Oedipal injunction to repudiate and devalue the mother (object-relations). In both cases, an originally undifferentiated state of the sexes suffers the process of differentiation and hierarchization through the advent of a repressive law. "In the beginning" is sexuality without power, then power arrives to create both culturally relevant sexual distinction (gender) and, along with that, gender hierarchy and dominance.

The Lacanian position proves problematic when we consider that the state prior to the law is, by definition, prior to language and yet, within the confines of language, we are said somehow to have access to it. The circularity of the reasoning becomes all the more dizzying when we realize that prior to language we had a diffuse and full pleasure which, unfortunately, we cannot remember, but which disrupts our speech and haunts our dreams. The object-relations postulation of an original identification and subsequent repudiation constructs the terms of a coherent narrative of infantile development which works to exclude all kinds of developmental histories in which the nurturing presence of the nuclear family cannot be presupposed.

By grounding the metanarratives in a myth of the origin, the psychoanalytic description of gender identity confers a false sense of legitimacy and universality to a culturally specific and, in some contexts, culturally oppressive version of gender identity. By claiming that some identifications are more primary than others, the complexity of the latter set of identifications is effectively assimilated into the primary one, and the "unity" of the identifications is preserved. Hence, because within object-relations the girl-mother identification is "founding," the girl-brother and girl-father identifications are easily assimilated under the already firmly established gender identification with women. Without the assumption of an orderly temporal development of identifications in which the first identifications serve to unify the latter ones, we would not be able to explain which identifications get assimilated into which others; in other words, we would lose the unifying thread of the narrative. Indeed, it is important to note that primary identifications establish gender in a substantive mode, and secondary identifications thus serve as attributes. Hence, we witness the discursive emergence of "feminine men" or "masculine women," or the meaningful redundancy of a "masculine man." Without the temporal prioritization of primary identifications, it would be unclear which characterizations were to serve as substance and which as attributes, and in the case in which that temporal ordering were fully contested, we would have, I suppose, the gender equivalent of an interplay of attributes without an abiding or unifying substance. I will suggest what I take to be the subversive possibilities of such a gender arrangement toward the end of my remarks.

Even within the psychoanalytic frame, however, we might press the question of identification and desire to a further limit. The primary identification in which gender becomes "fixed" forms a history of identifications in which the secondary ones revise and reform the primary one but in no way contest its structural primacy. Gender identities emerge and sexual desires shift and vary so that different "identifications" come into play depending upon the availability of legitimating cultural norms and opportunities. It is not always possible to relate those shifts back to a primary identification which is suddenly manifest. Within the terms of psychoanalytic theory, then, it is quite possible to understand gendered subjectivity as a history of identifications, parts of which can be brought into play in given contexts and which, precisely because they encode the contingencies of personal history, do not always point back to an internal coherence of any kind.

Of course, it is important to distinguish between two very different ways in which psychoanalysis and narrative theory work together. Within psychoanalytic literary criticism, and within feminist psychoanalytic criticism in particular, the operation of the unconscious makes all narrative coherence suspect; indeed, the defenders of that critical enterprise tend to argue that the narrative capacity is seriously undermined by that which is necessarily excluded or repressed in the manifest text and that a serious effort to admit the unconscious, whether conceived in terms of a repressed set of drives (Kristeva) or as an excluded field of metonymic associations (Rose), into the text disrupts and inverts the linear assumptions of coherent narrativity. In this sense, the text always exceeds the narrative; as the field of excluded meanings, it returns, invariably, to contest and subvert the explicitly attempted narrative coherence of the text.

The multiplication of narrative standpoints within the literary text corresponds to an internally fragmented psyche which can achieve no final, integrated understanding or "mastery" of its component parts. Hence, the literary work offers a textual means of dramatizing Freud's topographical model of mind in motion. The nonliterary use of psychoanalysis, however, as a psychological explanatory model for the acquisition and consolidation of gender identification and, hence, identity generally fails to take account of itself as a narrative. Subject to the feminist aim to delimit and define a shared femininity, these narratives attempt to construct a coherent female subject. As a result, psychoanalysis as feminist metatheory reproduces that false coherence in the form of a story line about infantile development where it ought to investigate genealogically the exclusionary practices which condition that particular narrative of identity formation. Although Rose, Mitchell, and other Lacanian feminists insist that identity is always a tenuous and unstable affair, they nevertheless fix the terms of that instability with respect to a paternal law which is culturally invariant. The result is a narrativized myth of origins in which primary bisexuality is arduously rendered into a melancholic heterosexuality through the inexorable force of the law.

Juliet Mitchell claims that it is only possible to be in one position or the other in a sexual relation and never in both at once. But the binary disjunction implicit to this gendered law of noncontradiction suggests that desire functions through a gender difference instituted at the level of the symbolic that necessarily represses whatever unconscious multiplications of positions might be at work. Kristeva argues similarly that the requirements of intelligible culture imply that female homosexuality is a contradiction in terms, with the consequence that this particular cultural manifestation is, even within culture, outside it, in the mode of psychosis. The only intelligible female homosexuality within Kristeva's frame is in the prohibited incestuous love between daughter and mother, one that can only be resolved through a maternal identification and the quite literal process of becoming a mother.[11]

Within these appropriations of psychoanalytic theory, gender identity and sexual orientation are accomplished at once. Although the story of sexual development is complicated and quite different for *the* girl than *the* boy, it appeals in both contexts to an operative disjunction that remains stable throughout: one identifies with one sex and, in so doing, desires the other, that desire being the elaboration of that identity, the mode by which it creates its opposite and defines itself in that opposition. But what about primary bisexuality, the source of disruption and discontinuity that Rose locates as the subversive potential of the unconscious? A close examination of what precisely Freud means by bisexuality, however, turns out to be a kind of bi-sexedness of libidinal dispositions. In other words, there are male and female libidinal dispositions in every psyche which are directed heterosexually toward opposite sexes. When bisexuality is relieved of its basis in the drive theory, it reduces, finally, to the coincidence of two heterosexual desires, each proceeding from oppositional identifications or dispositions, depending on the theory, so that desire, strictly speaking, can issue only from a male-identification to a female object or from a female-identification to a male object. Granted, it may well be a woman, male-identified, who desires another woman, or a man, female-identified, who desires another man, and it may also be a woman, male-identified who desires a man, female-identified, or similarly, a man, female-identified, who desires a woman, male-identified. One either identifies with a sex or desires it, but only those two relations are possible.

But is identification always restricted within the binary disjunction in which it has been framed so far? Clearly, within psychoanalytic theory, another set of possibilities emerges whereby identifications work not to consolidate identity but to condition the interplay and the subversive recombination of gender meanings. Consider that in the previous sketch, identifications exist in a mutually exclusive binary matrix conditioned by the cultural necessity of occupying one position to the exclusion of the other. But in fantasy, a variety of positions can be entertained even though they may not constitute culturally intelligible possibilities. Hence, for Kristeva, for instance, the semiotic designates precisely those sets of unconscious fantasies and wishes that exceed the legitimating bounds of paternally organized culture; the semiotic domain, the body's subversive eruption into language, becomes the transcription of the unconscious from the topographical model into a structuralist discourse. The tenuousness of all identity is exposed through the proliferation of fantasies that exceed and contest the "identity" that forms the conscious sense of self. But are identity and fantasy as mutually exclusive as the previous explanation suggests? Consider the claim, integral to much psychoanalytic theory, that identifications and, hence, identity, are in fact *constituted* by fantasy.

Roy Schafer argues in *A New Language for Psychoanalysis* that when identifications are understood as internalizations, they imply a trope of inner psychic space that is ontologically insupportable. He further suggests that internalization is understood better not as a process but as a fantasy.[12] As a result, it is not possible to attribute some kind of ontological meaning to the spatial internality of internalizations, for they are only fantasied as internal. I would further argue that this very fantasy internal psychic space is essentially conditioned and mediated by a language that regularly figures interior psychic locations of various kinds, a language, in other words, that not only produces that fantasy but then redescribes that figuration within an uncritically accepted topographical discourse. Fantasies themselves are often imagined as mental contents somehow projected onto an interior screen, a conception conditioned by a cinematic metaphorics of the psyche. However, identifications are not merely fantasies of internally located objects or features, but they stand in a transfigurative relation to the very objects they purport to internalize. In other words, within psychoanalytic theory, to identify with a figure from the past is to figure that figure within the configuration of interior psychic space. Identification is never simply mimetic but involves a strategy of wish fulfillment; one identifies not with an empirical person but with a fantasy, the mother one wishes one had, the father one thought one had but didn't, with the posture of the parent or sibling which seems to ward off a perceived threat from some other, or with the posture of some imagined relation whom one also imagines to be the recipient of love. We take up identifications not only to receive love but also to deflect from it and its dangers; we also take up identifications in order to facilitate or prohibit our own desires. In each case of identification, there is an interpretation at work, a wish and/or a fear as well, the effect of a prohibition, and a strategy of resolution.

What is commonly called an introject is, thus, a fantasied figure within a fantasied locale, a double imagining that produces the effect of the empirical other fixed in an interior topos. As figurative productions, these identifications constitute impossible desires that figure the body, active principles of incorporation, modes of structuring and signifying the enactment of the lived body in social space. Hence, the gender fantasies constitutive of identifications are not part of the set of properties that a subject might be said to have, but they constitute the genealogy of that embodied/psychic identity, the mechanism of its construction. One does not have the fantasies, and neither is there a one who lives them, but the fantasies condition and construct the specificity of the gendered subject with the enormously important qualification that these fantasies are themselves disciplinary productions of grounding cultural sanctions and taboos—a theme to which I will momentarily turn. If gender is constituted by identification and identification is invariably a fantasy within a fantasy, a double figuration, then gender is precisely the fantasy enacted by and through the corporeal styles that constitute bodily significations.

In a separate context, Michel Foucault challenges the language of internalization as it operates in the service of the repressive hypothesis. In *Discipline and Punish*, Foucault rewrites the doctrine of internalization found in Nietzsche's *On the Genealogy of Morals* through the language of *inscription*. In the context of prisoners, Foucault writes, the strategy has not been to enforce a repression of their desires but to compel their bodies to signify the prohibitive law as their ownmost essence, style, necessity. That law is not internalized, but it is incorporated, with the consequence that bodies are produced which signify that law as the essence of their selves, the meaning of their soul, their conscience, the law of their desire. In effect, the law is at once fully manifest and fully latent, for it never appears as external to the bodies it subjects and subjectivates.

"It would be wrong", Foucault writes, "to say that the soul is an illusion, or an ideological effect. On the contrary, it exists, it has a reality, it is produced permanently around, on, within, the body by the functioning of a power that is exercised on those that are punished. . . ."[13] The figure of the interior soul understood as "within" the body is signified through its inscription *on* the body, even though its primary mode of signification is through its very absence, its potent invisibility, for it is through that invisibility that the effect of a structuring inner space is produced. The soul is precisely what the body lacks; hence, that lack produces the body as its other and as its means of expression. In this sense, then, the soul is a surface signification that contests and displaces the inner/outer distinction itself, a figure of interior psychic space inscribed on the body as a social signification that perpetually renounces itself as such. In Foucault's terms, the soul is not imprisoned by the body, as some Christian imagery would suggest, but "the body becomes a prisoner of the soul"[14].

The redescription of intrapsychic processes in terms of the surface politics of the body implies a corollary redescription of gender as the disciplinary production of the figures of gender fantasy through the play of presence and absence in the body's surface, the construction of the gendered body through a series of exclusions and denials, signifying absences.

But what determines the manifest and latent text of the body politic? What is the prohibitive law that generates the corporeal stylization of gender, the fantasied and fantastic figuration of the gendered body? Clearly, Freud points to the incest taboo and the prior taboo against homosexuality as the generative moments of gender identity, the moments in which gender becomes fixed (meaning both immobilized and, in some sense, repaired). The acquisition of gender identity is thus simultaneous with the accomplishment of coherent heterosexuality. The taboo against incest, which presupposes and includes the taboo against homosexuality, works to sanction and produce identity at the same time that it is said to repress the very identity it produces. This disciplinary production of gender effects a false stabilization of gender in the interests of the heterosexual construction and regulation of sexuality. That the model seeks to produce and sustain coherent identities and that it requires a heterosexual construction of sexuality in no way implies that practicing heterosexuals embody or exemplify this model with any kind of regularity. Indeed, I would argue that in principle no one can embody this regulatory ideal at the same time that the compulsion to embody the fiction, to figure the body in accord with its requirements, is everywhere. This is a fiction that operates within discourse, and which, discursively and institutionally sustained, wields enormous power.

I noted earlier the kinds of coherences instituted through some feminist

336 / Judith Butler

appropriations of psychoanalysis but would now suggest further that the localization of identity in an interior psychic space characteristic of these theories implies an expressive model of gender whereby identity is first fixed internally and only subsequently manifest in some exterior way. When gender identity is understood as causally or mimetically related to sex, then the order of appearance that governs gendered subjectivity is understood as one in which sex conditions gender, and gender determines sexuality and desire; although both psychoanalytic and feminist theory tend to disjoin sex from gender, the restriction of gender within a binary relation suggests a relation of residual mimeticism between sex, conceived as binary[15] and gender. Indeed, the view of sex, gender, and desire that presupposes a metaphysics of substance suggests that gender and desire are understood as attributes that refer back to the substance of sex and make sense only as its reflection.

I am not arguing that psychoanalytic theory is a form of such substantive theorizing, but I would suggest that the lines that establish coherence between sex, gender, and desire, where they exist, tend to reenforce that conceptualization and to constitute its contemporary legacy. The construction of coherence conceals the gender discontinuities that run rampant within heterosexual, bisexual, and gay and lesbian contexts in which gender does not necessarily follow from sex, and desire, or sexuality generally, does not seem to follow from gender; indeed, where none of these dimensions of significant corporeality "express" or reflect one another. When the disorganization and disaggregation of the field of bodies disrupts the regulatory fiction of heterosexual coherence, it seems that the expressive model loses its descriptive force, and that regulatory ideal is exposed as a norm and a fiction that disguises itself as a developmental law that regulates the sexual field that it purports to describe.

According to the understanding of identification as fantasy, however, it is clear that coherence is desired, wished for, idealized, and that this idealization is an effect of a corporeal signification. In other words, acts, gestures, and desire produce the effect of an internal core or substance, but produce this on the surface of the body, through the play of signifying absences that suggest, but never reveal, the organizing principle of identity as a cause. Such acts, gestures, enactments, generally construed, are performative in the sense that the essence of identity that they otherwise purport to express becomes a *fabrication* manufactured and sustained through corporeal signs and other discursive means. That the gendered body is performative suggests that it has no ontological status apart from the various acts which constitute its reality, and if that reality is fabricated as an interior essence, that very interiority is a function of a decidedly public and social discourse, the public regulation of fantasy through the surface politics of the body. In other words, acts and gestures articulate and enacted desires create the illusion of an interior and organizing gender core, an illusion discursively maintained for the purposes of the regulation of sexuality within the obligatory frame of reproductive heterosexuality. If the "cause" of desire, gesture, and act can be localized within the "self" of the actor, then the political regulations and disciplinary practices which produce that ostensibly coherent gender are effectively displaced from view. The displacement of a political and discursive origin of gender identity onto a psychological "core" precludes an analysis of the political constitution of the gendered subject and its fabricated notions about the ineffable interiority of its sex or of its true identity.

If the inner truth of gender is a fabrication and if a true gender is a fantasy instituted and inscribed on the surface of bodies, then it seems that genders can be neither true nor false but are only produced as the truth effects of a discourse of primary and stable identity.

In *Mother Camp: Female Impersonators in America*, anthropologist Esther Newton suggests that the structure of impersonation reveals one of the key fabricating mechanisms through which the social construction of gender takes place. I would suggest as well that drag fully subverts the distinction between inner and outer psychic space and effectively mocks both the expressive model of gender and of the notion of a true gender identity. "At its most complex," Newton writes, "[drag] is a double inversion that says, 'appearance is an illusion.' Drag says [Newton's curious personification], my 'outside' appearance is feminine, but my essence 'inside' {the body} is masculine." At the same time it symbolizes the opposite inversion: "my appearance 'outside' {my body, my gender} is masculine but my essence 'inside' myself is feminine."[16] Both claims to truth contradict one another and so displace the entire enactment of gender significations from the discourse of truth and falsity.

The notion of an original or primary gender identity is often parodied within the cultural practices of drag, cross-dressing, and the sexual styliza- tion of butch/femme identities. Within feminist theory, such parodic iden- tities have been understood to be either degrading to women, in the case of drag and cross-dressing, or an uncritical appropriation of sex-role stereotyping from within the practice of heterosexuality, especially in the case of butch/femme lesbian identities. But the relation between the "imitation" and the "original" is, I think, more complicated than that critique generally allows. Moreover, it gives us a clue to the way in which the relationship between primary identification, that is, the original meanings accorded to gender, and subsequent gender experience might be reframed.

The performance of drag plays upon the distinction between the anatomy of the performer and the gender that is being performed. But we are actually in the presence of three separate dimensions of significant corpore-

338 / Judith Butler

ality: anatomical sex, gender identity and gender performance. If the anatomy of the performer is already distinct from the gender of the performer, and both of those distinct from the gender of the performance, then the performance suggests a dissonance not only between sex and performance but between sex and gender, and gender and performance. As much as drag creates a unified picture of "woman" (what its critics often oppose), it also reveals the distinctness of those aspects of gendered experience which are falsely naturalized as a unity through the regulatory fiction of heterosexual coherence. In imitating gender, drag implicitly reveals the imitative structure of gender itself—as well as its contingency. Indeed, part of the pleasure, the giddiness of the performance is in the recognition of a radical contingency in the relation between sex and gender in the face of cultural configurations of causal unities that are regularly assumed to be natural and necessary. In the place of the law of heterosexual coherence, we see sex and gender denaturalized by means of a performance which avows their distinctness and dramatizes the cultural mechanism of their fabricated unity.

The notion of gender parody defended here does not assume that there is an original which such parodic identities imitate. Indeed, the parody is *of* the very notion of an original; just as the psychoanalytic notion of gender identification is constituted by a fantasy of a fantasy, the transfiguration of an other who is always already a "figure" in that double sense, so gender parody reveals that the original identity after which gender fashions itself is itself an imitation without an origin. To be more precise, it is a production which, in effect, that is, in its effect, postures as an imitation. This perpetual displacement constitutes a fluidity of identities that suggests an openness to resignification and recontextualization, and it deprives hegemonic culture and its critics of the claim to essentialist accounts of gender identity. Although the gender meanings which are taken up in these parodic styles are clearly part of hegemonic, misogynist culture, they are nevertheless denaturalized and mobilized through their parodic recontextualization. As imitations which effectively displace the meaning of the original, they imitate the myth of originality itself. In the place of an original identification which serves as a determining cause, gender identity might be reconceived as a personal/cultural history of received meanings subject to a set of imitative practices which refer laterally to other imitations, and which, jointly, construct the illusion of a primary and interior gendered self or which parody the mechanism of that construction.

Inasmuch as the construct of women presupposes a specificity and coherence that differentiates it from that of men, the categories of gender appear as an unproblematic point of departure for feminist politics. But if we take the critique of Monique Wittig seriously, namely, that "sex" itself is a category produced in the interests of the heterosexual contract,[17] or if we consider Foucault's suggestion that "sex" designates an artificial unity that works to maintain and amplify the regulation of sexuality within the reproductive domain, then it seems that gender coherence operates in much the same way, not as a ground of politics but as its effect. The political task that emerges in the wake of this critique requires that we understand not only the "interests" that a given cultural identity has, but, more importantly, the interests and the power relations that establish that identity in its reified mode to begin with. The proliferation of gender style and identity, if that word still makes sense, implicitly contests the always already political binary distinction between genders that is often taken for granted. The loss of that reification of gender relations ought not to be lamented as the failure of a feminist political theory, but, rather, affirmed as the promise of the possibility of complex and generative subject-positions as well as coalitional strategies that neither presuppose nor fix their constitutive subjects in their place.

The fixity of gender identification, its presumed cultural invariance, its status as an interior and hidden cause may well serve the goals of the feminist project to establish a transhistorical commonality between us, but the "us" who gets joined through such a narration is a construction built upon the denial of a decidedly more complex cultural identity—or non-identity, as the case may be. The psychological language which purports to describe the interior fixity of our identities as men or women works to enforce a certain coherence and to foreclose convergences of gender identity and all manner of gender dissonance—or, where that exists, to relegate it to the early stages of a developmental and, hence, normative history. It may be that standards of narrative coherence must be radically revised and that narrative strategies for locating and articulating gender identity ought to admit to a greater complexity or it may be that performance may preempt narrative as the scene of gender production. In either case, it seems crucial to resist the myth of interior origins, understood either as naturalized or culturally fixed. Only then, gender coherence might be understood as the regulatory fiction it is—rather than the common point of our liberation.

Notes

1. Remarks, Center for the Humanities, Wesleyan University, Spring 1985.
2. Julia Kristeva, "Woman Can Never Be Defined," *New French Feminisms*, ed. Elaine Marks and Isabelle de Courtivron, (New York: Schocken, 1984).
3. Juliet Mitchell, *Psycho-analysis and Feminism*, (New York: Vintage, 1975), p. 377.
4. Jacqueline Rose, "Femininity and its Discontents," *Sexuality in the Field of Vision* (London: Verso, 1987), p. 90.

5. Luce Irigaray, "Any Theory of the Subject Has Already Been Appropriated by the Masculine," *Speculum of the Other Woman*, trans. Gillian Gill (Ithaca, NY: Cornell University Press, 1985), p. 140. See also "Is the Subject of Science Sexed?," *Cultural Critique*, Vol. 1, Fall 1985, p. 11.

6. For an interesting discussion of the political desirability of keeping the feminist subject incoherent, see Sandra Harding, "The Instability of the Analytical Categories of Feminist Theory," *Sex and Scientific Inquiry*, ed. Sandra Harding and Jean F. O'Barr (Chicago: University of Chicago Press, 1987).

7. See Jacqueline Rose's argument in "Femininity and its Discontents," *Sexuality in the Field of Vision, pp. 90–94*.

8. Sigmund Freud, *Three Essays on the Theory of Sexuality*, trans. James Strachey (New York: Basic Books, 1975), p. 1.

9. Freud, *Three Essays*, p. 7; see also "The Ego and the Superego," *The Ego and the Id*, trans. Joan Riviere (New York: Norton, 1960), pp. 22–23.

10. See Freud, Chapter 33, "Femininity," *New Introductory Lectures*, trans. James Strachey (New York: Norton, 1965), p. 116.

11. For a fuller exposition of Kristeva's positions, see my article "The Body Politics of Julia Kristeva" in the French Feminism issue of *Hypatia: A Journal of Feminist Philosophy*, Vol. 3, no. 3, pp. 104–108.

12. Roy Schafer, *A New Language for Psychoanalysis*, (New Haven, CT: Yale University Press, 1976), p. 177.

13. Michel Foucault, *Discipline and Punish* (New York, Panthenon, 1977), p. 29.

14. Foucault, *Discipline and Punish*, p. 30.

15. The assumption of binary sex is in no sense stable. For an interesting article on the complicated "sexes" of some female athletes and the medicolegal disputes about how and whether to render their sex decidable, see Jerold M. Loewenstein, "The Conundrum of Gender Identification, Two Sexes Are Not Enough," *Pacific Discovery*, Vol. 40, No. 2, 1987, pp. 38–39. See also Michel Foucault's *The History of Sexuality, Volume I: An Introduction*, trans. Robert Hurley (New York: Vintage, 1980), pp. 154–155, and *Herculine Barbin, Being the Recently Discovered Memoirs of a Nineteenth-Century French Hermaphrodite*, trans. Richard McDougall (New York: Pantheon, 1986), pp. vii-xvii. For a feminist analysis of recent research into "the sex gene," a DNA sequence which is alleged to "decide" the sex of otherwise ambiguous bodies, see Anne Fausto-Sterling, "Recent Trends in Developmental Biology: A Feminist Perspective" (Departments of Biology and Medicine, Brown University).

16. Esther Newton, *Mother Camp: Female Impersonators in America* (Chicago: University of Chicago, 1972), p. 103.

17. Monique Wittig, "The Category of Sex," *Feminist Issues*, Vol. 2, p. 2.

Index

341

Contributors

Seyla Benhabib teaches philosophy and women's studies at SUNY, Stony Brook. She is the author of *Critique, Norm and Utopia: A Study of the Foundations of Critical Theory*, co-editor with Drucilla Cornell of *Feminism and Critique: Essays on the Politics of Gender in Late Capitalism*, and translator of Herbert Marcuse, *Hegel's Ontology and the Theory of Historicity*.

Susan Bordo, Associate Professor of Philosophy at Le Moyne College, is the author of *The Flight to Objectivity: Essays on Cartesianism and Culture* (New York: SUNY Press, 1987) and the editor (with Alison Jaggar) of *Gender/Body/Knowledge: Feminist Reconstructions of Being and Knowing* (New Brunswick, NJ: Rutgers University Press, 1989). Her current project is *Food, Fashion, and Power*, a study of gender, culture, and the construction of the body.

Judith Butler is Associate Professor of Humanities at Johns Hopkins University. She is the author of *Subjects of Desire: Hegelian Reflections in Twentieth-Century France* (New York: Columbia University Press, 1987) and of *Gender Politics and the Categories of Sex* (New York: Routledge, forthcoming).

Christine Di Stefano is Assistant Professor of Political Science at the University of Washington where she teaches political theory. She is completing a book which offers a feminist reinterpretation of the political theories of Hobbes, J.S. Mill, and Marx and hopes to pursue future research on prospects for the concept of "autonomy" within contemporary critical theory in the wake of feminist and postmodern assaults on the modern subject.

Jane Flax is Associate Professor of Political Science at Howard University and a psychotherapist in private practice in Chevy Chase, Maryland. Her papers on feminism, psychoanalysis, and philosophy have appeared in a number of books and journals. The University of California Press will publish her book *Thinking Fragments: Psychoanalysis, Feminism and Postmodernism in the Contemporary West* in 1989.

Nancy Fraser teaches philosophy, women's studies, and contemporary literature and theory at Northwestern University. She is the author of *Unruly Practices: Power, Discourse and Gender in Contemporary Social Theory*, (Minneapolis: University of Minnesota Press and Polity Press).

Donna Haraway teaches and writes feminist theory addressed to the politics, histories, and cultures of modern science and technology. She is Professor in the History of Consciousness Board at the University of California, Santa Cruz, where she also participates in the Women's Studies Program. She is the author of *Primate Visions: Gender, Race, and Nature in the World of Modern Science* (New York: Routledge, 1989) and *Simians, Cyborgs, and Women: The Reinvention of Nature* (London: Free Association Books, forthcoming 1990). She is currently writing on feminist theory, science fiction, and fictions of science and on the material and semiotic productions of the immune system in late capitalism.

Sandra Harding is Professor of Philosophy and Director of Women's Studies at the University of Delaware. She is the author of *The Science Question in Feminism* (Cornell and Open University Presses, 1986; to be published in German and Italian translation in 1989), which won the Jessie Bernard Award of the American Sociological Association in 1987 and was selected as one of the five best books of 1986 by *The Socialist Review*. She is also the editor of *Can Theories Be Refuted?* (Reidel, 1976) and *Feminism and Methodology: Social Science Issues* (Indiana University Press, 1987), and co-editor of *Discovering Reality: Feminist Perspectives on Epistemology, Metaphysics, Methodology and Philosophy of Science* (with Merrill Hintikka, Reidel, 1983) and *Sex and Scientific Inquiry* (with Jean O'Barr, Chicago University Press, 1987).

Nancy Hartsock is Associate Professor of Political Science and Women's Studies at the University of Washington. She is the author of *Money, Sex and Power: Towards a Feminist Historical Materialism* and former editor of *Quest: A Feminist Quarterly*.

Andreas Huyssen, Professor of German at Columbia University, is an editor of *New German Critique* and an author of books on Romanticism and the *Sturm und Drang*. He also co-edited *The Technological Imagination, Postmoderne: Zeichen eines Kulturellen Wandels*, and *Modernity and the Text: Revisions of German Modernism* (forthcoming, Columbia University Press).

Linda Nicholson teaches Philosophy of Education and Women's Studies at SUNY Albany. She is the author of *Gender and History: The Limits of Social Theory in the Age of the Family* (New York: Columbia University Press, 1986).

Elspeth Probyn is a doctoral candidate and teaches part-time in the Department of Communication Studies, Concordia University, Montreal, Quebec. Her articles on feminist and cultural theory have appeared in various journals, including *The Canadian Journal of Social and Political Theory; Cultural Studies; Communications; Canadian Women's Studies Journal*; as well as in the anthologies *Body Invaders: Panic Sex in America* and *Sight Works*.

Anna Yeatman is an Australian, whose first degree was in Politics (Political Theory) from an Australian university, and whose graduate degrees were in Sociology from U.S. universities. Her current position is Senior Lecturer in Sociology, Flinders University of South Australia. She is completing a book *Feminists, Femocrats, Technocrats: Essays on the Contemporary Australian State*.

Iris Young teaches philosophy at Worcester Polytechnic Institute. She has written numerous articles on political philosophy and feminist theory. A collection of her essays in feminist theory is forthcoming from Indiana University Press.